American Assassins

American Assassins
The Darker Side of Politics

JAMES W. CLARKE

Princeton University Press
Princeton, New Jersey

FOR

Julie and Michael

AND

THE GOOD TIMES

Contents

Preface   *xi*

Chapter One • **Introduction**   3

Chapter Two • **Region and Class**   18
    John Wilkes Booth (Abraham Lincoln, 1865)   19
    Leon Czolgosz (William McKinley, 1901)   39

Chapter Three • **Nationalism**   63
    Oscar Collazo and Griselio Torresola (Harry S Truman, 1950)   64
    Sirhan Sirhan (Robert F. Kennedy, 1968)   76

Chapter Four • **Rejection**   105
    Lee Harvey Oswald (John F. Kennedy, 1963)   107
    Samuel Byck (Richard M. Nixon, 1974)   128

Chapter Five • **The Feminine Dimension**   143
    Lynette Alice Fromme (Gerald R. Ford, 1975)   144
    Sara Jane Moore (Gerald R. Ford, 1975)   156

Chapter Six • **The Nihilist Perspective**   166
    Giuseppe Zangara (Franklin D. Roosevelt, 1933)   167
    Arthur Herman Bremer (George Wallace, 1972)   174

Chapter Seven • **The Psychotics**   194
    Richard Lawrence (Andrew Jackson, 1835)   195
    Charles J. Guiteau (James A. Garfield, 1881)   198
    John Schrank (Theodore Roosevelt, 1912)   214

Chapter Eight • **Family and Money**   223
    Carl Austin Weiss (Huey Long, 1935)   224
    James Earl Ray (Martin Luther King, Jr., 1968)   239

Chapter Nine • **Conclusions**   258

Notes   272
Bibliography   299
Index   313

List of Illustrations

(facing page 148)

Richard Lawrence (Andrew Jackson, 1835)
Photo: Library of Congress

John Wilkes Booth (Abraham Lincoln, 1865)
Photo: Library of Congress

Charles J. Guiteau (James A. Garfield, 1881)
Photo: Library of Congress

Leon Czolgosz (William McKinley, 1901)
Photo: Wide World Photos

John Schrank (Theodore Roosevelt, 1912)
Photo: Library of Congress

Giuseppe Zangara (Franklin D. Roosevelt, 1933)
Photo: Wide World Photos

Carl Austin Weiss (Huey Long, 1935)
Photo: Wide World Photos

Griselio Torresola (Harry S Truman, 1950)
Photo: Wide World Photos

Oscar Collazo (Harry S Truman, 1950)
Photo: Wide World Photos

Lee Harvey Oswald (John F. Kennedy, 1963)
Photo: Wide World Photos

Sirhan Sirhan (Robert F. Kennedy, 1968)
Photo: Wide World Photos

James Earl Ray (Martin Luther King, Jr., 1968)
Photo: Wide World Photos

Arthur Herman Bremer (George Wallace, 1972)
Photo: Wide World Photos

Samuel Byck (Richard M. Nixon, 1974)
Photo: Wide World Photos

Sara Jane Moore (Gerald R. Ford, 1975)
Photo: Wide World Photos

Lynette Fromme (Gerald R. Ford, 1975)
Photo: Wide World Photos

Preface

THERE ARE risks in writing a book about sixteen complicated people. Given the scope of the study, complete biographies are impossible, so the task was to distinguish between the important and the unimportant details of the subjects' lives in my attempt to understand and explain their actions. What follows is not, therefore, a series of exhaustive biographies but rather what I hope will be sixteen biographical sketches that taken together advance our understanding of assassination in America.

My research relies as much as possible on primary sources, but the existence, quality, and availability of information spanning a 140-year period varies: in some cases, it is voluminous; in others, it is scant. Working within these constraints, I sought not only to present facts but also to convey the moods and feelings that pervaded these dark events. Put differently, I tried to see the world as the subjects saw it and to explain their behavior in that context.

Empathy often follows understanding, and some of these stories may be disturbing in that sense. But my purpose is to present accurate information—not apologies. If some of these subjects seem more human than they have been depicted in the past, it is because they are, and not because I made them that way. This is not, however, to imply approval or justification for their actions; to understand is not to excuse, or even forgive.

I AM GRATEFUL to a number of persons who offered help and encouragement over the years of research and writing: James C. Davies of the University of Oregon, Dorothy Ross of the University of Virginia, and David Winter of Wesleyan University commented extensively on the manuscript; Robert Penn Warren read and offered interesting insights on the Huey Long case; John Mack of the Harvard Medical School read selected chapters, gave me the first opportunity to present a paper on the subject, and introduced me to Priscilla Johnson McMillan, whose encouragement, at that time, meant more than she probably realized. My colleagues at the University of Arizona and elsewhere, Jeanne Nienaber, Vine Deloria, Clifford Lytle, Thomas Volgy, Mitchell Seligson, Daniel O'Neil, Jerrold Rusk, Philip Chapman, John Ostheimer, Mary Thornberry, Janet Thompson, John Soule, Paul Bartlett, Conrad Joyner, Henry Kenski, John Crow, Edward Muller, and Lee Sloan read, criticized, and helped me improve specific chapters.

I would also like to acknowledge the assistance given me during my research by Judge William B. Keene of the California Superior Court in Los Angeles; Francis K. Cholko, formerly of the same court; Deborah Kanter of the California Administrative Office of the Courts; Donald Johnson of the Prince George's County Court, Upper Marlboro, Maryland; and Richard Fong of the United States District Court in Sacramento. On a less personal level, I also want to acknowledge the cooperation and documents supplied by the Federal Bureau of Investigation, the Secret Service, the Federal Communications Commission, the National Park Service, the Federal Aviation Administration, and the Small Business Administration. Needless to say, I am also most appreciative of the help provided by the staffs at the Library of Congress, the National Archives, and the Interlibrary Loan and Documents sections of the University of Arizona Library.

Ivor Crewe, editor of the *British Journal of Political Science*, and Margaret Hermann, editor of *Political Psychology*, deserve mention for their willingness to publish evocative research—a rare quality among social science editors. Similarly, Paul Rosenblatt, Dean of the College of Liberal Arts at the University of Arizona, and John Wahlke, Head of the Department of Political Science at the same institution, are accorded my sincere gratitude for their professional integrity and support—also rare qualities, it seems, among university administrators. And I am grateful to Sanford Thatcher of the Princeton University Press for his confidence and willingness to ride with me, as we say out here in the desert.

Thanks are due my friends William and Katherine White of Washington, D.C. and Margaret Perry of the Canton Public Library in Collinsville, Connecticut for their kindness and hospitality, as well as my dear mother and sister, for putting up with me on my trips east.

Finally, I am indebted to a very competent staff at the University of Arizona for all the typing, retyping, footnote corrections, and so forth that went into this effort over the past couple of years: Mary Sue McQuown, Kari Askey, and Peggy Ellig did a superb job of typing; Daniel McCool helped enormously in checking footnotes; and Jane Bakos, Janet Griffing, Yasue Kidd, Sally Garnaat and Susan Brochick all assisted in a variety of ways that enabled me to write. And to my copy editor, Catherine Thatcher of the Princeton University Press, my gratitude for her help in making this manuscript more readable. I, of course, bear sole responsibility for what follows.

American Assassins

Chapter One · Introduction

We are left sitting in the dark, still wondering how such a deed could have been done by a man in his sound and sober senses in fair and free America and appalled at the possibility of a sane man murdering an American President.
> —An observation made after the
> McKinley assassination in 1901

By codifying acts of violence as expressions of mental illness, we neatly rid ourselves of the task of dealing with criminal offenses as more or less rational, goal-directed acts, no different in principle from other forms of conduct.
> —Thomas S. Szasz, 1963

And yet it goes on, and on, and on . . . why?
> —Robert Kennedy on the murder
> of Martin Luther King, Jr., 1968

BETWEEN 1835, when Richard Lawrence's pistols misfired and Andrew Jackson's life was spared, and 1981, sixteen[a] assassination attempts directed at nationally prominent political figures have occurred in the United States. There is something paradoxical about such events in a nation with a well-established democratic tradition of electoral stability, where authority to govern is peacefully transferred from party to party and from one administration to another as the political preferences of the electorate are expressed at regular intervals. But assas-

---

[a] This figure includes the March 30, 1981 attack on President Reagan, which occurred after this book was written. Although complete information on President Reagan's assailant is not available at this pre-trial date, some preliminary and tentative observations about his case are reported in the concluding chapter. Thus the substance of the book focuses on fifteen incidents, through 1975, involving sixteen assassins and would-be assassins.

sinations, like elections, represent a recurring and perplexing phenomenon in American politics. Why?

Is the commonness—some might say the banality—of assassinations in the United States symptomatic of a culture gone haywire, where handguns are as available as wristwatches, where theater audiences throng to view the blood-drenched screens of horror movies, and where only the very brave or very foolish walk city streets at night? Is this form of political violence a normal consequence of a highly competitive society that continues to define its heroes in terms of the rugged individualism of a frontier past—a society where success is now defined in unreachable and frustrating terms for substantial segments of its people, and too many corrupt politicians accumulate wealth and power at their expense? Or is assassination merely the attempt of a mentally ill person—someone deranged, a deviate, unlike most of us—who in the grip of some delusion attempts to redress imagined grievances, or perhaps in a twisted sense of hero worship or jealousy attempts to lock himself forever in the pages of history with some famous political figure? These are just some of the questions addressed in this book.

Names—John Wilkes Booth, Lee Harvey Oswald, Sirhan Sirhan, James Earl Ray, Arthur Bremer, and more recently, John Hinckley—symbolize the darker side of American political life: sad, bloody, irremovable stains on our national consciousness. But the strong emotions—the sadness, outrage, and indignation—that their acts and the acts of their more obscure counterparts triggered has also clouded our understanding of them and, as a result, the assassination phenomenon in America. Probably no group of political actors is more poorly understood than American assassins. My purpose in this book is to identify the sources and dimensions of this misunderstanding and to suggest how these persons and their acts can be more accurately explained. Sixteen individuals who attacked nationally prominent political leaders in fifteen separate incidents were selected for study. The subjects, both assassins and would-be assassins, their victims, actual or intended, and the dates of the attacks are as follows:

1835	Richard Lawrence	(Andrew Jackson)
1865	John Wilkes Booth	(Abraham Lincoln)
1881	Charles Guiteau	(James Garfield)
1901	Leon Czolgosz	(William McKinley)
1912	John Schrank	(Theodore Roosevelt)
1933	Giuseppe Zangara	(Franklin Roosevelt)
1935	Carl Weiss	(Huey Long)

1950	Oscar Collazo	(Harry S Truman)
	Griselio Torresola	
1963	Lee Harvey Oswald	(John F. Kennedy)
1968	James Earl Ray	(Martin Luther King, Jr.)
1968	Sirhan Sirhan	(Robert Kennedy)
1972	Arthur Bremer	(George Wallace)
1974	Samuel Byck	(Richard Nixon)
1975	Lynette Alice Fromme	(Gerald Ford)
1975	Sara Jane Moore	(Gerald Ford)

PROBLEMS IN PAST RESEARCH

The first would-be assassin of an American president was Richard Lawrence. In 1835, Lawrence tried to kill President Andrew Jackson but failed. Lawrence was quite obviously insane and was acquitted to spend the rest of his life in a mental institution. Since that time, fifteen other attempts have been made on the lives of nationally prominent political leaders.

In each instance, an effort has been made to categorize the attackers in much the same way that Lawrence was correctly diagnosed. To do this, however, a number of important facts had to be omitted, altered, or discounted through interpretation. The result is what I have labeled a pathological theory of assassination. It has been offered with minor variations as an explanation for every subject considered in this book. The dynamics of this explanation translate into something like the following. Assassins are acutely disturbed persons who suffer from such a diminished sense of self that their lives become increasingly isolated, bitter, and unbearable. Accordingly, this profound sense of failure translates into a generalized distrust of others to the extent that compensatory delusions of persecution and grandeur begin to domi-nate the subject's life. This distortion of reality is ultimately expressed in the irrational act of assassination. Some observers draw heavily on psychoanalytic concepts to explain this condition, but the conclusions are essentially the same: the act is irrational and the assassin is, there-fore, "delusional," "deranged," or "schizophrenic."

Unfortunately, terms such as psychopathology (or sociopathology or personality disorder),[b] paranoia, and schizophrenia are used so indiscriminately that they possess very little conceptual or diagnostic clarity. In one sense, it may be reasonable to argue that all premeditated

[b] These terms are used interchangeably in the literature.

murder is pathological. But there are some rather obvious conceptual problems in applying such common labels to assassins and would-be assassins as different, for example, as John Wilkes Booth, Charles Guiteau, Lee Harvey Oswald, James Earl Ray, and Sara Jane Moore. Unfortunately, more often than not, it is precisely these labels that one discovers in the literature.[1] Only the vocabulary changes over time, as newer terms replace older ones. Thus the "dementia praecox" of the nineteenth century has become the "paranoid schizophrenia" of the twentieth; the "psychopath" of the 1960s has become the "sociopath" of the 1970s. The substance of the labeling remains the same; that is, these persons are presumed "sick" and their acts are, in tautological fashion, evidence of that sickness.

The political rationale for this questionable assertion is illustrated in the following statement made after President Garfield's assassination in 1881:

> But this question of . . . insanity also involves the vaunted stability of our government in the estimation of the outside world. It is not supposable by our people that a sane man would seek to destroy a President without adequate personal cause, and in the absence of a political conspiracy. The idea of a political conspiracy, encompassing the life of a great party leader for party purposes, *must not* be entertained in this country. The royal world abroad, whose peoples have their own assassins to contend with, must not be furnished reason to conclude, that, in America the assassin is moved by the same impulses which control the assassin under monarchical forms of government. This would be admitting that the President of the United States *might* become a tyrant, a fact, that the Constitution, in so carefully defining and limiting his power, explicitly excludes.[2]

It was such reasoning that "explained" John Wilkes Booth's motive in 1865 as an insanely jealous desire for fame and recognition,[3] Leon Czolgosz's anarchist beliefs in 1901 as "delusions,"[4] and Sirhan Sirhan's Arab nationalism in 1968 as a confused expression of unresolved oedipal conflict.[5][c]

[c] Typical of such questionable appraisals was an article entitled "Social Psychopathology of Political Assassination," which appeared in the prestigious *Bulletin of Atomic Scientists* (Slomich and Kantor, 1969). In this piece, a social psychologist and a political scientist collaborated to offer the following generalizations about past assassins—all of which are without empirical support:

In addition to the possible political bias in such appraisals, another disturbing methodological flaw is apparent: in much of the literature there is scant evidence of any primary research. Rather, the references reveal a heavy reliance on *secondary* sources as well as a kind of incestuous process of citing each other's work to "document" the same questionable assertions. Many articles written since 1950, for example, have relied on Robert Donovan's very readable but undocumented book, *The Assassins*, for their facts, rather than on primary sources. And there is a seemingly unquestioning acceptance of earlier interpretations despite the dubious scholarly merits of such interpretations.[d]

BOOTH . . . an unemployed actor who was a fanatic advocate of the beaten Confederate cause (p. 9).

GUITEAU . . . a disappointed, mediocre, deranged office-seeker (p. 9).

CZOLGOSZ . . . an anarchist suffering from severe mental derangement, probably a form of schizophrenia (p. 9).

ZANGARA . . . a deranged anarchist (p. 10).

OSWALD . . . a disoriented, hate-ravaged, mother-dominated failure (p. 9).

SIRHAN . . . a withdrawn fanatic with multiple identity problems (p. 10).

Their assessments of the Puerto Rican Nationalists Oscar Collazo and Griselio Torresola and James Earl Ray come closer to the truth but still miss the mark. The "psychological condition" of the Puerto Ricans, the authors imply, clouded their ability to recognize the benefits of United States policy in Puerto Rico. James Earl Ray is characterized, as so many Americans can be, as a person willing to sell himself for financial gain; but his alleged "habitual self-degradation" mistakes Ray's incompetence for masochism (p. 10).

One might expect that psychiatrists would be less susceptible to such gross and inaccurate generalizations, but that is not the case. An article in the journal *Postgraduate Medicine* characterizes Oswald and the assassins who preceded him as "stand[ing] midway between the aggressive and paranoid psychopath" who share a common "desire for recognition" (Freedman, 1965, p. 655). A *Journal-Lancet* article written in the same year by another psychiatrist offers the diagnostic generalization that "[American] assassins, in my opinion, had schizophrenia, in most cases a paranoid type" (Hastings, July 1965, p. 300). Four years later, essentially the same conclusion is offered in an article published in *Diseases of the Nervous System*, a publication described as "A Practical Journal on Psychiatry and Neurology." In this article, the authors conclude that, with the possible exceptions of the two Puerto Rican Nationalists, "each assassin was seriously deranged." But they go on to suggest that even the Puerto Ricans may qualify for this diagnosis because their political motive "seems to be a nearly delusional judgment" (Weisz and Taylor, 1969, p. 663).

[d] Such misconceptions and bias are also reflected in the views of respected journalists. Thus, in his best-selling *The Making of the President 1964*, Theodore White asserts that "John F. Kennedy was killed by a *lunatic*, Lee Harvey Oswald, who had momentarily given loyalty to the *paranoid* Fidel Castro of Cuba. And Oswald was, in turn,

In this fashion, Donovan's influential observation that most assassins are "men suffering from mental disease, who pulled the trigger while in the grip of delusion,"[6] is repeatedly "confirmed." Consequently, the circularity continues, with many journalists and psychiatrists incorporating and extending the same inaccurate stereotype.[e]

Most disturbing is the fact that this circular and pyramiding body of questionable literature provides the basis for the conclusions of important official documents such as the *Report to the National Commission on the Causes and Prevention of Violence*,[7] not to mention that such misinformation apparently defines the operational understanding of assassins for the Federal Bureau of Investigation and the Secret Service. Both rely heavily on the literature just discussed.[f] Given

within two days, slain by another *madman*, Jack Ruby" (1965, p. 29, emphasis added). And in his *Playboy*-commissioned *Assassination in America*, James McKinley writes that assassins fit a "mold" of short, opinionated, loner males from broken homes with distorted views of themselves "just this side of megalomania" (1977, p. 57).

[e] The same problems can be observed in the law enforcement journals. Thus, virtually every cliché contained in the psychiatric literature and respected journalism is accepted and amplified in an article published in the *Journal of Police Science and Administration*. The article was written by an attorney and former "special agent of the Federal Bureau of Investigation for 12 years" (Hassel, 1974). We are told that a probable factor in "the composite social and psychological makeup of this *type* of killer" is the fact that assassins tend to be white males who are "short and slight of build" (pp. 399-400). Observe that this generalization fails to include the Arab, Sirhan Sirhan, or, after the article was published, the obese Samuel Byck and the two women, Lynette Fromme and Sara Jane Moore. Likewise the suggestion that "most 'had domineering mothers and weak and ineffectual fathers' " (p. 400) is diminished by the necessary exclusion from such categorizing of John Wilkes Booth, Charles Guiteau, Leon Czolgosz, Giuseppe Zangara, Carl Weiss, and depending on the definition of "weak," Lynette Fromme, Sara Jane Moore, and Sirhan Sirhan.

Noting also the conceptual ambiguities of the psychiatric literature, the author concludes, nonetheless, that "it is clear that all the assassins acted under some *delusion* strong enough to lead to murder" (p. 401, emphasis added). Examples offered of such delusions include the statement that "John Wilkes Booth believed himself to be an instrument of God, as did Guiteau" and Sirhan's belief that "Kennedy proposed sending 50 military aircraft to Israel" (pp. 401-402). Each of these examples represents a faulty grasp of the facts, as we will see. There are also many other questionable assertions contained in this piece, such as the conclusion that assassinations have caused "no substantial change in public policy" (p. 403).

[f] In a personal communication from the Secret Service dated October 16, 1979, the following bibliography on assassins was suggested to me:

Donovan, Robert J., *The Assassins*, Harper & Brothers, New York, revised 1964.

Hastings, Donald W., M.D., *The Journal-Lancet*, "The Psychiatry of Presidential Assassination," Reprinted from Volume 85, March, April, May, July 1965. Copyright 1965, by Lancet Publications, Inc., Minneapolis.

Kirkham, James F., Sheldon Levy and William Crotty, *Assassination and Political Violence: A Staff Report to the National Commission on the Causes and Pre-*

the problems in this literature, it is tempting to speculate about Lee Oswald, Samuel Byck, Lynette Fromme, and Sara Jane Moore—all of whom had made threatening remarks and gestures that the FBI and/ or Secret Service were aware of before their attacks: Why were they ignored or dismissed from protective surveillance? Was it because they did not then seem as "deluded" or "schizophrenic" as assassins were *supposed* to be before their acts?

Finally, one other problem can be identified in the literature on assassins. This is a general problem that afflicts many psychiatric and psychological diagnoses, even those based on actual clinical examinations of the subjects. Most of the conclusions that have been put forth about each of these subjects fails to consider the *political context* of the assassination or the assassination attempt. Instead, attention is focused on the subject's personality as it is thought to be revealed in various questionable projective tests, such as the Rorschach and Thematic Apperception Tests and clinical interviews. In addition to the highly subjective nature of these diagnostic methods, such tests are invariably conducted after the subject has been arrested and, consequently, under the most intimidating situational circumstances of confinement, fear, and uncertainty. It is hardly surprising that these examinations often reveal fear and anxiety. Whether such stress-related responses should be interpreted as "paranoia" or "schizophrenia" is another matter. To respond otherwise under such circumstances would appear, to some, more bizarre.

This problem was particularly apparent in the post-arrest examinations of Sirhan Sirhan and Arthur Bremer. To the extent that psychiatric diagnoses depend on such tests (as they almost always do) to the exclusion of the larger context of the subject's behavior, the conclusions are *reductive*. That is, they reduce the complexities of the act to the *presumed* pathology of unconscious motives and personality of the subject as defined by the social and political values of the examiner. Rarely is any systematic consideration given to the larger social and political contexts of the subject's behavior. Given such weaknesses in test procedure and interpretation, it is not surprising that questions arise concerning the empirical support and objectivity of such diagnoses. Frequently a less constricted assessment reveals that the "pathology" or "deviance" reported appears to be well within the range of ordinary behavior. The inescapable conclusion is that it is only the

vention of Violence, Volume 8, Government Printing Office, October, 1969.

Investigation of the Assassination of President John F. Kennedy, Hearings Before the President's Commission on the Assassination of President Kennedy, Government Printing Office, 1964.

criminal act itself that in this process of tautological and nonempirical reasoning lends "validity" to such suspicious verifying symptoms of mental illness.

PROBLEMS IN CLASSIFICATION

There are abundant problems in classifying human beings, and nowhere are these difficulties more apparent than in attempts to classify mental disturbances and deviant behavior. The American Psychiatric Association's attempts to classify mental illnesses in their official *Diagnostic and Statistical Manual* have generated a troublesome history of disputes that reflects poorly on the scientific basis of psychiatry.[8] Beyond the serious questions of validity, an even more embarrassing literature has emerged concerning the reliability of diagnostic criteria, tests, and procedures, which appear to be, at best, highly subjective, at worst, biased toward often unwarranted diagnoses of pathology.[9]

Perhaps the most well-known illustration of these difficulties in classification and diagnosis is Rosenhan's study, which revealed that eight pseudo-patients were classified as mentally ill by the staffs of various psychiatric hospitals, even though the pseudo-patients exhibited no abnormal behavior.[10] Just as assassins have been *presumed* and labeled insane because of their acts, the only basis for the diagnoses of mental illness in the Rosenhan study was a *presumption* of mental illness merely because the pseudo-patients were encountered in psychiatric hospitals. In other words, there are rather fundamental problems of equating labeling with diagnosis. Similar criticisms have been made about the weaknesses of projective tests, such as the Rorschach and Thematic Apperception Tests, in distinguishing *between* the ordinary person and the mentally disturbed, as well as *among* the latter.[11]

Part of this difficulty in classification appears to be the reductionist failure to consider the *context* of behavior in evaluations of the subject's personality. And in the case of assassins, that context must extend beyond the social to the political.

CRIMINAL RESPONSIBILITY

For over one hundred years, the courts have generally followed the so-called M'Naghten Rule as the standard test of criminal insanity.[12] Accordingly, a determination of insanity was based upon whether the defendant knew right from wrong at the time the crime was committed.

If that definition is applied to the sixteen subjects considered here, only three would, in my view, qualify as being legally insane: Richard Lawrence, Charles Guiteau, and John Schrank. As will be seen, none of the three had a clear conception of what they had done. All the others did.

The M'Naghten Rule has been modified in some states over the years to take into account other aspects of behavior beyond merely the ability to make cognitive distinctions between right and wrong. Some consideration has been given to emotional factors in self-control. For example, it has been argued that some persons are subjected to irresistible impulses that render their cognitive grasp of right and wrong ineffective in controlling their behavior.

In 1954, what has become known as the Durham Rule was adopted in a decision by the United States Court of Appeals in the District of Columbia. The rule states that "an accused is not criminally responsible if his unlawful act was the product of mental disease or defect."[13] This controversial ruling exposed the considerable ambiguity about what constituted "mental disease." For example, in addition to congenital mental defects, some states consider alcoholism and drug addiction to be mental illnesses. In 1962, the same court redefined its Durham Rule adding further ambiguities in an attempt to clarify its earlier ruling.[14] In this restatement of Durham, the court noted that what is considered a mental illness for clinical purposes may or may not be important in determining whether a person can be held responsible for a crime. In other words, some persons who are mentally ill are, nevertheless, accountable for their behavior unless it can be proven that the mental illness was directly associated with their criminal conduct. Given the highly subjective and nonempirical conception of mental illness, this refinement has added little clarity in actual practice. The scientific evidence linking empirically verifiable mental illnesses with impaired judgments resulting in criminal behavior remains obscure.[15]

Also in 1962, the American Law Institute drafted what it called a Model Penal Code that addressed these problems. The code states in part:

A person is not responsible for criminal conduct if at the time of such conduct as a result of mental disease or defect he lacks substantial capacity either to appreciate the criminality of his conduct or to conform his conduct to the requirements of law.[16]

This definition is embraced in the concept "diminished capacity," which was employed unsuccessfully in the defenses of Sirhan Sirhan (against his wishes) and Arthur Bremer.[g] In both cases, it was the only realistic defense that could have been argued because of the overwhelming and undeniable evidence of their crimes. It is also unlikely that any of the other subjects would have qualified for acquittal under this doctrine. Again, in my view, there was convincing evidence of diminished capacity in only three of the sixteen subjects considered in this research: Lawrence, Guiteau, and Schrank.

Regardless of which definition of criminal responsibility is applied, there is little agreement either within the courts or among psychiatrists and psychologists about what constitutes mental illness and to what degree it may be considered a mitigating factor in criminal responsibility. Insanity, like culpability itself, remains a highly elusive concept that invites controversy: a point this book will illustrate.

Before he became Chief Justice of the Supreme Court, Warren E. Burger referred to the insanity defense as a "fiction" that is often abused by attorneys and psychiatrists alike.[17] The well-known psychiatrist Thomas Szasz is also troubled by the tendency of many of his professional colleagues to consider any deviant behavior symptomatic of mental illness. Of particular concern to Szasz is the questionable empirical basis of the "schizophrenia" diagnosis that is so widely applied to so many different kinds of persons. The notion of schizophrenia, according to Szasz, is "the result not of empirical or scientific work, but of *ethical and political decision making.*"[h] It is, he concludes, "the greatest scientific scandal of our scientific age."[18] And this is not an isolated observation. A growing literature suggests that the contaminating effect of social value judgments is a very serious problem in psychiatric diagnoses.[19] And, as the following chapters will reveal, this same observation seems to apply to much of the research on American assassins.

As a practical matter, attorneys and juries seem to share this skep-

---

[g] The defense was, however, employed with startling success in the trial of Dan White for his 1978 murders of San Francisco Mayor George Moscone and Supervisor Harvey Milk. White was convicted of "voluntary manslaughter" and received a prison sentence of seven years and eight months, with the possibility of an early parole for the double, and what many considered premeditated, murders. The jury accepted the defense's controversial argument that White had not acted willfully but only as a result of emotional stress aggravated by his high intake of snack food.

[h] This issue was raised in Smith v. Schlesinger, 13 F.2d 462 (D.C. Cir. 1975), where the court formally recognized the probability that the "political or social biases" of the examining psychiatrists may have contaminated their diagnosis of the defendant. Recognizing the scholarly literature underscoring this problem, the court held that it was imperative that medical diagnosis of mental illness be free of "social judgement[s] about the desirability of an individual's lifestyle and associations" (p. 474).

ticism about psychiatric diagnoses. Given the conflicting and often contradictory testimony of expert psychiatric witnesses in many trials, juries tend to exercise their own subjective judgments about a defendant's guilt. This was clearly the case in both the Sirhan and Bremer trials where the embarrassing weaknesses in psychiatric testimony were skillfully exposed by shrewd and contemptuous attorneys on both sides of the cases.

An Alternative Approach

The psychologist M. Brewster Smith, noting the problems in studying complex political behavior, suggested that a number of factors beyond the personality of the subject must be considered. According to Smith, the cultural, political, and social contexts of the behavior under consideration must be taken into account as well as the immediate situation or circumstances in which the behavior occurs.[20] That is the approach of this study.

Drawing upon primary sources as much as possible, I have attempted to reconstruct the lives and times of American assassins. To do this, I have researched materials contained in, or supplied by, the National Archives, the Library of Congress, the Federal Bureau of Investigation, and the Secret Service, as well as a number of other government agencies. Congressional hearings and investigations proved to be another valuable source. Beyond that, I have examined trial transcripts available in various federal and state courts around the country. From this wide variety of sources, I have read personal diaries, autobiographical manuscripts, medical histories, newspaper accounts, and listened to hours of tapes. This primary material was supplemented with pertinent biographical and historical work and other careful secondary sources.

In order to understand the motives of the sixteen subjects considered in this work, I attempted to reconstruct two realities: the *objective* reality of the times and the *subjective* reality of the subject. By comparing the degree to which these subjective and objective realities were congruent, I was able to make some determinations about what motivated these individuals. In so doing, I was then able to make judgments about the *rationality* of their acts in the sense that they had meaningfully contemplated the consequences before embarking upon them.

In all but one case, James Earl Ray, I found that the subjects acted initially on the basis of some *frustration*. As others have observed in a variety of different contexts, aggression is frequently preceded by frustration.[21] Having noted the frustration, I then investigated its *source*, finding in some cases that it was *personal* and in others that it was, contrary to the stereotype, *political*. My next objective was to determine the actual *target* of the aggression. Obviously, the target was a political figure, but was this person a *real* or *surrogate* target? In other words, was the aggression against these political leaders *direct* or *displaced* from some other real frustrating agent?

Finally, drawing on the psychiatric literature I have just criticized, I attempted to make some judgments about the existence of any symptoms of mental disturbance, as they are commonly defined. In each case, I looked for signs of emotional and cognitive distortion, hallucination, delusion, fragmented reality contact, and disturbed social relations. Taking the answers to all these questions together, I was able to make some suggestive judgments about the motives, rationality, and criminal culpability of each of the subjects. Moreover, it soon became apparent that certain *patterns* were observable. I subsequently identified these patterns as *types* of assassins and labeled them largely as a convenient way to organize and present this work (and not as an attempt to impose a new classification scheme). But I will also argue for the considerable heuristic value of this typology in understanding American assassins and, consequently, the assassination phenomenon in America. Only two of the sixteen subjects could not be categorized according to this method. Let me briefly describe each type.

TYPE I assassins view their acts as a probable sacrifice of self for a political ideal. They are fully cognizant and accepting of the meaning, implications, and personal consequences of their acts. Inherently personal motives, such as a neurotic need for recognition, are secondary to their primary political purpose. Type I's may or may not attempt to escape, but the sacrificial theme that characterizes their zeal and commitment suggests that capture, like death, is an acceptable, if not preferred, risk. Emotional distortion is present only to the extent that political ideals supersede survival instincts. If captured, the Type I does not recant on his or her motivating principles or seek clemency or personal publicity. Unlike Types II, III, and IV, their extremism is rational, selfless, principled, and without perversity.

TYPE II assassins are persons with overwhelming and aggressive egocentric needs for acceptance, recognition, and status. There is none of the cognitive distortion associated with psychoses. Emotionally they are characterized by moderately high levels of reality-based anxiety that exerts a strong influence on their behavior. Without delusion, they fully appreciate and accept the personal consequences of their acts. The primary characteristic they share is what Harold Lasswell has called a "political personality."[22] That is, a personality which is inclined to project personal motives on public objects and rationalize them in terms of some larger public interest. According to Lasswell, such persons seek power in order to compensate for low estimates of self that are most frequently a result of a deprivation of love and affection in their personal lives—e.g., possibly the indifference of a parent, the rejection of a spouse, or other comparable experiences. Thus there are always *significant others* in the personal lives of Type II subjects. Under these circumstances, in every instance, the exercise of power in a public manner generates the attention that had been denied in the past. And, in some cases, the act may serve, in a revengeful way, to place the burden of guilt on those persons in their disturbed personal lives who have denied or rejected them. Although Lasswell had public office seeking in mind, assassination too may be used to compensate for personal rejection and failure. Assassins of this type anticipate capture or death and prepare for it: The neurotic Type II assassin is an anxious, emotional, and ultimately depressed person who is primarily concerned with his or her personal problems and frustrations and only secondarily with causes or ideals.

TYPE III assassins are psychopaths (or sociopaths) who believe that the condition of their lives is so intolerably meaningless and without purpose that destruction of society and themselves is desirable for its own sake. Unlike ordinary psychopaths whose rage is usually directed at specific segments of society (e.g., sexually or racially defined victims), this type of killer strikes at persons who personify the majority or those who represent a cross-section rather than any particular segment. Type III subjects possess no positive political values and are belligerently contemptuous of morality and social convention. The amorphous rage and perversity that characterizes the lives of these persons may finally take form in some extreme act like suicide, mass murder, or assassination; but in the case of assassination, there is no political motive. Except for their perverse anger, they are emotionally dormant: the pendulum swings of emotion associated with some psychoses are absent. They also differ from Type I assassins in that they are rational in a negative and perverse Dostoyevskian sense and thoughtfully aware of their motives and the consequences of their acts. Feeling neither joy nor sadness and indifferent to death, they are unable to relate to others. Thus, unlike Type II's, there are no significant others in their empty lives. The Type III subject accurately perceives reality but is limited in his capacity to respond to it emotionally. To paraphrase G. K. Chesterson, he is not someone who has lost his reason, rather he is someone who has lost everything *but* his reason.

TYPE IV assassins are characterized by severe emotional and cognitive distortion that is expressed in hallucinations and delusions of persecution and/or grandeur. Their contact with reality is so tenuous that they are usually unable to grasp the significance of their actions or understand the response of others to them. As a rule, their acts are mystically or "divinely" inspired—in a word, irrational or insane.

Observe that these definitions refer to ideal or hypothetical types and do not presume the exclusivity of the four classifications. Obviously, most human behavior is distributed along an infinite continuum reflecting subtle gradations of individual differences. The delusions of a Type IV, for example, may be couched in the ideological language of a Type I. And as I have indicated, the Type II assassin invariably rationalizes his or her act in terms of some larger political ideal. Also the violent and perverse rage of the Type III assassin may seem psychotic to those who overlook the reasoned and controlled manner in which that rage is expressed.

The sixteen subjects are classified according to these definitions in Figure 1. Note that the assassins of Huey Long and Martin Luther King, Jr. represent two very different, special cases.

FORMAT OF THE BOOK

The chapters that follow are, in a sense, stories. As much as possible, I have tried to let the facts speak for themselves. I have also tried to do the same for the subjects, so that their words, and not only my analyses and interpretations, are an important part of the story on each.

Assassins are not likeable people in most instances. But of course that is a political judgment on my part. Would we say the same about the would-be assassins of Adolph Hitler or other Nazi leaders? In writing this, I have attempted not only to communicate facts but, in a departure from the usual standards of academic writing, I have tried to convey a mood about these people and their times. Complex behavior such as personal violence cannot be understood completely without some sense of mood and emotion. In some of the subjects there is nothing for most readers to empathize with. This is especially true for Type III and IV subjects. But many of the thoughts and

Figure 1

Classification of American Assassins and Would-Be Assassins and Their Intended Victims

Type I

John Wilkes Booth
(Abraham Lincoln)

Leon Czolgosz
(William McKinley)

Oscar Collazo
Griselio Torresola
(Harry S Truman)

Sirhan Sirhan
(Robert Kennedy)

Type II

Lee Harvey Oswald
(John F. Kennedy)

Samuel Byck
(Richard Nixon)

Lynette Alice Fromme
(Gerald Ford)

Sara Jane Moore
(Gerald Ford)

Type III

Giuseppe Zangara
(Franklin Roosevelt)

Arthur Bremer
(George Wallace)

Type IV

Richard Lawrence
(Andrew Jackson)

Charles Guiteau
(James Garfield)

John Schrank
(Theodore Roosevelt)

Atypicals

Carl Weiss
(Huey Long)

James Earl Ray
(Martin Luther King, Jr.)

emotions of some of the others may be disturbingly familiar to a good number; the beast slumbers in us all.

Violence is most often an emotional act—something we *feel* rather than think. Even the cold, calculating, and premeditated violence of assassination is, in most cases, a highly charged emotional expression of something more than simple aggression. The major undertaking in the following chapters is to determine exactly what that something is.

Chapter Two · Region and Class

Booth and Czolgosz

I know how foolish I shall be deemed for undertaking
such a step as this, where on one side I have my friends
and every thing to make me happy, where my profession alone has gained me an income of *more than* twenty
thousand dollars a year, and where my great personal
ambition in my profession has such a great field of
labor.
　　　　　　　　　　　　　　—John Wilkes Booth

I killed the President because he was the enemy of
the good people—the good working people. I am not
sorry for my crime.
　　　　　　　　　　　　　　—Leon Czolgosz

UNLIKE the stereotype of mental impairment described in Chapter One,
the two assassins discussed in this chapter can be understood only in
the context of the political events that defined their motives; neither
was mentally deranged. The assassination of Abraham Lincoln was a
direct result of the regional conflict that had taken such a terrible toll
of American lives from 1861 to 1865. William McKinley's death was
expressly linked to the bitter class struggle that characterized a major
segment of American politics during the last quarter of the nineteenth
century. Yet most accounts of both assassinations have little to say
about how these eras of conflict might have stirred the passions of the
two assassins John Wilkes Booth and Leon Czolgosz. Instead we are
led to believe that both assassinations can be understood as the acts
of irrational men who killed only to satisfy their warped, egocentric
need for acclaim and notoriety. Thus Booth has been described as a
frustrated "ham" actor, jealous of the fame of his father and older
brother. Czolgosz's sanity was not questioned until after his execution
when, on the basis of the most subjective interpretations, the case was

made that he was obviously "deluded" or insane because he believed William McKinley was antagonistic toward working-class people.

Such conclusions about Booth and Czolgosz provide examples of the most naive, or perhaps politically inspired, kind of psychological reductionism. As the facts will show, such ideologically biased interpretations are inaccurate. Both Booth's and Czolgosz's acts were politically inspired. If their reasons for taking such extreme measures were irrational, then one must conclude that the thousands, perhaps millions, of other Americans who hated Presidents Lincoln and McKinley were also irrational.

Who were those other Americans? In Booth's case, they were Southerners who supported the Confederate cause and others, outside the South, who vigorously opposed the bloodiest war in American history. In Czolgosz's case, they were the masses of immigrant workers who were being brutalized during the most oppressive quarter-century in American history by the industrial establishment that William McKinley represented.

Neither Booth nor Czolgosz were deluded as were the Type IV assassins; nor did they share the purposeless negativism of the Type III's, or the compensatory motives of Type II subjects. Each acted on the basis of political principles that they maintained to their dying breaths.

JOHN WILKES BOOTH (1838-1865)

It is commonly assumed that President Lincoln's assassin, John Wilkes Booth, killed to achieve the fame that had eluded him in a floundering career as an actor. Booth's stage career, it is reasoned, had never achieved the distinction of his famous father, the English-born tragedian Junius Brutus Booth, or his older brother Edwin. Realizing this in 1864, and confronted with a bronchial condition that threatened his ability to perform, Booth, in a classically compensatory manner, supposedly decided to resolve his personal disappointments and failures and achieve lasting fame by striking a dramatic political blow for the Confederate cause. Probably the most widely respected and quoted proponent of this view is Stanley Kimmel in his *The Mad Booths of Maryland.*[1]

Drawing upon Kimmel, Booth has been dismissed elsewhere in even less qualified language as merely a deluded, acrobatic, noisy, and alcoholic actor.[2] Other secondary work has imposed a rather strained psychoanalytic interpretation on this general explanation that goes even further in stressing Booth's neurotic motives.[3] Yet even in Kimmel's carefully researched work, numerous facts appear that raise doubts about his interpretation.

The most important qualification of Kimmel's explanation, however, is that it virtually ignores the political context of the assassination: facts such as Lincoln's unpopularity in the North as well as the South, the vicious opposition within his cabinet and the Congress, and the controversy surrounding his re-election in 1864. To ignore the political circumstances and events of the Civil War era is to miss the most important element in Booth's motives. And virtually every account of the assassination that shares Kimmel's conclusion about Booth does just that.

In most cases, the omission is a result of the erroneous assumption that the nation's esteem and affection for Lincoln preceded his death. The fact is that until Appomattox, a week before his death, Lincoln was one of the most criticized and vilified presidents in American history, commonly referred to as "the baboon, the imbecile, the wet rag, the Kentucky mule."[4] Although winning re-election in 1864 by a convincing margin (55 percent of the popular vote), that victory can be best understood, not in terms of Lincoln's personal popularity, but rather in terms of the ineffectiveness and confusion of the opposition—both within his own party as well as among his Democratic opponents—and a final reluctant resignation of party leaders to the principle that in time of war it is best not to change horses in midstream. When considered in this political context, the facts of Booth's life—both his upbringing and his career—suggest a different view of the man and his motives.

Youth and Career

John Wilkes Booth was born on May 10, 1838 near Baltimore. He was almost twenty-seven years of age when he shot himself in a burning barn surrounded by soldiers on April 26, 1865. Of the ten children born to Junius Brutus Booth and his second wife, Mary Ann Holmes Booth, John Wilkes, or "Johnny" as he was called, was their favorite. A beautiful child with shiny black hair and classically sculpted features, he exuded the brightness and exuberance of a happy childhood. His mother and his older sister Asia adored his kind and gentle ways, while his tempestuous but doting father admired his fiery spirit and athletic ability. As we will see, this positive view of Booth was shared by virtually everyone who ever knew him.[5] He made friends easily and was loyal and generous to a fault.[6] Even after he had achieved fame as an actor, Booth did not forget his childhood friends. Throughout his life his friendships endured, uncontaminated by his success, and they would span a sociological range from stable boys and clerks to debutantes and high-ranking public officials.

As a youth, Booth attended private schools where he studied history and the classics, reading Milton, Byron and Shakespeare, and committing much of the latter to memory in preparation for a stage career virtually assured by family tradition. He also played the flute.[7] He learned to ride early and well, and his sister later remembered fondly their spirited gallops together chasing imaginary villains through the wooded Maryland countryside.[8] A lover of the outdoors, Booth's respect for living creatures prevented him from becoming the hunter and angler so encouraged by the culture of nineteenth-century America. Rather his interest ran toward botany and geology; he was an observer rather than a conqueror of nature. His sister described him as "very tender of flowers, and of insects and butterflies; lightning bugs he considered as 'bearers of sacred torches' and would go out of his way to avoid injuring them."[9]

An unusually articulate youth, Booth's gaiety and exuberance for life had a contagious quality that partly explains his popularity with those who knew him. Often his activities were punctuated with melodramatic exclamations that delighted his friends. His sister recorded one occasion where he exclaimed:

Heaven and Earth! How glorious it is to live! how divine! to breathe this breath of life with a clear mind and healthy lungs! Don't let us be sad. Life is so short—and the world is so beautiful. Just to breathe is delicious.[10]

Booth was fourteen when his famous father died in 1852. During his lifetime, the elder Booth had become the most famous Shakespearean actor in America. Although his career kept him away from home frequently during his son's formative years, there was no question of his love for the handsome boy who had inherited so much of the old man's spirit and flamboyance. Edwin, Booth's talented but more taciturn older brother, had spent a youthful stage apprenticeship with his father and thus logically assumed many of the roles and much of the acclaim previously enjoyed by the elder Booth. The oldest brother, Junius Brutus, Jr., was also an actor, but being some seventeen years older than John Wilkes, a sibling rivalry, which often placed strains on the relationship between the two younger brothers, never developed between them.

When Booth began his acting career at the age of seventeen, three years after his father's death, there is no question that some rivalry developed with respect to his by-now-famous older brother Edwin. No doubt both were intent on carrying on the proud and highly successful tradition their father had established. What is less clear, however, is the familiar contention that Booth fared less well in the views of audiences and critics than did Edwin—the basic premise of the argument upon which so many have explained the Lincoln assassination.

The evidence appears to support the premise only for the first three years of John's career, when his inexperience was acknowledged in his reviews. The sense of inferiority Kimmel claims Booth experienced during these early years of apprenticeship, performing in the shadow of a late and lamented father and an older brother, was no doubt justified. The fact that Booth had himself billed as "J. Wilkes" rather than invoking the renown of the Booth name attests to that fact. It also suggests Booth's desire to make a reputation on his own merits rather than capitalizing on the fame of his father and brother. Determined in this respect, Booth took his critical knocks, as most young actors do, as an obscure "J. Wilkes" before emerging triumphantly on the Richmond stage in the autumn of 1858 where he delighted audiences and was proclaimed then and until his death as the handsomest actor on the American stage.[11]

The argument that Booth's sympathies for the Confederacy had their origins in the applause of Southern audiences and the critical disdain he received in the North has no basis in fact. After his first three apprenticeship years, Booth was never to receive a bad review—North or South. He was a star, a matinee idol whose talents approximated those of Edwin, while his physical attractiveness and flair on stage exceeded his older brother's and placed him in a position of undeniable ascendancy in the American theater. In fact, the *only* reservations about his abilities cited by Kimmel are those expressed by Edwin in private correspondence.[12] Contrary to Edwin's assessment, Booth's reviews across the country were sufficiently enthusiastic to trigger professional envy from an older brother. Consider the following representative critical comments taken from Booth's reviews:

> An artist of the highest order. [*Richard III*, New York, January 1862]

> . . . the most brilliant [Richard III] ever played in the city. [Chicago, January-February 1862]

In Baltimore, his performances were thought superior to Edwin's. Even in New York where Edwin was a special favorite of theater audiences, complementary comparisons were made. His performances also cut through the typical Bostonian reserve of the *Daily Advertiser*, which allowed that with some reservations about "proper treatment of the voice," it was "greatly pleased" by his Richard III.[13] When he returned to Boston in January 1863 for an appearance in *The Apostate* with brother Edwin in the audience, he was "wildly cheered."[14]

In February of the same year, Booth played Macbeth at the Arch Street Theatre in Philadelphia where one of his first appearances as a fledgling actor had been poorly received. Nearby at the Chestnut Street Theatre, Edwin Forrest, perhaps America's first matinee idol, was performing in the same role. In a convincing demonstration of his great appeal, audiences ignored Forrest and lined up to see the handsome new star of the American stage—John Wilkes Booth. And reviews indicate that they were not disappointed.[15] Advanced billings for Booth's April appearance as Richard III in Washington described him as "a star of the first magnitude."[16] Reviewers later acknowledged that he had established himself as a reigning favorite in the capital. Attracted by such reviews, President Lincoln saw Booth perform in *The Marble Heart* on November 9, 1863.[17] Later that month, the Washington *Daily National Intelligencer* praised his performance of Romeo in the Shakespearean drama as "the most satisfactory of all renderings of that fine character."[18]

Recognition of Booth's talents were not limited to audiences and critics only. Established professionals in the theater acknowledged his superior talents. John Ellsler, Director of the respected Cleveland Academy of Music, who knew and admired all the Booths, observed that John Wilkes had "more of [his famous father's] power in one performance than Edwin can show in a year." He went on to predict that John Wilkes Booth would become "as great an actor as America can produce."[19]

Such appraisals continued as long and wherever Booth performed. At a March 1864 appearance in New Orleans, he gave an emotional performance before a typically appreciative audience in the same role and on the same stage where his father had given his last performance.[20] Similar praise followed his engagements in Boston later that year, where crowds waited after the performance outside the stage exit hoping for another glimpse of the handsome actor as he left the theater.[21] On November 25, 1864, he appeared for the first and last time with his brothers Edwin and Junius in *Julius Caesar* before an ecstatic audience of over two thousand "Bravo"-shouting New Yorkers who crowded the Winter Garden Theatre for a command performance.[22] Again, it should be emphasized that from 1858 through his last performance at Ford's Theatre less than a month before the assassination, there is *no* evidence that Booth received other than the most complimentary reviews of his work.

In this context, it is surprising that he remained so well-liked by his peers in the acting profession. Although numerous young women succumbed to Booth's dashing good looks and personal charm, he remained a discrete and invariably kind and sensitive Lothario. Such refinement set him apart from the typical nineteenth-century American male; women found him irresistible. Clara Morris, a contemporary of Booth's on the American stage, described him as "so young, so bright, so gay, so kind." Recalling an incident where Booth, hurrying from the stage door of the theater, inadvertently knocked over a small child, the actress described how Booth picked up the little street urchin and carefully wiped the tears from his grimy face. Then satisfied that the child was not injured, Booth kissed him and pressed a pocketful of change into his hand before dashing off. The significance of the act was that it was so characteristic of Booth:

> He knew of no witness to the act. To kiss a pretty clean child under the approving eyes of mamma might mean nothing but politeness, but surely it required the prompting of a warm and tender heart to make a young and thoughtful man feel for and caress such a dirty, forlorn bit of babyhood as that.[23]

Nor was Booth's kindness and generosity confined to star-struck young women and children. He remained a close and loving son and brother to his mother and sister Asia.[24] More interesting, however, is that men from seemingly all walks of life valued the friendship of the engaging young actor. Even male peers within his competitive and egocentric profession genuinely seemed to like and admire Booth. A fellow actor, Sir Charles Wyndham, described him as "a man of flashing wit and magnetic manner. He was one of the best raconteurs to whom I ever listened."[25] Another actor who knew Booth explained that he was liked because of his quick good humor, his love of fun, and his unassuming ease with people regardless of social rank. He never permitted his celebrity status to become a barrier to old friends. He was also generous with his money.[26]

Thus an accurate view of John Wilkes Booth—the view of his contemporaries—represents a stark contrast to the image of a frustrated, highly neurotic actor obsessed with achieving fame. Booth's character emerged out of a childhood of great love and affection—a beautiful, self-confident child who never knew unkindness or hardship. Raised in the cultured, if eccentric, environment of a theatrical aristocracy, the transition to the stage was swift, smooth, and highly successful.

The acclaim denied to so many in the acting profession was well within grasp by his twenty-first year. By the time of his death, some six years later, his reputation as a fine actor and matinee idol was established. Booth's popularity and success were reflected in his income: in 1862, he wrote that he was averaging 650 dollars per week for his performances—an extraordinary sum for that period.[27] At the time of his death, even after he had cut his performances drastically because of his war-related activities, he wrote that he was earning "more than twenty-thousand dollars a year."[28]

To bolster the unconvincing explanation that professional jealousy and an obsessive "greed for fame" motivated Booth, the argument, as previously observed, has also been made that he was threatened with a loss of his voice due to a recurring bronchial condition.[29] Recognizing that his career was limited, he then supposedly turned to political extremism only as a means of eclipsing a loathesome brother's theatrical ascendancy. While this argument cannot be substantiated or denied in the absence of medical evidence, it is true that Booth's sixth performance in New Orleans in March, 1864 was cancelled because of a "cold."[30] But there is simply no other evidence attesting to the alleged seriousness or chronic nature of this problem as Kimmel suggests. Rather it is *assumed* that Booth had permanently damaged his voice and was thus forced to acknowledge that his acting career was over. It is further *assumed* that this circumstance heightened his "neurotic sense of inferiority."[31] Such is the highly questionable basis of the Kimmel explanation.

The Political Context

Political events in 1864, rather than assumptions about chronic laryngitis and sibling rivalry, provide a more accurate context in which to assess Booth's motives. Nearing the completion of his first term in office, Abraham Lincoln enjoyed none of the esteem accorded to him after his death. Lincoln had been elected president, a minority candidate of an upstart new party, with less than 40 percent of the popular vote. He had won only because the Democratic party had divided ranks with two candidates, J. C. Breckenridge and Stephen A. Douglas, splitting 47.5 percent of the vote while the remaining 12.6 percent went to Constitutional Union party candidate John Bell. Undaunted by his lack of a popular mandate, Lincoln quickly embarked upon a course of action with a single overriding purpose in mind—the restoration of the Union between the North and South.

Needless to say, Lincoln was hated in the rebellious states. Not so obvious in history texts, however, was his unpopularity in the North, where growing opposition to the war required drastic—some would say dictatorial—executive actions to control the festering and volatile dissent. Lincoln quickly, and on his own initiative, suspended the constitutionally guaranteed writ of *habeas corpus* and authorized the arbitrary arrest of any suspected opponents of his war policies. In 1863, for example, some 38,000 persons were arrested in the North and imprisoned without trial for suspected anti-war activities. Soon after the first shots were fired at Fort Sumter, he had—without Congressional approval—called up the militia and expanded the size of the regular army. He arbitrarily, and again without congressional approval, transferred some two million dollars to Union agents in New York for assistance in stifling the anti-war movement. Ignoring Congress, he instituted unpopular conscription in 1862 by executive order. He aggressively appointed and removed a succession of politically ambitious Union generals before finding a satisfactory commander in Grant. He issued the Emancipation Proclamation, freeing the slaves in the rebellious states without consulting Congress. He issued executive orders establishing provisional courts in conquered states and appointed military governors in Arkansas, Louisiana and Tennessee without Congressional approval or clear constitutional authority. In general, President Lincoln ignored the Congress and the Constitution during his first term in office and dramatically exploited his executive authority.

A nation averse to strong central government, sympathetic to states' rights, and embued with notions of Jacksonian democracy did not respond kindly to this unimpressive-looking, obscure midwesterner who was presiding over the bloodiest war in American history with the iron hand of a despot—a war that would kill and maim over a million American boys, many of them drafted as reluctant participants in what had become an All-American holocaust.[32] Such negative public sentiments were reflected most vigorously in the Congress, where Lincoln was especially reviled by members of his own party. He was also condemned and ridiculed by his own cabinet appointees. Prominent and influential newspaper editors charged him with abuses ranging from incompetence to war profiteering. On one side, Democrats blasted him for waging an unconstitutional war against political self-determination; on the other, radical Republicans condemned his restraint in prosecuting the war. By 1864, it was difficult to identify any important segment of support for the President. Strong criticism had developed in the North in response to costly military defeats at Southern hands, racist opposition to emancipation, and resistance to the draft in an exceedingly bloody war to free Negroes most Northerners considered less than human.[33]

Opposition to Lincoln and the draft was particularly vigorous in New York and Philadelphia, as well as smaller towns on the eastern seaboard and Ohio, Kentucky, and Wisconsin in the Midwest, not to mention the strong Southern sympathy in the marginally loyal Border States. Following on the heels of New York Governor Horatio Seymour's denunciation of Lincoln in a July Fourth speech in 1863, draft resisters rioted in New York City, attacking blacks and abolitionists in a murderous three-day rampage.[34]

By early 1864, many prominent Union supporters considered Lincoln's presidency an unqualified failure[35]; it was certain that his renomination would be challenged. As the peace movement grew in 1864, influential newspapers in New York and Philadelphia attacked the use of black soldiers and condemned the Emancipation Proclamation.[36] Moreover, Lincoln's vilification was not confined to this country: London papers also sneered at his manners and ridiculed his homeliness while condemning his policies.[37]

A discouraged Lincoln anticipated defeat in 1864 and prepared a memorandum on the transition as serious challenges to his renomination were mounted by Salman P. Chase, his Treasury Secretary, and former general and "Great Pathfinder" John C. Fremont, as well as another general, Benjamin Butler.[38] Largely as a result of the fragmented quality of his opposition, rather than his own popularity, Lincoln was finally renominated in Baltimore by an unenthusiastic party amid feelings of sullen resentment.[39] Prominent Union supporters such as William Cullen Bryant, Theodore Tilton, and Horace Greeley considered Lincoln a failure as president but saw no acceptable alternative.

Undoubtedly, the curious nomination and party platform of opposition Democrats contributed importantly to the beleaguered Lincoln's subsequent re-election. The Democrats nominated another former general, George McClellan, as a candidate committed, like Lincoln, to an uncompromising military solution to the war. They then saddled the general with an incongruous peace platform written by chief antiwar advocate and vice-presidential nominee Clement L. Vallandigham—a man who had been arrested and deported to the South by a military court for his treasonous Confederate sympathies.[40] Confronted with a choice between such a contradiction or the unpopular Lincoln, the electorate held its nose and voted for the incumbent, giving him an unanticipated impressive victory.[41]

Lincoln's surprising re-election and mandate signaled an ominous message for the South. Given Lincoln's unpopularity in the North and the growing anti-war sentiment in that part of the country, many war-weary Southerners had prayed for his defeat and a negotiated end to the war that would recognize, as many Northern papers advocated, an independent Confederacy.[42] The loss of life on both sides during Grant's Wilderness Campaign in May and June 1864 was staggering—an estimated 90,000 casualties. Lincoln, like another president a hundred years and a different war later, was widely blamed for this carnage that many, anticipating a shorter, less costly war, now considered unnecessary. For the South, his re-election meant that the destructive war of attrition Grant was now conducting would grind on toward its humiliating ultimate objective—unconditional surrender. It was a time of desperation in the South. Lincoln, as Commander in Chief of the Union armies now intent on destroying men, not merely capturing territory, was intensely hated throughout the South. The *Richmond Examiner* asked: "What shall we call him? Coward, assassin, savage, murderer of women and babies? Or shall we consider them all embodied in the word of fiend, and call him Lincoln the Fiend."[43]

Booth's Politics and Plan

Few persons loved the South and hated Abraham Lincoln more than John Wilkes Booth. From the beginning of the war, Booth had made his Southern sympathies clear in the most outspoken and unequivocal manner. His hatred for the President was both personal and political, and it grew more intense as the conflict dragged on. He held Lincoln responsible for a bloody and unnecessary war and, as a man of some refinement, he was contemptuous of what he saw as Lincoln's personal coarseness of style and manner. In Booth's eyes, Lincoln was not qualified by birth or training to be president.[44]

As a performer, Booth was permitted to travel throughout the country—North and South—during the war. He used this privilege to smuggle quinine and other war-related material, as well as information, into the South at every opportunity.[45] As prospects for a Southern victory began to dim after Lee's defeat at Gettysburg in 1863, Booth's activities intensified. By 1864, he was preoccupied with the war effort, severely curtailing his professional commitments—not because of bad reviews or throat problems—but because his priorities were now elsewhere.

It is worth noting that Booth's theatrical tours regularly took him to areas of the most intense opposition to the President. In addition to Southern cities, Booth regularly toured New York, Philadelphia, and Baltimore, not to mention the capital itself where the anti-war movement was very strong. It is little wonder that he correctly viewed himself as participating in a widely popular cause.

In September 1864, the same month that Lincoln was renominated for a second term, Sherman's forces swept through Atlanta burning and pillaging as they went. To the north, Lee's army was being forced into a last stand outside Richmond. The situation for the Confederates was desperate. It was at this time that Booth became part of a plan to abduct the President so that subsequently Lincoln could be ransomed for the release of Confederate prisoners of war who were sorely needed to restore Lee's badly depleted ranks. In October, Booth went to Montreal on the first of many trips he would make across the border over the next few months to meet with Confederate agents.[46] While there, he opened a bank account and packed his theatrical wardrobe and paraphernalia in a trunk for future shipment to Richmond. Any doubts about the plan were put aside with Lincoln's November re-election. It was now evident that drastic measures would be required to prevent Southern defeat.

Various alternatives were discussed by Confederate agents: plots to sabotage government ships and buildings; raids from Canada on cities such as Buffalo, Detroit, and New York; attacks on prisoner of war camps to release Confederate soldiers; a plot to burn New York City; and a plan to distribute clothes infested with yellow fever, smallpox, and other contagious diseases in Washington[47]—all desperate measures to stem the tide of a war going very badly.

In this context, the plan to abduct the President seems less bizarre. Earlier in April 1864, General Grant had refused a Confederate proposal for a prisoner exchange; a successful abduction could possibly achieve that end. In any case, it was worth the gamble. In November, Booth initiated actual preparations to carry out the abduction. He began to recruit among old friends and acquaintances for persons willing to assist in the operation. He also made trips into southern Maryland to plan the route by which the handcuffed president would be transported across Southern lines. During the year, Booth had spent large sums of his own money in such espionage activities.

Intent on having his purpose and motives for the abduction clearly understood, Booth drafted a sealed letter of explanation and left it with his sister Asia's husband, John Sleeper Clarke, for safekeeping. The letter, which remained unopened until it was discovered after the assassination, reveals the scope and depth of Booth's feeling and his rationale for his anticipated crime:

My Dear Sir:

You may use this as you think best. But as some may wish to know when, who and why, and as I know not how to direct, I give it (in the words of your master).

To whom it may concern,

Right or wrong, God judge me, not man. For be my motive good or bad, of one thing I am sure, the lasting condemnation of the North.

I love peace more than life. Have loved the Union beyond expression. For four years I have waited, hoped and prayed for the dark clouds to break, and for the restoration of our former sunshine. To wait longer would be a crime. All hope for peace is dead. My prayers have proved as idle as my hopes. God's will be done. I go to see and share the bitter end.

I have ever held the South were right. The very nomination of Abraham Lincoln, four years ago, spoke plainly war—war upon Southern rights and institutions. His election proved it. Await an overt act. Yet, till you are bound and plundered. What folly! The South was wise. Who thinks of argument or patience when the finger of his enemy presses the trigger? In a *foreign war*, I too, could say, country right or wrong. But in a struggle *such as ours* where the brother tries to pierce the brother's heart, for God's sake, choose the right. When a country like this spurns *justice* for her side, she forfeits the allegiance of every honest free man, and should leave him untrammelled by any fealty soever, to act as his own conscience may approve.

People of the North, to hate tyranny, to love liberty and justice, to strike at wrong and oppression, was the teaching of our fathers. The study of our early history will not let me forget it and may it never.

This country was formed for the *white* man and not for the black. And looking upon *African slavery* from the same stand-point as held by the noble framers of our Constitution, I, for one, have ever considered it one of the greatest blessings for themselves and for us that God ever bestowed upon a favored nation. Witness heretofore our wealth and power; witness their elevation and enlightenment above their race elsewhere. I have lived among it most of my life, and have seen less harsh treatment from master to man than I have beheld in the North from father to son. Yet heaven knows that *no one* would be more willing to do more for the negro race than I, could I but see a way to *still better their* condition.

But Lincoln's policy is only preparing the way to their total annihilation. The South *are not nor have they been fighting for the continuance* of slavery. The first battle of Bull Run did away with that idea. The causes since for war have been as *noble, and greater far than those that urged our fathers on. Even though we should allow that they were wrong at the beginning of this contest, cruelty and injustice* have made the wrong become the right, and they now stand before the wonder and admiration of the world, as a noble band of patriotic heroes. Hereafter reading of *their deeds*, Thermopylae will be forgotten.

When I aided in the capture and execution of John Brown who was a murderer on our western border, who was fairly *tried and convicted* before an impartial judge and jury, of treason, and who by the way, has since been made a god, I was proud of my little share in the transaction, for I deemed it my duty, and that I was helping our common country to perform an act of justice. But what was a crime in poor John Brown is now considered by themselves as the greatest and only virtue of the Republican party. Strange transmigration. Vice is to become a virtue, simply because more *indulge* in it.

I thought then, *as now*, that the Abolitionists *were the only traitors* in the land, and that the entire party deserved the same fate as poor old Brown, not because they wish to abolish slavery, but on account of the means they have endeavored to use to effect that abolition. If Brown were living, I doubt whether he *himself would set slavery against the Union. Most, or many in the North do, and openly curse the Union, if the South are to return and attain a single right* guaranteed to them by every tie which we once *revered as sacred*. The South can make no choice. It is either extermination or slavery for *themselves* worse than death to draw from. I know *my* choice.

I have also studied hard to discover upon what grounds the right of a state to secede has been denied, when our name, United States and Declaration of Independence, both provide for secession. But this is no time for words. I write in haste. I know how foolish I shall be deemed for undertaking such a step as this, where on one side I have my friends and every thing to make me happy, where my profession alone has gained me an income of *more than* twenty thousand dollars a year, and where my great personal ambition in my profession has such a great field of labor.

On the other hand the South have never bestowed upon me one kind word, a place where I have no friends except beneath the sod: a place where I must either become a private soldier or a beggar.

To give up all the *former* for the *latter*, besides my mother and sisters whom I love so dearly, although they differ so widely in opinion, seems insane; but God is my judge. I love *justice* more than a country that disowns it; more than fame and wealth; heaven pardon me, if wrong, more than a happy home. I have never been upon the battle field, but, O my countrymen, could all but see the *reality* or effects of this horrid war, as I have seen them in *every state* save Virginia, I know you would think like me, and would pray the Almighty to create in the Northern mind a sense of *right and justice* even should it possess no seasoning of mercy, and then he would dry up this sea of blood between us, which is daily growing wider. Alas, poor country, is she to meet her threatened doom? Four years ago I would have given a thousand lives to see her as I have always known her, powerful and unbroken. And even now I would hold my life as naught, to see her what she was. O, my friends, if the fearful scenes of the past four years had never been enacted or if what had been done were but a frightful dream from which we could now awake with over-flowing hearts, we could bless our God and pray for his continued favor. How I have loved the *old flag* can never be known.

A few years since the world could boast of none so pure and spotless. But of late I have been seeing and hearing of the *bloody deeds* of which she has been *made the emblem*, and would shudder to think how changed she has grown. Oh, how I have longed to see her break from the midst of blood and death that circles round her folds, spoiling her beauty and tarnishing her honor! But no: day by day she has been dragged deeper into cruelty and oppression, till now in my eyes her once bright red striped look [like] *bloody gashes* on the face of heaven.

I look now upon my early admiration of her glories as a dream.

My love as things stand today is for the South alone. *Nor do I deem it a dishonor in attempting to make for her a prisoner of this man to whom she owes so much misery.* If success attends me, I go penniless to her side. They say she has found that last ditch which the North has so long derided and been endeavoring to force her in, forgetting they are our brothers, and it is impolite to goad an enemy to madness. Should I reach her in safety and

find it true, I will proudly beg permission to triumph or die in that same ditch by her side.
A Confederate doing duty on his own responsibility,

J. Wilkes Booth[48]

Booth coolly and rationally recruited five men (all of whom he had known earlier) to assist him: John Surratt, a Confederate spy and a person well acquainted with the geography of southern Maryland; David Herold, a simple-minded but extremely loyal person who also knew the country; George Atzerodt, an experienced boatman who was familiar with the river crossings that would be required; Lewis Payne[a], a burly, physically powerful ex-Confederate soldier familiar with firearms; and finally, another ex-Confederate soldier, an old boyhood friend, Samuel Arnold. The qualifications of all but possibly Herold, who had only his loyalty to recommend him, suggest Booth's choices were not as ill-considered as some have made them out to be. A number of other persons were indirectly involved in the conspiracy (and theories abound about those who were not involved but were aware of the plot), but these were the main actors.[49]

The plan was to abduct Lincoln on his way to the play, "Still Waters Run Deep," which was being performed at the Soldier's Home on the outskirts of Washington. On either March 16 or 20,[b] 1865, the conspirators prepared for the abduction. They hoped to stop the President's carriage, overpower him and any aides (he was rarely escorted by more than one), then drive the handcuffed chief executive south where fresh horses would carry the group beyond to the protection of the Confederate lines.

The plan failed, however, because Lincoln did not appear. Rather, he had asked Treasury Secretary and political adversary Salmon P. Chase to go in his place. The carriage of a startled Chase was stopped by a group of riders, who, seeing the President was not on board, then galloped off.[50]

Military events soon made it clear that abduction was no longer a viable strategy. Lee's army could not hold its positions at Petersburg much longer without an enormous sacrifice of life; surrender appeared inevitable. But on April 4, Confederate President Jefferson Davis, fearing the terms of surrender, urged a continuation of the war as a guerrilla campaign "operating in the interior . . . where supplies are more accessible, and where the foe will be far removed from his own

---

[a] Variously known as Lewis Powell or Lewis Paine.
[b] The exact date remains uncertain.

base." He went on to ask the South for a renewed commitment to "render our triumph certain."[51]

Lee, closer to the suffering of his troops than the truculent Davis, saw no reason to continue a senseless slaughter. On April 7, he asked for terms, and two days later he formally surrendered his army. Desperate, Davis continued to press for a continuation of the war west of the Mississippi. With General Joe Johnston's Confederate army still in the field blocking Sherman's way north, he reasoned, perhaps there was a way out yet. Davis, the Southern zealot, was grasping for straws. So was Booth.

The Assassination

After the abduction plot had failed, Booth began to consider other more drastic measures that could throw the Union war effort into disarray permitting the South to regroup militarily long enough, at least, to enhance the possibility of a negotiated settlement rather than an unconditional surrender dictated by the despised Lincoln. The plan that evolved was to strike down by assassination key government and military leaders, thus producing complete chaos in Washington. The targets: the President, Vice-President Andrew Johnson, Secretary of State William H. Seward (who would become President in the event of the death of a succeeding Vice-President), and General Ulysses S. Grant, commander of the Union army. In so doing, the conspirators hoped to eliminate in one stroke the government's formal political and military leadership.

On April 14, after learning of the President's theater plans with General Grant, a determined Booth decided that this was the opportunity he had been awaiting. It was time to strike. He again wrote a letter to explain what he was about to do and gave it to a fellow actor, John Matthews, in a sealed envelope instructing him to deliver it personally to the publisher of the *National Intelligencer* the next day. An unnerved Matthews tore open the letter after the assassination, then fearing the consequences of having it in his possession, destroyed it. He recalled the closing paragraph, however:

> The moment has at length arrived when my plans [to abduct] must be changed. The world may censure me for what I am about to do, but I am sure posterity will justify me.[52]

To this Booth signed his name and those of fellow conspirators Payne, Atzerodt, and Herold. Reserving for himself the President and General Grant, who was expected to accompany the President, Booth assigned

Atzerodt to kill Vice-President Johnson and Payne to kill Secretary of State Seward with Herold's assistance.

Why did Booth choose a public theater for the act? And why the leap to the stage after the fatal shot, unless it was for recognition? Booth's choice of Ford's Theatre was in part fortuitous, but it was also a very rational, calculating decision. As a famous actor, he had unlimited access to Ford's. This meant that he could enter and leave the theater when and where he pleased without questions. Thus, he could enter and climb the stairs to the President's box without suspicion. He leaped to the stage after the shooting because that was the quickest, most direct way out of the crowded theater. To go back down the stairs and through the lobby would have meant almost certain capture. This is not to suggest that Booth was averse to the publicity. As his letters and diaries indicate, he was convinced that what he was doing was right and that public opinion would support the elimination of this "tyrant" who had ruled the country and had conducted the bloodiest war in American history. But the desire for notoriety, in this case, was a distinctly secondary consideration—neither necessary nor sufficient as a motive for his act.

Except for whatever fleeting personal satisfaction Booth may have derived from Lincoln's death, the plan was a failure: Payne's attempt to kill Seward ended bloody but unsuccessful; Atzerodt could not bring himself to execute a man he did not know: he made no attempt on the Vice-President's life.[53] Grant had declined the President's theater invitation because of plans to visit a daughter in New Jersey. Thus, only the President died.

The conspirators, except for John Surratt, were quickly arrested, although much controversy surrounded the investigation of the conspiracy and many questions remained about its thoroughness and the possibility of other conspirators.[c] If it hadn't been for Booth's broken leg, which he suffered in his leap to the stage, he and the ever faithful Davy Herold, who accompanied him on his flight toward an anticipated sanctuary in Virginia, might have escaped.

Booth's diary records his despair after the event as he realized that his act was poorly timed and misunderstood. The nation was tired of killing after four long years of war. North and South, a war-weary

[c] David Herold, George Atzerodt, Lewis Payne, and Mary Surratt (the latter in a highly questionable judgment) were hanged on July 7, 1865. Other conspirators not directly involved, Samuel Arnold, Samuel Mudd, Edward Spangler, and Michael O'Laughlin were given prison sentences. John Surratt escaped to Europe. After his capture in Cairo in November 1866, he was returned to the country for trial. He was released in August 1867 after the jury failed to reach a verdict.

nation welcomed Appomattox. A year earlier, the result may have
been different, but except for zealots like Jefferson Davis and Booth
Americans were ready to lay down their arms and return to their
homes and farms. Now in great pain, making his way through the
Maryland swamps, Booth wrote:

> April, 13, 14, Friday, The Ides
> Until today nothing was ever thought of sacrificing to our coun-
> try's wrongs. For six months we have worked to capture. But our
> cause being almost lost, something decisive and great must be
> done. But its failure was owing to others who did not strike for
> their country with a heart. I struck boldly, and not as the papers
> say. I walked with a firm step through a thousand of his friends,
> was stopped but pushed on. A colonel was at his side. I shouted
> Sic semper before I fired. In jumping I broke my leg. I passed all
> his pickets. Rode sixty miles that night, with the bone of my leg
> tearing the flesh at every jump.
> I can never repent it, though we hated to kill. Our country
> owed all our troubles to him, and God simply made me the
> instrument of his punishment.[d]
> The country is not what it was. This forced union is not what
> I have loved. I care not what becomes of me. I have no desire to
> outlive my country. This night [before the deed] I wrote a long
> article and left it for one of the editors of the *National Intelli-
> gencer*, in which I fully set forth our reasons for our proceedings.
> He or the Gov't. . . . [the entry ends][54][e]

A week later, a depressed Booth laments that his act has been misunderstood:

> Friday 21
> After being hunted like a dog through swamps, woods, and last
> night being chased by gunboats till I was forced to return wet,
> cold, and starving, with every man's hand against me, I am here
> in despair. And why? For doing what Brutus was honored for—
> what made Tell a hero. And yet I, for striking down a greater
> tyrant than they ever knew, am looked upon as a common cut-
> throat. My action was purer than either of theirs. One hoped to

[d] The final phrase of this sentence is often cited out of context as evidence of Booth's
alleged delusion of divine inspiration.

[e] In the last incomplete sentence, Booth probably intended to express his frustration
that "he [John Matthews] or the Gov't" suppressed his letter of explanation.

be great.ᶠ The other had not only his country's, but his own, wrongs to avenge. I hoped for no gain. I knew no private wrong. I struck for my country and that alone. A country that groaned beneath this tyranny, and prayed for this end, and yet now behold the cold hand they extend me. God cannot pardon me if I have done wrong. Yet I cannot see my wrong, except in serving a degenerate people. The little, the very little, I left behind to clear my name, the government will not allow to be printed [the letter he had left with John Matthews]. So ends all. For my country I have given up all that makes life sweet and holy, brought misery upon my family, and am sure there is no pardon in the Heaven for me, since man condemns me so. I have only heard of what has been done (except what I did myself), and it fills me with horror. God, try and forgive me, and bless my mother. Tonight I will once more try the river with the intent to cross. Though I have a greater desire and almost a mind to return to Washington, and in a measure clear my name—which I feel I can do. I do not repent the blow I struck. I may before my God, but not to man. I think I have done well. Though I am abandoned, with the curse of Cain upon me, when, if the world knew my heart, that one blow would have made me great, though I did desire no greatness.

Tonight I try to escape these blood-hounds once more. Who, who can read his fate? God's will be done. I have too great a soul to die like a criminal. O, may He, may He spare me that, and let me die bravely.

I bless the entire world. Have never hated or wronged anyone. This last was not a wrong, unless God deems it so, and it's with Him to damn or bless me. And for this brave boy with me, who often prays (yes, before and since) with a true and sincere heart— was it crime in him? If so, why can he pray the same?

I do not wish to shed a drop of blood, but "I must fight the course." 'Tis all that's left me.⁵⁵

Given the tone and intensity of Booth's remarks, it is difficult to take seriously an often-quoted subsequent remark he allegedly made to a farm girl, who, unaware of who he was, said to him that she thought Lincoln's assassin had killed for money. Booth was said to have replied that in his opinion "he wasn't paid a cent, but did it for notoriety's sake."⁵⁶

ᶠ The sentence, "one hoped to be great" is also cited out of context as evidence of Booth's alleged desire for fame, despite the fact that the reference is clearly to another earlier assassin.

Had Booth been seeking the fame he already possessed, it is likely that he would have welcomed a well-publicized trial where he could have spoken with the dramatic persuasiveness of the skilled actor he was in his own defense. He could have given expression to the many eloquent political statements he had penned in letters and diary. Rather, he chose to die alone "bravely." With that in mind, as he leaned heavily on a crutch, surrounded by Union troops who had encircled his refuge in a barn, he shouted back when asked to surrender:

> Captain, I know you to be a brave man, and I believe you to be honorable: I am a cripple. I have got but one leg; if you withdraw your men in "line" one hundred yards from the door, I will come out and fight you.[57]

When the officer-in-charge replied that it was his intention to take him and Herold prisoners, Booth shouted back: "Well, my brave boys, prepare a stretcher for me."[58] He then negotiated with the soldiers to permit his panicked companion to surrender alone. Soon after Herold left the barn, it was set afire by the soldiers. Seeing no other honorable alternative, Booth raised his pistol and fired a shot behind his right ear, smashing instead his spinal column and leaving him paralyzed but conscious to die a slow agonizing death. Throughout an ordeal so painful that he pleaded to be killed, he did not recant on his principles. Shortly before he died, he whispered to a soldier bending over him, "Tell mother I die for my country."[59]

Conclusions

Much of the misunderstanding about Booth and his motives has been the result of the failure to consider the political context of his actions. It has been assumed that Lincoln was the revered leader in life that he became after his death: the fact that his assassination is frequently referred to as a martyrdom attests to this point. Thus, it has been further assumed that only a deranged person could have killed so noble a human being. Consequently, writers have interpreted virtually every aspect of Booth's life from this incorrect perspective. As I have indicated, it is unlikely that a "ham" actor would have received the consistently good reviews that Booth did. It is also unlikely that a person consumed with the egocentric and anxiety-induced needs for acclaim attributed to Booth would have had so very many friends and admirers from all walks of life.

Booth was wrong, obviously, on moral grounds; moreover, he was wrong politically, as subsequent events illustrated. But he was not deranged, nor did he kill for neurotic compensatory or nihilistic reasons. His motives were more akin to those of the German officers who conspired and attempted to kill Hitler to end the madness of World War II than they were to a deranged person. Such a conclusion is difficult to accept because it conflicts so directly with the mythology surrounding a slain national hero. But during most of his presidency, Abraham Lincoln was viewed by many Americans, especially in the South, as a cruel, despotic man. As a more restrained but still bitter Jefferson Davis wrote some years later about Lincoln, "[The South] could not be expected to mourn" an enemy who had presided over such misery.[60]

Leon Czolgosz (1873-1901)

On September 6, 1901, Leon Czolgosz shot and fatally wounded President William McKinley as the latter stood greeting a line of well-wishers at the Pan-American Exposition in Buffalo, New York. The President died eight days later. Czolgosz, who was arrested at the scene, was tried and convicted of first degree murder and executed forty-four days later on October 29. His trial had lasted less than eight hours. Czolgosz freely acknowledged his guilt without remorse. He refused to cooperate with his court-appointed attorneys and offered no defense after his guilty plea was denied.[61]

When the calm and composed assassin was strapped into the electric chair at New York's Auburn Prison he turned to the grim-faced witnesses and "in a clear distinct voice" repeated the explanation he had given since his arrest: "I killed the President because he was the enemy of the good people—the good working people. I am not sorry for my crime. I *am* sorry I could not see my father."[62]

Problems of Past Research

Before his execution, Czolgosz had been examined for the prosecution and defense by five psychiatrists, or alienists as they were then called; all concluded that they could find no evidence of insanity.[63]

After the execution, two other psychiatrists of the day became interested in the case. Walter Channing and his assistant L. Vernon Briggs were skeptical about the official conclusion that Czolgosz was sane. Then citing the fact that the five doctors who actually examined Czolgosz did not carefully consider his personal history, the two began an investigation of Czolgosz's family and past.

In October 1902, Channing published an article in *The American Journal of Insanity* disputing the earlier conclusion that Czolgosz was sane.[64] Channing made much of the fact that as a child Leon was "quiet and retired" and only played with "a few" other children. Channing also thought it was significant that as Leon grew older he spent a lot of time alone reading. Odd also, he argued, that Czolgosz apparently only had one girlfriend but she had broken off the relationship; after that he allegedly had difficulty even speaking to women. Strange, Channing thought, that Czolgosz especially did not like his stepmother and refused to eat his meals with her, preferring instead to cook his own food or simply to drink milk and eat bread alone. He also slept a lot, Channing noted. Channing considered these characteristics to be of great "pathological significance." Of special importance in Channing's view was the "nervous breakdown" Leon appeared to have in 1897 when he became ill and depressed before leaving his job in a wire mill a year later. Czolgosz refused to work after that—a fact Channing also considered of major significance in his diagnosis of the assassin's mental condition.[65]

Nineteen years later, Dr. Channing's associate, Dr. L. Vernon Briggs, presented these same facts in an interesting book entitled *The Manner of Man that Kills*.[66] Like his late associate, Briggs also concluded that Czolgosz was insane, afflicted with paranoid schizophrenia or "dementia praecox" as it was called then.

The Channing and Briggs interpretation and conclusion have become the most widely known and accepted assessment of Czolgosz's life and motives in the McKinley assassination. Robert Donovan's influential book on assassins relies on Briggs.[67] Donald Hasting's later article draws heavily on both Donovan and Briggs.[68] Virtually all the work written on Czolgosz since Briggs' book have accepted his analysis.[69]

Acknowledging the fact that Briggs and Channing have written the most complete and accurate history of Czolgosz's life before the assassination, there remains, however, two fundamental problems in their conclusions: first, neither author has considered the political and social context of the crime; second, each, for that reason, provides a highly reductionist and questionable interpretation of Czolgosz's motives that is not supported by any of the evidence they themselves report.

In his book, Dr. Briggs attempted to bolster his diagnostic conclusions about Czolgosz by citing the opinions of other authorities who, without having examined Czolgosz or his life history in any systematic manner, agree with his diagnosis. For example, Briggs quoted Dr. Allan

McLane Hamilton, who in 1881 was convinced of Charles Guiteau's *sanity*; Hamilton later was equally convinced that Czolgosz was *insane*. Citing the assassin's "prepossessing personality," Hamilton concluded that Czolgosz was "clearly demented" because "[he] seemed to take little or no interest in his trial." Hamilton also viewed Czolgosz's dying belief that President McKinley was "the enemy of working people" as evidence of his insane "delusions." And, following Channing, Hamilton agreed that Czolgosz's refusal to eat his stepmother's food, as well as his refusal to work, was evidence of paranoia.[70] Briggs also cites approvingly another authority of the day, Dr. Sanderson Christieson, who offers the following insights concerning Czolgosz:

> Such a monstrous conception and impulse as the wanton murder of the President of the United States, arising in the mind of so *insignificant a citizen*, without his being either insane or degenerate could be nothing short of a miracle, for the reason that we require like causes to explain like results. *To assume that he was sane, is to assume that he did a sane act*, i.e., one based upon facts and for a rational purpose.[71] [Emphasis added.]

Dr. Christieson agreed with Hamilton that Czolgosz's beliefs about the slain president were evidence of "insane egotism." Briggs then quotes Dr. Christieson's list of other symptoms of the assassin's alleged insanity as supporting evidence. These include his reticence, alleged hypochondria, the fact that "he was notoriously prone to fall asleep in a chair at any hour of the day," and his decision to quit his job and subsequent refusal to seek another.[72]

Moreover, Briggs contends that Czolgosz's anarchist sympathies were probably delusional. This conclusion is based on a survey of anarchist publications after the assassination which revealed a diversity of views concerning the McKinley assassination that ranged from approval to condemnation. Such lack of agreement, Briggs implies, suggests Czolgosz must have *imagined* that his act was consistent with anarchist beliefs. To support this assertion, Briggs cites the reluctance of anarchists he contacted after the assassination to acknowledge any support for Czolgosz's act.[73] Briggs' insensitivity and failure to comprehend the political context of the assassination is underscored by this naive conclusion. Given the mood of hostility in the government toward any socialist, and especially toward anarchist groups, it is little wonder that some reticence was observed among the anarchist groups he contacted.

The failure to consider the context of any behavior is a serious omission in evaluative research and one that most alienists at the turn of the century were guilty of. Leon Czolgosz's decision to kill William McKinley on that warm late afternoon in September 1901 can be understood only if analyzed in the context of the economic and political circumstances of American society in the last quarter of the nineteenth century.

The Context: 1873-1901

Leon Czolgosz was twenty-eight years of age when he was executed. Conceived in what is now Czechoslovakia, he was born in Alpena, Michigan, near Detroit, within a month of his mother's arrival in the United States. Leon was her fourth child. She would have five more children before she died twelve years later after childbirth at the age of forty-two. Before she slipped into a final coma from the internal hemorrhaging and inadequate medical care that claimed her life, she was frequently delirious. Her husband recalled that she often repeated this statement to the children she loved and knew she was leaving: "My children, the time will come when you will have greater understanding and be more learned."[74] After the assassination, Emma Goldman, the well-known anarchist and feminist who was a contemporary of Czolgosz, would contend that it was Leon's greater understanding of American society that motivated him to act.[75]

When Leon Czolgosz was born in 1873, the American industrial revolution was underway. Society was changing rapidly as the economy began to shift from a predominantly agricultural base to one of heavy industrialization. Hard times in eastern and southern Europe and a demand for industrial labor were the reasons for the successive waves of immigrants, like the Czolgosz family, who came impoverished to America seeking a better life. While there is no question that opportunity existed in America to a greater degree than on the Continent, the last quarter of the nineteenth century remains one of the most exploitative and oppressive periods in American history.

The country was run by industrialists such as Vanderbilt, Rockefeller, Carnegie, and Frick, masters of capital like Morgan and Gould, and their spokesmen in government with names like Blaine and Aldrich and Hanna, and every president elected since Lincoln—all eminently forgettable men because of their personal insignificance in office. Like the Congress, most served simply to ratify and forward the policies advocated by big banks, big railroads, big oil, and big iron and steel. And the policies of industrial capital can be characterized as aggressively hostile and remarkably indifferent to human concerns.

In the name of progress, American Indians were being systematically exterminated by rank-seeking commanders in massacres at places like Sand Creek and Wounded Knee and also through the destruction of the buffalo herds, upon which many tribes depended for food, shelter, and clothing. The decimated remnants of these once proud and colorful people were herded onto disease-ridden reservations as the railroads and speculators took over their land.

In the South, the marginal gains of radical reconstruction were quickly negated after 1877 as newly freed black slaves were again, as a matter of public policy, stripped of their constitutional rights guaranteed by the Fourteenth and Fifteenth Amendments. And even the Thirteenth Amendment, which had freed them from slavery, was effectively neutralized by the imposition of an exploitative system of sharecropping that soon had blacks bound again by shackles of economic indenture.

In the growing cities of the industrial Northeast and Midwest and the coalfields of Pennsylvania, Ohio, West Virginia, and Kentucky, workers—a large proportion of them eastern and southern Europeans who did not even speak the language—labored under intolerable circumstances. Wages low, hours long, safety ignored, and rights nonexistent, the life of the American worker was difficult, dirty, dangerous and, all too frequently, short. It was such a life that Leon Czolgosz and others like him lived in the grimy steel and glass industries that scar the riverbanks in eastern Ohio and western Pennsylvania.

Labor was becoming restive under the brutal and unfair authority of American capital. When the economy slipped into a depression in 1873, the year of Czolgosz's birth, wages were cut back. Unions, weak as they were at that time, fought back. Unionized workers went on strike in textile mills, coalfields, and foundries from Chicago to New York, but the strikes were quickly broken by the overwhelming economic and political strength of industry. Striking unionists were fired and replaced with nonunionists; those who were fired were blacklisted, so that future employment would be difficult; legal harassment with political backing followed for those who fought back. With approximately 60 percent of the average workingman's pay going for food alone, most families did not have enough for adequate housing or medical care. For American labor, there was little to celebrate in 1876 when the nation observed its first one hundred years of freedom and independence.

A year later, when Leon Czolgosz was four, railroad workers walked off their jobs in Pennsylvania to protest a scheduled 10-percent reduction in their wages. The walk-off marked the beginning of a chain-reaction strike that eventually consumed the major railroads of the nation. The strike lasted from May 15 until August 1 when federal and state troops subdued the last remaining strikers in Scranton, Pennsylvania. The first striker was killed on July 17 in Martinsburg, West Virginia by the state militia. Three days later, the state militia shot and killed eleven unarmed persons in Baltimore. On July 22, the Pennsylvania state militia shot and killed twenty strikers in Pittsburgh while sustaining the loss of several of their own killed and wounded as workers lashed back. The next day in Pittsburgh, the National Guard shot into a crowd of unarmed demonstrators killing eleven more. On July 25, more were killed in Chicago, as police fired into crowds of strikers. The killing continued in Chicago for another day.[76] The response dictated by industrial and political leaders and carried out by "coal and iron police" and state militias was vicious but hardly surprising. West of the Mississippi the U.S. Cavalry was exacting a terrible toll on American Indians who were also resisting the exploitation of the same railroad interests.

In 1879, at the age of six, Leon Czolgosz began to shine shoes and sell papers in Detroit to supplement his father's meager income. After an uneven five years of schooling in Polish parochial and public schools, he was forced to quit and begin work in a Michigan factory at the age of twelve in 1885. That same year his mother died.[77]

The following year, on May 4, 1886, a bomb exploded during a labor rally of some 1,500 people who had gathered in Chicago's Haymarket Square. The bomb killed eleven persons, including seven policemen, and more than one hundred persons were injured. Eight anarchists were arrested for the crime and, in spite of an absence of any evidence linking them to the crime, all were tried and convicted, and five were sentenced to die. The Haymarket Square affair and its aftermath remained as a major news item for nearly a year and provided a catalyst for the bitter continuing disputes that divided capital and labor.

The day before their scheduled hanging, one of the condemned men, Lingg, committed suicide in his cell. The next day, November 11, 1887, the remaining four—Spies, Fischer, Engel, and Parsons—died bravely on the gallows, proclaiming their cause to the last breath:

SPIES: "There will come a time when our silence will be more powerful than the voices you strangle today."
FISCHER: "Hurrah for anarchy."
ENGEL: "Hurrah for anarchy. This is the happiest moment of my life."
PARSONS: "Let the voice of the people be heard."[78]

And with those defiant words, they dropped to their deaths, becoming revered martyrs of the American labor movement.

Leon Czolgosz was an impressionable fourteen-year-old factory laborer when news of this gross injustice reverberated through the labor movement. The anarchists' deaths also made an indelible impression on a teen-aged Emma Goldman, who in her autobiography years later would recall with reverence the inspiration their brave deaths provided.[79]

The Czolgosz family moved to Natrona, Pennsylvania, in the Pittsburgh area in 1889. Leon found work there in a glass factory. Making seventy-five cents a day for a ten- to twelve-hour shift, the conditions of the sixteen-year-old youth's job were difficult: he had to carry red hot glass from the ovens to cooling racks.[80] The heat was intense in such factories. Two suits of long woolen underwear were worn beneath an outer layer of clothing to provide some insulation from the searing temperatures. But even so, workers frequently developed severe abdominal pains and muscle cramps from dehydration. Bent over with pain, workers drank salty pickle brine for relief.

Slavic immigrants confronted other difficulties in the Pittsburgh area. Thomas Bell (Tomas Belejcák), a Slavic-American writer who grew up in Braddock, Pennsylvania (near Natrona), describes the impressions of his youth in these gray turn-of-the-century mill towns and explains his reasons for writing about them:

> I saw a people brought here by steel magnates from the old country and then exploited, ridiculed, and oppressed. . . . The life of a Slovak boy in Braddock 30-40 years ago was a bitter one. As a small boy I could not understand why I should be ashamed of the fact that I was Slovak. While Irish and German kids could boast of the history of their ancestors, I did not know anything about the history of my people. I made up my mind to write a history of the Braddock Slovaks. . . . I wanted to make sure that the hardships my grandfather, my father, my mother, and my brother, sisters, and other relatives lived through would not be forgotten.[81]

In 1892, the Czolgosz family moved back to the Cleveland area just before the Homestead strike broke near Pittsburgh on June 29. Steel workers, a large number of them Slavic, had limits on their ability to control the resentment Bell expressed. When the Carnegie Steel Company arbitrarily decided to reduce the meager wages these workers received, their anger boiled to the surface. Workers walked off their jobs in protest and blocked the entrances to the Homestead plant.

Rather than negotiate, company manager Henry Clay Frick hired some two hundred Pinkerton detectives to disperse the mob and break the strike. Outraged by Frick's callousness, the strikers refused to leave the scene. Bloodshed followed as Pinkerton agents fired into the crowd killing sixteen and wounding many others in a confrontation on July 6. On July 23, the outspoken and outraged anarchist Alexander Berkman tried to assassinate the despised Frick in his Pittsburgh office but failed. Overwhelmed by the brutal response, workers gave up on the strike. The loss of the Homestead strike was considered a severe blow to the cause of American labor.[82]

Back in Cleveland, Leon got another laborer's job in the Newberg Wire Mills. Here too working conditions were primitive and dangerous. Menacing hot steel wire stretched under pressure from machines, leaving unprotected workers exposed to a potentially lethal whiplash if the steel broke, as it frequently did. Leon was lucky. When the wire broke once on his shift, he survived with only a bloody gash that scarred his cheek. The six-day work week and hours remained the same, but the wages were better—twenty-six cents and thirty-three cents an hour for the ten-hour-day and twelve-hour-night shifts respectively; but, most importantly, he did not have to contend with the enervating heat of the glass factory. As a result, he was less tired than he had been and was able to spend more of his time doing what he enjoyed most—following his late mother's admonition to read and learn. His brother, Waldek, considered him "the best scholar of them all" during the time he had been able to attend school.[83]

When the depression of 1893 hit, the wire mill attempted to reduce wages; the workers, including Leon, went on strike and were promptly fired. Six months later, Czolgosz used an alias, Fred C. Nieman, to avoid the company blacklist and successfully regained a job at the same mill.

During the time he was unemployed, he began to question his Catholicism. The teachings of the church and the advice of the priests did not square with the radical papers and pamphlets he had been spending increasing amounts of time reading. Both he and his brother, Waldek, had prayed for help during the difficult period they had been on strike, but their prayers had gone unanswered. Moreover, they felt the priests they knew were fairly comfortable men who were largely indifferent to the economic difficulties of their parishioners. The two brothers decided "the priests' trade was the same as the shoemaker's or any other." In other words, they believed the priests were primarily interested in money just like any other businessmen.[84] For this reason, they broke with the church and relied upon the radical political literature of the day, which they believed honestly addressed the basic problems in American society. And, unlike the conservatism of the church, the socialists and anarchists offered solutions in this world, not the next. Leon's brother-in-law, Frank Bandowski, who had been an officer in a socialist organization for some time, joined the two brothers in their study and discussion sessions. Leon and Waldek eventually joined Bandowski's group and attended meetings with him. Before long, however, disagreements between members who supported Eugene Debs and others who did not split the organization, but Leon, Waldek, and Frank continued to read and study together.

One of their favorite books was Edward Bellamy's *Looking Backward 2000-1887*. Published in 1888, Bellamy's book envisioned a utopian society of state socialism by the year 2000. Next to the Bible, which he continued to read, it was Leon's favorite book; he studied it as one would study a textbook. Leon, Waldek, and Frank were, by all indications, close friends and political allies. After his arrest, his two relatives demonstrated considerable courage, given the hostility that prevailed, by visiting him in prison.[85]

About the time Leon had left the church and was heavily involved in what might be considered his political self-education, another great labor uprising occurred—the Pullman strike of 1894. It was a bitter strike, accompanied by the worst kind of nineteenth-century corporatism. The strike exposed the corporate creed "that property was the highest good and the chief end of society . . . that social justice and human rights should remain forever subordinant to considerations of property."[86] With intransigent railroad tycoons George Pullman and Richard Olney championing that creed, the battle lines were drawn when the fiery Eugene Debs, leading the American Railway Union, challenged the Pullman Company's right to use economic coercion to force its workers to rent company-owned housing. The Pullman Company had also arbitrarily reduced the wages of its workers.[87]

President Grover Cleveland, siding with the company, brought the full force of federal troops in to prevent the destruction of railroad property; Debs was quickly jailed for his activities. Frustrated with industry and disillusioned with a government that responded in every dispute as an arm of industry, Debs, like Czolgosz, found an outlet in the radical literature he read and studied during his confinement. Debs went on to lead the largest Socialist movement in American history. It is probable that no other strike had a greater radicalizing influence on the American working class than the Pullman strike of 1894. During this time, the issues between industry and labor were starkly defined in word and deed.

The callousness, corruption, and brutality of this corporate Gilded Age was not lost on even the rural masses who were now swelling the ranks of the newly emerging Populist party. A genuine people's movement succeeded in nominating the Populist William Jennings Bryan to head the Democratic ticket in the presidential election of 1896. With the support of individuals like Tom Watson of Georgia, spokesman for poor southern farmers, and Eugene Debs, defender of the industrial working class, Bryan's candidacy posed a major challenge to the economic status quo.

That challenge resulted in the most massively organized and financed Republican campaign ever waged until that time. Managed by the Ohio industrialist-politician Marcus Hanna, the comfortable and agreeable Republican nominee William McKinley ran on a platform that proclaimed with religious solemnity the "sanctity of contracts," "national honor," and "peace, progress, patriotism and prosperity." Worried by the Democratic/Populist definition of the issues as "the people" versus "the great trusts and combinations," Wall Street was willing to reach deep into its bulging coffers to aid Mark Hanna's Republican cause of silencing this ominous threat from the Left. The nation's largest corporations rallied to the call. Firms such as Rockefeller's Standard Oil, J. P. Morgan's banking empire, New York Life, as well as the Pennsylvania and New York Central railroads contributed unprecedented amounts to McKinley's campaign.[88]

The purple platitudes about God, country, and the virtues of American life that the carefully managed candidate proclaimed were designed to appeal to the well-dressed, church-going protestant mainstream of American life. And these same values of Protestantism, corporatism, and Americanism became one and the same in Hanna's astutely programmed campaign advertising.

The more subtle message of the campaign spoke to the issue of political power in America—who should exercise it and why. The McKinley victory of 1896 stands as the indisputable triumph of nineteenth-century industrial capitalism, or as Lawrence Goodwyn has termed the election, "the conclusive triumph of the corporate ethos."[89] Hanna's skillful campaign had succeeded in isolating the poor, immigrant working-class on the Left. Many Democrats in the industrial Northeast who did not identify with the ethnic working-class voted Republican in an affirmation of their belief in American values and "progress." The result was a major realignment in the electorate that left American labor politically weakened until 1932.[90]

For the American Left, it was a disheartening election, from which they would never truly recover. For Leon Czolgosz, the election was a confirmation of what he, Waldek, and Frank Bandowski had been discussing and reading in the anarchist journals and pamphlets that were stacked in his bedroom: namely that the oppressive American corporate structure could only be changed through revolution.

The Lattimer Mines Massacre

In 1897,[g] Leon contributed four hundred dollars to the family's purchase of a farm outside of Cleveland.[91] His father had remarried, and although Leon did not like his domineering stepmother and tried to avoid her as much as possible, he did enjoy the farm. Owning a farm represented a big step toward the self-sufficiency, freedom, and financial independence virtually every immigrant hoped to find in America. For Leon, the farm was a pastoral escape from the noise, ugliness, and danger of the wire mill.

Across the Allegheny mountains near Hazleton, Pennsylvania, Slavic coal miners lived much the same way as the Czolgosz family. Isolated by language, culture, and poverty in the rural setting of the anthracite coalfields, the life of the Slavic worker was bleak regardless of whether he worked in the hillside mines or the iron and steel mills on the rivers. Eastern and southern Europeans were invariably relegated to the least desirable jobs. Lacking the gregarious qualities of the Italians and Irish, Slavic workers seemed to their employers especially foreign and difficult to understand. Michael Novak's perceptive description of the Slavic workers of that period is worth quoting at length:

> In the gregarious, informal, quick-talking America described by Tocqueville, the Slavs were not as articulate and sociable as many other immigrants. As their clothes were dark and their demeanor dour, so their manners were also somewhat forbidding. As newcomers, they were strange enough. Their personal style was stiff, formal, distant. Their languages were more distant from English than were Latin or Germanic tongues. Taught by life to be thoroughly suspicious of authorities but outwardly deferential, they were hard to flatter, cajole, amuse, or kid.
>
> The wit of the Irish did not penetrate their defenses. The wink and elbow of the con man and the regular guy made those defenses tighten. The signals they received and those they gave were not easy to recognize. They lived in poverty so extreme it scandalized their neighbors. Their capacity for saving was prodigious.

[g] Various dates have been suggested for the farm purchase, ranging from 1892 to 1897. The date is not of great significance.

These immigrants were not, then, a wholly attractive people. If one places oneself in the shoes of those who experienced their coming, one sees how frictions and misunderstandings must have festered. Sheer verbal communication was, for the most part, out of the question, and the rituals and gestures of nonverbal expression must have been so skewed that great feelings of hopelessness and frustration had to well up. Among some of the Slavs, it was considered rude and impolite to smile on formal occasions or in the presence of superiors. Even to look superiors straight in the eye was considered an impudent and rebellious act. On this point alone, conflict with Anglo-American mores was assured.[92]

In September 1897, Slavic miners at the Lattimer Mines near Hazleton walked off their jobs to protest an "alien tax" on their wages that the Pennsylvania legislature had just passed. Since most were only working at half-time already because of earlier cutbacks, the new tax meant practically all their remaining wages would be siphoned off for rents, groceries, and medical care at company-owned enterprises. With the new tax, virtually nothing would be left to save in order to bring other members of their families to this country, or, as many planned to do, to return to Europe someday.[93]

On September 10, over four hundred miners began a protest march that would cover the six miles from Hazleton to the Lattimer Mines. Unarmed and orderly, the march was conceived as a peaceful protest against company wage policies and the new state tax. At about 3:00 P.M., the marchers were intercepted by the Hazleton sheriff and some one hundred fifty armed deputies who took up positions along the road leading to the mine superintendent's office. As the miners approached, the sheriff, revolver drawn, walked toward the front rank of the shuffling column and ordered them to disperse. When the marchers continued to file silently by, the sheriff grabbed one and thrust his pistol into the man's chest. A second miner pulled the sheriff's arm away from the first. At that point, the sheriff raised his pistol to the second man's forehead and pulled the trigger. But the gun misfired. The panicked sheriff shouted "Fire" and his deputies let loose a murderous fusillade of rifle and shotgun fire. The shooting continued for one to five minutes amid cries of "shoot the sons of bitches." As the workers scattered, they were chased and shot in the back by their relentless attackers. When the firing began to slacken, the groans and cries of the wounded filled the dusty, smoke-filled air. Angry deputies walked among the bodies and answered the pleas for water with,

"We'll give you hell, not water, hunkies!" Nineteen died and some thirty-nine were wounded.[94]

The enormity of this massacre shocked even radicals who were by then conditioned to the excesses of corporate violence. There can be little doubt that Leon Czolgosz was aware of the event, and even less that he followed the trial that began the following February to determine the guilt of the sheriff and his deputies.

The massacre assumed national significance as protest rallies were held in Slavic settlements throughout the country. A "National Prosecuting and Welfare Committee of the Lattimer Victims" was formed by Slavic groups to handle court and relief costs.[95] But the trial was a sham. On March 9, 1898, the all-male, Protestant, and Republican jury brought in its verdict of not guilty.[96] The Slavic community was outraged.

The Nervous Breakdown

In the fall of 1897, in the wake of the Lattimer Mines Massacre, Leon Czolgosz became ill from what appeared to be an emotional and physical breakdown. His brother Waldek said that he just seemed "gone to pieces like."[97] His symptoms? Shortness of breath, fatigue, heart palpitations, stomach discomfort, and loss of appetite—the well-known symptoms of acute depression. Refusing to seek hospital admittance, and, given the quality of medical care available to his mother before her death, cynical about doctors ("There is no place in the hospital for poor people; [only] if you have lots of money you will get well taken care of"), Leon suffered alone and in silence.[98] Although possibly unaware of the link between his mental state and its physical symptoms, Leon was aware of the cause of his depression: foremost was the intolerable injustice of industrial employment epitomized by events such as the Lattimer Mines Massacre. As he told his brother, "I can't stand it any longer."[99] And he refused to return to his job at the wire mill.

A secondary source of continuing irritation was his domineering stepmother, whom he had always resented as she did him. He now refused to take his meals with the family when the "old woman," as he called her, was present, preferring instead to eat alone in his room. Moreover, he even refused to eat the food she prepared. It is important to note, however, that he did eat with the family when she was absent, and he frequently prepared the family meals himself.[100] His refusal to eat with this woman had nothing to do with a paranoid fear that she would poison his food as others have alleged. He simply could not bear to be around her.

Except for Waldek and Frank, Leon had little to say to anyone during the period of his depression. Although he did occasionally play with his sister's children, most of his time was spent reading and sleeping. According to his brother, Leon was aware that his family was "uneducated" and did not understand him.[101]

Waldek, concerned about his brother's health and also afraid that he would lose his job, insisted that Leon see a doctor. But the several doctors Leon eventually saw could find no physical cause for his problems.[102] It seems certain, however, that Leon understood that the causes of his problems were *external*, not internal. During this period he continued to read voraciously, and the substance of his reading was invariably political: he consumed all the anarchist and socialist literature he could get his hands on. Periodically, he would travel the five miles into Cleveland where he would purchase newspapers, journals, and books. On some of these trips he also made discrete visits to houses of prostitution.[h] He also became a casual visitor at political rallies and meetings where he picked up any pamphlets that might be available. Returning to the farm he would read and study until he had exhausted his supply before returning again to replenish his growing political library. His collection consisted of virtually "everything pertaining to working men, strikes, etc."[103] He was obsessed with the need for radical social change in America.

On August 29, 1898, he formally quit the wire mill job, which as a practical matter he had avoided for nearly a year. But in spite of his earlier festering bitterness, Czolgosz had never expressed any hostility on the job. Except for his participation in the strike of 1893, he was a cooperative, reliable, and skilled worker. His foreman said there was none better on his shift.[104]

But this was typical, as Novak has suggested, of the Slavic workers of his day. Quiet and obedient, even to the point of appearing obsequious to persons who did not understand their culture, resentments were most often expressed away from their employers. Domestic quarrels, such as Leon had with his stepmother, sullen moodiness and explosive outbursts of temper characterized Slavic neighborhoods. So also did a pattern of heavy drinking, which Novak describes as "a ransom paid to demons" that stirred the reservoirs of resentment deep within them.[105]

---

[h] He acknowledged that he had contracted gonorrhea as a result of these visits (MacDonald, 1902, p. 379).

Czolgosz was typical of this culture in most respects, except that he controlled his anger better than most. His intellectual curiosity, fed by extensive reading and increasing attendance at anarchist and socialist meetings, provided him with a more sophisticated grasp of the predicament the immigrant working class in America confronted. He understood that the familiar eddies of domestic violence and melancholy, swirling in the tides of alcoholism that characterized immigrant populations of the day, were symptoms of political and economic oppression and not, as Protestant ministers proclaimed from their pulpits, moral weakness. It was this realization and not "dementia praecox" that was at the core of Leon Czolgosz's "breakdown" following the Lattimer Mines incident.

Prelude

For the next year and a half, Czolgosz's life continued much as it had since he had quit work. His major activity was reading. Occasionally he hunted rabbits, entertained his sister's children, and prepared evening meals for the family—if his stepmother was absent.[106] Apart from his continuing political discussions with Waldek and Frank, he had little to say, beyond functional conversations, to anyone else in the family. On his trips to Cleveland, however, he did go to the theater with a friend, Walter Nowak, who also attended the same political meetings. But eventually Nowak stopped attending because the meetings had become too radical.[107]

Czolgosz was contemptuous of his faint-hearted former friend. He believed in revolution. The assassination of King Humbert I of Italy on July 29, 1900 greatly interested him.[108] The king had been killed by the Italian-American anarchist Gaetano Bresci, who had been praised in anarchist publications around the world.

In the spring of 1901, Leon announced to his family that he had decided to move on, perhaps to Chicago or further west to look for different kinds of employment. He told his brother that he could not bear to return to the kind of factory work he had left. Perhaps in the West, he said, he could find a job "binding wheat or fixing machines or something."[109] With that in mind, he asked the family to return his share of the farm investment. It took awhile, but that summer his father finally agreed and returned a first installment of seventy dollars from the four hundred dollars he had contributed.

In the meantime, Czolgosz had heard the fiery anarchist crusader Emma Goldman when she spoke at a meeting in Cleveland on May 6, 1901. Czolgosz was impressed.[110] On May 19, he returned to the anarchist headquarters on 4 Elivell Street and talked with Emil Shilling, the association's treasurer. Schilling reported that they discussed class and revolutionary aspects of the labor movement. He recalled that he gave Czolgosz a book about the Haymarket Square martyrs and invited the young man home to dinner where their conversation continued. One of the issues discussed was whether King Humbert's assassination had been a result of a conspiracy or simply that of an individual acting alone.[111]

Schilling did not care for Czolgosz, finding him arrogant and poorly informed about the theoretical aspects of anarchism. Apparently the feeling was mutual. On his second visit, Czolgosz returned the book he had been loaned with the curt explanation that he did not have time to read it. It is virtually certain that Czolgosz already had read as much as there was to read about the Haymarket affair and considered the loan an insult. When Schilling offered him a beer, Czolgosz refused and countered by offering Schilling a cigar. Miffed, Schilling "told him to smoke it himself."[112] It was very clear that hard feelings of pride had developed between the two during the intellectual sparring of their first visit.

Czolgosz did not find in the party functionary, Schilling, the revolutionary vision and charisma he had observed in Emma Goldman. Cautious and suspicious, Schilling carefully weighed every answer he gave to Czolgosz's very direct inquiries. And to that extent he aroused the contempt of the idealistic Czolgosz just as did his condescending offer of a book whose contents were well-known by every literate radical.

Sometime in late May or early June, Czolgosz visited Schilling again. This time he talked at length about Goldman and how impressed he had been when he had heard her speak. During the intermission of her talk, he had spoken with her briefly to inquire about reading material she would recommend; she had treated him kindly.[113] He asked Schilling how he could meet her again. Schilling explained that Goldman was in Chicago and advised him simply to introduce himself to her there.

On July 11, he caught a westbound train in Cleveland, repeating to his family before leaving that his purpose was to look for work. He wrote from Fort Wayne, Indiana on July 14 to say he was continuing west and would write again later.[114] That was the last contact he had with his family until after the assassination.

Czolgosz's precise movements and activities after this point are difficult to pinpoint with any certainty. The pattern, however, is fairly clear. What he wanted had nothing to do with finding work in the

West, as he told his family; rather he intended to become involved in what he hoped would be the revolutionary activities of the anarchist movement. He had spent the last few years in study and reflection about the need for radical political change in America; now he was prepared to act. All he needed was more direction and support. Thus, for the next six weeks he traveled between Cleveland, Chicago, and Buffalo, establishing contacts with anarchist groups and, in effect, volunteering his services. In the brief meeting he eventually had with Emma Goldman in Chicago, he asked her to introduce him to other activists. Similarly, in Cleveland and Buffalo he made the same inquiries, which led to the suspicion among those he contacted that he might be a government infiltrator. The intensity of his manner, the probing nature of his questions, and, especially, his conviction that violence must be a necessary component of the class struggle alarmed many party functionaries (or so they claimed after the assassination).

He was an enigma to the persons he met. His basic reticence and lack of verbal sophistication, so characteristic of Slavic men of his day, was punctuated with intense questions and ideological statements. This lack of style was misunderstood by the doctrinaire leftist intellectuals he talked with. Abe Isaak, editor of the Chicago-based anarchist publication, *Free Society*, became convinced that this intense young man was really a government agent. In the September 1, 1901 issue of *Free Society*, he published an alert:

ATTENTION

The attention of the comrades is called to another spy. He is well-dressed, of medium height, rather narrow-shouldered, blond and about twenty-five years of age. Up to the present he has made his appearance in Chicago and Cleveland. In the former place he remained but a short time, while in Cleveland he disappeared when the comrades had confirmed themselves of his identity & were on the point of exposing him. His demeanor is of the usual sort, pretending to be greatly interested in the cause, asking for names or soliciting aid for acts of contemplated violence. If this same individual makes his appearance elsewhere, the comrades are warned in advance and can act accordingly.[115]

By this time, Czolgosz—who had been using his wire-mill alias, Fred C. Nieman, since he left Cleveland—had checked into a room above John Nowak's saloon in downtown Buffalo.[116] A day or two later, he purchased a new .32 caliber Iver Johnson revolver for $4.50 at a hardware store.[117] He had given his old pistol, the one he had used to hunt rabbits on the farm, to a previous landlord in lieu of the $1.75 rent he had owed.[118]

It is possible that Czolgosz's decision to kill the President may have been prompted by the *Free Society* notice questioning his purpose. He did say after his arrest that "something I read in *Free Society* suggested the idea," but he never identified what it was. Nor did he ever comment on the *Free Society* allegation.[119] Emma Goldman, for example, was concerned that the unsubstantiated charge may have prompted Czolgosz to demonstrate the sincerity of his commitment.[120] It is a question that must, unfortunately, remain unanswered. But the overall pattern of his behavior suggests that he had the assassination in mind long before the notice appeared.

The Assassination

President McKinley, accompanied by his wife, arrived in Buffalo on the evening of September 4 aboard a special Lake Shore & Michigan Southern Railway train. The Pan-American Exposition was being held in Buffalo that year, and the President was making a first official visit.

It was hard not to like the President. A large affable individual with a penchant for speeches presented in the most florid patriotic prose, he was a man of the times. McKinley was happily oblivious to the circumstances of life for the working masses whose labor, under intolerable conditions, provided the soft cushion of affluence that he and men of his class so much enjoyed. He epitomized the small-town, well-dressed, church-going values of protestant-turn-of-the-century America. This portly, tuxedoed, socially insulated Christian man, so solicitous of the frail wife who accompanied him, thus had no idea that danger lurked in the shuffling, shabbily dressed masses of American life he understood no better than the strange languages they spoke.

Thursday, September 5, had been proclaimed President's Day, and the President and his entourage toured the Exposition grounds accompanied by a detail of mounted National Guardsmen, bands, and city police. McKinley was scheduled to address an immense crowd of Exposition visitors. Leon Czolgosz was among the cheering throng, attempting to edge closer to the speaker's platform, but the press of the crowd made it impossible. Czolgosz stood helpless as the President, surrounded by local and foreign dignitaries, colorfully dressed Marines, and the parasols of wealthy women, began his speech by extolling the virtues of progress and prosperity:

Expositions are the timekeepers of progress. They record the world's advancement.

He went on to describe the nation's "unexampled prosperity":

We hope that all that are representatives here may be moved to higher and nobler efforts for their own and the world's good and that out of this city may come not only greater commerce and trades . . . [deafening applause] . . .

Then later, with ministerial solemnity, he concluded with a benediction:

Our earnest prayer is that God will graciously vouchsafe prosperity, happiness, and peace to all our neighbors and like blessings to all the people and powers of earth.[121]

Then amid the cheers, the President, wearing a tall silk hat and black frock coat, nodded and smiled benignly to the applauding dignitaries and crowd as his doting wife moved to his side. He exuded the good will of a self-satisfied and comfortable man as he accompanied her to an awaiting carriage amid the playing of the bands. One can imagine Czolgosz's resentment as he witnessed this spectacle of privilege that was so far beyond the grasp of the weary masses he knew.

On Friday, September 6, the President was scheduled to appear at a public reception in the ornate Temple of Music on the Exposition grounds. Before the afternoon reception, he and his party boarded a special train for a short sightseeing trip to Niagara Falls. Czolgosz followed but was frustrated again in his attempt to get close enough for a shot. He returned to the Exposition by streetcar and was one of the first in the lengthening reception line that was forming inside the temple. The President returned shortly after 4 P.M. and was guided to a position of honor amidst potted palms and bay trees.[122]

The first man to shake the President's hand looked intently into his eyes and said dramatically "George Washington, Abraham Lincoln and President McKinley."[123] The President smiled approvingly and eased the admirer on with the pleasant indifference of a man accustomed to such praise.

As the line shuffled toward the President, Czolgosz discretely removed the pistol from his pocket and concealed it in his handkerchief-wrapped hand. The white cloth looked like a bandage and did not arouse the curiosity of the security guards who casually scrutinized the line of well-wishers. The President was flanked by his personal secretary, George B. Cortelyou, on his right and the director of the

Pan-American Exposition, John G. Milburn, to his left. As Czolgosz approached, the President extended his hand. Czolgosz casually extended his left hand as if to greet the President, then suddenly pushed the President's hand aside as he stepped forward and fired two fatal shots through the tuxedo vest and bloused white shirt while smiling directly into the President's face.[124] The startled McKinley stiffened, then staggered backward but remained on his feet as soldiers swarmed over his assailant. Dazed, McKinley murmured "Be easy with him, boys."[125] It was almost four years to the day after the Lattimer Mines Massacre.

At the police station, a badly beaten Czolgosz was questioned as the wounded President was rushed to the Exposition Hospital and prepared for emergency surgery. The hastily assembled doctors were hampered by confusion, inadequate surgical instruments and, ironically, poor lighting.[i] The President died of a gangrenous infection eight days later. His physicians were never able to locate the fatal bullet even after a four-hour search during the autopsy.[126] His doctors claimed that the President's chances for recovery had been seriously limited by his obesity (as had their search for the bullet) and "a rather low vitality" that was characteristic of his sedentary lifestyle.[127]

Retribution

Czolgosz was arraigned on first-degree murder charges on September 23. When the Judge asked for his plea, he uttered the only word he would speak in the courtroom during his brief trial: "guilty." The judge explained that a guilty plea could not be entered and instructed the clerk to enter a plea of not guilty. Czolgosz tried unsuccessfully to dismiss his court-appointed attorneys; failing that, he refused to participate in his own defense. The trial was a farce. His attorneys spent more time apologizing for the onerous task they had been assigned than they did defending their silent client. In fairness, there was little to defend. The trial was swift and to the point. Within eight hours it was over, and Czolgosz was sentenced to die, as he expected.

Before the trial began, however, Czolgosz did make several statements concerning his motives and went to his execution without deviating from them. Immediately after the shooting he told his interrogators that he shot the President because he felt it was his "duty" to do so. He resented the President's indifference and hostility toward

---

[i] Ironic because the main features of the Exposition were electrical displays. The central attraction was a 389-foot Electric Tower with a gilded one and a half ton Goddess of Light glowing from her perch at the top.

the "working people." "I didn't believe," he said, "[that] one man should have so much and another should have none." He added that he understood and accepted the consequences of his act.[128]

The day after the shooting he was questioned by several doctors. He repeated essentially the same explanation:

> I don't believe in the Republican form of government and I don't believe we should have any rulers. It is right to kill them.

On another occasion, he commented on the resentment incurred by the slain President's speeches:

> McKinley was going around the country shouting prosperity when there was no prosperity for the poor man. I am not afraid to die. We all have to die sometime.[129]

Then explaining that he was an anarchist, he added:

> I fully understood what I was doing when I shot the President. I realized I was sacrificing my life. I am willing to take the consequences.[130]

Throughout the pre-execution examinations, he remained calm, polite, and remorseless.[131] Witnesses testified that he maintained his principles and composure to the end. They reported that as Czolgosz entered the execution chamber, "he appeared calm and self-possessed, his head was erect and his face bore an expression of defiant determination."[132] He died a few minutes after 7 A.M. on October 29, 1901 in a "cool and courageous manner."[133] An autopsy revealed nothing more than a "good-looking, youthful" corpse. There were no organic abnormalities.[134]

When Waldek asked to claim his dead brother's body for burial, prison authorities denied the request. Instead the body of Leon Czolgosz was lowered casketless into a prison grave bubbling with the contents of "six barrels of quicklime and a carboy of sulphuric acid."[135]

Conclusions

Following the assassination, some anarchists—now under siege from a government committed to the eradication of the "social disease" that resulted in the President's death—condemned Czolgosz's act and labeled him a "lunatic."[136] Others, less timid, viewed him as a courageous martyr in the fight against political and economic oppression.[137] One who shared the latter opinion was Emma Goldman, who viewed the assassin in the same way she viewed the Haymarket martyrs. She endorsed the "social necessity" and selflessness of his act, saying at the time:

> The boy in Buffalo is a creature at bay. . . . He committed the act for no personal reasons or gain. He did it for what is his ideal: the good of the people. That is why my sympathies are with him.[138]

Writing years after the event, Goldman explained the controversy over Czolgosz as one that divided American-born and Jewish anarchists, who condemned the assassination, and their European-born comrades, who considered it a meaningful act of political significance.[139] It was such ethnic and cultural differences that accounted, in part, for the lack of cohesiveness that continued to weaken leftist movements in the United States.

Much of what has been written about the assassination since those troubled times has discounted the rationality and political motive of Leon Czolgosz. Rather than examining the political context of Czolgosz's act, purportedly significant details of his life have been sifted out to support the claim that he was insane. For such observers, the extraordinary nature of the crime itself provided sufficient evidence of insanity.

Typical of such reasoning are Drs. Channing and Briggs, whose collaborative conclusions were outlined earlier. Both doctors based their conclusion that Czolgosz was insane on the assertion that his belief that President McKinley was an "enemy of the working people" was the "essence of his delusion."[140] Moreover, his other anarchist beliefs—for example, the rejection of organized religion and marriage—were considered evidence of the "moral chaos" of insane persons. Further, based on the denials of acquaintanceship with Czolgosz and the reluctance to endorse his act that Briggs observed in his post-assassination interviews with known anarchists, both doctors concluded that Czolgosz's anarchism was also a delusion.[141][j] Channing also dismissed the absence in Czolgosz of any evidence of "divine" inspiration or spiritual "mission" associated with two earlier psychotic assassins, Lawrence and Guiteau, suggesting that Czolgosz undoubtedly shared such a delusion in spite of his denials. Channing explained:

> We must remember that this man was an ignorant Pole [*sic*], who spoke his own language most of the time, and it would have been quite impossible for him to have made use of words that a man like Guiteau, who had a great facility of speech, might have used.[142]

[j] For a discussion of the sentiment aroused against anarchists following the assassination as well as its consequences, see Fine (1955).

Even respected historians such as McKinley biographer Margaret Leech have fallen into such glib and inaccurate generalizations. Ignoring the fact that Czolgosz refused to make any public statements about the crime or to seek notoriety of any kind, Leech concludes that he killed McKinley to "attract attention." To support her conclusion, she makes much of Czolgosz's choice of the alias "Nieman":

> There was bleak self-revelation in the alias which he often used, and which he would use again when the time came for the police to question him: Fred Nieman, Fred Nobody (Nieman in German means Nobody). But on this September afternoon, for the first time in his thwarted twenty-eight years, Czolgosz was going to be somebody.[143]

Interesting speculation, but the fact is that Czolgosz used the alias Nieman because, as he explained, it was the English derivation of his mother's maiden name, Nebock.[144]

The other associated "symptoms"[k] of Czolgosz's insanity also fade under the glare of close examination—for example, his eating alone (he resented his domineering stepmother and refused to share the table with her), his fatigue (he worked a seventy-two hour work week most of his life), his reticence (Slavic culture), and his social isolation (but he was close to his brother and brother-in-law and he did have other friends in Cleveland).[l]

Earlier, one plausible alternative motive was mentioned: the possibility that Czolgosz had seen the *Free Society* allegation which suggested that he might be a government spy. Consequently, he may have acted to demonstrate his loyalty. If true, this would shade Czolgosz's Type I classification with the neurotic tones of the kind of compensatory act associated with Type II subjects. Was he, like Lee Oswald (in part) and Sara Jane Moore, seeking acceptance from a political group? Possibly, but Czolgosz's rational political concerns were much more convincing than either Oswald's or Moore's.

The insanity label is clearly without any empirical support. What we see is not a psychotic but a young man who was as much a product of the times as William McKinley. A man whose beliefs, considered

---

[k] Czolgosz's father had heard that one of Leon's maternal aunts in Europe was "crazy." Leon claimed no knowledge of this. If true, this represents the only potentially significant evidence of the Czolgosz alleged mental illness. Ironically, it has been ignored in all such diagnoses (Briggs, 1921, p. 289; Lawson, 1923, p. 201).

[l] After the execution, Waldek wore a button picture of his dead brother on his coat lapel. Frank Bandowski kept Leon's political library as a fond remembrance of his old friend (Briggs, 1921, pp. 301, 305).

in the context of the life he knew, were no less removed from reality than the platitudes of the President he killed.

There were a number of realities in nineteenth-century America. There was a black reality of servitude, a red reality of extermination, a working-class reality of poverty and exploitation, and William McKinley's comfortable reality of "greater commerce," "happiness," and "vouchsafe[d] prosperity." The rationality of behavior can only be evaluated accurately in the context within which it occurs. Commenting on this point in the February 14, 1902 issue of *Free Society*, Abe Isaak argued that if Czolgosz's anti-establishment views were, in fact, symptomatic of the "moral chaos" of insanity, then all anarchists must be insane. And, of course, that was precisely the point: the insanity diagnosis was transparently ideological.

A leading publisher of the day, Henry Holt,[m] apparently not completely convinced that Czolgosz was insane, grappled with the disturbing implications of a politically inspired assassination:

> We are left sitting in the dark, still wondering how such a deed could have been done by a man in his sound and sober senses in *fair and free America* and *appalled at the possibility of a sane man murdering an American President*.[145] [Emphasis added.]

Rather than acknowledge that possibility however, even contemporary experts find insanity a convenient, if questionable, explanation.[146] To do otherwise, it seems, would be to acknowledge some flaw in the image of a "fair and free America"—the comfortable America of William McKinley and wealthy industrialists.

There is irony in Dr. Briggs' pronouncement that "the principal *cure* for anarchism . . . must, after all, be educative," when one recalls that a grief-stricken little boy tried to achieve throughout his life the whispered hope of his dying mother: to attain "greater understanding and be more learned."[147]

---

[m] Founder of Holt, Rinehart & Winston.

Chapter Three · Nationalism

COLLAZO, TORRESOLA, AND SIRHAN

> I intend to continue where I left off, to keep on fight-
> ing for Puerto Rico's independence until I die.
> —Oscar Collazo (after his release
> from prison, September 1979)

> Kennedy got what was coming to him.
> —Sirhan Sirhan (March 1969)

LIKE their nineteenth-century counterparts, Oscar Collazo, Griselio Torresola, and Sirhan Sirhan can only be understood within a political context. In the case of the two Puerto Rican would-be assassins of President Truman, Collazo and Torresola, there has been less disagreement about their motives than there has been with other subjects. This is largely due to the fact that terrorist activities of Puerto Rican Nationalists still continue; thus it becomes difficult to label an entire movement insane or deluded.

Such is not the case for Arab terrorist Sirhan Sirhan, who continues to be viewed as yet another disturbed young man who killed Robert Kennedy for personal rather than political reasons. Some believe he did it for fame and notoriety; others of the psychoanalytic persuasion are convinced that he was the victim of an unresolved oedipal conflict and, as a consequence, viewed Kennedy as a hated father surrogate. In this chapter, evidence is presented that clearly defines Sirhan's cold, calculating political motives. Had such an event occurred in Europe, there would have been little question that it was a terrorist act. Perhaps now, with greater American awareness of the bitter and seemingly, to the Western mind, irrational hostility of Middle East politics, Sirhan will be viewed in a clearer, more accurate, if not sympathetic, perspective.

In both the Truman and Kennedy attacks, the primary motive was nationalism. Each was an expression of resentment about United States foreign policy. Consider first the case of the Puerto Ricans.

Oscar Collazo (1915-) and
Griselio Torresola (1927-1950)

Near dawn on October 30, 1950—five days before Puerto Ricans were to vote on a new home-rule constitution—members of the Nationalist Party of Puerto Rico quietly took up positions around the Insular Police Headquarters at Bario Mucana, Penuelas, Puerto Rico. Twenty-six police officers were on duty. At 4:00 A.M., the Nationalists opened fire wounding six of them. Five hours later, at 9:00 A.M., a policeman was shot and killed in the town of Ponce on the southern coast of the island. Shortly after, at 10:30 A.M., Nationalist guerrillas attacked the police station in the northern coastal town of Arecibo. An hour later, Nationalists fought Insular Police and National Guard troops from houses they had barricaded in the town of Utuado in the island interior. At noon, they attacked the governor's mansion and the general post office in San Juan killing a policeman and losing four of their own members in the ensuing exchange of gunfire. Police counter-attacked, and a sustained battle developed at the home and party headquarters of Pedro Albizu Campos, the Harvard-educated leader of the Nationalist movement. While the siege continued at Campos' home, Nationalists bombed the police station in the interior town of Jayuya later that night and shot down six policemen as they ran from the burning building. The guerrillas then set fire to most of the town before National Guardsmen arrived and drove them off.[1] The gunfire at Campos' headquarters would continue three more days.

The Backgrounds of Collazo and Torresola

The next day, American newspapers carried news of the insurrection. In the Spanish Harlem section of New York City, members of the Nationalist Party followed the papers and discussed developments. Two party members in particular were concerned, Oscar Collazo and Griselio Torresola, both of whom were committed Nationalists active in party affairs. Torresola had been born and raised in one of the siege towns, Jayuya, and Collazo had spent a good part of his youth there. Although Collazo was nearly thirty-seven—twelve years older than Torresola—they had known each other as youths in Jayuya and had joined the Nationalist Party in the 1930s as young men there. Both had served in various leadership positions within the party. Griselio's brother Elio was also active in the Nationalist movement and would later be arrested for his role in the October 30 insurrection. His sister,

Doris, would be severely wounded during the battle at the party head-quarters.[2]

Both Torresola and Collazo knew Albizu Campos personally. Collazo first met the fiery Puerto Rican leader in 1932, and their friendship and cooperative political activity never ceased. Virtually the entire Torresola family was involved in the Nationalist movement and were even closer to Campos and his family.[3] Torresola's sister Doris worked directly with Campos as his personal secretary.

Campos had risen to prominence in the Nationalist movement after tearing an American flag from a speaker's stand and denouncing U.S. colonialism before a mass rally in San Juan on April 16, 1925. He continued in this role until 1936 when he was arrested and convicted of conspiracy to overthrow United States rule in Puerto Rico. He was imprisoned for his involvement in the bloody Rio Piedras riots on October 24, 1935 and his role in the assassination of a government police chief in 1936. When he was released from the Federal Penitentiary in Atlanta in 1943, he traveled to New York where he lived until 1947 in the same tenement building as Oscar Collazo. Part of this time he was hospitalized for a heart condition and a paralytic condition in one arm. A good friend and admirer, Collazo was a regular hospital visitor during these periods.[4] In December 1947, Campos returned to Puerto Rico where he resumed his activities as leader of the movement and established a party headquarters in San Juan.[5]

Unlike their well-educated leader, neither Collazo nor Torresola had much formal education; both came from impoverished backgrounds. Collazo left school after completing the eighth grade; Torresola left after two years of high school. But both were intelligent, aware men. Collazo especially was a voracious reader of newspapers, history, and political biography. Each had married young, as was the custom, and had fathered a daughter before their first marriages had broken up.

Collazo left Puerto Rico for New York in 1937 to look for work. His father had been a small sugar-cane farmer who had been wiped out by failing health and, in Collazo's opinion, an American embargo on Puerto Rican sugar in the 1920s; he died shortly afterward.

Collazo lived in New York from 1937 on except for periodic sojourns in Puerto Rico. He worked in a variety of menial jobs there and in Connecticut, until he finally developed a skill as an apprentice metal polisher. He was always considered a good worker and was well-liked by his employers and fellow employees.[6]

Throughout these early years in the United States, his activities in the Nationalist party continued. He served as head of the Manhattan junta of the party from 1940 to 1943; from 1944 to 1946, he was editor of the party magazine, *Puerto Rico*; and in 1949, he was elected secretary of the Nationalist party board in New York City.[7]

In 1939, Collazo met Rosa Mercado at a political meeting. Rosa was a forty-year-old divorcee with two daughters. She was also a committed Puerto Rican Nationalist. As their friendship developed, Rosa managed to get Oscar a job as a polisher in the metal products company she worked for in Connecticut. A month later they were married on August 3, 1940. It was to be a close and good marriage. Oscar became a kind, loving, and adored father to his two stepdaughters, and Rosa welcomed his daughter as her own. Soon after, they moved to a small apartment in the Puerto Rican section of New York. They were a devoted family bound by their love and respect for each other and also their unwavering commitment to the Nationalist cause. By November 1950, the Collazos had been happily married for ten years.[8]

On August 21, 1948, Griselio Torresola first stepped onto American soil at the airport in Teterboro, New Jersey. He left behind him in Puerto Rico a wife he thought he had divorced[a] and an infant daughter. Unlike Collazo, Torresola did not actively seek employment. He signed up for government relief and immediately became involved in Nationalist party politics in New York. His party activities brought him into contact with a young strikingly attractive Puerto Rican woman, Carmen Dolores. Well-educated by the standards of the time for women, she had completed two years at the University of Puerto Rico before leaving for New York in November 1948. Carmen claims she married Griselio in an unofficial ceremony shortly afterward. In any case, they moved into a couple of rooms at the Hotel Clendenning at 202 West 103rd Street. Her husband worked briefly at a store on Fifth Avenue called El Siglio but soon quit and applied again for relief in order to devote all of his time to politics. In May 1950, she bore his second daughter. Like Griselio, she was a committed Nationalist.[9]

The October Insurrection

On Wednesday, September 20, 1950, Torresola flew to Puerto Rico to meet with Albizu Campos in San Juan.[10] The next day he talked with Campos, leaving afterward with two notes of instructions signed by the party leader. The first is dated September 21, 1950 and reads as follows:

---

[a] The divorce was contested and had not been granted at the time of his death (FBI Document 100-7689, p. 6).

My dear Griselio:

If by some circumstance it may become necessary that you assume leadership of the Movement in the United States, you will do it without any kind of qualms. We leave everything concerning this affair to your high patriotism and sound discretion.

I embrace you
[signed] Albizu Campos[11]

The second note read:

Griselio will draw the funds which he deems necessary to attend to the supreme necessities of the cause. He will be responsible directly to the Treasurer General. The Delegate will lend him all the cooperation necessary that his mission may be a triumph.

[signed] Albizu Campos[12]

Torresola returned to New York on Friday, September 22, on an American World Airways flight.[13] For the next month or so, his activities continued much as they had before his visit with Campos. Most of both his and his wife's social life was associated with political activities of the Nationalist party, but that was not unusual. He chose to remain unemployed, managing to support his wife and baby on the $129-a-month relief check he received.

Toward the end of October, the pattern of activity changed. Increasing numbers of visitors began to come to the Torresola's Hotel Clendenning rooms. Arriving in twos and threes, both men and women would enter, stay for a short time, and leave. All were associated with the Nationalist party.[14] One can assume that the primary subject of these meetings was the information Torresola had received from Campos. There is little question that he confided to his fellow Nationalists that a revolt would be staged before the November 4 home-rule referendum in Puerto Rico. To the Nationalists, the advantages of "home rule" were illusory; the referendum was simply another attempt to siphon off the growing Puerto Rican discontent with the colonial domination exercised by the United States.

October 29-31

Although Torresola and Collazo had known each other from their early days in Jayuya, they were not close personal friends; they saw each other only at political meetings. Thus it was somewhat surprising when Torresola knocked on the door of the Collazo's Bronx apartment at 173 Brook Avenue at about 9:00 P.M. on October 29. Earlier that evening, he had met with a small group of party activists at his hotel room.[15]

Torresola had a copy of the Puerto Rican newspaper *El Diario de Nueva York* in his hand and said he wanted to talk with Collazo alone about the political situation in Puerto Rico. Keep in mind that this was hours before the first shots were fired in Penuelas. The two left together and walked four blocks to the Willis Avenue Bridge where they stopped and talked for "almost two hours." It is not certain whether Collazo had known about the planned revolt, but it is probable that he did, given his involvement in the higher levels of party leadership. He may not have known, however, that the insurrection was planned for the next day. In any event, Torresola proposed that they both go to Puerto Rico to aid in the revolution. Collazo was considered something of an intellectual in the movement, and this, combined with his long history of party leadership and responsibility, probably prompted Torresola's suggestion. After more discussion about the historical context of the situation—for example, Collazo reminded Torresola of past failures at places like Ponce and Rio Piedras where Government police had killed a number of Nationalist demonstrators—Collazo agreed to go. Then, almost as an afterthought, he told Torresola that he had no weapon. Torresola replied that if Collazo could give him some money, he could quickly pick up a gun. Collazo gave him fifty dollars and they parted close to midnight, agreeing that they would fly to Puerto Rico to join the fight as quickly as they could make arrangements.[16]

The next day, October 30, news of the insurrection was broadcast on radio reports and splashed across the front pages of the afternoon newspapers in New York. That evening, some twenty to twenty-five persons filed in and out of the Torresola's hotel rooms. According to one of those present, all had family members involved in the revolution and had come for any additional information that Torresola might have on developments.[17]

Earlier that evening, Torresola had walked a few doors down West 103rd Street to the apartment of Manuel Lopez. Lopez later reported that Torresola was very excited about news of the revolt and asked him to return to Puerto Rico with him to join in the fight. Lopez declined, saying he could not leave his pregnant wife, but he did accompany Torresola back to his apartment. At the apartment, the phone rang continuously as a steady stream of Puerto Rican males arrived.[18] Presumably, Torresola made similar proposals to each. Then shortly before 9:00 P.M. he left the hotel and walked to meet Collazo at the Willis Street Bridge as planned.

Torresola's optimism about the revolt was diminished somewhat when he met with Collazo. Collazo had worked as usual that day but had listened to radio reports on the revolt and read the newspapers when he returned home that evening. He was upset because the news reports made it appear that the conflict was between the Puerto Rican government and the Nationalist party only, while omitting the important fact that American domination was the fundamental issue in the hostilities. He went on to explain to the less sophisticated Torresola how crucial this omission was to the success of the Nationalist cause. Most Americans, he explained, did not know where Puerto Rico was located, let alone understand anything about the political history of the island. Until the American public understood, he continued, how Puerto Rico was seized as a result of the Spanish-American War and forced to submit to the colonial domination and economic exploitation of the United States government, there would be no sympathy and support in America for the Nationalist cause.

With that in mind, Collazo suggested that they could accomplish more by going to Washington rather than San Juan. As he explained later:

> I told him that a better idea would be to come to Washington; as long as the American people didn't know what Puerto Rico was, or where Puerto Rico was, or which was the real Government of Puerto Rico, they would never care what was happening in Puerto Rico; that by coming to Washington and making some kind of demonstration in the capital of this nation, we would be in a better situation to make the American people understand the real situation in Puerto Rico; that Puerto Rico has no government; there is no Government of Puerto Rico.[19]

After more discussion, Torresola, who had been anxious to return to Puerto Rico, agreed that Washington would better serve their purposes. They decided that the best way to get the publicity they needed was to attack the President just as their compatriots had attacked the governor's mansion that day in San Juan. But since neither one had ever been to Washington, they were unable to plan their venture beyond agreeing to buy new clothes the next morning and to take an afternoon train to the capital.[20]

Sometime during the day, Torresola had purchased a Walther P-38 pistol for thirty-five dollars. After their discussion, and, again, almost as an afterthought, he gave Collazo the gun and fifteen dollars change. Collazo was unfamiliar with guns, but Torresola assured him that he would show him how to use it later.[21]

Both men had told their wives the previous day that they were considering leaving for Puerto Rico to fight if the revolt continued. That night when they returned to their respective apartments they told their anxious wives that they would be leaving for the island the next day. Both wives later substantiated Collazo's claim that he and Torresola did not reveal their plan to go to Washington. It would have been too upsetting, they reasoned, since both recognized their chances for survival would be slim.[22]

The next morning, Rosa Collazo called her husband's employer, the Gainer Corporation in New Rochelle, and told them that Oscar was ill and would not be coming to work that day. Collazo then asked her to go to the post office and withdraw one hundred dollars from their postal savings account. When she returned, Collazo took the money and left at about 9:00 A.M. He returned a few hours later with a new pin-stripe suit, shirt, underwear, and a small valise he had bought for the trip. He had also purchased two one-way train tickets at the Pennsylvania Station. Still thinking he was bound for San Juan, his wife cried and pleaded with him not to go as he packed his things. At 2:00 P.M., the Collazos left the apartment and walked to 138th Street near Brook Avenue and Bronx Place where he hailed a cab. He kissed his wife saying, "Good bye, pray for me."[23]

Torresola had much the same kind of morning. He arose early and went to sign for a relief check he was to receive on November 6. He returned at about 10:30 A.M., also with a new pin-stripe suit. He and his wife then left with the baby and walked to various stores buying a blue valise, two white shirts, and a light gray necktie. They returned home about noon, and Carmen pressed off the new suit, packed his suitcase, and prepared lunch for her husband.

Meanwhile he dressed and then stood at a bureau writing. He told Carmen to mail one of the notes he had written to his daughter by his first marriage in Puerto Rico. The second note he had written to their infant daughter, Rebecca. Both notes were dated October 31, 1950 and said "Remembrances of your Daddy [signed] Griselio." After eating, he left some money with Carmen, kissed her and his daughter good-bye, and left.[24]

The two short, slightly-built men met at Pennsylvania Station and caught the 3:30 P.M. train for Washington. On the trip, they read accounts of the fighting in Puerto Rico in the *New York Times* and also in the Philadelphia papers they purchased when the train stopped there.[25] They arrived at Union Station at about 7:30 P.M. and walked along Massachusetts Avenue looking for a hotel. They decided on the Harris Hotel at 17 Massachusetts Avenue, N.W., the first one they saw, and entered separately, each using an alias to register. Collazo signed in as Anthony de Silva of 150 Aldridge Drive, Aldridge Village, Connecticut, and Torresola as Charles Gonzalez of 167 Ponce de Leon Avenue, Miami, Florida.[26]

By chance, they were given adjoining rooms. Since they were unfamiliar with Washington and had no idea where the President's temporary residence in the Blair House was located, they decided to take a cab tour of the area. On that tour the cab driver, at their request, pointed out the Blair House.[27] They then returned to their hotel and went to bed.

The Attack

The next morning, the two had breakfast together and decided over coffee that they had best take another look at the Blair House in the daylight. They hailed another taxi and were driven down Pennsylvania Avenue to the White House area. The next hour was spent walking around as inconspicuously as possible making mental notes of the security guards and the location of the two sentry boxes that stood at either end of the large Georgian-style mansion. The small leafless trees along the sidewalk permitted an unobstructed view of the four-story building and the canopied front entrance. The house was separated from the sidewalk by only a small hedge and a thin stretch of grass.

Although neither of the two knew it, the President's unprotected bedroom window was located directly above the main entrance, a very short distance from the sidewalk where hundreds of sightseers like themselves strolled in the November sunshine. An American president had not been attacked since 1933 when Giuseppe Zangara tried to kill President Truman's predecessor, Franklin D. Roosevelt, and security was remarkably lax by present standards. It would have been very easy for one of the casual strollers outside the President's window simply to hurl a grenade or bomb into the bedroom where he, like most people, spent seven to nine hours a day.

But Collazo and Torresola had not had the time to plan that carefully. In fact neither was even sure the President was in the Blair House that day.[28] And as far as they were concerned, it did not really matter that much. Neither one disliked Mr. Truman personally. As Collazo explained later: "I never had any feeling of hatred or dislike for Mr. Truman or any other American or anybody else for that matter."[29]

Their primary purpose was to awaken the American public to conditions in Puerto Rico. They believed the only way this could be accomplished was to sacrifice *themselves* in some dramatic way. Americans did not care about Puerto Ricans, but maybe they would change if they realized Puerto Ricans were willing to die for their cause:

> Our intentions were to make a demonstration on the steps of the Blair House. In the Blair House was the residence of the President of the United States and we wanted the American people and the people of the world to know that Puerto Rico was a possession of the United States and at that time, particularly, the Puerto Rican people were being murdered by the American authorities in Puerto Rico, we wanted them to realize that . . . we figured out that a demonstration would never be serious enough . . . to attract the attention of the American people if we were not hurt or wounded or killed in some way . . . especially if two Puerto Ricans were killed in front of his [the President's] residence.[30]

After their reconnaissance, they had lunch and returned to the hotel. As yet Collazo did not know how to use his semi-automatic pistol. For the next two hours Torresola oiled their weapons and showed Collazo how to load and fire his. They also planned their attack.[31] With these preliminaries out of the way, they called another cab and rode downtown, getting out on Pennsylvania Avenue near Lafayette Park, across from the White House, a short block from the Blair House. After a quick conversation, they took one more casual walk past their target and returned to the corner of 15th Street and Pennsylvania Avenue. Pausing there, they decided to approach the Blair House entrance from opposite directions in order to appear less suspicious. Torresola crossed Pennsylvania Avenue and walked down the sidewalk across from and past the Blair House where he recrossed the street and began his approach from the west. Meanwhile, Collazo walked slowly east past Lafayette Park to give his partner time to make his return.[32]

It was approximately 2:15 P.M. and unbeknownst to his two would-be assassins, President Truman had just stretched out for his customary afternoon nap in the front bedroom. Oddly enough, as Collazo approached the east sentry box, he was not wearing the glasses his weak eyes required. They were in his pocket.[33] As he closed to within a few yards of security guard Donald T. Birdzell, Collazo drew his pistol from the waistband of his trousers, aimed, and pulled the trigger— but he had failed to release the safety. In a frantic movement, he fumbled with the weapon attempting to release the safety lever. Suddenly the safety snapped off and the pistol discharged accidentally striking the startled Birdzell in the knee and knocking him to the pavement. As the wounded security guard began to crawl away from his attacker out into the street, Collazo fired off the remaining eight shots in the clip at the other security guards now converging on him. But he hit no one else as he moved toward the front steps of Blair House in a fusillade of returning fire. Missing death by fractions of inches from bullets that cut his nostril, right ear and tore a hole in his hat, he paused on the steps to reload.

Torresola, in the meantime, began firing with deadly accuracy, fatally wounding guard Leslie Coffelt with three shots, then whirling, he hit another guard, Joseph H. Downs, with three more shots. Then while pausing an instant to reload as he stood by the hedge separating him from the building, the dying Coffelt killed him instantly with one shot that struck him in the right ear. He fell, hands clasped together, head bowed, knees drawn up in a grotesque fetal position in the shadow of the Blair House hedge.

Moments later, Secret Service Agent Vincent P. Mroz stopped Collazo on the entrance steps with a single shot to the chest. Collazo fell unconscious face-down with his hat still on, blood trickling down the side of his face from his bullet-knicked ear.

Three days later, the siege ended in San Juan with the surrender of Albizu Campos on November 4. Some twenty-eight persons had been killed, a score wounded, and hundreds arrested.[34] But the movement would continue.

The Trial

Collazo's wound proved to be not as serious as it first appeared, and his life was spared. He was charged with four counts of homicide (in the death of Officer Coffelt) and assault. His trial ended on March 7, 1951 with a guilty verdict on all counts. He was sentenced to die.

During the trial, an unidentified attorney had contacted Collazo's court-appointed counsel and offered him five hundred dollars to permit him to take over the assassin's defense based on the temporary insanity plea Collazo had consistently rejected.[35] When Collazo learned of this, he was furious. Convinced that the man was sent by the Puerto Rican government, Collazo repeated his position to the court that he "would not accept any insanity plea, either temporary or any kind of insanity plea."[36] Collazo went on to explain that the government wanted him to appear insane because it did not want the public to learn that the Nationalist movement had a legitimate and rational basis of support on the island. In Collazo's words, they wanted him to plead insanity not to save his life but only to "discredit my cause."[37] And, in fact, there was absolutely no evidence of insanity.[b]

Thanks to President Truman, who, on July 24, 1951, granted the clemency Collazo refused to request for the same reason he had rejected an insanity plea, Collazo's life was again spared. The President commuted his sentence, without comment, to life imprisonment.

The Aftermath

Throughout his trial and his long subsequent confinement, Collazo never recanted from the principles that brought him to the steps of the Blair House on that warm November afternoon in 1950. Just three years after Collazo was found guilty of attempting to assassinate the President, four Puerto Rican Nationalists, and former associates, attacked the U.S. House of Representatives. On March 1, 1954, Lolita Lebron, Rafael Cancel-Miranda, Irving Flores-Rodriguez, and Andres Figuero-Cordero opened fire from House Gallery 11, shouting Nationalist slogans and wounding five Congressmen before they were overpowered. Each was tried and, like Collazo, remained adamant in maintaining the principle of Puerto Rican independence as their only defense. And, accordingly, each was convicted and sentenced to long prison terms. Like Collazo, the four refused during the long years of imprisonment to petition for clemency, maintaining throughout that they were political prisoners.[38]

The Release

Then on September 10, 1979, in a surprise move, President Carter commuted their sentences, as well as the sentence of the balding, white-haired convicted would-be assassin, Oscar Collazo, to the time already served. A jubilant but remorseless Collazo, Cancel-Miranda, Flores-Rodriguez, and Lolita Lebron[c] were greeted after their release as heroes at an Hispanic rally at Roberto Clemente High School in Chicago. Cancel-Miranda defiantly tore up his clemency papers before the crowd; Mrs. Lebron shouted into the microphone that their release "was done for political expediency and not because of a concern for human rights." A happy but more subdued Oscar Collazo, now sixty-four, told the cheering throng of Hispanics: "The fight for freedom is always

[b] A court-appointed psychiatrist expressed the same judgment after examining Collazo.

[c] Figuero-Cordero had been freed in 1977 suffering from terminal cancer. He died shortly thereafter.

a long fight and always a hard fight. I have nothing to be disappointed about."[39]

Later in New York City, where they were scheduled to appear (strangely enough, given the nature of their crimes) before the United Nations on September 11, they told more cheering Puerto Ricans that they would fight to their "last breath" for "the liberation and freedom of Puerto Rico."[40]

Then before boarding a plane for their return to Puerto Rico, a small frail-looking Oscar Collazo, wearing the glasses he had forgotten twenty-nine years earlier, told the New York crowd: "Repression brought about the violence. Not the aggressiveness of the Nationalist Party but the aggressiveness of the United States Government." And he concluded: "I intend to continue where I left off, to keep on fighting for Puerto Rico's independence until I die."[41]

An estimated crowd of five thousand people greeted the triumphant foursome when they landed in San Juan on September 12. Refusing to renounce violence, the four vowed the movement would continue until independence was won.[42]

On December 3, 1979, Puerto Rican Nationalists ambushed a U.S. Navy bus outside of San Juan, killing two sailors and wounding ten others—two critically—with automatic weapons fire. It was the first attack on American military personnel in Puerto Rico in nearly ten years.[43]

Conclusions

During his trial, the prosecuting attorney asked Collazo, "What, if anything, had Birdzell [the security guard] done to you, sir, to warrant your shooting at him?"

Collazo replied, "Just the same thing, what did the Puerto Ricans ever do to the Americans either, but they were shot at by the Americans and killed."

The attorney countered, "You had never seen him before?"

Collazo responded, "No, sir, and the Puerto Ricans had never seen the Americans either, but they were shot at by the Americans and killed."[44]

Oscar Collazo has never expressed any doubts or remorse about what he attempted to do on November 1, 1950. As his answers illustrate, it all made sense, given his values and priorities. He believed completely in the morality of his cause and was willing to die or spend the rest of his life in prison for it. And his values and priorities were shared not only by his slain associate Griselio Torresola but by those who fought for Campos in Puerto Rico during the insurrection, the four who attacked Congress three years later, and the guerrillas who ambushed the Naval personnel in San Juan in December 1979.

As Type I subjects, Collazo and Torresola were political zealots set apart from the Types II, III, and IV assassins by their very clearly defined and purely political motives. They were hardly the "couple of lame-brained New York Puerto Ricans" they had been labeled the day after the attack.[45] There was no evidence of emotional or cognitive distortion in either. Neither suffered from delusions or hallucinations or imagined themselves divinely inspired. And they both enjoyed normal social relations and strong family loyalties and confidence. Nor was there suggestion of compensatory personal motives in their act. Collazo shunned personal publicity, rejected an insanity plea, refused to request clemency, and remained true to his principles during his long silent years of imprisonment.

Neither Collazo nor Torresola hoped to change the world by their attack. Each realized that the most they could accomplish was the creation of greater awareness among Americans about the conditions they opposed in Puerto Rico. There was no thought that independence would be won as a result of their act. Collazo always recognized, as he said after his release, that "the fight for freedom is always a long fight." He was well aware that the Blair House attack was only one possible step toward their objective. Feeling no specific hostility toward Mr. Truman, their act was simply a symbolic protest against American oppression. As Collazo later explained, the success of their act did not hinge at all on the President's death but rather their own. The cause was paramount, the ideological theme of the political zealot unmistakable.

SIRHAN SIRHAN (1944-)

Of the sixteen assassins considered in this study, Sirhan Sirhan stands out as possibly the shrewdest, most devious and remorseless of the lot. For those reasons, he is, perhaps, the most unattractive. Probably no other assassin, with the possible exceptions of John Wilkes Booth and Carl Weiss, hated his victim more. But he is hardly the mentally unbalanced paranoid schizophrenic that his defense attorneys and psychiatrists attempted to portray.

Sirhan's trial stands out as the longest, most detailed defense of an assassin based on psychiatric evidence. Only the trial of the psychotic

Charles Guiteau nearly a century before and Arthur Bremer's trial three years later compare in terms of the sheer volume of psychiatric (or alienist) testimony. Thus, the Sirhan trial provides an excellent illustration of the attempts by attorneys and psychiatrists to deny the rationality of a politically inspired murder on the basis of the (California) doctrine of "diminished capacity"—the doctrine which holds that a person cannot be convicted of first degree murder if he or she were unable, for whatever reason—alcohol, drugs, or mental impairment—to premeditate the act in a rational manner. In other words, anything that diminishes a person's mental capacity lessens the actual responsibility for the crime committed. One of the central figures in the evolution of this doctrine is Dr. Bernard L. Diamond, an attorney and psychiatrist at the University of California, Berkeley, who participated in Sirhan's defense.

Another participant in Sirhan's defense was the well-known New York attorney Emile Zola Berman. Berman volunteered his services free of charge, eliciting praise from many who viewed the Jewish attorney's willingness to defend a Palestinian Arab—whose hatred of Jews was, by his own admission, at the basis of the primary motive in the assassination—an extraordinary act of humanitarianism. But Berman's willingness to assist in the trial may not have been merely an act of good will because it hinged upon a defense based on "diminished capacity": he strongly opposed any attempt to address Sirhan's political motives in the trial. It was imperative in his view to deny a rational political motive, to portray Sirhan as "mentally ill," and to keep the Arab-Israeli issue out of the defense.[46] And despite Sirhan's continuing protestations, this was the strategy selected by the defense after the judge rejected an initial attempt to plea-bargain a second degree murder conviction and a life sentence.

In addition to the trial testimony and documents, the most interesting and useful source of information on the Sirhan case is Robert Blair Kaiser's book *"R.F.K. Must Die!" A History of the Robert Kennedy Assassination and Its Aftermath.*[47] Kaiser worked as an assistant to the team of defense attorneys and thus was able to report unusually detailed information on many facets of the case available nowhere else. Especially important are Sirhan's off-the-record statements about the assassination and the trial, as well as conversations among his attorneys and psychiatrists. While some of my interpretations and my basic conclusions do not always agree with Kaiser's, his excellent book is an informative and truly unique contribution to the literature on assassins.

The Event

Shortly after midnight on June 5, 1968, a weary but happy Robert Kennedy stepped to the podium in the Embassy Ballroom in the Ambassador Hotel in Los Angeles to acknowledge his victory in the California presidential primary election. Moments later, his speech finished, he made his way through a dimly lit food service corridor in order to avoid the onslaught of well-wishers. Anticipating this move, Sirhan Bisbara Sirhan had positioned himself behind a food tray rack in the corridor. As the Senator approached, Sirhan stepped from behind the rack snarling, "Kennedy you son of a bitch,"[48] as he raised his .22 caliber Iver Johnson revolver to within an inch of the forty-two-year-old New York senator's head and fired. The fatal first hollow-point bullet exploded through the right mastoid bone, disintegrating into the right hemisphere of Kennedy's brain. Two more shots struck the Senator's right armpit as he fell to the floor.[49] His relentless attacker continued to fire five more shots that struck and wounded five other persons as he was being wrestled onto a steam table where he was held until police arrived. Moments later, police officers Travis White and Art Placentia pushed the handcuffed assassin into their patrol car as an hysterical mob clamored for his blood. Jesse Unruh, leader of Kennedy's California campaign, accompanied the two officers, concerned that nothing happen to prevent the Senator's attacker from standing trial.

Once in the car Unruh asked Sirhan why he had done it. Sirhan's reply, "I did it for my country,"[50] was the same comment he had made earlier at the scene of the crime according to an eye witness, Dr. Marcus McBroom. Both the Unruh and McBroom accounts of Sirhan's statement were reported by United Press and the Associated Press but denied by the *New York Times*. Later both police officers denied hearing Sirhan make the statement, and Unruh claimed he could not remember. In his book *Why Robert Kennedy Was Killed*, Godfrey Jansen cites this as evidence that a systematic attempt was made to deny Sirhan's political motives from the beginning.[51]

Whether Sirhan made the statements or not on June 5, the record shows that he offered the same explanation repeatedly during the months before and during his trial. Moreover, the explanation is implicit in the notebooks Sirhan kept prior to the assassination. The record also reveals that an attempt was made to present Sirhan's pre-assassination political writings as evidence of his alleged paranoia rather than as an expression of rational political anxiety, hatred, and preparation for his act, given the assassin's background, values, and perception of Senator Kennedy's position on the Arab-Israeli issue. To understand the source and intensity of Sirhan's political views, it is necessary to review his experiences as a Palestinian child living in Jerusalem during the period of brutal conflict in early 1948.

Childhood and Identity

Sirhan was born on March 19, 1944 in Jerusalem. His father had a comfortable job with the city water department, and the family—six brothers and a sister—lived in an attractive stone house in the Musrara section of the city. In December 1947, the undeclared prelude to the first Arab-Israeli war broke out. Although armed conflict had been common since 1920, when Great Britain had assumed the League of Nations mandate for Palestine, it intensified in the period 1945 to 1948 as Zionist guerrilla forces fought both British and Palestinian Arab troops to establish a new state of Israel in what was, at that time, Palestinian territory. In 1947, Zionist pressures continued to build with the realization that their objective was within reach: Palestine would soon become a sovereign, independent nation, the new homeland for thousands of Jewish refugees from post-war Europe. By December of that year, the conflict intensified as snipers monitored and controlled movement on the streets and terrorist bombs made any public assembly exceedingly dangerous. Shouts and machine-gunfire regularly shattered the barbed-wire tension of Jerusalem nights. The air reeked of fire, smoke, and death as the battle for a homeland locked the inhabitants of that ancient city in the cold terror and brutality of a religious war.

Sirhan Sirhan had just turned four in the midst of this period, but the terror he witnessed with childish bewilderment remained with him, as such traumas invariably do, etched in his memory like painful scars that never quite heal and are easily reopened. Much violence occurred in the mixed Palestinian and Jewish section of the city where the Sirhans lived. In late December or early January 1948, the perplexed child witnessed a bomb explosion at the Damascus gate that left the street strewn with the bloody, mutilated bodies of Arab victims. Later, as the little boy played with one of his older brothers, gunfire rattled when a Zionist truck rumbled down the street. The driver swerved to avoid the sniper's attack, running over and killing the older child as Sirhan screamed in horror and disbelief. It would be months before the little boy could accept the finality of his brother's death. On another occasion, he was the first to discover the corpse of an Arab neighbor lying in a pool of blood along the same street. Later he and his family observed portions of a British soldier's body that dangled from a church tower after being blown to pieces by a terrorist bomb; a finger was found in the Sirhan's yard. On yet another occasion, he was among those who fled in panic as a driverless, bomb-laden truck rolled silently down a street to explode on impact; the deafening blast destroyed three buildings.[52]

Such experiences were not uncommon in Jerusalem, as the Zionist Stern Gang and the Irgun terrorists systematically attacked Arab resistance with the efficiency and cold-blooded resolve of persons who had survived the holocaust and now vowed never again to seek quarter or grant it to their enemies. It *was* a war of survival as a people.[53]

In this context, the words Deir Yassin have the same significance for Palestinian Arabs as does Buchenwald for Jews, Sand Creek and Wounded Knee for American Indians, and My Lai for the Vietnamese who know about it. Deir Yassin is the name of a small Arab village where some 250 old men, women, and children were massacred by Zionist attackers on April 10, 1948. For Arabs, Deir Yassin remains a symbol of Zionist brutality as immoral and evil as the atrocities the Zionists themselves had fled in Europe.[54] It is not surprising that Sirhan Sirhan's political hostility is so easily traced to this formative period of his life.

Shortly after the Deir Yassin massacre and the declaration of Israel's independence on May 14, 1948, the Sirhan family fled their home in the middle of the night, leaving all their possessions behind. The family was about to begin a nine-year period as poverty-stricken refugees living on the fringes of a hostile Israeli society on land that was no longer theirs.

An uneasy armed truce was declared between Israel and the Arab states in 1949. Hostile feelings between Jews and Arabs continued to grow, however, and the truce was frequently broken by raids and reprisals. Some forty thousand displaced Palestinian refugees lived in camps along Israel's borders contributing to the tensions. During this period, the Sirhan family stayed in a fifteen-by-thirty-foot dome-ceilinged room, without furniture, lighted by a single kerosene lamp in the Old Walled City section of Jerusalem. The building also housed two other Arab families who had fled their homes in the conquered part of the city the Zionists now controlled. An Arab friend who lived in the same building confirmed the ugly circumstances of their lives.[55]

Sirhan's mother, Mary, apparently found solace from the family's hardships in religion.[56] A Christian convert, she raised her children in the Lutheran faith and was intensely religious herself. Fearing for her children's safety following the death of her oldest son, the mother did not permit them to play in the street with other children. The unrelieved stresses of a large family living in such small quarters and Mary Sirhan's preoccupation with her children's safety, combined with the generalized frustration and outrage over their situation, soon were reflected in the hostility of Sirhan's father, Bisbara, toward his wife and children.[57] The father's fits of temper and harsh beatings produced a rebellious attitude among the two oldest sons, Sharif and Saidallah, and a cowering obsequiousness in the younger children. Mary Sirhan increasingly withdrew into her messianic Christian beliefs, obsessed with the safety of her children. Under normal circumstances she could have been considered overprotective—but not in Jerusalem during those dangerous years.

From 1951 to 1956, Sirhan attended kindergarten through the fifth grade in a Lutheran school, compiling an overall "C" average in the fifth grade in spite of a demanding curriculum that included English as well as Arabic, geometry, arithmetic, science, geography, history, and religion. His best subject was religion, his worst, arithmetic.[58] Sirhan got along well in school. According to his teachers and classmates, he was mature beyond his years—possibly a reflection of the various crises he had survived—possessed a quiet engaging sense of humor for his age, and was well-liked.[59]

On October 29, 1956, Israeli troops launched a successful attack, advancing into the Egyptian Sinai Peninsula and signaling a resumption of the armed conflict that had been smoldering beneath the surface since the 1949 cease-fire. Although another cease-fire was declared on November 6 and Israel eventually relinquished its captured territory—which included the Gaza Strip—to a United Nations emergency force, it was clear that any hope the Palestinian refugees might have had of regaining their homeland was now fading.

Anticipating no possibility of change in their rapidly deteriorating situation, Mary and Bisbara Sirhan sought financial assistance to emigrate to the United States. With the aid of Lutheran missionaries and the United Nations Relief and Works Agency, the family, without the two eldest sons, left Jerusalem on December 14, 1956. Sirhan was twelve years old.[60]

After arriving in New York, the family traveled to Pasadena, California, where the missionaries had suggested they relocate. They moved into a modest three-bedroom frame house on Howard Street—a shaded, respectable, lower-middle-class neighborhood. The stresses within the family did not ease, however, and before the year ended, Bisbara had left his family and returned to Jordan. In one sense, his departure was a relief: according to those who knew him, he was a mean, self-centered man who treated his family badly. But his absence also added a sense of abandonment to the feelings of isolation the family already was experiencing in a totally new and alien environment.

Senator Kennedy's Political Career

In May 1948, Robert Kennedy completed his studies at Harvard and flew to Israel to cover the establishment of the new state of Israel for the *Boston Globe*. While there, an associate filmed him thoughtfully surveying the war-ravaged scene. Twenty years to the month later clips from that film would be shown in a Los Angeles television campaign documentary shortly before the June 4 California primary. The film would have a decidedly unsettling effect on Sirhan Sirhan.[61]

After his trip to Israel, Robert Kennedy returned home and enrolled in law school at the University of Virginia. In 1951, the year Sirhan began kindergarten in Jerusalem, he graduated and quickly went to work managing his older brother's successful Massachusetts campaign for the U.S. Senate in 1952. In 1953, he became counsel, along with Roy Cohn, to the Senate Permanent Investigations Subcommittee chaired by Senator Joseph R. McCarthy.

McCarthy had launched the most callous and virulent anticommunist crusade in American history in 1950.[62] Through the use of unsubstantiated public statements, indiscriminate accusations, and publicized hearings, McCarthy used his committee to destroy the careers of numerous persons in public and private life. McCarthy pursued this vicious course, which many considered an outrage to public decency, before he was formally "condemned" by the Senate for his activities in December 1954. Robert Kennedy continued to serve on the subcommittee until 1956, despite McCarthy's public condemnation. His affiliation with McCarthy together with his older brother's seeming senatorial indifference[d] to McCarthy's excesses were to become an issue of some concern to liberals whose support the Kennedy family would seek for John Kennedy's presidential bids in 1956 and 1960 respectively.

As the Kennedy brothers moved onto the national political scene, older liberals would also recall Joseph P. Kennedy's noninterventionist position toward Germany when he was Ambassador to Great Britain from 1937 until his resignation in November 1940. Kennedy had consistently supported the Chamberlain government's overtures to Hitler.

[d] Senator John F. Kennedy did not vote on McCarthy's condemnation.

Memories of these controversial pages in the Kennedy family's political history would remain barely under the surface even as late as 1964 when, in the melancholy last light of Camelot, Robert Kennedy mounted his senatorial campaign in New York. Liberals in that state—many of them Jewish, with family and friends who had been victims of Hitler and/or McCarthy—would feel uneasy about the rash, but now seemingly mellowed, younger brother's bid for the U.S. Senate. On the positive side was his strong support for minorities as attorney general in his brother's administration; but his relentless investigation and prosecution of Teamster president James Hoffa was, for some civil libertarians, a chilling reminder of the previous decade.

Some also criticized his abrupt move from Massachusetts to New York, for no other reason than to establish residency for his Senate campaign, as yet another Machiavellian move made possible only by the wealth and power of the Kennedy family. And to challenge whom but Kenneth Keating—a liberal and also a loyal and consistent supporter of Israel in the U.S. Senate. Then again in 1968, Robert Kennedy's decision to challenge President Johnson's renomination was made only after anti-war candidate Eugene McCarthy had demonstrated the strength of anti-war sentiment by defeating Johnson in the New Hampshire primary. McCarthy supporters were angered when Kennedy announced his candidacy on March 16, 1968; it was difficult, even for Kennedy supporters, to deny the opportunistic nature of his announcement. Thus in spite of his strong support for social reform and civil rights and his eventual opposition to the Vietnam War, Robert Kennedy still would find it necessary to deny that he was as "ruthless" as his past political career seemed to indicate.

In addition to his liberal positions on minorities and his opposition to the war, another issue Kennedy had used to win the confidence and support of the wealthy and influential New York Jewish community was his strong advocacy of Israeli interests in the Middle East. In part, the Senator's strong unequivocal support for Israel can be understood as compensatory politics. The checkered Kennedy political history required such a commitment to allay a generation of fears and resentments among many American Jews. Jewish support was absolutely essential in New York and also vital to his presidential campaign in 1968.

Sirhan in America

Adjustments to life in America were difficult for the Sirhan family. Many of their problems were clearly a result of cultural and language barriers. One brother had difficulty finding employment because he could not speak English. Another was arrested for threatening the life of an American girl whose friendship he had misunderstood. A sister, who had secretly married an American, died of leukemia in 1964. Another brother was arrested for drug dealing. Only Sirhan and his brother Adel seemed to avoid any major difficulties during this period, although they, too, found life in America considerably more difficult than they had been led to believe.

A major element in all their difficulties was the fact that they had come to the United States reluctantly, and only as a last resort. Their true home was Palestine, and they had been forced to leave. Thus they were resistant to American acculturation and continued to speak Arabic, listen to Arabic music, read Arabic newspapers, and observe Arabic customs, all in the hope that someday they could return to their homeland.[63]

Given the fact that Sirhan arrived in the United States at the brink of that most difficult time of life—adolescence—his adjustment during this stressful period appears remarkable. While maintaining a strong Arab identity in music, language, and politics—he would listen to the poetic Arabic music of vocalist Umm Kulthum for hours—he also seemed to adjust better than his brothers to American life. He learned English quickly and successfully completed the elementary grades at Pasadena's Longfellow Elementary School before entering John Muir High School. There he accumulated a record of mostly above average grades but graduated only number 558 in a competitive class of 829 students on June 13, 1963.[64] It was clearly a respectable record, however, especially given his unusual background.

While at Muir he got along well, as he always had, with his teachers and classmates. Never a social recluse, he joined the officer cadet corps and was elected to the student council both his junior and senior years.[65] Fellow members of the council recalled him as a cooperative and enthusiastic person.[66]

After graduating from high school, Sirhan entered Pasadena City College for the fall 1963 semester, but there was a notable change in his scholastic performance. In four semesters, he accumulated grades of mostly D's and F's, largely because he simply did not attend classes. He was dismissed in May 1964.[67] His lack of interest and poor performance were directly associated with his dearly beloved sister's illness. Her suffering and death during this period, by his own testimony, had a great impact on him. He had been very close to her—much closer than he had been to any of his brothers.[68]

After dropping out of college, Sirhan worked as a gas station attendant and then a gardener for the next year. Both his employers spoke well of him. Late in 1965, he got a job as a stable boy and "hot-walker" at the race track in Santa Anita. His ambition, consistent with his small size—five-feet-five-inches and about 120 pounds—was to become a jockey. He gradually worked his way up to a job as an exercise boy, which meant he would actually ride rather than walk and clean up after the horses. In the summer of 1966, he left Santa Anita for another job as an exercise boy at the Granja Vista Del Rio Ranch in Corona, California. His jockey ambitions were cut short, however, when he suffered a bad spill at full gallop on a fog-shrouded morning in September 1966. Although an examination and a night at the Corona Community Hospital revealed no serious injuries, Sirhan soon began to complain of blurred vision and pain; in July 1967, he filed a workman's compensation complaint that resulted in a two-thousand-dollar settlement paid to him the following February. Meanwhile Sirhan had gotten a two-dollar-an-hour job at a health food store in Pasadena. The owner knew his mother. But by this time he was growing tired of menial work and, in March 1968, soon after he had received the compensation for his injury, he quit.[69]

The Motive

After graduation from high school Sirhan seemed to be at loose ends. For a young man upset by his sister's illness and death, unhappy and bored with college, dissatisfied with the variety of menial jobs available to a high-school graduate, life in the United States was a growing disappointment.[70]

Sirhan had always been a politically well-informed person, especially on the subject of the Middle East. He was also an avid reader of newspapers—both Arab and American—and his library card reflects his preoccupation with books on this topic.[71] A college friend also acknowledged that Sirhan used to talk with him at length about the Middle East situation. He was adamant in his often-stated desire to return to Jordan someday. His future, he felt, was there—not the United States.[72] With that in mind, he was very sensitive to political developments in that part of the world. And, unsurprisingly, his hatred of Jews and Israel was the deep, smoldering, unforgiving hatred of the persecuted and dispossessed. Anyone who ever discussed politics with him at anytime in his life quickly observed his hostility toward Israel.

Sometime during high school he had underlined passages in two history books that described the assassinations of Archduke Ferdinand

and President McKinley. The last underlined sentence in the McKinley passage reads: "After a week of patient suffering the President died, the third victim of an assassin's bullet since the Civil War." Sirhan added a neatly written, "many more will come," in the margin.[73] Although it is unlikely that he had anything definite in mind, it is clear that his past experiences had prepared him to accept the efficacy of violence as a political instrument.

After high school he began to attend regular meetings of the Organization of Arab Students, where members recalled his strident Arab nationalism and his hatred of Zionists. He equated Zionists with Nazis in their cruelty and immorality.[74] Thus it was with intense anger and humiliation that Sirhan read, listened to, and watched reports on Israel's invasion of the Sinai on June 5, 1967. His political hero was Egyptian President Nasser,[75] but Nasser's forces were defeated with shocking swiftness by the Israeli army and air force. Israeli units gained total control of the Sinai in only three days. Then in three more days, they turned toward the Jordanian frontier to capture the Old City of Jerusalem (where Sirhan had spent part of his childhood) and the strategically important Golan Heights. The brief but devastating engagement that ended on June 10 became known as the Six Day War. For Arabs throughout the world it was their most humiliating defeat. For Palestinian Arabs such as Sirhan, it meant that prospects of ever regaining their homeland were now more remote than they had ever been.

Sirhan's frustrations were expressed in his political arguments and eventual difficulties with his last employer, John Weidner, before he angrily quit his job at the health food store. He told Weidner, for example, that he had no intention of becoming an American citizen because he was an Arab. Moreover, he added that he resented the fact that the United States was a supporter of the Zionists who had taken his homeland. Sirhan told Weidner that wealthy American Jews controlled politicians and the media to ensure the continuation of policies favorable to Israel. Zionists, Sirhan claimed, were as wicked as the Nazis Weidner had fought in World War II.[76]

During the time Sirhan had worked at the ranch in Corona, he became interested in occult sciences and mind control. He believed that mastery of the subject would enable him to achieve his personal and political objectives.[77] After his injury at the track, his interest intensified as he began both to read books on mind control and to practice exercises in his room. The exercises ranged from self-hypnosis to attempts to exert subconscious control over others.[78] Early in 1968, he joined the Ancient Mystical Order of the Rosae Crucis, a San Jose organization that promised self-improvement through control of the mind.[79]

Thus from the Six Day War to the end of 1967, two major concerns seemed to weigh on Sirhan's mind: his disappointment with life in the United States and the realization that his dream of ever returning to Jordan was quickly fading. Arab newspapers, which he continued faithfully to read,[e] daily reported Israel's increasing power and expanding military presence in the Middle East.

With such events paramount in Sirhan's thoughts, there is little doubt that he read in the Arab papers that the *New York Times* reported on January 9 and 10, 1968, Senator Kennedy's proposed sale of fifty Phantom jet bombers to Israel.[f] Sirhan was enraged when he learned of the proposal. He had been an admirer of President Kennedy and thought of him as a reasonable person who had attempted to understand the Arab position. He had had similar hopes for his younger brother. Now his disappointment was profound.[80]

Sirhan kept a notebook in which he recorded his disappointments and hopes; he also used it to practice his mind control exercises, and the two activities became inseparable. The entries were often seemingly incoherent or disjointed statements written over and over again. The idea behind this approach was that once the expressed objective became imprinted on the subconscious, commitment and success in attaining the objective were virtually assured. On Friday, January 31,

[e] Sirhan was also a regular reader of the *B'nai B'rith Messenger* to, in his words, "know what the Zionists are up to" (Trial testimony, Sirhan, vol. 17, pp. 4896-4897).

[f] On January 9, the *Times* reported that Israeli jets had knocked out Jordanian artillery positions on the east bank of the Jordan River (p. 12). In another article by Max Frankel, President Johnson was quoted as promising visiting Israeli Premier Levi Eshkol that the United States would sell Israel "planes and other weapons." Because Israel had lost forty planes in the Six Day War, it sought a replacement purchase of fifty Phantom Jet fighter-bombers from the United States. Forty-eight A-4 Skyhawks had already been ordered before the Six Day War. Thus Israel was hoping to add nearly one hundred new jet bombers to its air force.

In a related article concerning an address Senator Kennedy made before faculty and students at Manhattan Community College, Richard Witkin wrote: "Mr. Kennedy said he thought the United States should supply Israel *whatever* weapons it needed to offset whatever Russia was supplying the Arabs so that Israel can protect itself. *He specifically included the 50 supersonic jets the Israelis have been seeking*" (January 9, 1968, p. 25; emphasis added).

The next day, January 10, the *Times* reported that Senator Kennedy had met privately with Premier Eshkol at the Premier's suite in the Plaza Hotel and had assured him that "he favored supplying Israel with 'whatever assistance is necessary to preserve Israel's borders and protect the integrity of its people' " (January 10, 1968, p. 14). It is most unlikely that news of this importance would have been overlooked in the Arab papers Sirhan faithfully read.

1968, Sirhan scrawled what was the first of a series of trancelike notebook entries declaring repeatedly that "RFK must die." It is also important to note that the last two lines of the entry pose a question and an answer: "Who killed Kennedy? I don't know I don't know."[81] From this point on, Sirhan Sirhan began to prepare himself psychologically to assassinate Robert Kennedy, provided he got the chance. However, in January 1968, Robert Kennedy was only a senator from New York—not yet a presidential candidate—and it must have seemed unlikely, even to Sirhan, that such an opportunity would arise.

The probabilities changed suddenly on March 16, however, with the Senator's announcement of his candidacy for the Democratic presidential nomination. Then on March 31, President Johnson announced his decision not to seek re-election. With a familiar California loser, Richard M. Nixon, virtually assured the Republican nomination, and only the phlegmatic Eugene McCarthy and the Johnson-tainted Hubert Humphrey to defeat for the Democratic nomination, it seemed obvious to Sirhan that the popular pro-Israeli senator from New York would be the next president of the United States. Already on record supporting the sale of more bombers to Israel, Kennedy's election, in Sirhan's view, would signal the beginning of the end for the Palestinian Arabs struggling to survive on the Israeli border. Kennedy had to be stopped.[82]

Preparations

Sirhan's notebook entries during this period reveal a rather well-defined plan of preparation for the assassination. Much like the ancient sect of Arabs from whom the term "assassin" is derived,[g] and with whom Sirhan identified, he began to ready himself for his difficult task. His preparations were based on the Rosecrucian assumption that one can accomplish any objective by writing it down over and over while in trancelike concentration on its realization; or in Sirhan's words: ". . . how you can install a thought in your mind and how you can have it work and become a reality if you want it to."[83] Sirhan began to record his intent to assassinate Robert Kennedy and to establish his own defense on the basis of the claim that he could not remember what he had done.

Although the fact has been largely ignored, Sirhan's notes during this period anticipate in remarkable detail his behavior immediately

---

[g] Assassin or "hashshashin" in Arabic means user of hashish, the mind-altering intoxicant smoked by a secret order of the Ismaili sect (c. 1090) of Islam to prepare themselves to commit politically inspired murders.

preceding and following the assassination. Before he shot Kennedy, Sirhan had had four drinks—Tom Collinses. He then was seen drinking coffee with a young woman. After the shooting, he claimed no memory of the event—although it is interesting to note that he never asked *why* he had been arrested.[84]

With this in mind, observe how closely his notebook entry of January 31, 1968 parallels his actual behavior before and after the shots were fired on June 5. After writing over and over "RFK must die," "Robert F. Kennedy must die," "Robert Kennedy is going to die," he wrote "Who killed Kennedy? I don't know I don't know I don't know." He then wrote:

> girl the girl the girl no no no no no practice practice practice practice practice Mind Control mind control mind control
>
> 1234 1234 1234 1234 give me a Tom Collins were you drunk yes yes yes where is the [girl or gun][h] I don't know go home go hom home car car car car car I want coffee cofee cofee at the party at the party [illegible]

And then:

> Kathleen Kathleen Kathleen Kathleen NO [illegible] NO Kathleen She did not tell me her name NO NO I don't know she wanted she wanted coffee NO NO NO NO[85]

While the identity of "Kathleen" remains a mystery,[i] the similarity between this entry and the actual events on June 5 is remarkable. It strongly suggests that the notebook contained not the incoherent writings of a paranoid schizophrenic but the efforts of a determined assassin to prepare himself psychologically for an assassination as well as for his anticipated capture and defense if he survived.

Elsewhere in the diary the entries vary from statements of political belief to more trancelike writings—sometimes in English, sometimes in Arabic—that reflect objectives Sirhan hoped, in this manner, to achieve. Although political objectives were paramount to him, the trancelike writings reveal his desire for money, two particular women he had met briefly,[j] and "a new Mustang."[86]

His political entries did not vary too much. A sampling:

[h] Nearly illegible, but could be either word.
[i] He may have been referring to a former high-school classmate, Kathleen Rafferty, who had no connection with the assassination.
[j] Although Sirhan could not be labeled a ladies' man, there is ample evidence that he liked women, found them easy to talk with, and enjoyed a normal sex life that probably compared well with most young men of his age and circumstances.

Ambassador Goldberg must die—Goldberg must be eliminated[k]

Sirhan is an Arab

American capitalism will fall an[d] give way to the worker's dictatorship.

Long live Nasser

Taking note of President Kennedy's assassination he wrote:

I believe that the U.S. is ready to start declining, not that it hasn't— it began in Nov. 23, 63.

And he had particular contempt for American politicians:

I advocate the overthrow of the current president of the fucken United States of America.

The American politician leads his people through any course that he wants them to—this is possible because the people lack the initiative or are indifferent to the actions of their leaders. Their leaders say: ["]You have the right to speak against your government and support its Changeover—but remember—through Democratic means Only—if otherwise we will blast the hell out of you—and besides, you wouldn't want to do anything like that, it is stupid, costly and wasteful. Just let us run the country, hire our relatives to work for us—and earn fat checks["]. . . . Well my solution to this type of government is to do away with its leaders. . . . The President-elect is your best friend until he gets into power then he suck[s] every drop of blood out of you—and if he doesn't like you—you're dead—[87]

The persistent theme of his writings, however, was his trancelike preoccupation with Senator Kennedy's assassination:

Kennedy must fall.

Robert F. Kennedy must be sacrificed for the cause of poor exploited people.

Kennedy must die.[88]

---

[k] Sirhan's specific hatred for Goldberg began when he saw the U.N. Ambassador in a televised United Nations debate on the Arab-Israeli conflict in 1967 (Trial testimony, Sirhan, vol. 17, pp. 5019-5020).

Activities: March to May 18, 1968

An attempt was made during the trial to dismiss the notebooks as further evidence of Sirhan's sick mind—his paranoid delusions.[89] But considered in the context of his experiences in Palestine and the very clear positive slant of United States foreign policy toward Israel, the evidence of paranoia seems much less convincing: his concerns were not imagined.

He shared those concerns not only with fellow Arab students at the meetings of the Organization of Arab Students but also in informal conversations he had with other political friends. One of these was Walter Crowe, a high-school friend who went on to attend Pasadena City College with Sirhan. Crowe was a typical campus radical of the period. In 1965, he had organized an ad hoc committee for black civil rights. Then he had tried to form a chapter of the SDS (Students for Democratic Society) but was unsuccessful. In 1966, he joined the W.E.B. DuBois Club, and in 1967 he organized an eight-member student club of the Communist party at UCLA where he had since transferred.

In March 1968, he spent a bar-hopping evening with Sirhan talking politics and watching topless dancers. They discussed Mideast politics—the Six Day War, the loss of Arab territory, the predicament of the Palestinians, and the activities of Al Fatah, the Arab terrorist organization—but without much intensity, according to Crowe.[90] Sirhan's notebook entries during the period reveal a great deal of intense political hostility, however. And the hostility was directed primarily at Robert Kennedy, especially after Kennedy announced his candidacy for the Democratic presidential nomination. It was also at this time that Sirhan began to practice shooting with what was to be the murder weapon.[91]

A few days after the assassination of Martin Luther King, Jr. on April 4, Sirhan discussed the King assassination with a friend of his, a black trash collector, Alvin Clark of Pasadena. Sirhan was angry about King's death and asked Clark if he thought black people would retaliate. Clark replied that he didn't know what they could do even if they wanted to strike back. Then Sirhan asked Clark how he was going to vote in the California primary. When Clark replied that he was going to vote for Senator Kennedy, Sirhan expressed surprise and anger and asked why Clark would vote for that "son of a bitch." He then announced that Clark's vote would be wasted "because I'm planning on shooting him."[92]

Later, on May 2, Sirhan met once again with his friend Walter

Crowe, and Crowe told Sirhan about his Communist party activities at UCLA. He went on to explain to Sirhan that the Arab-Israeli conflict was actually a war of national liberation—an internal struggle by Palestinians against the Israeli oppressors that could be best understood in terms of Marxist theory. He added that the terrorist activities of Al Fatah had boosted the morale and self-respect of Arabs everywhere. Sirhan agreed and observed that the revolutionary objectives of Al Fatah required total commitment.[93] After the assassination, an anguished Walter Crowe would wonder whether his discussion of the strategic and tactical importance of terrorism had influenced Sirhan.[94] Only after the trial began would he realize that Sirhan's thoughts about assassinating Robert Kennedy were first recorded in January when he learned of the Senator's endorsement of the bomber sale to Israel— some two months before their first conversation together in March and five months before their second in May.

The Stalk

At 9:45 A.M. on May 18, 1968, Sirhan wrote in his notebook:[95]

My determination to eliminate RFK is becoming . . . more of an unshakeable obsession.

Following below in his trance-inspired mechanical scrawl he had written over and over again:

R.F.K. must die—RFK must be killed—Robert F. Kennedy must be assassinated

And then, most significantly:

Robert F. Kennedy must be assassinated before 5 June 68.

Why June 5, 1968? It was the first anniversary of the humiliating Six Day War. It also just happened to be the day after the California presidential primary, which was central to the Senator's presidential aspirations. As Sirhan later explained to author Robert Kaiser: "June 5 stood out for me, sir, more than my own birth date. I felt Robert Kennedy was coinciding his own appeal for votes with the anniversary of the Six Day War."[96]

Any lingering doubts Sirhan might have had about Kennedy's Israeli commitment were removed two days later, on May 20, when the television campaign documentary "The Story of Robert Kennedy" was shown in Los Angeles. Midway through the film, the narrator described Kennedy's 1948 visit to Israel as battle scenes and milling crowds of frightened refugees were shown. Noting that Kennedy had lived with Israeli troops and witnessed war firsthand, the voice added that the Senator had joined in to "celebrate" Israel's independence. During this trip, the narrator continued, Kennedy had made a decision. And then with the Israeli flag waving in the background, the rather innocuous decision was announced: "Bob Kennedy decided his future lay in the affairs of men and nations." But the impression on persons sensitive to the Arab-Israeli conflict was that Kennedy's future was tied to the *Israeli* cause. Sirhan could remember little else about the film.[97]

But, in fact, the film was not that crucial to a decision he had already made. It was merely reinforcing. Earlier that same day, Senator Kennedy had made a campaign appearance before a group assembled in the banquet room of Robbie's Restaurant in Pomona. A bartender who was acting as a security check at a stairway leading to the room stopped a young man and woman who claimed they were with the Kennedy party.[1] The young man, if not Sirhan, looked very much like him, carried a coat over his right arm and became very angry when their explanation was challenged. But the couple left without further discussion. The incident and resemblance were verified by two other onlookers.[98] This was probably the first in a series of known attempts Sirhan would make to get within striking range of Kennedy.

On Sunday, May 24, Sirhan continued his stalk of the candidate at a political rally in the Los Angeles Sports Arena. He was later identified as moving about the fringes of the crowd as the rally ended, but again the opportunity did not develop and Kennedy was spared.[99]

On May 26, a column by political commentator David Lawrence appeared in the Pasadena *Independent Star-News*. The title of the column was "Paradoxical Bob" and went on to criticize what Lawrence considered to be Kennedy's inconsistency in opposing the war in Vietnam while advocating military aid for Israel. Sirhan clipped out the column and carried it with him until his arrest.[100]

That same evening, May 26, an Associated Press wire reported that Kennedy again urged the sale of fifty jet bombers to Israel in a speech he had made earlier that day in Portland, Oregon. Sirhan later that night heard on radio station KFWB "All News Radio" that Kennedy had promised a Zionist audience in Beverly Hills that he would send jet bombers to Israel.[101] Such reports only strengthened Sirhan's resolve.

Kennedy's pro-Israeli position and his connections with wealthy

---

[1] Police could not identify or locate the female suspect.

Jewish liberals in the film industry were hardly obscure facts in his California campaign. He regularly made well-publicized appearances in synagogues, and photographs often appeared of him wearing a yarmulke when he addressed Jewish audiences. All this was obvious, even without the explicit Jewish appeal presented in his televised campaign film.

Two days later, on May 28, Sirhan attended an uneventful meeting of the Rosecrucian Society in Pasadena.[102] Then on Saturday, June 1, he drove to the Lock, Stock, and Barrel Gun Shop in San Gabriel and purchased two boxes of .22 caliber hollow-point high velocity ammunition and drove to a pistol range in Corona to practice. He had practiced with the gun only half a dozen times since he first shot it in March after hearing the announcement of Kennedy's presidential candidacy. The gun had been purchased in February by Sirhan's brother, Munir.[103]

The next day, Sunday, June 2, after again practicing at the Corona range, he went to a Kennedy campaign rally at the Ambassador Hotel in Los Angeles. Sirhan's stalk continued in the lobbies and banquet rooms of the Ambassador but without success.[104] Time was growing short. Sirhan was committed to the June 5 deadline he had programmed himself to meet.

On Monday, June 3, the day before the primary, Kennedy was scheduled to speak in San Diego at a rally at the El Cortez Hotel. Sirhan made the two-hour trip to San Diego in his battered 1956 De Soto and then returned that evening to Pasadena—once more without success.[105][m]

The next day, Tuesday, June 4, was crucial for both Kennedy and Sirhan. The outcome in the June 4 California primary was a critical event in Kennedy's quest for the presidential nomination. For Sirhan, who was convinced that Kennedy would win, it meant he had only twenty-four hours left to meet the objective he had been preparing himself for at least since March and thinking about since January.

The day of the election Sirhan drove to the San Gabriel Valley Gun Club where he again spent the afternoon practicing rapid-fire shooting. He left the range when it closed at 5 P.M. and went to a Bob's Big Boy restaurant where he had a hamburger.[106] Then he drove into Los Angeles to the Ambassador Hotel at 3400 Wilshire Boulevard where Kennedy and his supporters had gathered to await the election results. After parking his car, he wandered around the hotel visiting at least one other political gathering and downed the first two of his four Tom

---

[m] Although Sirhan denied this, it is almost certain that he did follow Kennedy to San Diego.

Collinses in the process—just as he had prepared himself to do in the self-induced trances he recorded in his notebook. He then walked to the second floor banquet area where Kennedy supporters crowded in anxiously to await the results. There he had, as planned, two more Tom Collinses. A little later, Sirhan left the hotel briefly, walked to his car, and got the pistol he had left there, tucked it into the waistband of his trousers beneath his jacket and returned to the hotel where he began to drink coffee and talk with an unidentified woman—again as planned.[107]

At about 10:00 P.M. Sirhan walked over to a hotel electrician, Hans Bidstrup, and asked him how long the Senator would be staying at the hotel. He then inquired whether Kennedy's bodyguards remained with him all the time.[108] Sometime during this period, Enrique Rabago, an unemployed auto mechanic who had come to celebrate Kennedy's anticipated victory with a friend, Humphrey Cordero, began to small talk with Sirhan. When Rabago expressed his hope that Kennedy would win, Sirhan replied: "Don't worry if Senator Kennedy doesn't win. That son of a bitch is a millionaire. Even if he wins, he won't do anything for you or me or the poor people."[109]

About 11:45 P.M., Sirhan approached Jesus Perez, a kitchen helper, and Martin Patrusky, a waiter, and asked if Kennedy would be coming through the kitchen. Neither Perez nor Patrusky could answer his question. While talking with the two, Sirhan looked around the kitchen area.[110] He assumed that it was likely, given the size of the crowd assembling, that Kennedy would leave the Embassy Room by way of the pantry. Thus he positioned himself by the tray rack and waited.

Arrest and Trial

Apart from Sirhan's reply to Jesse Unruh—"I did it for my country"—in the police car after his arrest, Sirhan claimed he could not remember the shooting and refused to give his name or reveal any information about himself. At the police station, he seemed calm, careful, especially lucid, and quite glib about subjects *he* wanted to discuss—for example, the trial of a Los Angeles district attorney, Jack Kirschke, who had killed his wife and her lover, and the Boston strangler case—but refused to discuss the assassination.[111] This refusal, combined with several other of his utterances, suggests that Sirhan was very aware of what happened and, given his concerns, behaved quite rationally. First, as indicated earlier, it is curious that while claiming a loss of memory, he at no time asked *why* he had been arrested.[112] Second, when a police officer asked him if he was ashamed of what he had done, he replied angrily, "Hell no!"[113] Third, although he refused to ask the police anything about the crime, he was very anxious to see the newspapers the following day.[114] Fourth, his interest in the Kirschke and Boston strangler cases was probably based on his awareness that in both instances the defendants got lighter sentences than had been anticipated for double and multiple murders. Fifth, concerned that drugs might be used to get information from him, Sirhan refused to drink coffee or water until someone else first took a drink.[115] Sixth, he was aware that the law required that he be brought before a magistrate within seventy-two hours (actually it was forty-eight hours).[116] And finally, the most telling evidence of his total awareness was his concern about the police finding the incriminating notebooks he had left in his bedroom.

When a representative from the American Civil Liberties Union met with him the day after the shooting to arrange for legal counsel, Sirhan, in what under the circumstances seemed to be a totally bizarre command, said "Tell my mother to clean up my room. It's a mess."[117] His hope was that his mother would find the notebooks and destroy them. But it was too late. Sirhan's brothers had identified him, and police had already found the notebooks.[118] Sirhan correctly recognized that the notebooks would provide indisputable evidence of premeditation.

Indeed the notebooks provide the key to understanding the motives of Sirhan. The battery of psychiatrists that had been assembled by Sirhan's attorneys viewed the notebooks as further evidence of the paranoia and schizophrenia that they believed their extensive testing of Sirhan had revealed.[119] The prime source of those tests was Dr. Martin M. Schorr, a clinical psychologist from San Diego who had volunteered to assist in Sirhan's defense. Before Sirhan's trial, in a July 10, 1968 letter addressed to Russell E. Parson, one of Sirhan's attorneys, Schorr wrote:

> I would like to help you very much in the matter of pre-planning jury selection on the basis of the personality dynamics of the client, since so many headaches can be avoided if proper jury selection tuned to the emotional needs of Sirhan can be met, prior to the trial.[120]

After Dr. Schorr had signed on to the case, he was given the permission he so anxiously sought to administer a battery of psychological tests to Sirhan on November 25 and 26, 1968. On the basis of Sirhan's responses on the Rorschach Inkblot Test, the Bender-Gestalt Test of Intelligence, the Thematic Apperception Test, the Minnesota Multiphasic Personality Inventory, and his answers during an interview, Dr.

Schorr diagnosed Sirhan's mental condition as "paranoid psychosis, paranoid state."[121]

Dr. Schorr explained the psychodynamics of the condition in the all-too familiar language of unresolved oedipal conflict: Sirhan didn't really want to kill Kennedy, according to Schorr's analysis, he wanted to kill his father for whom he felt "strong antagonism." Consequently, he generalized this hostility to all "men in authority, of persecutors, of all that is unjust in Israel."[122] Schorr claimed Sirhan "had never advanced beyond the primitive stages of love for his mother—a common pattern in paranoia." Thus Schorr concluded:

> By killing Kennedy, Sirhan kills his father, takes his father's place as the heir to his mother. The process of acting out this problem can only be achieved in a psychotic, insane state of mind.[123]

Even Sirhan's attorneys had trouble with this explanation but accepted it with head-scratching amusement. Any evidence of Sirhan's "diminished responsibility" was welcome. It was their only hope, if they were to avoid a first degree murder conviction and a death sentence. The most they could expect from a jury was some form of institutionalization, medical or penal, for life.

The circumstances of Sirhan's crowded cell where the tests were conducted were alone enough to raise questions about the scientific basis of the psychologist's diagnosis. Dr. Schorr administered his tests and conducted his interviews with Sirhan in the presence of a team of security guards, one of Sirhan's attorneys, Russell Parsons, and a legal assistant, in addition to author Robert Kaiser, in the midst of the most elaborate and intimidating security arrangements. According to Kaiser, Sirhan's attorney and the legal aide—neither of whom had the greatest confidence in Schorr—laughed and wisecracked about the tests as they were being administered. At one point Parsons broke into laughter and said to Schorr, "I don't know who is crazier, you or Sirhan."[124n]

It is hardly surprising that Sirhan's anxiety about his situation was translated into "paranoid" responses on the tests he took. Imagine the situation: confined in a small windowless cell with a multiple twenty-four-hour guard, every move monitored, and facing a murder charge that could carry the death penalty; add to this his alien status as an Arab whose victim was a very prominent American—a hero to many. Who in such circumstances would not feel depressed, threatened, and

---

[n] When questioned about the testing situation during the cross-examination, Schorr claimed that the tapes of his interviews with Sirhan had been accidentally destroyed.

anxious?[125] Indeed, the absence of such responses would appear more bizarre. But Dr. Schorr labeled it paranoia—or the presence of persecutory delusions. To compound the difficulties in this questionable diagnosis, it was subsequently revealed during the trial that Dr. Schorr had plagiarized much of his explanation of the test results from a book by James A. Brussel, *A Case Book of a Crime Psychiatrist.*[126]

Unfortunately, in spite of the difficulties in Dr. Schorr's testing procedures and his diagnosis, as well as those of other psychologists called into the case, whose examinations were conducted under similar circumstances, such evidence provided the basis for much of the psychiatric testimony that was to follow.[127] It also set the tone of this testimony. Few persons were convinced that Sirhan was as sick and deluded as the psychiatrists and clinical psychologists who were summoned to his defense said he was. According to Kaiser, even Sirhan's attorneys privately rejected the notion of his insanity.[128]

Foremost among those rejecting this diagnosis was Sirhan himself. Although maintaining his claim that he had no memory of the shooting, he consistently stated that his primary motive was political. Rather than subject himself to a demeaning defense based on diminished responsibility, Sirhan, like Oscar Collazo, preferred to plead guilty. After Schorr had examined him, Sirhan angrily told his attorneys, "I don't want a trial. I don't want doctors proving I'm insane."[129] He maintained this position throughout his trial, frequently objecting strenuously to the psychiatric testimony designed to save his life.[130]

His family as well as other Arab observers also objected to the attempt to develop a defense based on Sirhan's mental state rather than on the Arab-Israeli conflict that provided a political context for his actions.[131] But the battery of expert witnesses who testified in his behalf rejected Sirhan's own explanation that he hated Robert Kennedy, saw him as a friend of the Zionists and the next President of the United States, and killed him for that reason. This in spite of Sirhan's surprisingly articulate discussion° on the witness stand of the history of Zionism, the Arab-Israeli conflict, and the atrocities he had witnessed.[132] Nonetheless, most of the doctors continued to cling to their familiar oedipal theme, bolstered with some rather questionable test results, that Sirhan was actually lashing out at one or the other of his parents when he shot Kennedy.[133] All refused to acknowledge that, given the political context of Sirhan's life and what Kennedy represented within that context, his motives and actions could have been as rational as those of any political terrorist.

° Some tests had also supposedly revealed a subnormal IQ of 89—thus the surprise.

The only reason Sirhan reluctantly agreed to go along with the diminished responsibility defense (after a fashion—he continued to object to suggestions of mental illness throughout the trial) was that he hoped that he might become part of a future prisoner exchange if he was able to avoid the death sentence.[134] This had been an important element in his plan all along. Or, as he had whispered to Robert Kaiser in court, "Better a live dog than a dead lion."[135] In 1962, the United States had exchanged Soviet spy Rudolph Abel for the return of American U-2 pilot and spy Francis Gary Powers, so there was recent precedent for such changes. But he had assumed incorrectly that the mitigating circumstances presented would be political rather than psychiatric.

Of the psychiatrists testifying for the defense, only Bernard Diamond seemed close to an understanding of Sirhan, but he, too, rejected Sirhan's rational political motive. Rejecting the oedipal theme advanced by others, Diamond testified that Sirhan had killed Kennedy irrationally in a self-induced trance brought on by the mirrors and lights in the hotel lobby. In Diamond's view, the killing was virtually accidental and was due solely to Sirhan's "dissociated" mental state. According to Diamond, had the mirrors and lights not been present, Sirhan would not have gone into his trance, and the assassination would not have occurred.[136] He described the defendant this way:

> I see Sirhan as small and helpless, pitifully ill with a demented, *psychotic* rage, out of control of his own consciousness and his own actions, subject to bizarre dissociated trances in some of which he *programmed himself to be the instrument* of assassination, and then in an almost accidentally induced twilight state he actually executed the crime, knowing next to nothing what was happening.[137]

Diamond rejected the possibility that all this could have been deliberate. He dismissed Sirhan's political views as "delusional fantasies." He also denied that the mind control exercises could have been part of a plan to prepare for a difficult and dangerous task. Sirhan practiced mind control, according to Diamond, merely to "improve his mind."[138]

During cross-examination, prosecuting attorney David Fitts asked how Sirhan's April conversation with Alvin Clark could be explained if the assassination was the unplanned accident Diamond insisted that it was (recall that in April Sirhan had told Clark that he was planning to shoot Kennedy):

DIAMOND: I don't believe he [Sirhan] said that, sir.
FITTS: Well the witness testified to it from the stand.
DIAMOND: I think the witness was incorrect.
FITTS: Is that a polite word for saying the witness was lying?
DIAMOND: No. It's just that he was incorrect.
FITTS: And the basis for your belief—you didn't see the witness on the stand?
DIAMOND: No.
FITTS: You don't know anything about the witness except for the statement you read?
DIAMOND: No.
FITTS: You were not here when he was present?
DIAMOND: I prefer to believe Sirhan.[139]

Only psychiatrist Seymour Pollack, for the prosecution, was willing to acknowledge Sirhan's primary political motive. In his report to the district attorney, Pollack concluded that although Sirhan may have been, in some sense, mentally disturbed, "[his] motivation in killing Senator Kennedy was entirely political, and was not related to bizarre or psychotic motivation or accompanied by peculiar or highly idiosyncratic reasoning."[140]

Although Pollack was alone in this assessment among the nine psychiatrists and psychologists who testified during the trial, the jury accepted his interpretation.[p] One probable reason for the jury's rejection of opposing testimony was that in spite of the diagnostic agreement among the others—that is, that Sirhan was suffering from paranoid schizophrenia—their explanations were often contradictory, poorly defended during cross-examination, and unconvincing. Only Diamond, for example, attempted to explain how the alleged paranoid schizophrenia caused the assassination in other than strained language of unresolved oedipal conflict. But his admission that he found his own explanation "an absurd and preposterous story, unlikely and incredible" did little to add to its credibility.[141]

On April 17, 1969, the jurors found Sirhan guilty of the first degree murder of Senator Kennedy. In so doing, they endorsed Sirhan's own explanation that his motives were political. Six days later, on April 23, they agreed with the assessment of prosecuting attorney John E. Howard who urged the jury "to apply the only proper penalty for political assassination in the United States of America":

---

[p] Pollack's occasional ambivalence about Sirhan's mental state can best be understood in terms of his strong opposition to the death penalty he felt Sirhan would certainly receive.

You may eliminate Sirhan from society altogether or merely eliminate him from your society. This defendant will regard permission to live as a further triumph of imprisonment, for life imprisonment is an entry into a form of custodial society that can only suffer by the inclusion of this defendant.[142]

Sirhan was sentenced to death in the gas chamber in spite of a handwritten plea for clemency made by the late Senator's brother, Senator Edward Kennedy.[143] His sentence was later reduced to life imprisonment when the United States Supreme Court declared the death penalty unconstitutional.

Conclusions

Sirhan Sirhan possesses all the characteristics of a Type I assassin. The only emotional and cognitive distortion present was self-induced in order to carry through his plan. To that extent, his "mind control" exercises served the same function as hashish did for his ancestors, the first Arab assassins. There was also no evidence of hallucination or delusion. When Robert Kaiser asked him if he saw himself as "an instrument of divine wrath," he shook his head and said smiling, "God didn't tell me to shoot Kennedy."[144] He understood completely what he had done and why, as well as the consequences. He had read extensively about previous assassins. Even his alleged loss of memory was part of a carefully calculated plan to avoid the death sentence. And his hope to become part of a future prisoner exchange was not only based on precedent but was substantiated in 1970 when on September 6, Arab terrorists in Europe hijacked four commercial jetliners bound for the United States and forced them to fly to the Middle East. The hijackers reportedly sought to exchange their captives for the release of Sirhan.[q]

Moreover, Sirhan has not yet given up the idea of a prisoner exchange. In a 1978 article in *Playboy* magazine,[145] a former cellmate of Sirhan's at Soledad Prison is quoted as saying that Sirhan told him that he was still hopeful that Arab terrorists would be successful in arranging the circumstances for his release. He recognizes that he is a hero to many Arabs. And his plan still may come to fruition. Eligible for parole again in 1984, the Arab-American Relations Committee is

---

[q] The passengers were later released, and the Palestine Liberation Organization denied that Sirhan was part of the attempted exchange (*New York Times*, September 8, 1970, A1).

now working for his release, having already made arrangements for his return to any one of five Arab countries.[146] And on February 4, 1981, the Associated Press reported that "friends of Sirhan Sirhan have appealed to Senator Edward M. Kennedy to support the early release of the man who assassinated his brother, Robert."[147]

Perhaps not until the seizure of the American Embassy in Iran and the confinement of the hostages have Americans realized that political leaders in the United States are widely hated with great intensity in many Arab countries. And nowhere is that hatred more intense than it is toward pro-Israeli politicians. In addition, the long history of Islamic cultures provides ample religiously based justification for violent retaliation against their enemies. Thus, Sirhan remains satisfied and confident that his act was justified. There is no evidence that his motives were purposeless or simply nihilistic. He was not, as his attorney Emile Zola Berman told reporters, "obviously mad."[148] His intent was to deny the presidency to a powerful pro-Israeli politician on the brink of the nomination: in that role, Sirhan believed that Robert Kennedy would have been an enemy to Arabs everywhere.

Sirhan has consistently remained without remorse for his crime; he has never once expressed sorrow or regret. His most common references to his victim are illustrative:

Kennedy, you son-of-a-bitch. (June 5, 1968)

The bastard isn't worth the bullets. (October 1968)

. . . a fuckin politician, who would have been a killer if he had been elected, he would have sent those fuckin' jets, I don't think I should be convicted at all. (December 1968)

That bastard is not worth my life. (January 1969)

Kennedy got what was coming to him. (March 1969)

In the first place, Robert Kennedy was a Fascist pig. Eldridge Cleaver said so. (May 1969)

Every morning when I get up, sir, I say I wish that son of a gun were alive, because I wouldn't have to be here now. (May 1969)[149]

Then, in a very rare interview, Sirhan discussed the assassination a decade later, in 1979, and although attempting to project the image of a completely changed, patriotic and born-again Christian hoping for parole or deportation, the theme persists. In words eerily similar to those he first recorded in his notebook in early 1968, his contempt for his victim remains as clear as his political motive:

As far as the loss of a human being, loved by his family and all that, loved by his children—on that basis my action was undefensible. I acknowledge that. And I am willing to pay the price. But as far as a politician, a self-seeker, getting votes and preferring one ethnic group against another in this great democracy, for personal interest, I have no   what's the word? I don't feel that he was even fair in that respect.[150]

Then expressing anger because convicted murderer Dan White received only a seven-year, eight-month sentence for slaying San Francisco mayor George Moscone and supervisor Harvey Milk, Sirhan demanded: "Who was Robert Kennedy? Was he a greater creation of God? Was he more loved by God than, say, Moscone or Milk?" And he concluded his interview on another familiar note: "I have been victimized by this country, deprived of my homeland, dispossessed."[151]

In addition to his remorseless reflections on the assassination, there are other aspects of Sirhan's behavior that also support his classification as a Type I assassin. The fact is that with rare exceptions, such as his 1979 interview, Sirhan has consistently shunned publicity. Had he killed for the neurotic compensatory reasons of seeking fame and glory, it is certain he would have sought rather than avoided public attention. In 1969, for example, he was very upset when he learned that Robert Kaiser was going to write a book about him, and his attorneys subsequently sought to prevent its publication. And that basic reclusive pattern continues over a decade later.

Similarly there is no evidence to support the notion that Sirhan was a loner who could not get along with other people—especially women. All the known facts reveal a basically quiet but friendly and conversant person who got along well with most people and especially enjoyed the companionship of women right up through the evening of the assassination.

In the final analysis, what we see in Sirhan is a coldly calculating and remorseless assassin who killed for political reasons—reasons that were difficult for many to grasp or accept in 1968 and 1969. But now with the increased awareness of the intensity of Arab and Islamic feelings and values in the Middle East, Sirhan's motives, no matter how objectionable and deplorable, cannot be dismissed as irrational. His values and political perspective are shared by millions of other Arabs.

Sirhan's crime on June 5, 1968 was no different than the atrocities of numerous Palestinian terrorists who continue to bomb and assassinate in attempts to reach their political objectives. He is no more irrational than the Black September terrorists who murdered the Israeli athletes at the 1972 Munich Olympics, or the two Zionist assassins who killed Lord Moyne in 1944, or the Zionists who participated in the Deir Yassin massacre in 1948. Sirhan was mad or irrational only to the extent that war and intense nationalism are mad or irrational.

Chapter Four · Rejection

OSWALD AND BYCK

There is no borderline between one's personal world
and the world in general.
—Lee Harvey Oswald

I think this all begins with the lack of respect.
—Samuel Byck

MANY AUTHORITIES agree that it is often a very fine line that separates
psychotic and neurotic behavior.[1] Given the fact that most neurotic
persons think of themselves as normal, the problem of classification,
as indicated earlier, becomes somewhat arbitrary, even among the
experts. With this qualification in mind, however, it is possible to
observe some significant differences between the Type IV assassins
discussed in Chapter Seven and the subjects discussed in this one. This
is not to say that the Type II subjects are carbon copies of each other
in either the nature of their neuroses or the circumstances and quality
of their lives. As will be seen, they are quite different people with
markedly different backgrounds.

The primary characteristic of Type II subjects is what Harold Lasswell has called a "political personality."[2] What this means, in effect,
is that the subject displaces personal motives on public objects, ra-
tionalizing the motives in terms of some larger public interest. According to Lasswell, such persons seek power in order to compensate
for low estimates of self. The low estimate of self, he contends, is most
frequently a consequence of a deprivation of affection experienced in
the individual's personal life—for example, the denial or rejection of
love by a parent, spouse, one's children, or other loved one. The
exercise of power in a public manner generates the attention, and,
occasionally, affection, that otherwise is denied. Lasswell had in mind
specifically persons who seek positions of authority.[3] However, the
same explanation can be applied to some similarly frustrated persons
who, lacking the skills or other personal attributes necessary for con-

ventional success, choose another more spectacular and tragic alternative—namely, assassination.

In addition to this main common characteristic, a number of other important qualities define the differences between the Type II and Type IV assassins. Unlike the Type IV's, the Type II assassins do not suffer from delusions or hallucinations. The cognitive distortion that does exist is mild and certainly within the range of ordinary subjectivity. Type II assassins maintain their grip on reality. They are not confused by events they cause or encounter; their personalities remain intact, without the disintegrating effects associated with psychoses. The tensions and anxieties generated in their social environments produce, along with their political personalities, a tendency toward paranoia. But, as we will see, their suspicions and fears are, more often than not, rather firmly grounded in the objective circumstances of their lives and to this extent may be reasonably considered rational. Lacking the self-imposed withdrawal and psychopathology of the emotionally desensitized Type III assassins, the subjects of the next two chapters are ruled by anxiety and emotion.

Lest the impression be created that Type II assassins are just everyday folks—they obviously were not—some further qualifications are in order. While their anxieties and fears may be based on the realities of their lives, the neurotic assassins differ from ordinary people to the extent that they rely more on ego-defensive behavior in order to deal with these threats. This is, in some cases, because they did not possess the qualities necessary to compete or cope successfully. Ultimately, as one coping strategy after another failed, each of these persons sought to resolve their frustrations by proving their value to themselves and the significant others in their lives. Their motives can only be understood in terms of the acceptance and recognition they had been denied or, in one case, had feared losing.

Four persons in my study fit this basic description: Lee Harvey Oswald, Samuel Byck, Lynette Fromme, and Sara Jane Moore. As the first women in American history who attempted to assassinate a president, Fromme and Moore illustrate interesting variations on this theme. For that reason they are considered separately in Chapter Five.

Volumes have been written and continue to be written about the 1963 Kennedy assassination and Lee Oswald. But most people have never heard of Samuel Byck who, on February 22, 1974, died in his attempt to hijack and crash dive, kamikaze fashion, a Delta jetliner into the White House to kill President Nixon. Both men illustrate the basic compensatory motives of Type II assassins. Consider first the case of Lee Harvey Oswald.

LEE HARVEY OSWALD (1939-1963)

There is little doubt that Lee Harvey Oswald killed President Kennedy on that sunny, clear November afternoon in Dallas. But two related major questions remain unanswered: Why did he do it? and, did he act alone? In the attempt to deal specifically with the first question, some observations will also be made regarding the second.

Childhood

Lee Harvey Oswald was born in New Orleans on October 18, 1939, the third of Marguerite Oswald's three sons. His father had died two months before. The death forced his mother to seek employment and, as a result, his brothers were placed in an orphanage where he joined them two years later.[4] When he was four years of age, he was withdrawn from the orphanage and taken by his mother to Dallas where she remarried five months before Lee's fifth birthday. After her marriage, the older brothers were sent to a military academy and Lee lived with his mother and new stepfather, who, according to his half-brother, John Pic, Lee loved as a father. But the marriage soon deteriorated and his parents were divorced in 1948.[5] This brief period between his fifth and eighth birthdays when, as it turned out, his parents' marriage was breaking up, was to be the closest Lee Oswald was to come to an ordinary family experience.

After the divorce, moving between Dallas and New Orleans, Marguerite Oswald worked at a variety of unskilled jobs to support herself and her sons until her two oldest boys, John and Robert, were old enough to enlist in the service. As a result, Lee was left alone much of the time that he was not in school compiling a surprisingly good, under the circumstances, "average" record.

The first serious evidence of the effect that his unpleasant childhood was having on him came in August 1952 when, shortly before school started, Marguerite abruptly decided to move to New York. There they lived briefly with her oldest son, John, before eventually moving to an apartment in the Bronx. Missing the friends and surroundings he knew, Lee found himself thrust into an alien urban culture where his new seventh-grade classmates ridiculed his rural-looking clothes, peculiar mannerisms, and southern accent. Confronted with such hostility, Lee withdrew and began to spend more and more time away from his classes watching television and reading magazines alone in the seedy apartment. His poor school attendance resulted in truancy charges, and he was subsequently sent for psychiatric observation to determine the cause of his increasing psychological as well as social withdrawal. In the post-examination report, the thirteen-year-old boy's problems were diagnosed to be the result of "intense anxiety, shyness, feelings of awkwardness and insecurity." The report concluded that:

> Lee has to be seen as an emotionally, quite disturbed youngster who suffers under the impact of really existing emotional isolation and deprivation, lack of affection, absence of family life and rejection by a self involved and conflicted mother.[6]

Likable and even charming when he wanted to be, this bright and good-looking, but disturbed, youngster was elected president of his eighth grade class when he returned to school in the fall of 1953. But he soon became distracted, surly, and, at times, disruptive. According to the reports of his probation officer, he began once more to avoid his assignments and, among other things, refused to salute the flag with his classmates.[7]

Although doing little in school beyond attending in order to avoid probation problems, Lee had become an avid reader. During this period, a major political issue was the controversial Rosenberg case. The eventual execution of Julius and Ethel Rosenberg on June 19, 1953 was nowhere more vigorously and emotionally contested than in New York City. It was during this time that someone handed Lee a Marxist pamphlet protesting the injustices of that trial and the impending execution. Oswald was later to say that this event in his troubled fourteenth year stirred his interest in Marxism. From this point on, he began to develop through his new Marxist perpective the idea that the unhappiness and difficulties of his life were not unique. Like the Rosenbergs and the innocent people who were to fall victim the following year to the indiscriminate attacks of Senator Joseph R. McCarthy, Lee Harvey Oswald began to see himself as a victim of capitalist oppression. Even his hostility or, at best, ambivalence toward his mother—"well I've got to live with her. I guess I love her"[8]—could be rationalized this way: she, too, was a victim—as she, in less doctrinaire fashion, constantly complained—of the same oppressive system.[9]

Indeed, it is interesting to observe the striking similarity between the personality of Marguerite Oswald and the evolving personality of her son. She was described by the psychologists who were treating

Lee in 1953 as "very self-possessed and alert," with a "superficial" affability that did not quite conceal "a defensive, rigid, self-involved person who had real difficulty in accepting and relating to people."[10] Essentially the same words would be used to describe her son by virtually everyone who knew him.[a] Lee was in every sense his mother's son. The stamp of her personality on his was undeniable.

It was in the midst of these difficulties with the New York school authorities that Marguerite, with Lee in tow, moved again. Back in New Orleans, where Lee finished the ninth grade, he was once again looked upon as an outsider.

Thus, with no family life to speak of, isolated and frequently harassed in school, and having few, if any, close friends, Lee Oswald was to make the first of four major decisions designed to alter the dismal circumstances of his life: he would join the Marines, following in the footsteps of his older brother Robert. He hoped to find the adventure, recognition, pride, and self-respect portrayed in Marine recruitment posters, not to mention an escape from Marguerite and school authorities.

The Marines (October 1956 to September 1959)

Soon after enlisting in the Marines in October of 1956 he realized that he had made a mistake. His fellow Marines were no more tolerant of his reclusiveness and surliness than his schoolmates in New York and New Orleans. Nor were Marine officers any more inclined to ignore his indiscretions than his teachers were. Moreover, they were perhaps even less inclined to acknowledge what he considered to be his superior abilities.[11]

At first withdrawing, he was soon dubbed "Ozzie the Rabbit" because of his pinched, unsmiling little mouth and his seeming vulnerability.[12] Ignoring the sex and violence that typify the reading material in most barracks, Oswald read Whitman's "Leaves of Grass" and Orwell's *1984*[13] and also began to study the Russian language and read a Russian newspaper.[14] Although he had his first sexual experiences with Japanese prostitutes and drank a little beer in the local slop-chutes, Oswald was not a typical hell-raising Marine. Unhappy with barracks life and discipline, his resentment began to surface in disputes with superiors that resulted in a court-martial conviction and

---

[a] Priscilla Johnson McMillan has made the same observation and attributes much of Oswald's subsequent behavior to an unconscious Freudian-like rejection of this unacceptable image of himself and a search for more acceptable mother substitutes, such as the Marine Corps and Russia (McMillan, 1977, pp. 223-228).

twenty-eight days in the brig. He had previously been court-martialed for the unauthorized possession of a pistol with which he had accidentally shot himself in the arm.[15]

Four weeks in a Marine brig, at that time, was an emotionally searing, personally degrading and embittering experience. Prisoners were forced to do trivial and repetitious tasks, required to stand at attention when not working or doing physical exercise, forbidden all but task-related conversations with fellow prisoners, required to ask permission to relieve themselves, and frequently harangued and harassed in humiliating boot-camp fashion. This totally punitive experience was designed to minimize recidivism. Few prisoners left Marine brigs without a great deal of resentment.

For Lee Oswald, already disillusioned, the experience was a confirmation of all he hated about the Corps as well as the wisdom of the plans he had been considering to defect to the Soviet Union. There appeared to be a direct relationship between his difficulties in the Marines, his interest in the Soviet Union, and the intensity with which he pursued his study of the Russian language.

The Soviet Union (1959-1962)

Securing an early discharge, ostensibly to care for his allegedly disabled mother, Lee instead left almost immediately for the Soviet Union with money he had saved in the service. Denouncing the United States in the most unqualified terms, he anticipated a warm reception in the nation he had elevated to the level of an ideal.[16] Instead, he was shattered by the cold indifference and skepticism of the Soviet bureaucracy when informed immediately after his arrival that he was not welcome to remain.

As a result of this blow, on October 21, 1959, Oswald attempted to commit suicide by drawing a razor through the flesh and tendons of his left wrist, Lee recorded his disappointment in his own "Historic Diary":

> I am shocked!! My dreams! . . . I have waited for 2 years to be accepted. My fondes dreams are shattered because of a peety offial, . . . I decide to end it. Soak rist in cold water to numb the pain, Than slash my leftwrist. Than plaug wrist into bathtum of hot water. . . . Somewhere, a violin plays, as I wacth my life whirl away. I think to myself "How easy to Die" and "A Sweet Death, (to violins). . . ."[17b]

---

[b] Oswald's misspelling is thought to be a result of dyslexia. His writing is quoted throughout without corrections.

Although eventually Soviet Union officials agreed to permit him to remain, there is no evidence that Oswald completely recovered from the initial trauma of rejection by what he had hoped would be his new homeland. Like the disappointment of unrequited love, he would often reflect on this bitter experience. His disillusionment would be complete when some four years later he was again rebuffed by another nation that had become his revolutionary ideal and hope for a new life—Cuba. And once again his response would be very similar: one calculated to demonstrate the sincerity of his commitment in the same self-flagellating, guilt-inflicting, egoistic manner.

Although his life in the Soviet Union was to take on new and appealing social dimensions—he made friends, dated pretty girls who found him attractive, and eventually married one of them—the drab, daily routine of Soviet life soon became unbearable. Having been denied admission to a university in Moscow, he was provided employment at a radio and television factory in Minsk. However, even the generous allowance that supplemented his factory salary and an unusually commodious apartment were not enough to compensate for the obscurity of his position and the boredom of Soviet life.[18] In January of 1961, he wrote in his diary:

> I am stating to reconsider my disire about staying the work is drab the money I get has nowhere to be spent. No night clubs or bowling allys no places of recreation acept the trade union dances I have had enough.[19]

Disillusionment

In June 1962, he returned to the United States with his Russian wife Marina and their infant daughter. Earlier in a preface[20] he had written to *The Collective*, his manuscript about life in the Soviet Union, he presented a brief autobiographical assessment of his own life at that point:

> Lee Harvey Oswald was born in Oct 1939 in New Orleans La. the son of a Insuaen Salesmen whose early death left a far mean streak of indepence brought on by negleck. entering the US Marine corp at 17 this streak of independence was strengthened by exotic journeys to Japan the Philipines and the scores of odd Islands in the Pacific immianly after serving out his 3 years in the USMC he abonded his american life to seek a new life in the USSR. full of optimism and hope he stood in red square in the fall of 1959 vowing to see his chosen course through, after, however, two years and alot of growing up I decided to return to the USA.[21]

But it was not a happy return because even though his positive view of the Soviet Union had been significantly altered, his negative view of the United States remained as intense as before. Thus, he was at loose ends. His great adventure had been a failure and now he was returning to an unhappy past he had hoped to leave.

After a brief and clearly strained reunion with his mother and brother Robert in Texas after their arrival in June 1962, Lee and his wife saw very little of his family. The pattern his life soon assumed was all too familiar: the self-generated isolation, the moving from one dead-end job and shabbily furnished apartment to another, and the ever-increasing alienation from all things American.[22]

His frustration and anger were reflected in his deteriorating marriage. He began to beat his wife at the slightest provocation, became sexually abusive, and was in general unreasonably cruel to her.[23] This type of behavior, however, only deepened his depression and moodiness and added further to the already heavy strains on the marriage.

Very depressed and discouraged, Oswald saw little hope for the future. Disillusioned with the Communist party's bureaucratization and betrayal of Marxist principles in the Soviet Union and confronted with the dismal realities of slum life in Fort Worth, Oswald wrote in despair:

> No man, having known, having lived, under the Russian Communist and American capitalist system, could possibly make a choice between them. there is no choice, one offers oppresstion the other poverty. Both offer imperilistic injustice, tinted with two brands of slavery.
>
> But no rational man can take the attitude of "a curse on both your house's." There *are* two world systems, one twisted beyond recognition by its misuse, the other decadent and dying in its final evolution.[24]

Marina Oswald's biographer Priscilla Johnson McMillan attributes great significance to this document, suggesting that "it gives a better idea than anything else he wrote of what appears to have been his conscious purpose in killing President Kennedy, and of the resigned, stoical and yet exalted spirit in which he went about it."[25]

Although Oswald does anticipate that "a coming economic, political or military crisis, internal or external, will bring about the final destruction of the capitalist system,"[26] this would appear to be no more than a familiar Marxist assessment of the end of capitalism rather than a revelation of the motives for his subsequent assassination of the President. Indeed, as a good Marxist, his stoical belief in the

historically inevitable collapse of capitalism denies the utility of individual violence in precipitating the final "crisis." He mentions this
fact repeatedly in his manuscript. On pages four and five he writes:

> We have no interest in violently opposing the U. S. Government,
> why should we manifest opposition when there are far greater
> forces at work, to bring-about the fall of the United States Gov-
> ernment than we could ever possibly muster.

And later, on page five, he states:

> Resoufullniss and patient working towards aforesaid goal's, are
> prefered rather than loud and useless manifestations of protest.

On page eight, he writes that failure to work and organize to prepare
for the crisis would be as big a mistake "as trying to use force now
to knock down the door." And in the next sentence, he declares:

> Armed Defenses of our ideals must be an accepted doctrine after
> the crisis, just as refrointing [refraining] from any demonstrations
> of force must be our doctrine in the mean time.

Thus, his anticipation of an impending "crisis" would appear to be
nothing more or less than a statement of Marxist doctrine. There is
little in this essay that sheds any light on his reasons for the subsequent
attacks on General Edwin A. Walker and President Kennedy. Indeed,
the utility of violence, as we have seen, is repeatedly denied. His
philosophical musings are important, however, to the extent that they
reveal his disillusionment with the Soviet Union and the United States
and the personal and political importance he was to attach to a Cuban
alternative.

General Walker and the Cuban Alternative

By March 1963, Oswald's political interest had begun to shift to the
Third World, and he renewed a particular abiding interest in Cuba.
With that shift, his depression began to lift. Long an admirer of Fidel
Castro, he began to formulate a plan that would prepare the way for
a new life in a truly revolutionary society. Uncontaminated by the
stultifying, gray-cold bureaucracy of the Kremlin, in Oswald's mind
Cuba represented a fresh new revolutionary ideal—a country that
would recognize and appreciate a fellow revolutionary like himself.
In Cuba, he could imagine assuming a leadership role in society—
certainly, he would be taken seriously and not relegated to the obscurity of an assembly plant as he had been in the Soviet Union. But

first he had to establish his credentials in a way that would impress a revolutionary military government that had seized power after years of skillfully directed guerrilla warfare.

Living in Dallas at the time was retired Major General Edwin A. Walker. Walker had recently gained national attention as the result of his right-wing political activities. A militant anti-communist of paranoid proportions, Walker urged an invasion of Cuba in the most unqualified terms, comdemned the Kennedy administration for its restraint, and vigorously opposed the civil rights movement. Forced to resign from the army as a result of his extremist views, Walker toured the country speaking in behalf of these causes. No one represented the racist imperialism Oswald associated with American society better than General Walker; no one, therefore, offered a more convenient and appropriate target at which to strike a blow for Cuba and, consequently, establish the revolutionary credentials of Lee Harvey Oswald. On a personal level, Walker would also provide a less demeaning target than his frail and pregnant wife, who had been absorbing the verbal and physical abuse of his frustration and anger.

Early in March, Oswald decided Walker should die. He began to make preparations for the assassination, taking care to document his act with photographs of Walker's home supplemented with elaborately drafted plans that could subsequently be produced as proof of his revolutionary act. On March 12, he ordered a 6.5 millimeter Mannlicher-Carcano rifle with a telescopic sight from a Chicago mail-order house.

Shortly after the rifle arrived, Oswald posed for the now-famous pictures of himself dressed in black, holding the rifle and copies of *The Militant* and *The Worker*, with his holstered .38 on his hip.[27] Making copies of the photograph for his daughter June, as he told Marina, "to remember Papa by sometime,"[28] he inscribed another "Ready for anything": the latter was intended for *The Militant*.[29] He also signed a third for his friend George de Mohrenschildt, who Oswald knew shared his contempt for Walker: "For George, Lee Harvey Oswald, 5-IV-63."[30c] He had by this time begun to practice with the rifle.[31]

The events that follow from this point in his life are important because they provide some insight into Oswald's motives and behavior leading up to his attack on President Kennedy. On Saturday, April 6, Oswald was fired from his job with a commercial photography firm. He was disappointed because it was probably the only job he had ever

c April 5, 1963.

held that, in his fashion, he had liked. He had learned of his impending dismissal earlier that week, but embarrassed and hurt, he had not told his wife.[32]

By the time of his actual dismissal, Oswald had made a detailed study of bus schedules and routes in Walker's neighborhood. On Sunday, he left the apartment with the rifle. When he returned later that afternoon, he did not have the rifle; it had been buried near Walker's home.[33] After supper, he left again and did not return until later that evening. On Monday, April 8, General Walker returned from a cross-country speaking tour. On Wednesday, April 10, Oswald tearfully admitted to his wife that he had lost his job, largely he felt, because of FBI harassment.[34] In actuality, in addition to his personality-related problems on the job, he had deliberately antagonized his employer by reading Russian language newspapers during his breaks.

In any case, his course of action was set, the job-loss only confirmed his decision to get Walker. Soon after, he prepared written instructions in Russian[d] for his wife in the event he was arrested or killed in the attempt. She found the note when he did not return for supper that evening:

1. This is the key to the mailbox which is located in the main post office in the city on Ervay Street. This is the same street where the drugstore, in which you always waited is located. You will find the mailbox in the post office which is located 4 blocks from the drugstore on that street. I paid for the box last month so don't worry about it.

2. Send the information as to what happened to me to the Embassy and include newspaper clippings (should there be anything about me in the newspapers). I believe that the Embassy will come quickly to your assistance on learning everything.

3. I paid the house rent on the 2d so don't worry about it.

4. Recently I paid for water and gas.

5. The money from work will possibly be coming. The money will be sent to our post office box. Go to the bank and cash the check.

6. You can either throw out or give my clothing etc. away. Do not keep these. However, I prefer that you hold on to my personal papers (military, civil, etc.).

7. Certain of my documents are in the small blue valise.

[d] The improved spelling and writing observed in this note is due to the fact that this is a translation from Oswald's original Russian version.

8. The address book can be found on my table in the study should you need same.

9. We have friends here. The Red Cross also will help you.

10. I left you as much money as I could. $60 on the second of the month. You and the baby [illegible—possibly baby's name] can live for another 2 months using $10 per week.

11. If I am alive and taken prisoner, the city jail is located at the end of the bridge through which we always passed on going to the city (right in the beginning of the city after crossing the bridge).[35]

At about 9 P.M. on Wednesday evening, he shot and barely missed Walker as the latter worked at a desk in his study. Planning the attack to coincide with the conclusion of evening services at a Mormon church near Walker's home, Oswald placed the rifle back where he had buried it near the scene, boarded a bus amid the departing Mormon parishioners, and returned home flushed with excitement.[36] The next morning, greatly disappointed to learn on the news that he had missed, he explained to his distraught wife that he wanted to kill Walker because he was a dangerous "Fascist" like Hitler had been, with the same potential for human destruction.[37]

Later as he read accounts of the police investigation into the incident, he laughed at their inability to identify the bullet and their presumption that he had fled in a car. The simplicity and success of his escape plan confirmed his opinion that the Dallas police were, as he explained to his wife, "fools."[38] Consistent with this contemptuous view of the Dallas investigation, Oswald was on the streets a few days later with a "Hands Off Cuba! Viva Fidel" placard hanging from his neck handing out pro-Castro pamphlets.[39]

On April 21, he alarmed his wife when he abruptly rose from his reading of the *Dallas Morning News*, quickly dressed, belted on his .38, and announced that Nixon was coming to town and "I am going to have a look." The headline in the paper read "Nixon Calls for Decision to Force Reds Out of Cuba."[40]

In fact, Nixon was not coming to town. Oswald had been bluffing simply to provoke his distraught wife. In any event, it did not matter since, by this time, Marina was convinced her husband was on the verge of an emotional breakdown. Unaware of his long-range Cuban plans, his attack on Walker and the disturbing Nixon bluff convinced her that he was coming unhinged. She urged him to get out of town before he was arrested and to look for work elsewhere. She assured him that she and the baby would join him as soon as he found another job. In the meantime, she would remain in Dallas with friends. Much to her relief, he agreed, and on the night of April 24 he boarded a bus for the city of his birth, New Orleans.

Fair Play for Cuba

After the Walker incident, Oswald's interest in Cuba continued to grow. He had first become interested in Cuba during his Marine Corps days when he and a fellow Marine talked, as many young Marines did during the period, of joining the Castro guerrilla forces in the Sierra Maestre Mountains.[41] Now, however, Castro was in power, and Oswald's concern centered on the Kennedy administration's clearly hostile policies toward the new revolutionary government: first there had been the Bay of Pigs invasion in 1961 and then, a year later, the Cuban missile crisis. There was little doubt in Oswald's mind that the Kennedy administration's aggressive acts toward Cuba were designed to bring down the Castro regime.

Soon after he arrived in New Orleans, he obtained a menial job as a greaser and oiler in a coffee processing plant. It was a dirty, uninteresting job, and Oswald did not invest much time or effort in it— he had other concerns. Within a month after his arrival, he wrote to the national headquarters of the Fair Play for Cuba Committee to request literature and instructions for establishing a FPCC chapter in New Orleans.[42]

In the meantime, his pregnant wife and infant daughter had arrived, and they settled into yet another rundown apartment on Magazine Street. On July 19, he was fired at the coffee processing plant.[43] Now without a job and living only on unemployment compensation, his political activities accelerated. He had "Hands Off Cuba!" handbills printed and by August 9 was on the streets, dressed in a white shirt and tie, distributing them. His activities were calculated to attract as much attention as possible. Twice on August 9 and 16, he was arrested when disputes developed between himself and anti-Castro Cuban exiles who objected to his demonstrations. Shortly after, he appeared on two radio programs where he discussed and debated, in a very sophisticated manner, his objections to the Kennedy administration's Cuban policy.[44] A voracious reader of newspapers and radical publications such as *The Militant* and *The Worker*, Oswald had become an especially well-informed and effective debater on the Cuban issue.

The publicity he was receiving as a result of his political activities and his bogus FPCC chapter (he was its only member) prepared the way for his next move. On September 9, it is virtually certain that he read in the New Orleans *Times-Picayune* that Fidel Castro had warned the United States that if CIA plots to assassinate Cuban leaders continued, Cuba would respond in kind. Having heard of CIA plots against his life, the *Times-Picayune* quoted Castro as saying: "United States leaders should think that if they are aiding terrorist plans to eliminate Cuban leaders, they themselves will not be safe."[45] Eight days later on September 17, Oswald applied for a Mexican visa.

During this same period, August to September 1963, it is probable that Oswald had contact with any number of persons in New Orleans on both sides of the Cuban issue. One such person was probably David Ferrie, a former flight instructor in the New Orleans chapter of the Civil Air Patrol to which Oswald belonged briefly as a youth in 1954 and 1955. Although Ferrie was an ardent anti-Castro activist with Mafia connections, Oswald's attempts to infiltrate such groups raises the probability that the two did meet, as witnesses testified, in Clinton, Louisiana, early in September 1963. It is also probable that both were trying to use each other, since it is as likely that Oswald knew of Ferrie's anti-Castro activities as it is that the latter was well aware of his former student's well-publicized Fair Play for Cuba efforts.[46] Thus Oswald was probably in contact with Ferrie in an attempt to obtain information on anti-Castro activities that he hoped to relay to the Castro government.[e]

Having failed that summer to complete arrangements for Marina and the baby to return to Russia where he had promised to join her later, he ordered her to return to Texas with family friend Ruth Paine. A day or two later, Oswald left by bus, also for Dallas, but for different reasons. En route to Mexico City, he had one more item of business he wanted to attend to before approaching Cuban Embassy officials there about a visa.

Arriving in Dallas, Oswald immediately made contact with two pro-Castro Cubans. They, in turn, took him to the apartment of a young Cuban exile, Silvia Odio. Odio was a member of the anti-Castro Cuban Revolutionary Junta. Her parents, wealthy Cuban aristocrats, had

---

[e] It has been suggested that during this time in New Orleans, Oswald may have come into contact with other Mafia functionaries through his uncle "Dutz" Murret. Murret was a bookmaker and was acquainted with a number of persons, such as Ferrie, who were associated with Mafia-related gambling operations in New Orleans. This, combined with organized crime's well-documented antipathy for the Kennedy administration, has led to the speculation that such persons may have conspired with Oswald to kill the President. Although intriguing and seemingly unanswerable questions remain, it is my contention that the circumstances of the assassination do not bear out this claim. For a discussion of the issue see the appendix to *Hearings on the Investigation of the Assassination of President John F. Kennedy* (vol. 9 and vol. 5, 1-471).

been Castro opponents and were subsequently imprisoned in Cuba for their activities. The purpose of the meeting was, in all probability, to infiltrate or gain more information about anti-Castro activities. However, Ms. Odio was suspicious of the three visitors, and the short meeting was concluded unproductively from their standpoint.[47] Oswald then proceeded on to Mexico City confident that, in spite of this minor disappointment, his record of pro-Castro activity was sufficiently impressive that his request for a Cuban visa would be quickly approved. After all, since his near successful attempt to assassinate the vehemently anti-Castro General Walker, he had succeeded in compiling a well-documented record of activity in behalf of the Castro regime.

On Friday, September 27, Oswald walked optimistically into the Cuban Embassy and requested an in-transit visa to visit Cuba on a trip that would eventually take him, he claimed, to the Soviet Union. Then announcing that he was a friend of the Cuban revolution, he produced a fistful of documents attesting to the fact: a Fair Play for Cuba Committee membership card, a newspaper photograph and clippings describing his FPCC activities and arrest in New Orleans, letters to the Communist party, a labor card and marriage license from the Soviet Union. He told the secretary, Sylvia Duran, that he was a member of the Communist party. When she asked why the Party had not arranged for his visa, he replied simply that he had not had time to do that. He told the bemused secretary that he had brought the strange documents to prove that he was a friend and supporter of Cuba. Pleasantly unimpressed, she told the nervous applicant that it was more complicated than that and suggested that he go down the street to have the necessary photographs taken while she checked with the Russian Embassy. Dismayed, Oswald rushed out for the photographs.

When he returned an hour or so later with the photographs, he was told that he must first have a Russian visa before an in-transit visa to Cuba could be approved. Oswald again bolted out and rushed down the street to the Russian Embassy where he was informed that it would be three or four months before a Russian visa could be approved. The frustrated Oswald no doubt recalled his first disillusioning encounter with the Soviet bureaucracy in Moscow—an experience that precipitated his melodramatic suicide attempt. In any case, he returned to the Cuban Embassy and lied, saying he had been granted the Russian visa. Noting his evasiveness, a suspicious Duran called the Soviet Embassy and learned the truth. Oswald was enraged. Angrily waving his membership cards and clippings, he protested that he had been jailed for his activities in behalf of the Cuban revolution. His credentials were beyond question, he cried, demanding the visa.

Unable to reason with the irate American, Duran asked the Cuban Consul, Eusebio Azcue, to speak with him. When Azcue tried again to explain the Cuban policy on visas, a flushed and crying Oswald screamed that he deserved better treatment for all that he had done for Cuba. It was during this outrage that Oswald probably[f] made threatening remarks about President Kennedy. Offended, an angry Azcue shouted that the revolution *didn't need friends like Oswald* and threatened to throw him out of the office if he didn't leave immediately. The "desperate" and wild-eyed Oswald left.[48]

A Warning to the FBI

Oswald arrived back in Dallas on October 3 after a long and frustrating bus trip from Mexico City. His trip notably unsuccessful, low on money and having suffered a final indignity—being harassed by Mexican officials, as only they can, at the border—Oswald was very discouraged when he stepped off the bus in Dallas.[49] Too drained and depressed to face his wife when he arrived, he spent his first night in Dallas at the YMCA after filing a claim for unemployment compensation and registering for employment at the Texas Employment Commission.[50] The next day, after some unsuccessful job hunting, he hitchhiked to Irving where Marina was living, empty-handed after yet another misspent political venture. Cuban bureaucrats, he complained to Marina, were as stupid and uncooperative as the Russians. Thus politically disillusioned, Oswald drew closer to his pregnant wife. For the next few weeks, his family would be uppermost in his anxious mind.[51]

With the second baby due anytime, the Oswalds decided it would be best for Marina to stay with the Paines in Irving, at least until the baby was born. Oswald would get a cheap room in Dallas and look for a job. Two weeks later, on October 14, Ruth Paine advised him of an opening at the Texas School Book Depository. He got the $1.25-an-hour job and began work on October 16.[52] Two days later, Marina

[f] In his book *Clearing the Air*, Daniel Schorr describes an interview that Fidel Castro granted to a British journalist in July 1967. In that conversation, Castro is quoted as saying that Oswald had made a threat against President Kennedy's life on his second visit to the Cuban Embassy. In particular, Oswald allegedly had said that "someone ought to shoot" the President, adding "maybe I'll try to do it" (Schorr, 1977, p. 177). In April 1978, Castro denied that he made this statement (Hearings, 1978, vol. 3, pp. 273-274). Two months later, Sylvia Duran claimed that she could not remember Oswald's threat but acknowledged that he might have made it because he was extremely angry (Hearings, 1978, vol. 3, pp. 53-54).

and the Paines presented him with a surprise birthday cake. He wept when they sang "Happy Birthday."[53] A few days later, he would weep again when his second daughter was born. Chastened by his recent disappointments, Oswald was for this brief October interlude perhaps more tender—and vulnerable—than he had ever been in his adult life. He adored his daughter and was more loving and kind to her mother than he had been since the early months of their marriage.

But there was an edge under this facade of family contentment, and it cut through the surface again just before the birth of his second child. The insensitive and often cruel way Oswald had treated his wife since their arrival from Russia had been aggravated by the difficult circumstances of their life in America. The impermanence, transience, and poverty had created a chronic state of bitterness in Marina that, even in the best of times, lapped at the edges of their relationship. With no other resources at her disposal, Marina expressed her resentment toward her husband in the only ways available to her—ridicule and indifference.

Often such ridicule had broad unmistakable sexual connotations—invidious comparisons of Oswald to other idealized males and unflattering remarks about the quality of their sex life in the presence of others.[54] For example, the evening after his birthday had been spent pleasantly together; he had held her affectionately, and they had talked quietly. Then Marina shattered the mood with a revelation that she had had an erotic dream about a former lover:

> "And what did you dream?" he asked.
> "We kissed, as we always did. Anatoly kissed so well it made me dizzy. No one ever kissed me like that."
> "I wish I did," he replied lamely.
> "It would take you your whole life to learn."[55]

Conversations like that would affect any young husband; Oswald was no exception. It would only rekindle the desire to demonstrate that he was not the failure, by societal standards, that he seemed to be. Having been told only a few weeks before in Mexico City that he did not possess the credentials of a Cuban revolutionary, a bedtime revelation that he fell short of the standard set by a former Russian lover had to be especially damaging. It was to be the last time he would try to prove himself in bed.

His attention again turned to politics. If he could not change the circumstances of his personal life, he would concentrate on changing the world. Two nights after his daughter was born, he sought out a familiar figure: General Walker. He went to hear him speak at a rally.[56]

By the end of October, he was fast withdrawing into a familiar pattern of isolation. Still living alone in Dallas and commuting to Irving on the weekends to see his family, the only warmth evident in this frustrated man was his undeniable love for his children. Others, according to Michael Paine who observed him during this period, were once again "cardboard."[57]

Living in a rooming house at 1026 North Beckley, eating alone, and enduring long evenings of quiet isolation broken by occasional trips to a laundromat or a Dobb's House Restaurant for a meal, Oswald's renewed political activity could not fill the emptiness of his life. He missed his children and the wife who had shown little interest in rejoining him in Dallas. He called them every day.[58]

On Friday, November 1, the FBI sent special agent James Hosty to Irving to interview Marina. The FBI had kept a file on Oswald since his defection and return from Russia. Now, having learned of his recent trip and activities in Mexico, a routine check on his whereabouts was considered in order. The same day, Oswald had formally resumed his political activities by applying for membership in the American Civil Liberties Union, mailing a letter to the Communist party describing the political situation in Dallas, and renting a post office box so that he could receive political mail more discretely (for example, mail for the Fair Play for Cuba Committee).[59] Earlier in October, he had been evicted from a room he had rented and blamed the eviction on a by-now-familiar pattern of FBI harassment. He subsequently registered for the room on North Beckley using an alias unknown to Marina, "O. H. Lee." He greatly resented the FBI presence in his life. When Oswald arrived in Irving later that Friday afternoon for the weekend, Ruth Paine related the matter of Hosty's visit. Oswald became quiet and visibly angry.

On November 5, Hosty returned again and this time talked only with Ruth Paine. Each day Oswald had called to inquire whether the agent had returned. Afraid to upset him, Ruth and Marina decided to wait until the weekend before telling him about the second visit. When they did, he was irate.[60] Early the next morning—Saturday, November 9—he drafted and then typed a letter to the Russian Embassy in Washington describing his difficulties in Mexico City and his recent harassment by "the notorious FBI."[61] On Tuesday, November 12, after a long Armistice Day weekend he mailed the letter, probably on the way to work. Sometime during the weekend or perhaps on Tuesday morning he had written a much more significant note. During his lunch break, he walked to the Dallas FBI office and delivered it.

Oswald took the elevator up to the FBI suite at 1114 Commerce

Street and stalked to the desk of receptionist Nancy Lee Fenner. "S. A. Hosty, please," he announced angrily, eyes flashing, nervously fingering the contents of the unsealed envelope in his hands. After a quick check, Ms. Fenner informed the clearly agitated stranger that Hosty was not in. Whereupon Oswald threw the envelope on her desk ordering, "Well get this to him." Then he turned and left.[62]

Somewhat startled Ms. Fenner noticed when she reached for the envelope that a portion of the letter was exposed. According to Ms. Fenner, it said, in effect: "Let this be a warning. I will blow up the FBI and the Dallas Police Department if you don't stop bothering my wife."[63] Despite its threatening message, the note was ignored until *after* the assassination when it was quickly destroyed.[g]

Thus Oswald seized this opportunity to protect his wife and family from what he considered to be an unwarranted intrusion by the FBI. Ironically, in a Friday afternoon telephone conversation three days later, Marina told her lonely, distressed husband that it would probably be better if he remained in Dallas the coming weekend rather than return to Irving for the customary weekend with his family. The reason, she explained, was that the Paines were planning a birthday party for one of their children and, since he did not care for Michael Paine, it would be less awkward if he did not attend. She went on to suggest to her silent husband that it might also be easier for everyone concerned if he did not visit every weekend as he had been doing. "As you wish," he replied without emotion. "If you don't want me to come, I won't."[64] Marina's remarks, in the wake of his recent protective efforts on her behalf, could only have added to his chronic depression. Except for a brief trip to a laundromat, he remained alone in his room the entire weekend.[65] On Sunday he did not call as he usually did.

Perhaps feeling a little guilty about the thought of her husband spending a lonely weekend in a rooming house, Marina, who had trouble dialing the phone, asked Ruth Paine to call him. When she asked for Lee Oswald, the voice at the other end informed her that no one by that name lived there. The next day when Lee called, Marina asked him about the incident. When he told her that he was living

---

[g] Agent Hosty later claimed he recalled the note stated, in effect: "If you don't cease bothering my wife I will take appropriate action and report this to proper authorities." Hosty destroyed the note approximately two hours after Oswald's death on November 24. He claimed his superior instructed him to do so. The note was not reported to the Warren Commission and knowledge of it did not become public until July 1975 (Hearings, 1975-1976: testimonies of James B. Adams, pt. 3, pp. 2-5; James P. Hosty, pt. 3, pp. 130-148; Kenneth Howe, pt. 3, pp. 179-180).

under an alias to avoid FBI harassment, she became furious. He lashed back. His lonely weekend of resentment boiling to the surface, he angrily explained once more that he had lost jobs and been evicted from a rented room the previous month because of the FBI's activities. He was enraged that his wife was so insensitive that she could not, or would not, recognize the threat posed by an organization that he had, unbeknownst to her, threatened to destroy only a week earlier.[66]

The President's Visit

From the second week of September, the Dallas papers had carried articles anticipating President Kennedy's scheduled November visit. The weekend Oswald had spent alone brooding and reading in his room (November 15-17), the papers revealed that the President's motorcade would travel through the downtown area on its way to a luncheon address at the Trade Mart. Oswald would have known there was a high probability that it would pass the Texas School Book Depository. On Tuesday, November 19, the probability was confirmed with the announcement of the President's specific route.[67]

Oswald's personal frustrations at a zenith, another plan to resolve the frustrations of life began to emerge. If this one worked, he would be able to even the score with the FBI, to prove his mettle and revolutionary credentials to the Cubans who had humiliated him, and to assert his manhood to the wife who had belittled him. It would be so easy—the rifle and scope, a virtual repeat of his attempt on Walker. He would follow the same format; leave the rifle, walk away from the scene, take a bus. There would be one difference this time, however, and he knew it: he would not escape for long. But it didn't matter. Indeed the whole purpose of the act hinged upon his identification, if not capture, as the assassin.

Unlike his feelings toward General Walker, Oswald had no personal animosity toward the President. But Kennedy was the chief architect of the nation's hostile Cuban policy and the leader of a government and society from which Oswald was totally alienated. The President's security was also an important responsibility of the FBI, which had caused so much recent distress in Oswald's personal life.

On Thursday morning, the day before Kennedy's visit, Oswald asked a fellow worker who lived near the Paines if he could ride to Irving with him that afternoon after work. He said he wanted to get some "curtain rods" for his "apartment."[68] His real purpose was to get the rifle that he would use the next day to kill the President.

However, probably because he had no strong personal dislike for

President Kennedy and perhaps dreading the calamitous situation that would follow his act, he sought a reunion with the wife he loved and the two tiny children he adored: a reconciliation of their bitterness and hurt would make his destructive plan unnecessary. Instead, his wife, still angry and resentful about his use of an alias and what that implied about his activities, greeted his unexpected arrival after a two-week absence coldly. Turning away from his kisses, she asked why he had come. When he told her he was lonely and missed her and the children, she looked at him indifferently and suggested that he "wash up."[69]

Throughout the evening, she treated him with the same cold indifference. Explaining that he was lonely and needed her and the children, he begged her repeatedly to live with him again as a family in Dallas. Scornful of his anguish, she refused, explaining she would be happier and the children would be better off remaining in Irving for the time being. Discouraged, he played quietly and lovingly with his oldest daughter and then, after tucking her into bed, he too retired early and alone:

> "I probably won't be out this weekend," he said.
> "Why not?"
> "It's too often. I was here today," he said hoping to evoke a sympathetic response.
> "Okay," she replied airily over her shoulder as she stood at the sink.[70]

After a sleepless night, Oswald arose on November 22 and prepared for work. Without kissing his wife as he usually did, he told her that he would prepare his own breakfast. He always did anyhow, but this morning he chose to tell her he would. After kissing the two children goodbye, he discretely removed his wedding ring and placed it in the delicate demitasse cup Marina's grandmother had given her. Then turning to his drowsy wife he announced that he had placed some money in the bureau. "Take it and buy everything you and Junie and Rachel need," he said as he left.[71] He had left $170—virtually all the money he had.

The events of the remainder of that tragic weekend are all too familiar. At 12:30 that bright November afternoon, Oswald shot and killed the President from his perch in the sixth floor window of the Texas School Book Depository. Forty-five minutes later, after making good his escape by bus and taxi, he hurried to his rooming house to pick up a pistol that he would use moments later to kill a police officer who had stopped him as he walked along the street. Arrested shortly afterward in a movie theater, he too would die less than forty-eight hours later from a gunshot wound sustained in the basement of the Dallas Police Headquarters.

Conclusions

In killing the President, Oswald had followed a well-established pattern in his behavior: his disillusionment with an unwelcoming Russian bureaucracy after his defection to the Soviet Union had precipitated a suicide attempt; a loss of a job for which he blamed the FBI immediately preceded his attempt on General Walker's life. In the same way, the frustration of his bitter experience at the Cuban Embassy, the hurt of his wife's reminders of past lovers and her indifference and refusal to live with him, the provocation of FBI surveillance, and the coincidence of a President's visit all combined to produce a national tragedy. In more specific terms, Oswald's motive in the assassination was personal and compensatory rather than political. He hoped to prove his value to the Cubans by killing a president who had effectively intimidated and threatened their small nation; he would also even the score with the FBI he despised by exposing their incompetence to a degree even he could not have anticipated; and in the process, he would leave the wife, who had turned him away, with a nagging sense of guilt for what he did that she will bear for the rest of her life.

Were others involved in the assassination? It seems unlikely, even though Oswald's Cuban activities undoubtedly led to contacts with a number of persons whose names have been mentioned as possible conspirators. Yes, he probably did contact his old Civil Air Patrol instructor, David Ferrie, and other anti-Castro persons, including some with Mafia connections, when he was in New Orleans the summer preceding the assassination. Yes, he probably had the same kind of contacts in Dallas. And, yes, he probably did go with two such persons to question Silvia Odio that late September night on his way to Mexico City. Since his plan was to establish his credentials as a pro-Castro activist, it is probable that his attempts to infiltrate anti-Castro groups brought him into contact with a wide variety of suspicious persons.

The tangled politics of the period reveal an open war on organized crime waged by the President's brother, the attorney general, at the same time that the CIA was conspiring with some of the same Mafia figures to assassinate Castro. Anti-Castro elements in this country blamed President Kennedy for failing them during the Bay of Pigs fiasco and, as a consequence, strengthening Castro's position; at the same time, Castro warned of a retaliation in kind if CIA plots against his life did not cease. Given such a confusing political situation with respect to the Kennedy administration, Cuba, and organized crime, it would be more surprising if Oswald, obsessed with Cuban affairs, had *fewer* or *no* contacts with persons representing these various interests. But the probability of such persons being involved in the assassination seems slight for a number of reasons: First, there was no evidence of a conspiracy in the attempt on General Walker's life, and the circumstances as well as Oswald's behavior both before and after that incident reveal a pattern that was to repeat itself fairly closely the following November. Second, it seems unlikely that Oswald would risk exposure and arrest by threatening to destroy the Dallas FBI and police department only ten days before the assassination if he was part of an emerging conspiracy to kill the President. This threat appears to have been purely personal and highly emotional. Third, the fact that he repeatedly sought to avoid the act in his pleas for reunion with his wife and children the evening before also suggest the absence of others in his plan. These pleas had the future orientation of a man who wanted to be with his family more than he wanted to kill the President: a nice apartment with a washing machine were the topics he discussed, not what to do when I'm gone as he had done before the Walker incident. Fourth, having failed at his attempt to have his family rejoin him, his acts the following morning were those of a man whose only hope is that the woman he loves will regret what she has done to him: the wedding ring placed in the cherished cup, the uncharacteristic generosity, and the you-get-everything-*you*-and-the-children-need-don't-worry-about-*me*-I'm-not-important message he was conveying, were the acts of an emotional man bent on a highly neurotic and personal compensatory act of tragic proportions.

Oswald knew exactly what he was doing and why. Arrested without travel documents, only a few dollars, and none of the other provisions one would expect to find on a man intent on escape, Oswald anticipated his capture: it was part of his plan. In his coldly selfish act, he would destroy a man he grudgingly admired in an attempt to establish himself as a sympathetic figure to the only significant entities, beyond his children, in his embittered life—his wife and his revolutionary hero, Fidel Castro.

The only significant evidence that Oswald might have been involved in a conspiracy is the acoustical analysis of the gunfire at the Dealey Plaza assassination site. The tests conducted at the request of the House Select Committee on Assassinations suggest that a second gunman may have fired one shot that missed from the grassy knoll in front of the President's limousine.[72] But other convincing supporting evidence has yet to surface. In the absence of such new evidence, too many extraordinary assumptions are required not only about the motives of the conspirators and about Oswald's chance employment in a tall building on the President's route before the President's Dallas itinerary was drawn up but about Oswald himself. Too much had to depend on a mercurial, anxiety-ridden young man who, the facts suggest, could have been turned away from his deadly assignment with a kind word and loving embrace.

SAMUEL BYCK (1930-1974)

A little after 7 A.M. on February 22, 1974, sleepy-eyed passengers shuffled into a line waiting at Gate C at Baltimore-Washington International Airport to board Delta Flight 523 for Atlanta. It was a cold, gray drizzling Baltimore morning. A jowly heavy-set man walked up behind the security guard and, suddenly drawing a .22 caliber pistol from beneath his dark raincoat, fired two shots. One of the shots tore through the officer's back, severing the main aorta, killing him instantly. As shocked passengers recoiled in terror, the man, with the lumbering agility and swiftness of a bear, leaped over the security chain, ran down the boarding ramp, and boarded the plane.

Confronting the crew in the cockpit, the perspiring and panting assailant fired a warning shot and ordered: "Fly this plane out of here." Then, following a second command to close the door, the flight attendants seized the opportunity to leave the plane. A shot was fired as they fled.

Turning again to the pilot and co-pilot, the man repeated his command to "take off." The pilot responded that he could not do anything until the wheel blocks were removed. Enraged, the man fired a shot that struck the co-pilot in the stomach screaming, "The next one will be in the head." He then grabbed a passenger and shoved her toward the control panel ordering her: "Help this man fly this plane." Just then shots were heard from outside the plane. Pushing the passenger back toward her seat, the man whirled and fired two shots hitting the already wounded co-pilot above the left eye and the pilot in the shoulder. Desperate, the wounded pilot called Ground Control:

PILOT: Ah, ground, this is . . . ah . . . Delta at the ramp C8 . . .
    do you read?
GC: Delta C, go ahead.
PILOT: Do you read?

GC: I cut Delta out. Go ahead, Delta.

PILOT: Emergency, emergency, we're all shot . . . ah . . . can you get another pilot here to the airplane . . . ah . . . this fellow he shot us both. Ground . . . I need ground . . . ah . . . this is a state of emergency. Get ahold of our ramp and ask the people to come on out to unhook the tug.

The pilot lost consciousness.[73]

Turning again toward the first-class cabin, the gunman reloaded his pistol and then seized another passenger by the hair and dragged her forward to the entrance of the cockpit where he again shot the wounded pilot and dying co-pilot as they slumped over the controls.

Just then a shot crashed through the window in the plane's door, splattering glass throughout the cabin and cutting the panic-stricken hostage on the thigh. Moved by her pleas for mercy, the man released his grip instructing her to return to her seat. As she moved away from him, two more shots were fired through the broken window, striking the would-be hijacker in the lower chest and stomach. Clutching his chest with both hands, he staggered and dropped to the floor. Then reaching for his pistol, he rested the barrel against his right temple and squeezed the trigger. Authorities later found a briefcase gasoline bomb under his body.

The Man

Who was this man who had killed two innocent victims and critically wounded a third before taking his own life? Where did he so desperately want to take the plane? What would be worth the carnage inflicted on that gray February morning? Who was Samuel Joseph Byck?

Sam Byck was born on January 30, 1930 and raised in Philadelphia, the eldest of three brothers. Byck's father was a kindly, well-meaning man who, Sam recalled fondly, played pinochle in the evenings with his sons. Unfortunately, to the disappointment of everyone in the family—especially his wife—the father was not much of an economic success. As a result of the financial difficulties the family had to endure, Sam seemed to feel a certain amount of ambivalence about him.

Sam attended Olney High School in Philadelphia but did not graduate. After bumming around in various jobs, he entered the army in 1954 at the age of twenty-four. He served uneventfully except for one AWOL scrape, received training in firearms and explosives, and was honorably discharged in 1956. When his father died in 1957, Sam, in an act either of contempt or extraordinary bad taste, married within a month of the funeral while the Jewish family was still in formal mourning.

After his marriage, he seemed to enjoy his new role as husband and father to the three daughters and a son who arrived in regular intervals. And he succeeded in most respects, except one: he could not keep a job. Outshone by his two younger brothers—one a successful businessman, the other a dentist—Sam's lack of success as a breadwinner began to place strains on his marriage and growing family. More importantly, the disturbing realization that he was just like his father was reflected in his increasing depressions.

As he failed in one job and business venture after another, his growing jealousy and resentment of his brothers deepened, as did the emerging cleavages in his marriage. Finally, he severed all relations with his brothers, even to the extent of formally mourning them according to Jewish custom, as if they had died.

In November 1968, he was arrested for receiving stolen goods. The case was dismissed the following May. About this time, Byck applied for a twenty-thousand-dollar loan through the Small Business Administration. His plan was to restructure his life on the basis of a rather novel scheme for retailing automobile tires in a brightly painted and remodeled school bus that he intended to park at various shopping centers. Unhappy with his marginal income as a tire salesman, Sam planned to operate his own business—not to mention compete with his greatly resented younger brother who was also in the tire business.

Politics

Under tremendous stress, he had himself admitted to the Friends Psychiatric Hospital on November 12, 1969 for in-patient treatment for anxiety and depression. Two weeks later, he received a letter from the SBA announcing their rejection of his loan application.[74] He was very upset and remained in the hospital until the Christmas holidays. He continued to seek out-patient care for the next two years and was diagnosed as having a "manic-depressive illness."[75]

But Byck did not believe his problems were the result of mental "illness." He had *real* problems: no job and a failing marriage. He began to see his mounting marital and career problems as symptomatic not of personal inadequacies but of political corruption and oppression. Such rationalization was subsequently reflected in his behavior. In March 1972, he established contact with the Black Liberation Army and later contributed some five hundred dollars and a couple of truck tires to the organization.[76] Like the blacks, the poor, and other casualties of political oppression he now identified with, Sam Byck believed he too was a victim. Only people who sold out to the system—like his brothers—could make it. But Sam Byck was no sellout. He had principles.

The more he read and thought, the more he became convinced that his economic difficulties, which were directly responsible for his rapidly deteriorating marriage, were the result of a corrupt, constitution-subverting political regime in Washington. He became a strong McGovern supporter and an outspoken critic of the Nixon administration. Then, on October 16, 1972, he had his first encounter with federal authorities. He was questioned by the Secret Service for allegedly suggesting that someone ought to kill President Nixon. Described by the Secret Service as "quite intelligent and well read," Byck jovially denied he had made such a statement. A psychiatrist who had treated Byck for his emotional problems told the investigators that he did not consider Byck a threat to himself or others. He described Byck as "a big talker who makes verbal threats and never acts on them."[77]

Byck's wife had asked him to move out the previous summer. The separation was hard on him. He claimed that he was permitted to see his children for only an hour on Sundays. His pleas for reconciliation were rejected. The loneliness of the Christmas holidays had been almost unbearable. Nothing had worked out. His life was a bust. At least his own father had been a good father, if not a successful breadwinner. Now with the separation, Sam was denied the opportunity to be even that. He wanted to die. But his death had to mean something; it was obvious that his life had not.

On January 12, 1973, Mark "Jimmy" Essex, armed with a high-powered rifle, killed six persons from his sniper's nest on the roof of the Howard Johnson's hotel in New Orleans before he was gunned down by police. Sam Byck was fascinated by the story. He clipped newspaper accounts of the incident and underlined the descriptions of slogans authorities found on the walls of the slain killer's apartment—slogans such as: "The quest for freedom is death. Then by death I shall escape to freedom"; "Political power comes from the barrel of a gun"; and most significantly: "Kill pig Nixon and all his running dogs."

Byck realized then what he wanted to do. Above the byline on an Essex article, he had written in large letters:

I'LL MEET YOU IN VALHALLA,[h] MARK ESSEX—OK!

SAM BYCK[78]

---

[h] According to Norse mythology, Valhalla is the Hall of Odin, where warriors who have died bravely in battle are received.

On January 16, he went to his estranged wife's residence and took the car. He left a note saying he would be away for awhile and then drove directly to Washington planning to attend the Nixon inauguration on the twentieth.

Once in Washington, he visited the inauguration site and talked with police about preparations. But then he left Washington and drove on to North Carolina before looping back north to Long Island where he visited relatives. He returned to the Philadelphia area and was located on January 22 sitting in the waiting room of his friend Bonny's tire store in Bristol. When questioned by authorities, who had been notified he was missing, Byck again denied that he had entertained any designs on the President's life. Rather, he explained, he simply could not tolerate the loneliness of his existence and left the area impulsively only to meet and talk with someone. He claimed that one of his missions in life was to establish lines of communication "between the races and peoples of the world." He was admitted to Philadelphia General Hospital for observation and released.[79]

In retrospect, it is clear that by January 1973, Sam Byck was set on a destructive course in which his problems were, in his mind, rapidly becoming every man's problems: if he could not communicate with his family, he would tackle the communications problems of the world; if he could not salvage his deteriorating marriage, he would save a deteriorating society from the government that, in his view, caused it. The cards were stacked against him, and his only recourse—the only way to salvage a degree of self-respect and release his terrible frustration and anger—was to get the dealer, the nefarious Richard M. Nixon.

Now consumed with his personal problems and suicidal, Byck did not surface again politically until August 1973. His wife had filed for divorce—the inevitable was happening as he observed helplessly. His displaced aggression became more direct and overt, if not focused.

Nearly four years had passed since his loan application had been denied by the Small Business Administration, but now he wrote angrily to Senator Schweiker to complain about the denial and the corrupt practices of the SBA.[80] That same month, he wrote another irate letter to the Federal Communications Commission protesting a radio editorial that endorsed capital punishment.[81] A week or so later, he wrote to the Israeli Consulate enclosing a map of Egypt on which he had circled the Sinai Peninsula. Above the circled area he had written: "Israelis go home and let my brothers alone." When questioned by the Secret Service, he replied only that he felt it was important, as a Jew, to let the Israelis know that he wanted peace in the Middle East and that "he cared."[82]

The divorce decree was granted in September. On the sixth of the month, Byck was arrested for picketing without a permit in front of the White House. His signs called for Nixon's impeachment. In October and November, Byck submitted numerous applications to the National Park Service requesting permission to demonstrate in front of the White House, but he appeared only on November 26 and 30.

In December 1973, he wrote again to Senator Schweiker requesting the names and offenses of persons granted executive clemency by President Nixon.[83] During this period, he also wrote to Senator McGovern to protest the Senator's vote for Gerald Ford's confirmation as vice-president: "How come you voted to confirm Gerald Ford when you and I both know Ford is Nixon's Echo-ooo-ooo-oo. P.S. From the mind of Ford came Edsels." Other letters were also written protesting against Mayor Rizzo and the Philadelphia City Council.[84]

On Christmas Eve, apart from his children, Sam Byck played Santa Claus instead to the nation. A lonely, pathetic figure in a Santa Claus costume, he paraded up and down in front of the White House stopping to ask passing children about their Christmas wishes. He carried a huge placard stating, "Santa sez 'ALL I WANT FOR CHRISTMAS IS MY CONSTITUTIONAL RIGHT TO PEACABLY PETITION MY GOVERNMENT FOR A REDRESS OF GRIEVANCES'." Another called for the President's impeachment.[85]

Pandora's Box

Christmas alone again, his forty-fourth birthday looming up on January 30, frustrated in his attempts to see his children (he had even hired an airplane to pull a Happy Birthday streamer for one of his daughters), Byck began to plan and justify his own death and, in so doing, his life. Isolated except for his tire-store friend, Bonny, and Bonny's family, Byck began to confide in his Sony tape recorder as he paced his apartment late into the winter nights. The tapes ramble as he talked about his love for his children, the unwanted divorce, the fuel shortage, his weight problem (5'9", 225 pounds) and bad back, his loss of jobs, the racism of the Philadelphia Phillies, his admiration for the late baseball player Roberto Clemente (who had died in a plane crash while working to aid hurricane victims in Puerto Rico), and so forth. But most of all he was obsessed with the corruption in Washington. Hardly any portion of the federal bureaucracy was spared as he lashed out at the SBA for denying his loan application; similarly he condemned the Department of the Interior, the Justice Department, and the FCC for alleged grievances. And, of course, the Nixon administration was singled out as the prime cause of the rampant corruption in Washington. His faded 1967 Buick was plastered with "Impeach Nixon" stickers.[86]

With Mark Essex as a role model, Byck also read about other assassins (he had photocopied a chronology of assassinations from the pages of the *Report to the National Commission on the Causes and Prevention of Violence*) and was intent upon making his own death and the President's, in his words, a "smashing success."[87] The plan that evolved was, indeed, spectacular. Rather than using the conventional firearms of past assassins, Byck planned to destroy not only the President but to incinerate a good portion of his entire administration by crashing a commercial jetliner directly into the White House. Byck explained his bizarre plan—"Operation Pandora's Box"—matter-of-factly on tape the day before:

> I will try to get the plane aloft and fly it towards the target area, which will be Washington, D.C., the capitol of the most powerful wealthiest nation of the world. . . . By guise, threats or trickery, I hope to force the pilot to buzz the White House—I mean, sort of dive towards the White House. When the plane is in this position, I will shoot the pilot and then in the last few minutes try to steer the plane into the target, which is the White House. . . . Whoever dies in Project Pandora Box will be directly attributable to the Watergate scandals.[88]

Concerned that his actions be understood, Byck sent copies of the tape quoted in part above to Leonard Bernstein, Jonas Salk, Jack Anderson, Senator Ribicoff, and other well-known persons. Denying that he was a "maniac or a madman," Byck went on to explain that he viewed himself as a political terrorist, like those in Northern Ireland and the Middle East.

Although most of the last tapes he made contain only oblique references to his personal problems, it is clear that such problems propelled him toward his tragic end.[89] On his birthday, he claimed that he had been a good father and stated resentfully that his ex-wife and children were partially responsible for his actions.[90] Five days later, he acknowledged that he had no reason to live now that his family had deserted him.[91] On February 8, he angrily denounced his mother, with whom he had been staying, because she had gone to Florida, adding that she would be returning soon "in a damn hurry."[92]

In his unfiled Last Will, dated February 20, two days before his death, Byck left everything he owned to his only friend "Bonny," the man at the tire store. At the bottom of the document he wrote bitterly:

"I will each of my children [names deleted] the sum of one dollar each. They have each other and they deserve each other."

His Last Tapes

But what does a man think about knowing that he has just a few more hours to live? As Byck drove from Philadelphia to Baltimore in the early morning hours of February 22, he talked into his tape recorder. He ruminated about the scarcity of gasoline and worries that he might run out before he reaches his destination. But, more importantly, these melancholy reflections, made lonelier somehow by the thumping windshield wipers in the background, illustrate how the threads of Sam Byck's personal tragedy have been woven into a tapestry of political justification for what he was about to do:

> . . . I don't feel as nervous as I thought I should feel. This is the last day of my life, if all goes as according to plan. . . . my watch says 12:30 [A.M.]. . . . I went to Bonny's house this evening . . . and, eh, I brought some books over for a couple of the six sick kids [names deleted]. I was very very touched because [one of the children] came over and gave me a hug. I felt very touched. . . . [that] family is one of the most beautiful families I have ever seen, if not the most beautiful family. Having a family like that really makes life worth living and they have shown me the only real kindness that anybody has for years now and what can I say, I will miss them very, very dearly.
>
> I hope they will forgive me for what I have done in the way of stealing Bonny's gun, but if it's any consolation to anybody, I felt that I would have killed somebody to get a gun, so by my stealing [his] gun it probably saved the life of at least one more innocent victim.
>
> I will try not to let nothing stand in my way from here on in. I will go step by step, try not to panic, which may be difficult. . . . I['m] beginning to think too much on what I'm doing. Anyhow, I want it to be known that whatever I have in this world, which isn't much, . . . only . . . a car and my papers and my tapes, which I've been mailing in a box

[voice trails off].

Wouldn't that be something if the so-called would-be assassin ran out of gas. Some people would have their lives to congratulate for the energy crisis, including my life. . . .

It's now 1:15 A.M., February 22, 1974. Today is Friday, Washington's Birthday. . . .

I suspect the way people are acting towards each other with this energy crisis . . . crisis, that's a big joke that, eh, they're acting very mean and rotten towards each other. And, eh, as far as I'm concerned, I would rather try to do something about the world I've lived in then just to try to hang around and . . . and . . . and tolerate some of the injustices and the indignities that I have seen. I don't know if I can live, or if I want to live in the type of world that I see developing with the type of people's emotions and bitterness that I see developing. . . .

. . . I was thinking, of course this is ridiculous, if I really had a choice about life or death, I guess I do have a choice, I'm choosing death. Nobody is forcing me to do it and it's not like that ya know, eh, I don't have any choice ya know, it's going to be either die or I can face, I could face doing it . . . eh . . . I don't have to die right now it's not necessary, but, eh, I don't know if I could go through life, eh, and then when I'm about to die whether it's in an accident or natural ya know, from heart attack or, eh, cancer or something like that and I, and I would be a nothing because *I don't think I would amount to anything in this life.* I'm not willing to pay the kind of price that you have to pay to be successful without being ambitious and screwing your fellow workers and being a fink and kissing ass and everything like that, I'm not willing to pay that price for success.

But, if I had sort of an after wish I would like to be alive, after I'm dead, I would like to be alive ya know, for about a week afterward to see what, eh, what people say and think, not that it makes any difference, I, eh, what they say or think about me, I mean they'll have their own opinions, *but I want to see who sheds an honest sincere tear, who's really gonna miss me.* I'll tell you something, I'm gonna miss myself. Yea, I'm not looking forward to dying. I'm gonna miss myself, that's for damn sure. But as Caesar said when he crossed, crossed the Rubicon, "The die is cast."

It's not really cast, I mean I can go back very easily. I could probably even, eh, finagle the gun back into Bonny's cabinet without him missing it and if not I could always tell him that I was fixin on killing myself and I, eh, got cold feet. He's quite a lovable guy, I'm sure he would understand and wouldn't make too much of a stink about it. *It's just a shame there aren't more people like him. If there were, I don't think I, I know I wouldn't be doing what I am planning to do.* . . . I would like to say it's like a horrible nightmare and that, eh, things are happening and, eh, it's just like a average thing here I'm just riding and riding.

Maybe in my own mind I don't believe that I'm gonna go ahead with what I think that I'm gonna go ahead with. That could be ya know. I think well, I'll get all the way down here and I'll turn around but I don't know . . . I'll probably go ahead with it. Ain't that awful to talk about killing people and myself dying and just by saying I'll go ahead with it. No, I have many reasons for going ahead with it. . . .

How 'bout that. We're gonna make it in with the needle touching empty, I guess. It would be a hell of a thing if they didn't have any gas and I'd have to wind up hitchhiking, eh, hitchhiking to the airport and attempting to, eh, hijack an airliner. Hitchhiker, a hitchhiker hijacks an airliner. That would be beautiful. . . .

I don't think I'm gonna turn back and I don't feel like ya know my life is passing before me, ya know, like the drowning man and all that jazz. I'm, eh, just riding and looking at the trucks and everything and reading the signs. I was thinking really that for all intents and purposes I'm not gonna be around too much longer.

I've got another half a dozen hours or so, something like that. But it all boils down to about a half a dozen hours right now. It'll boil down to a lot less in the, ya know as time goes by, but right now I hold forty-four illustrious years that have boiled down to about the next half a dozen hours.

The sign just said Baltimore twenty-eight miles. I wonder, I wonder how far the airport is? . . .

. . . I just feel, eh, resigned to what's going to happen. I think I feel that way. I really don't understand my emotions completely. I don't say I'm confused or mixed up. I just am going through this thing just like there is no tomorrow, or at least there'll be, eh, no there'll be no tomorrow because it's after twelve, after midnight. So, everything that's happening will be and, eh, this is the last time, it's almost two o'clock I guess or it's a little after two o'clock. And I'm gonna do this thing step by step and find out just how far I'm gonna get along with it, but eh, there's no malice in my heart. I feel that I'm doing something that just has to be done for, eh . . . for, eh . . . if it doesn't *we're* in an awful shape. I don't know. It's just I can't see the world that . . . eh . . . is going on around me. So . . . eh, that's that.

Now I'm going into the Maryland House [a restaurant] and

... eh ... have what should be my last meal. The condemned man's meal. The food in this place stinks anyhow. Oh, well, talk to you in a minute.

Then after eating he continues:

I suspect there will be some people that will say oh my, if I had done this and this wouldn't have happened and all the regrets and the remorse. I guess there will be some that will feel that way. Well, I don't know for sure whether it will have happened or not. All I know is that I'm a rather determined fellow and that I hold and prize things more dearly than the things that most people hold and prize dearly. Like, eh, the tangible things that they care about, eh, so-called good things that make up the good life. I think ... eh ... this is nice it's nice to have a good life since I really believe that you only go around once and that there is no hereafter for me or anybody for that matter. So, I feel that you should have a good life, but what price are you willing to pay? Are you willing to pay for these so-called good things with, eh, your dignity and your honor and your liberty? I ... eh ... I am not willing to pay this price and so I do what I am afraid to do but I do what I know must be done by somebody, and if not me, who could that somebody be?

His thoughts then turned to his one true friend:

I only feel sorry for Bonny because I know that when he gets over being angry at me for not confiding in him or not saying anything, he'll say to himself that he probably thought that he could have stopped me. But that's not really true because ya see there's no way of knowing, at least there wasn't for me, I didn't get that cruel smirk on my lips and that dark look in my eyes and do all kinds of weirdo type of things. No, I was just feeling fairly well-resigned, I guess is the word, and I just ... eh ... went ahead and did it and there were no outward signs or any inward signs, ya know, such as those and tapping of the toes or tapping of the fingers or what have you. ... must be almost three o'clock [A.M.]. So, there is no way of ... eh ... doing anything about it. There's no way of looking at a man's face and looking and seeing what he has in his mind.

So my dear friend, Bonny, you're all right. I don't know if you're all right, but you're as right as anybody I've ever met in this world and if I live to be a thousand I don't think I'll ever meet anybody quite as all right as you are. So, don't feel sorry that you think that there was anybody that could have foreseen what I was gonna do. Most of all myself . . . don't fret. . . .

He speculates about his innocent victims:

I . . . eh . . . suspect I'll just go ahead and do it even if it means my self-destruction and unfortunately, the destruction of innocent people who I don't even know. Maybe it's just as well that I don't, and this to me is the real tragedy of this adventure or mission or project or whatever you want to call it. But I guess in just about everything whether it's war or any sort of struggle that the innocent not only die, but in most cases, a lot of the innocent. . . . Well, in this case I'm trying to do the best I can to prevent as many deaths as I can.

It's three-thirty [A.M.], I'm in Baltimore and you wouldn't believe it, but people are lined up in front of the gas pumps now. . . . It's unbelievable.

. . . It's, eh, now a quarter after four. Airport areas. This used to be Friendship Airport. That's one thing this world doesn't have enough of or much of, that is friendship. *Very unfortunate that a good wholesome guy like me has to kill himself or get himself killed to try to make a point,* but if I make the point and if I can show you the futility or show the people the futility of this stupid greed when we live in a world that could be plentiful for everybody. If I could show you that millionaires do not have to be billionaires to be happy, they should not have to be, while other people do without. If that lesson can be learned, and I doubt if it can, it hasn't been learned for thousands of years, but somebody has to resist just somebody has to resist or else there is no end to tyranny.

I'm ending this tape right here. It's, eh, almost five o'clock and I'm parked at the airport and, eh, I think I lost my wallet. So, this really looks like a one-way street now. Maybe there was an element that I would chicken out. So, here I am, almost five o'clock . . .

[Voice trails off in a lengthy pause.]

This will be the last tape that I will make for [deleted, probably "Bonny"]. It's now after five o'clock at, eh, Washington Baltimore Airport and I'm trying to get some sleep, would you believe it. I am very tired. I hope if this cannon goes off that I wake up cause I'm sleepy. I didn't sleep all night. Just made it in here without too much gas to spare. Lost my wallet on the way, all I had in there I think was maybe about ten dollars and my drivers license . . . and my drivers license . . . and my registration card. I had a hole in my pocket and it went through it. Oh, well, I'm so punchy that I was about to say I'll be glad when this day is over, this night is over . . . I guess I will.

Someday men will learn to walk upright, someday other men might, might be aware that these people, their brothers have feelings. They don't like to be squeezed, they like to be respected. Someday this may happen; of course I'll never live to see it happen and neither will many, many people that will follow me. . . .

This will be actually the next to the last tape. The other one has just oh, I don't know . . . a . . . eh . . . a couple hundred feet which will be instructions . . . eh . . . of no, what I want done if possible, if I'm dead, and I suspect I will be, eh, I'd like to be . . . eh . . . well Bonny has everything anyhow. I'm sending him the title to the car and the keys. . . .

I wonder if they'll [the Secret Service and FBI] figure that I'm a product of these two plots that are going on. One in California with Patricia Hearst and the other in Atlanta with the editor. I wonder if they'll think that all this crap triggered me off. If they do, they're a bunch of damm fools because I've been planning this thing for well over a year. Planning it, thinking about it, trying not to think about it and I realized that at once I had conceived it, once I had conceived the Pandora Box, the Mission Pandora Box that it would be the downfall of me. And so it shall be. *It's the end.*[93] [Emphasis added throughout.]

Then sitting in his white and beige 1967 Buick in the airport parking lot, Byck records his last tape in a drizzling rain less than an hour before his death. In it he dwells on his political rationale:

It's a quarter to six and I'll be moving toward the airport in about . . . uh . . . one hour.

If there is a moral to this madness I suspect it may be the expression, "Am I my brother's keeper?" And the answer would have to be, positively, yes. For we are all brothers and if any one of us is hurting, then we all stand to get hurt.

I've never owned a pistol or even fired a pistol. It's rather strange. I'm not possessed by guns . . . only when I realize[d] it that killing and being killed may have to be done before men begin to respect other men. *I think this all begins with the lack of respect.* So I've got the gun and the time is beginning to run out on me for it's five of six now. If that flight is ready, it should be departing at 7:15. . . . *One man's terrorist is another man's patriot.* See what happens in Ireland. Who's the patriot and who's the terrorist? It all depends on which side of the fence you happen to be on at the time. Of course, the Israelis call the Arabs terrorists but they forget about [an] organization called the Stern Gang and the IRGUN and that's the way it is when a man has to fight a greater force, and would be ridiculous for him to meet that force head on and have himself destroyed uselessly.

Then he becomes a terrorist. He acts clandestine secret acts and he strikes dirty. And that's what it is about being a terrorist. . . .

I feel not like a hero but like a terrorist. . . . I don't know what they call it when they burn you uh—cremated. I think a tombstone that I would like to have is that "He didn't like what he saw and he decided to do something about it." *I just wish that I don't get to be known as a . . . uh . . . maniac or a madman.* There are a lot of things I am, but these are two things that I'm not, a maniac or a madman.

He concludes with a very revealing explanation of his motive:

It's always easy for a . . . uh . . . the authorities to look outward for the causes, say . . . uh . . . this guy acted as a madman, a mad dog, and this guy acted like a maniac, when basically these hostile actions, or at least *my hostile actions, are inward, that of being robbed and cheated out of my dignity.* . . .

And then follows the projection from personal to political:

. . . and seeing my country being raped and ravished almost before my very eyes. And I won't stand idly by and allow it to happen.

They can call me misguided, if they like, but of course being misguided or being guided is only a matter of again, of who is interpreting the action and what side of the fence you are sitting on.

I feel that I am guided, that I have a purpose, and I think that I have made it abundantly clear what I think my purpose is. . . .[94] [Emphasis added throughout.]

Conclusions

It seems reasonable to suggest that if Samuel Byck had had other options in his personal life, he would not have chosen to die as he did. He acknowledged this when he said: "It's just a shame there aren't more people like Bonny. . . . if there were, . . . I know I wouldn't be doing what I'm planning to do." He simply had nothing to live for. So in death he tried to establish his personal value—the respect he had lost—through an elaborate political rationalization of his attempt to kill an unpopular and corrupt president. And in so doing, in a manner similar to Lee Oswald, he hoped to place the burden of guilt on the real causes of his misery—an unloving wife and children and an indifferent mother who had rejected and deserted him.

In this context, it seems clear that his displaced anger toward the Small Business Administration, other government agencies, and the President were merely symptomatic, rather than causal, factors in his attempt on the President's life. This is not to suggest that his political resentments were irrational: they were widely shared by many Americans during this period. But like Oswald, the extreme intensity of these resentments can only be understood in the context of Samuel Byck's peculiarly personal problems as the neurotic and compensatory act of a Type II would-be assassin.

Chapter Five · The Feminine Dimension

FROMME AND MOORE

Well you know when people around you treat you like a child and pay no attention to the things you say you have to do something.
— Lynette Fromme

I did not want to kill somebody, but there comes a point when the only way you can make a statement is to pick up a gun. . . .
— Sara Jane Moore

IN 1975, for the first time in American history, two serious attempts were made on a president's life in less than three weeks. Moreover, the attempts were made—again for the first time in American history—by two women. Although classified as Type II subjects, both Lynette Fromme and Sara Jane Moore reveal important distinctions from their male counterparts. Oswald and Byck closely resemble Harold Lasswell's description of the "political personality." Of the two women, only Moore comes close to that description, and then only with some qualifications. Fromme represents a more complex variation of neurotic behavior.

The major dimension of Fromme's behavior is revealed in her obsessive/compulsive commitment to cult leader Charles Manson. Unlike the Type II males, her motive in attacking President Ford was not to attract attention to herself or to make anyone else feel guilty for what she had done. Rather she hoped to stand trial so that Manson could be called as a witness in her defense. With the media attention such a trial would command, Fromme reasoned, Manson's message would, at long last, reach the ears of the world. She viewed him as a Christ figure with a solution for the world's problems. A false belief? Undoubtedly, but as the evidence will show, she was not insane.

Lasswell's political personality characteristics come much closer to describing Sara Jane Moore to the extent that she did try to use a political act to resolve her personal dilemma; subsequently she also offered a political rationale for her assassination attempt. But she differs from Oswald and Byck in one important respect: whereas Oswald and Byck acted, in large part, to *place* guilt on significant others in their lives, Moore acted to *resolve* her own guilt stemming from her betrayal of the radical friends she had made while serving as an FBI informant.

Thus there is an important quality that separates these two female subjects from their Type II male counterparts: the *personal* motives of the women are less ego-defensive and punitive. Fromme wanted to help Manson—the one person who had ever taken her seriously—get the new trial he had been denied; she believed he could clear himself. Similarly, Moore sought the forgiveness of perhaps the first group of people in her life who had ever taken her seriously. In this sense, both women shot at the President as a result of a warped sense of *love* and *concern* for significant others in their lives. It seems apparent that they would not have attacked a president neither took very seriously for political reasons. Moore, for example, considered President Ford "a nebbish,"[1] and Fromme viewed him in much the same way—merely a puppet of the Nixon regime. In a political sense, each acknowledged the existence of worthier targets, but such targets would not have served their primary personal concerns. In contrast, Oswald and Byck acted punitively in anger and disappointment, hoping to place *blame and guilt* on others for what they had done.

In this respect, it is also interesting to observe the one striking similarity between the male and female counterparts: neither was taken seriously by authorities. Like Oswald and, to a lesser degree, Byck, both Fromme and Moore had provided rather pointed warnings of their potential for violence; and their threats were dismissed or ignored.

Lynette Alice Fromme (1948-)

In an untitled manuscript, Lynette Fromme describes her introduction to Charles Manson on the beach in Venice, California. Earlier the same day, after an argument, her father had ordered her out of "his" house with instructions "never to come back." Alone and frightened, she sat on a bench clutching her books and her eye makeup, not knowing what to do or where to go. As she sat staring at the ocean through her tears, suddenly "an elfish, dirty-looking creature" flashing a smile "that went from warm daddy to twinkley devil" startled her with, "so your father kicked you out." He talked with her, made her laugh and feel relaxed—strange emotions for this troubled young girl— and then he invited her to go with him:

> He smiled a soft feeling and was on his way. I grabbed my books, running to catch up with him. I didn't know why—I didn't care— and I never left.[2]

This episode marks the beginning of a psychological and spiritual conversion and journey that led through the formation of the Manson "family" of young dropouts, the ghoulish Tate-LaBianca murders two years later, the trial and conviction of Manson and four followers for those murders, and ended, perhaps, as a federal judge pronounced a sentence of imprisonment for life on the twenty-six-year-old Manson disciple for the attempted assassination of President Gerald R. Ford on September 5, 1975.

Losing and Finding Daddy

On the surface, Lynette Fromme appears to have had a typical American childhood in the middle-class Los Angeles suburbs of Santa Monica, Westchester, and Redondo Beach. She had taken ballet lessons as a youngster, twirled batons and ropes and memorized cheers during adolescence, listened to the Beach Boys, and, like most of her middle-class counterparts, graduated from high school in 1967 without any clear idea of who she was or what she wanted to do.

This typical teenage ambivalence was translated into political terms as the placidity of the 1950s was disrupted by the jarring events of the following decade. Lynette Fromme's generation—the first to be socialized in a television-dominated era of "Howdy Doody" and the "Mouseketeers"—witnessed on flickering black and white screens new and, some would say, unprecedented challenges to authority and the status quo in American society: President Kennedy was assassinated in 1963 when she was fourteen; a year later, heavy-handed university officials precipitated a free-speech movement at Berkeley that evolved into a nationwide mass protest against all oppression and the escalating Vietnam War. In the South, police and sheriff's deputies were hosing, clubbing, jailing, and, in some instances, killing civil rights demonstrators; and bloody racial riots erupted in Watts and Detroit in 1967.

Religion was divided. Most established faiths, with historical predictability, ducked the moral issues and held to a defense of the status quo; others declared God dead but offered no alternative. It was a period of turmoil and profound moral ambiguity.

In this context, it is not surprising that the parents of Lynette Fromme, as the parents of many teenagers of that period, found themselves at odds with their daughter's increasingly independent spirit. It was especially difficult for them because she was a daughter, and the usual sex-related concerns of parents of teenage daughters were aggravated by the new ideologically based challenges to all authority, including theirs.

The disputes between Lynette and her father became particularly bitter. A no-nonsense aeronautical engineer, her father did not adjust easily to change. Moreover, it was difficult for him to take Lynette seriously. A diminutive freckled-faced kid with big wide eyes and fluffy auburn hair, Lynette always seemed like the cute little baton twirler she no longer was, nor wanted to be. Her more important problem was that she had no idea what she wanted to be or do except find acceptance and understanding. After a brief enrollment at El Camino Junior College and a final argument with her enraged father, the saga described at the beginning of this chapter began.

In the bizarre life she was to live with Manson after her departure from home, Fromme's commitment to the bearded flashing-eyed guru was complete. In Manson, she found a father who loved and accepted her and a spiritual force who explained and made sense of a very confusing world. These qualities were much more important than the sexual relationship that aroused the curiosity of so many commentators. Even in the sexual context, Lynette seems to have viewed Manson always more as a father than a lover: "I felt so close to him and layed my head on his shoulder, wanting a daddy to hold me. . . . As all daughters I had wanted all the attention I could get from my daddy."[3]

Nor was this need for fatherly acceptance reflected only with respect to Manson. Prior to the Tate-LaBianca murders, when the Manson family lived at a vacated movie ranch in the California desert, Lynette established a close relationship with the eighty-one-year-old owner of the ranch, George Spahn. Later, before the Ford incident in Sacramento, she had an ongoing friendship with Harold Boro, a retired man of sixty-five who had befriended her, loaned her money, his car, and, unwittingly, the .45 caliber pistol she used to threaten the President's life. In the documentary film, *Manson*, Fromme states: "Every girl should have a daddy just like Charlie."

Manson's Influence

Related to the importance of Manson as an emotional prop in her chaotic life was her belief that he literally represented Christ. Manson, raised in the West Virginia-Southern Ohio Bible Belt of hell-fire-and-hallelujah fundamentalism before drifting West, was quite familiar with the significance of the prophesied second-coming of Christ. According to these prophecies, those who had accepted Christ as their savior and were, so to speak, born again would live with Christ in a paradise created when evil was destroyed at Armageddon. For Lynette, Christ had already returned for the second time in the form of Manson, and the battle was on against evil—as defined by Charlie. Manson's bearded Christ-like appearance, flashing eyes, and mystical utterances only added to this aura of spiritual authenticity.

Thus, members of Manson's family struck at the decadence of Hollywood affluence in the Tate-LaBianca spree hoping to precipitate a racial Armageddon of sorts. An attempt was made to leave evidence suggesting the crime was committed by blacks in the hope that a domestic racial war would develop, after which Manson would move in to fill the vacuum left by the triumphant, but racially inferior, blacks' inability to govern.[4] Manson-as-Christ-figure, however, was arrested and, Fromme believed, unjustly tried, and figuratively crucified with a life sentence for first degree murder. Mourning his anticipated fate, Fromme and other followers, at times with heads shaved, sat outside the courthouse in Los Angeles during the entire lengthy trial, their foreheads scarred with X's they had sliced into their flesh.[a] Nor would the mourners ever forget that during this time, President Nixon, like the Pharisees of old, publicly declared his belief in Manson's guilt.

Her Mission

After Manson's conviction and incarceration, Lynette Fromme's mission in life was set: she was to resurrect Charlie so that the world could be saved from the destructive course it was on. Moving to the state capital in Sacramento, she shared an apartment at 1725 P Street, near the capital complex, with two other Manson disciples, Sandra Good and Susan Murphy.

The women lived quietly, eschewing the drugs, alcohol, and free-

---

[a] The forehead scars recall another familiar prophecy of the "last days" before Christ's return: the mark of the "beast" or antichrist. It is not clear whether Manson considered himself Christ or the antichrist. It is certain that, whatever his conception of himself, it was viewed positively by his followers.

wheeling sex of an earlier period for an ascetic life of meditation, gardening, and vegetarian food. They were described as "model tenants."[5] With a small income based on Sandra Good's trust fund and handouts from various friends around the country, they threw themselves into plans to combat the destructive influences that Charlie had warned about—influences that seemed now to be everywhere: in particular, the choking industrial pollution in American cities and the logging and decimation of the irreplaceable redwood forests in northern California.

With such concerns in mind, the three set up among themselves a self-styled "International People's Court of Retribution" whose purpose it would be to begin the systematic extermination of polluters until they ceased their world-contaminating activities.[6] The initial targets were designated corporate executives and their wives. To carry out this planned terrorist campaign, they sought support from people they knew around the country. In a tape sent to a friend, Edward Vandervort, in Pennsylvania, Fromme instructed him on how to make a terrorist phone call:

Muster up your meanest voice, think of your dying world, and call. Speak slowly and precisely and clearly and as mean and frightening as you can. . . . I know you'll do it good. . . . Tell them the following:

"Your product or activity (or you may mention the name of it) is killing, poisoning the world. There is no excuse for it. (Now say this slowly): If you do not stop killing us, Manson will send for your heart. If the company pollutes the air (you may say lungs) close the shop. Flee the country. Or watch your own blood spell out your crime on the wall. Remember Sharon Tate."[7]

In a follow-up letter postmarked June 17, 1975, Lynette wrote, in part, to the same party:

Ed,
I just sent you a list of corporations to call. This one is to take care of NOW. William Roesch—President of Kaiser Company, makers of more forms of pollution than I can count—sellers of lives and souls—killers of U.S. more than anyone.
William Roesch.
With an address in Bridgeville, Pennsylvania.
Do not threaten him first. Kill him. Destroy him.
Here's How.

RICHARD LAWRENCE (Andrew Jackson, 1835)

JOHN WILKES BOOTH (Abraham Lincoln, 1865)

CHARLES GUITEAU
(James Garfield, 1881)

JOHN SCHRANK
(Theodore Roosevelt, 1912)

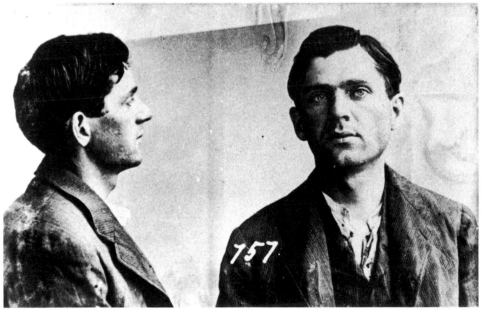

LEON CZOLGOSZ (William McKinley, 1901)

(*Above*)
GIUSEPPE ZANGARA
(Franklin Roosevelt, 1933)
(*Below*)
CARL WEISS
(Huey Long, 1935)

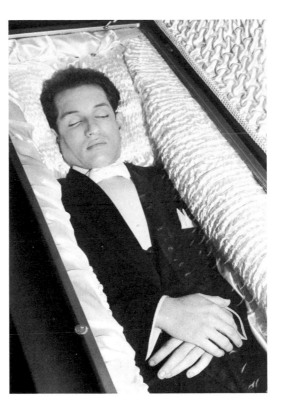

(*Above*)
GRISELIO TORRESOLA
(Harry Truman, 1950)
(*Below*)
OSCAR COLLAZO
(Harry Truman, 1950)

(*Above*)
LEE HARVEY OSWALD
(John Kennedy, 1963)
(*Below*)
SIRHAN SIRHAN
(Robert Kennedy, 1968)

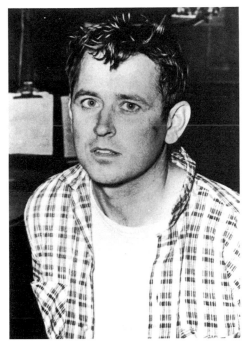

JAMES EARL RAY
(Martin Luther King, 1968)

SAMUEL BYCK
(Richard Nixon, 1974)

ARTHUR BREMER
(George Wallace, 1972)

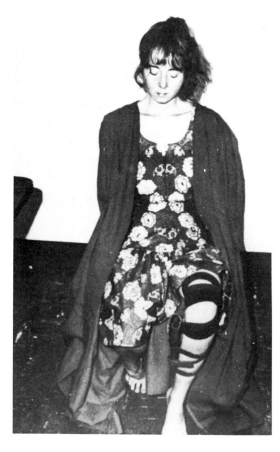

(*Above*)
SARA JANE MOORE
(Gerald Ford, 1975)

(*Below*)
LYNETTE FROMME
(Gerald Ford, 1975)

1. Case it out. Check for kids. We want to avoid hurting any kids. But get him and the wife however you can. Use gloves.
Be careful and sly. Could wear paint clothes. Take with you an aerosol can of BAN deodorant. Take also a can of pink paint and a large paint brush.
When bodies are dead, paint as much as you can of them with PINK paint. (faces, arms, etc.)
Put the aerosol can in the man's mouth.[8]

Then in a departure from the earlier taped instruction in which she mentioned Sharon Tate, Fromme now advised: "Do not write anything about *Helter Skelter* or any other words you got out of that book. Or anything about Manson."[9]

Thus a plan for a terrorist campaign directed at corporate executives, which would follow the European terrorist model being implemented in Germany and Italy, began to unfold. Government leaders were curiously excluded from the hit list of top executives and their wives. Politicians were viewed as merely the lackeys of the corporate elite that ruled the country. This conception of political power was hardly novel in its Marxist perspective. Indeed, it was one shared by the radical Symbionese Liberation Army who held Patty Hearst captive at this time—although no evidence has been produced that links Fromme or her associates with the SLA.

It soon became apparent, however, that her Pennsylvania collaborator was reluctant to implement this scheme. Frustrated, Fromme came to the conclusion that such plans could not be implemented without Manson. Only he could command the kind of commitment necessary for a true revolution.

With this in mind, she wrote in June 1975 to Los Angeles Supreme Court Judge Raymond Choate—the presiding judge at Manson's trial. She told the judge that Manson, with whom she maintained a regular correspondence, had asked her to visit the judge to request that he reduce the convicted killer's sentence. Fromme went on to say that she had failed to do that and apologized. The judge, apparently accustomed to such blandishments, thought little about the letter until a month later when he received an unsettling phone call from Lynette. In this conversation, she asked about him and his four children and then went on in a sinister voice to inquire about how he felt about all the killing in Vietnam and the "killing of the ecology." The judge later explained: "She said she wanted to talk to me because she was going to do something desperate. At first I thought she meant she was going to kill herself, but she specifically said she didn't mean suicide." Choate told police he thought she might have been threatening him and his family but could not be sure.[10] She was, of course.

Still nothing actually happened. Even her threats were dismissed by authorities as childish. Once again no one would take her seriously; no one would listen.

About this time, Lynette and her roommate Sandra Good began to wear red robes to draw attention to their concerns and tried without much success to get stories about their mission in the press. The red attire, Lynette explained, was to signify a new religious order that would pray for Manson's release/resurrection from prison. She went on:

> We're nuns now, and we wear red robes. We're waiting for our Lord [Manson] and there's only one thing to do before he comes off the cross [prison], and that's clean up the earth. Our red robes are an example of new morality. We must clean up the air, the water and the land. They're red with sacrifice, the blood of sacrifice.[11]

Again the biblical referents are clear. Fromme and Good, with missionary zeal, hoped to save as much of the world as possible in order to hasten the Second Coming of Christ, who, in their view, was the imprisoned Manson. Salvation was possible only through the shed blood of Christ and His resurrection, in their tortured but interesting interpretation, from the tomb of San Quentin. Still the press's interest in their bizarre attire and curious purpose was short-lived, and within a day or two, the two proselyters found themselves in the same shaded obscurity of the white frame tenement house on P Street.

In July, after a dramatic increase in correspondence from Manson,[12] Lynette asked a Sacramento reporter to do a story on a "press release" from Manson in which the latter attacked Nixon. The release, presumably written by Manson, read in part:

> Nixon declared the Manson family guilty before the trial was over, leaving them no defense. All laws were broken to put Manson in prison.
>
> If Nixon's reality wearing a Ford face continues to run this country against the law without any real truth, trust and faith— if Manson is not allowed to explain what you are too sheltered to face, your homes will be bloodier than the Tate-LaBianca houses and My Lai put together.

The last line proved to be very significant: *"It will take a courtroom to explain it"* (emphasis added).[13] When the reporter refused to do a story on the statement, Fromme angrily warned him: "It's your life that's on the line—that message has got to go out."[14]

Shortly after this episode, on August 2, 1975, Lynette wrote to a writer, Charles Rossie. Mr. Rossie had sought an interview with Manson the year before but was refused. Manson sent the request to Fromme and now, with his permission, she wrote to Rossie. The letter is important because it provides much insight into what was motivating Lynette throughout the summer of 1975. Her hope was that Rossie, as a last resort, would provide the media exposure for Manson's ideas that she so desperately wanted in order to generate popular support for a new trial for the convicted killer. She wrote in part:

> I am enclosing a double sided statement concerning both Nixon and what will happen to Los Angeles, even as I find it unlikely that you will use or pass this grim warning.[15]

In an obvious reference to Christ, she went on to describe Manson's qualities and the hope he held out to a troubled world:

> I am certain that you could find in history men with as strange and mystical, individual and yet all-encompassing qualities as Manson, if one could only think to compare. A braver (real) man would take a good long look at a phenomenon to see not what others think or fear about it—but WHAT IS. This is difficult for the schooled mind to see. . . . the American mind is left blocked by dozens of already tried solutions, to the OVERALL problems, that have fizzled.[16]

Then she exhorted Rossie:

> As a member of the media it is your responsibility to take into consideration the thought that the Man Family has presented. [On other occasions, Fromme had attached great spiritual significance to Manson's name—Man's Son.]

She continued with a condemnation of the "old school of thought" and the decadence of American life style represented in Tennessee Williams' plays. But, she contended, there is hope:

> There is around the corner of evolution a new experience, awareness and perception beyond anything we have yet experienced— and this itself is so feared that it has been locked up [by the ruling corporate elite]. The death of an old thought is the completion of a long line of grandmother's ways, and hard for most to let go of.[17]

Again she admonished Rossie: "The media CAN be used to unwind the tangles of a world running in circles toward what it fears most."[18] The solution, of course, was Manson: "Manson can *explain* the self-destructive thought. He can *explain* the Christ thought" (emphasis added). But he must have the opportunity to bring this message of salvation to the world, she continued, otherwise our lives will terminate in the "drug store[s], booze bottles and morgues" of a decadent and polluted Tate-LaBianca society.[19]

The first step in removing the "concrete billboard cancer reality killing the world," according to Fromme, was to

> put Nixon and the Pope in a *courtroom with Manson and family* and we will see what has been running our ignorances, what truth has been kept in closets, and who are the real servants of the people and earth. . . . Manson can explain it. . . . It is an exceptional man who tells the truth others do not want to hear. Those of us not exceptional, caught up in foolish formalities signifying nothing, may learn to face ourselves through him—but only while he lives. If he dies [*or remains silenced behind bars*], the truth along with him dies.

The urgency of her appeal was conveyed in a threat: "If [Manson is] not allowed to explain, there will be many more young murderers, beginning with the person typing this letter."[20] In a postscript, Fromme expressed her desire to debate *Helter Skelter* author and prosecuting attorney in the Manson trial, Vincent Bugliosi, who she felt grossly misrepresented Manson and the family. She went on to suggest that Rossie arrange a talk show appearance with Bugliosi, Sandra Good, and herself on CBS.

Seizing the Ford Opportunity

Before Rossie could respond, a frustrated and very discouraged Lynette Fromme learned that President Ford would be visiting Sacramento. All other means of obtaining the sought-after forum for Charlie had failed. But now a new opportunity presented itself. As the President and his entourage checked into the Senator Hotel adjacent to the Capitol Complex, Lynette Fromme, with her borrowed .45 caliber automatic and red robe, prepared for their anticipated rendezvous the next day.

After a breakfast meeting the following morning, the President left the hotel at 9:55 A.M. to walk across the attractively landscaped Capitol grounds to meet California Governor Jerry Brown. As the affable

Ford smiled and waved at onlookers, he noticed a small childlike woman standing to his left. The President noticed her red dress and turban before she reached under the robe and quickly leveled the ugly-looking weapon directly at his genitals. She was, he estimated, "approximately two feet from me" when a bodyguard grabbed the weapon, wrenching the would-be assassin to the ground. Surrounded by a flying wedge of Secret Service agents, Ford was hustled out of danger toward the Capitol.[21]

It is questionable whether Fromme intended to kill the President. Her frustration had never been directed specifically at Ford except to acknowledge that he was simply another willing instrument of the ruling corporate elite. All her efforts over the past few months had been directed toward gaining the kind of exposure that would, hopefully, lead to a new trial for Manson. There was little to be gained in killing the President even in retribution—except perhaps in the sense that he was a Nixon surrogate who had pardoned the despised former president. In this context, however, it is unlikely that Ford could have ever taken his predecessor's place or provided the same satisfaction as a surrogate victim; the hatred for Nixon among Manson followers was highly personalized. Ford as symptom was no substitute for Nixon the cause.

Frustrated in her attempt to gain publicity for Charlie, Lynette threatened the President with a weapon in order to focus the nation's attention on her subsequent trial. As she explained the day after her arrest: "Well you know when people around you treat you like a child and pay no attention to the things you say you have to do something."[22] A major witness in her defense, she assumed, would be Charles Manson, with the forum he needed to gain his pardon and save the world. In a pre-trial interview with the press, Lynette explained once more that the world would continue on its destructive course "until our Christ [Manson] is taken off the cross." She added that Charlie "could do a lot" for the world if given the chance.[23]

The Trial

Hoping to represent herself at the trial and expecting to be free to say what she wanted and to choose her own witnesses, Fromme had in mind a political trial on the order of the Chicago Seven. She was soon frustrated by presiding U.S. District Court Judge Thomas J. McBride who denied her request and ordered that she be represented by a court-appointed attorney. Fromme angrily dismissed the first attorney and with great reluctance accepted a second. After repeated disruptive attempts to explain her behavior, she was finally ordered removed from the courtroom.

Frustrated, she tried unsuccessfully to plead guilty and then refused to participate in the trial. She watched most of the proceedings in a cell on closed-circuit television. This, of course, made her defense most difficult. Repeated opportunities were provided for her to testify but she refused unless she could do so on her terms. The following was typical of the exchanges that occurred throughout the trial:

> JUDGE MCBRIDE: "Good morning, Miss Fromme. Do you wish to participate in the trial today?"
> MISS FROMME: "No."

On this occasion, the judge inquired whether she intended to waive her right to confront witnesses who testified against her:

> MISS FROMME: "Your Honor, I feel all the laws were broken when Manson was put in prison."
> JUDGE MCBRIDE: "All right, thank you."

Whereupon the defendant would be escorted from the courtroom.[24]

Fromme's defense was based on the argument that she did not intend to harm the President. Rather her purpose was only to provoke arrest for an incident that would guarantee the widest possible publicity for her cause. The fact that there was no bullet in the chamber of the weapon was cited by her attorney as evidence of her real purpose. Similarly, there were arguments back and forth whether she had actually squeezed the trigger. Witnesses such as William Melcher, Assistant District Attorney for Los Angeles County, found it difficult to believe that Fromme wanted to kill Ford. Melcher, who had known the defendant since the Manson trial five years earlier, stated in a pre-trial hearing that, in his opinion, there was little risk in reducing the $1 million bail to $350,000 because Lynette had what she wanted in the trial—"the ears of the world." Fromme herself, from the moment she was pushed to the ground and disarmed, repeated to her captors, "It didn't go off." Whether she said this defensively as a statement of fact, hoping to avoid additional rough treatment, or as an expression of surprise, was a key point of contention in the trial. Soon after her arrest she had explained: "I wasn't going to shoot him. I just wanted to get some attention for a new trial for Charlie and the girls."[25]

The jury rejected her explanation, and Lynette was found guilty of attempting to assassinate the President. She was given a life sentence like Charlie.

Conclusions

Whether Lynette Fromme was guilty of attempting to kill the President, as the jury decided, or sought only publicity in a terrifying bluff, her fanatical commitment to the pseudo-religious cause symbolized by the bizarre Charles Manson cannot be questioned. Found sane, free of drugs and alcohol, and competent to stand trial, Fromme's view of the decadence, waste, and pollution of modern society falls within the mainstream of contemporary social criticism. Her solution, a bizarre version of fundamentalist Christianity to which she was totally committed, is extreme but no more so perhaps than the beliefs of millions of others who live their lives on the basis of some equally curious interpretations of myth and reality extending from the Old Testament to Jonestown.

Lynette Fromme was a proselyter—a person who put nothing above her faith and who would do almost anything in her missionary compulsion to spread the gospel according to Manson, even if it meant symbolic acts such as the Tate-LaBianca murders or the attempted assassination of a president. To this extent, she possesses some of the qualities of Type I subjects. The major difference between Fromme and the four Type I assassins was her compulsive primary commitment to a *person* rather than an ideology. The desperation she felt was directly linked to her belief that, without Manson, the ideology was dead. This obsession with the bearded-guru-as-savior accounts for her highly neurotic emotional dependency on him—a dependency that was, as we have seen, a major unyielding component in virtually everything she did. In this sense Manson defined reality for his followers; his views were accepted as an article of faith.

Was such dependency the result of an insane delusion? Hardly, in a clinical sense, unless we want to label all deviant religious and political ideologies delusional.

One is reminded of the sad tale of Nicholas II and Alexandra and how the destruction of Czarist Russia was hastened by Alexandra's total—some would say, irrational—reliance on the Manson-like Rasputin. Like Alexandra, Lynette's religious beliefs imposed a highly selective perceptual screen that enabled her to eliminate or rationalize the evil concealed in the devious mysticism and strange, seemingly supernatural, prescience of her Rasputin. Manson's charismatic grip on her defied logic and common sense. But like the early Christians who died rather than renounce their belief in another bearded vagabond who claimed he was the Son of God, the scorn of the world only strengthened her commitment and, indeed, prompted her to await the President among the shade trees in Sacramento.

Sara Jane Moore (1930-)

Two and a half weeks after Lynette Fromme tried to shoot President Ford in Sacramento, a second attempt was made on his life in San Francisco. As the President, amid heavy security, left the St. Francis Hotel and walked quickly toward his waiting limousine, a shot exploded from across the street. Ford flinched, clutched his chest, then ashen-faced but unharmed was immediately pushed down and into the back seat of the limousine that sped away.

Across the street, police had pounced on a heavy-set, middle-aged woman, knocking her to the ground and twisting a .38 caliber revolver from her grasp—another woman, but this time hardly a flower-child.

Growing Up in West Virginia

Sara Jane Kahn was born in Charleston, West Virginia, on February 15, 1930. Her father, Olaf, an engineer, worked for DuPont, one of the many chemical plants that border the Kanahwa River that flows through the Charleston valley serving as a conduit for industrial waste. Although hardly the lumber and coal baron Sara was later to imply, her father did provide a comfortable middle-class home for his wife and five children. Her mother Ruth found time, even with five children, to play the violin in the Charleston Chamber Music Society.[26] As a result, the family attended many concerts and was much more involved in the arts than one might expect in an area best known for its stereotyped hillbilly image.

Sally, as she preferred to be called, played the flute in the Stonewall Jackson high-school band and was very active in the school's drama program; she was selected to play the lead in the senior play. Her picture—that of a slim and pretty, dark-haired girl—appeared in the 1947 high-school yearbook in a melodramatic pose from the production. Her childhood dream was to become a famous actress.[27]

Described by her high-school friends as quiet and bookish, Sally was a serious student who brought home A's on her report card. She was not drawn toward boys or the frivolities of high-school social life. Nonetheless, strains began to develop between her and her father— like Lynette Fromme's father, another no-nonsense disciplinarian who regularly attended the Randolph Street Baptist Church with the family.

Much to the annoyance of the elder Kahn, Sally developed an interest in the occult and read widely on the subject for a period during her youth.

Van Watson, who owned a neighborhood grocery store—"Van's Never Closed Market"—recalled that Sally, always with a couple of books tucked under her arm, used to stop by on her way to and from school to buy candy. Unlike another regular at Van's at that time—young Charles Manson, whose mother clerked for Van—Sally seemed serious and responsible to everyone but her father.[28] Finally, completely frustrated with his seemingly unwarranted punitiveness, Sally ran away from home briefly at the age of sixteen. When she returned, she delivered a second rebellious salvo by announcing that she was leaving the fundamentalist confines of the Baptist congregation for the modernist pews of the Episcopalians: an act verging on heresy for a fundamentalist Baptist of that time and region and one undoubtedly viewed by her father as being directly associated with her continuing interest in the occult.

Immediately upon her high-school graduation in 1947, Sally entered nurse's training at St. Francis Hospital, a Roman Catholic institution. Although one of the few professions readily accessible to women at that time, the Catholic affiliation again jarred the exasperated Olaf.

Finding the punitive rigidity of Catholic nuns no easier to bear than her father's, however, Sally deliberately had herself expelled before the end of her first year. She accomplished this, according to a source close to the situation, by "doing something that was very indiscreet and uncouth, then telling about it—the sort of thing that was tabu in a Catholic nursing school."[29] The act itself was not revealed.

Love and Marriage

During a subsequent brief stint in the Women's Army Corps, Sally, still rebelling, impulsively married a young Marine, but the marriage ended within a month. For some reason, perhaps the trauma of the experience, she was found wandering about in Washington apparently suffering from amnesia. After treatment at Walter Reed Hospital, she was released. This was to be the first of five tempestuous and unsuccessful marriages. In 1950, within a week after her first marriage was annulled, she married an Air Force officer and bore him a son and a daughter before a divorce in 1953. A month later, they remarried. Two years and another son later, Sally again filed for divorce.[30]

In 1958, now living in California, Sally remarried—this time an older, minor executive in the motion picture industry. Finding the care of her three children cumbersome in her new marriage, Sally arranged with her former husband to have them sent to her parents back in Charleston, with the understanding that she would send twenty dollars a month to help with the additional expenses. Her payments, always erratic, finally stopped; her ex-husband disappeared.

Overwhelmed with responsibility for the three youngsters, Olaf Kahn secured a warrant for his daughter's arrest. At long last, weary with attempts to force her cooperation, the Kahns adopted their grand-children, with Sally's consent, in 1963. Shortly thereafter, Olaf Kahn died. Sally was notified of his death but did not attend the funeral. Moreover, that was the last her family was to hear of her for twelve years—until her attack on President Ford.[31]

Now free of her maternal responsibilities, the ambitious and intel-ligent Sally studied and soon passed the rigorous examination to be-come a certified public accountant. The years of intense study had taken their toll, however, and her fourth marriage was deteriorating. Then either through fate or, paradoxically, design, Sally bore a fourth child—a son—only three years after giving up her other children. If the little boy, named for his father, was to mark a new beginning, it failed. Within a year, his parents had separated and his mother, in her haste to wed a prosperous Bay Area physician, had remarried on December 22, 1967, without benefit of divorce—unbeknownst, of course, to her new husband.

Now comfortably ensconced in an expensive home in the East Bay suburb of Danville, Sally, putting aside her interest in a fifty-thousand-dollar-a-year accounting career,[32] quickly settled into the middle-class vacuity of country club activity. But the reality of the utter purpose-lessness of this materially comfortable life style began to disturb her. The club and candy-striper mentality of her neighbors bored her; bridge didn't interest her; and how many San Francisco art shows could a person attend before the clichés, both verbal and canvas, became unendurable? Feeling her life was without meaning, she be-came very depressed, separated in 1971, and, in 1973 her fifth marriage was annulled (on the grounds that she had failed to obtain a divorce from her previous husband before she had remarried).

Radical Politics

On her own again, but now—for the first time—with no marriage prospects in sight, Sally used her generous child support payments to put her son in a private school while she took a job as head of the accounting department at a country club in Alamo, California. Withdrawal symptoms soon set in, however, as the day-to-day routine of an accounting department began to wear on her. Failing to open mail, working in the dining room instead of her office, hating the job but refusing to acknowledge it, Sally took out her frustrations on subordinates. Finally it worked. She was fired.

Completely soured on the status-seeking pursuits that had consumed most of her adult life and were reflected most clearly in the occupational hierarchy of her marriages—enlisted man, officer (twice), business executive, physician—Sally did an about-face, turning now to the street scene of San Francisco and radical politics. Searching for a new and different identity and life, she was eventually to discard her pant suits and wedgies, bridge clubs and art shows, for jeans, boots, and radical politics.

She now began to explore this new world that contrasted so starkly with the life she had known. When Patricia Hearst was kidnapped by members of the Symbionese Liberation Army and a ransom was demanded, Sally, who now had assumed her mother's maiden name, Moore, volunteered her accounting skills to the People In Need program set up by Randolph Hearst. The program was established in response to the ransom demand of Patricia's kidnappers that Hearst distribute two million dollars worth of food to the poor.[33]

As a result of her dedication, energy, and skill, Moore quickly attracted Hearst's attention and confidence and soon found herself as a major liaison between the millionaire and members of the radical community. One of these members was an ex-convict, "Popeye" Jackson, who headed the United Prisoners Union, which was thought to have contacts with the SLA.

Thriving on the adventure and excitement of her new role, Sally threw herself into a crash program on radical politics attempting to learn as much as she could about the participants and their unfamiliar beliefs. As a result of her work for PIN and her intense curiosity, she became fascinated with people like "Popeye" Jackson and cultivated his friendship. She had never known anyone like him. A black, streetwise ex-convict with a political perspective, if not ideology, Jackson introduced the sheltered middle-aged woman to, as she described it,

> this murky world of drugs, of wholesale screwing, of filthy language. Frequently, I was the only person at parties who did not openly use drugs. This was the fringes of the [radical] movement—and it was really a shock to see how they lived.[34]

Moore began to attend political rallies and listened intently as radicals such as Kathy Soliah spoke in behalf of the SLA and the need for revolutionary social change in America. She was intrigued as she became aware of the variety of groups that made up the movement, for example, the October League, the Communist Labor party, the Prairie Fire Organizing Committee, the May First Movement. As she became exposed to the intellectual side of the movement, Sally recalled: "I was learning that there was a whole . . . left movement that had been around all the time, that I lived right here and knew nothing about."[35]

It was during this period of infatuation that she was approached by the FBI. Having observed her contacts with the radicals as a result of her PIN activities, the Bureau asked her to work for them as an informant in April 1974. Moore was flattered, excited by the importance of her task, and not a little amused by the cloak and dagger antics of the agents—"just like a very bad movie script."[36] After forty-four years of middle-class, soap-opera tedium, Sara Jane Moore embarked on a true adventure—a mission of some significance. She recalled her induction: "The picture they [the FBI] painted was the very thing designed to make a nice, middle-class lady go off and save the country."[37]

The FBI instructed her to establish contact with and observe a young man named "Tom" who was suspected of having SLA contacts. They were also interested in any information she could provide on her friend Popeye Jackson, although Jackson was a person they did not take too seriously.

Acceptance and Conversion

Several things occurred as a result of her involvement with the ideologically committed activists (as opposed to the street people). Before long, her view of the groups she was infiltrating began to change as she learned more about them: she began to respect and then to like them. They accepted her as a human being—not merely a dumpy, middle-aged divorcee—and for perhaps the first time in her life, she was taken seriously. In addition, she began to understand and appreciate that real political radicalism was not based on the drugs and recreational sex of Popeye Jackson's world. In her words:

> I began to see that the leftist people I was working with were not enemies of this country—they were dedicated people working for qualitative change. They were not evil. Yes, they recognized revolution, they were dedicated to the armed overthrow of the Gov-

ernment—because they did not think there was any other way to do it.[38]

She found herself drawn to these people she admired. Moreover, they became her friends.

As her view of the radicals changed, she also became aware, for the first time, of the very real risks involved in what she was doing. She realized that what had begun as a naive little adventure was much more serious:

> I became aware of how dangerous it was in terms of those people [the radicals]. I was looking at people getting arrested on the basis of information like that which I was telling the FBI—I was looking at people getting killed. . . . I was afraid of the Bureau. It kills people.[39]

Rejection, Fear, and Guilt

More important than her fear was the *guilt* she now felt about her informer's role. In July 1974, after only three months with the FBI, Sally could take it no more. She confessed to the young man she had been observing that she was an FBI informant. He found it hard to believe, but after conferring with others, she was condemned and ostracized with the words, "Go make your own way." Cut off from the group, Moore was distraught, realizing now how very dependent upon these people she had become:

> I didn't realize how thoroughly I was going to be isolated. When you're in a group, you're getting mailings, you're talking to people, you're going to meetings. . . . When they cut you off, you're really cut off.[40]

Isolated in what had suddenly become an even more alien and threatening environment, Moore was afraid. And there was some rational basis for her fear: in a matter of months, school principal Marcus Foster had been murdered in Oakland by political terrorists, Patty Hearst had been kidnapped, and six SLA members had been shot down in a flaming gun battle in Los Angeles. By this time, Sally had moved into a flat on Guerrero Street in San Francisco's tough Mission District, far from her familiar digs in the suburbs. For a while, she didn't know where to turn. Slipping back into a familiar mode, she even placed an advertisement with a dating service describing herself as a woman who "enjoyed opera, theater, needlework, backpacking, entertaining, a lovely home, her art collection, her wonderful little son and pleasant work." She hoped to attract a "well-educated man who can be comfortable in any atmosphere, who can laugh and be enthusiastic, with a sense of curiosity and wonder at the world."[41]

Her real need, unstated, was rescue from the terrifying world in which she now found herself. Then lonely, depressed, and fearing retribution from the radicals she had betrayed, she chose what, at the time, appeared to be her only option: she went back to the FBI.

When the FBI learned she had blown her cover, she was told that she was no longer of use as an informant and was advised, for her own safety, to remove herself from all contacts with the movement. Now threatened with complete isolation, Sara desperately sought to demonstrate that she was still of some value to the Bureau's surveillance operations. In October 1974, as William and Emily Harris traveled from Pennsylvania back to the Bay Area with Patty Hearst in tow, the FBI decided to recycle her as an informant on a limited basis.[42]

But guilt once again began to weigh heavily because her sympathy and loyalty remained with her friends in the radical movement whom she now both missed and feared. In January 1974, she sought out attorney Charles Garry, who was representing the San Quentin Six. Relating her dilemma, she asked for his advice. According to Moore, Garry suggested that the only way she could possibly regain the confidence of the Left was to confess her sins—not just to the group she had associated with most closely, as she had already done—but to everyone who might have been adversely affected. Moore accepted the advice, contacted various leaders within the movement and, with some shading of detail, made her confession.[43]

The result was predictable: the leadership was somewhat sympathetic, tending to accept the sincerity of her conversion to the faith, but the rank and file was angry—so angry, that they scared poor frightened Sally right back to the unpleasant but better-than-nothing security of the FBI. No longer able to endure the dissonance created by her conflicting emotions, she began to rationalize her FBI affiliation: "I began to see that [keeping up her association with the FBI] was really the only way I could serve the left." Thus this unlikely refugee from East Bay bridge parties became a double agent, informing both the FBI and the radicals of the other's activities. Did this duplicity bother her? Sure, but

> nobody knew I was doubling. There were not two but three Sally Moores operating at that point: one the Sally Moore moving toward armed protest and starting to work with people dedicated to violence, telling no one—not the FBI, not friends on the left;

two, the Sally Moore, converted informant, struggling to find acceptance with the theoreticians and "respectable" Communists; and, three, Sally Moore, FBI informant, reporting on who was asking me what about my "past," as well as on the new groups and people I was meeting.[44]

It is clear, however, that the intense conflicts described in this statement could not be endured for long. Pressure at any point would destroy the precarious balance upon which her life now literally depended.

The pressure was to come from the radicals in the form of doctrinaire requests that she put her confession in writing. Obviously concerned, she got instructions from the FBI and then complied. The document, which was read by six movement people, was considered too revealing, and therefore dangerous, and was destroyed to keep it out of the hands of authorities. Shortly afterward, on June 8, 1975, Sally's friend Popeye and his girlfriend were shot and killed as they sat in a car near her apartment. She was distraught. Although unnamed in her confession, Popeye's identity was apparent to anyone familiar with the movement. Was she responsible? A few nights later, her question was answered when she picked up her telephone to hear an ominous, "You're next." The balance was destroyed; her life was on the line. Accused by the Left, too hot for the FBI (they referred her to the San Francisco police for protection), and aware that accepting police protection was tantamount to an admission of her guilt, Sally was desperately in need of some way to dramatize an undeniable break with the FBI and her true loyalties to the Left. Cut loose from everyone and everything she had identified with, something had to be done to end the terrifying fear, rejection, and isolation of her personal life.[45]

Penance

On September 5, Lynette Fromme tried to shoot President Ford in Sacramento. By the time the President's San Francisco visit on September 21 and 22 was announced, Sally had decided what she had to do, or so she thought. A lethal .44 caliber pistol had been purchased and trips made to a shooting range for practice; the stage was set for the fateful September weekend. When she was finished, she reasoned, no one—not even the most committed—could ever again question her loyalty, sincerity, and commitment.[46]

As the weekend approached, her anxiety grew. In a surprise raid on Thursday morning, September 18, the FBI had arrested Patty Hearst in the San Francisco apartment of Steve Soliah and Wendy Yoshimura.

Moore was on the verge of panic fearing that she would be blamed for the arrest. Two days later, unable to cope with the stress, she called the San Francisco police to say that she was considering a "test" of the presidential security system. She told the police she carried a gun.[47] Her hope, obviously, was to be taken into protective custody—not for the President but herself.

The next morning, Sunday, a policeman interviewed her, confiscated her .44 caliber pistol, and alerted the Secret Service.[48] Late that night, two Secret Service agents met with her but concluded that she was psychologically incapable of assassination, adding "that she was not of sufficient protective importance to warrant surveillance during the President's visit."[49] One by one her options were being closed; she was desperate. She felt that she had to do something at once to protect herself.

After a troubled night, she arose on Monday morning, pulled on a pair of yellow polka-dot slacks and cowboy boots, took her nine-year-old son to school, and drove out to her old haunts in middle-class Danville to purchase a .38 caliber Smith and Wesson revolver from right-wing gun dealer, Mark Fernwood.[50] Still apprehensive and ambivalent about what she planned to do, Sally drove recklessly at excessive speeds back to the city while loading the gun, hoping to attract attention and arrest. But it didn't work. She arrived in the city, parked her car, and walked to the St. Francis. Asked about her thoughts while she stood waiting for the President to appear, Moore described her continuing ambivalence:

> There was a point when anything could have stopped me and almost did. The most trivial little thing and I would have said, "Oh this is ludicrous. What am I doing standing here?" . . . There was a point whe[n] I was trapped. . . . I was actually up on the ropes, my hand in my purse, my finger on the trigger and the hammer back on the gun. I couldn't move, even if I had wanted to leave. I did try to leave once, but the crowd was just so tight. . . . There was a point where I thought, "This has to be the most ridiculous thing I have done in my entire life. What the hell am I doing here, getting ready to shoot the President?" I turned around to leave. Couldn't get through the crowd.[51]

Finally, after a three-hour wait outside the St. Francis Hotel while the President was addressing a World Affairs Council luncheon, he emerged at 3:30 P.M.—shortly before the time Sally had decided to leave to pick up her son after school. She raised the pistol and fired in what was less an attempt to kill than an act of contrition.

Conclusions

It was such ambivalence that seemed to have been the most distinguishing characteristic of Sally Moore's life. It was reflected in her family relationships, her marriages, her life styles, and finally her politics. Although stoutly and consistently defending her political motive after her arrest, the circumstances of her life reveal that her politics was, in essence, a means of regaining the personal acceptance she so badly needed from those who had rejected her.

In an almost allegorical explanation of her actions after the arrest, Moore alludes to her personal dilemma and frustration: "It [the assassination attempt] was a kind of ultimate protest against the system. I did not want to kill somebody, but there comes a point when *the only way you can make a statement* is to pick up a gun" (emphasis added).[52] The "statement" Sara Jane Moore wanted to make was not basically against the corrupt "system" that Gerald Ford represented (although she undoubtedly shared that opinion). Rather, politics was merely the vehicle for the more important *personal plea* for forgiveness she was making to her radical friends. Having failed in all previous efforts, Moore felt that she had reached the point where only political extremism and personal sacrifice could convey the sincerity of her contrition. To that extent her act was compensatory.

Consistent with such reasoning, Moore entered a plea of guilty to the charge of attempted assassination after a psychiatric examination confirmed her competence. Like Fromme, she was given a life sentence. Things had worked out fairly well for her. Satisfied that she had been forgiven, relieved that she had missed, Sara Jane Moore serenely began a new phase of her life in prison—a certified revolutionary with impeccable credentials.

Chapter Six · The Nihilist Perspective

ZANGARA AND BREMER

> I reached the point where I felt some kind of secret, abnormal, base gratification when I returned to my corner on some awful Petersburg night and felt intensely conscious that again that day I had committed another vile act, that what was done could never be undone again, and then inwardly, secretly I would gnaw, gnaw at myself for it, pestering and sucking the life out of myself until the bitterness eventually turned into some kind of shameful, damned sweetness and finally into a real definite pleasure.
> —Dostoyevsky, *Notes from Underground*

> I don't believe in nothing.
> —Giuseppe Zangara

> Ask me why I did it & I'd say "I don't know," or "Nothing else to do," or "Why not," or "I have to kill somebody."
> —Arthur Bremer

THE TYPE III SUBJECTS of this chapter—Giuseppe Zangara and Arthur Bremer—reflect a special kind of psychopathology.[a] What sets them apart from other psychopathic killers such as Richard Speck, Theodore Bundy, Gary Gilmore, and John Wayne Gacy is this: Speck, Gilmore, and Gacy *privately* directed their very controlled but perverse rage at victims who happened to represent some *segment* of society that each hated for a variety of reasons. Speck and Bundy chose young women;

[a] The terms psychopathology and sociopathology can be used interchangeably to refer to the characteristics of an antisocial personality.

Gilmore chose two young Mormon men; and Gacy, on a much more personal level, killed the young men he had seduced.

The rage of the Type III subject is more generalized, more inclusive of the *whole* society from which they are alienated. Unlike the ordinary psychopath, their victims are selected because they symbolize, or are representative of, a cross-section of society rather than a specific segment. Their victims may be the anonymous randomly selected targets of a sniper, such as Charles Whitman in the Texas tower, or Mark Essex on the roof of a New Orleans hotel; or they may be well-known political figures who represent society, such as the two politicians selected by Zangara and Bremer.

Zangara and Bremer differ from the other assassins and would-be assassins primarily in their perversity. Although their emotions were as distorted—some might conclude even disconnected—as the Type IV subjects discussed in Chapter Seven, their ability to perceive and reason remained virtually unimpaired. They led the most isolated lives of all the subjects considered. They hated society; they were close to no one and were totally alienated from life. It was from this alienation that their perversity and hostility developed. So complete was their self-estrangement that their capacity for love or empathy for anyone or anything was moribund. Zangara and Bremer knew only what they hated: there was nothing they loved, including themselves. It was this amorphous rage that was released by each when he opened fire on his victim. Each was thoughtfully aware of what he was about to do, why he was doing it, and the consequences. Their purpose was not political in any ideological sense: both would have been satisfied with any popular authority figure regardless of political persuasion. Rather, their motives were highly personal: they wanted to end their own lives in the most outrageous display of nihilistic contempt possible for a society they hated.

GIUSEPPE ZANGARA (1900-1933)

Not too much is known about Giuseppe Zangara. He was born in Ferruzzano in southern Italy on September 7, 1900, and lived there until August 18, 1923, when he sailed with his uncle, Vincent Cafaro, for the United States on the ship *Martha Washington*. Ten years of an isolated life later, he died in the electric chair at Raiford, Florida for the unintentional assassination of Mayor Anton Cermak of Chicago.

About all that is known about Zangara is what he volunteered after his arrest. No one knew him well. Even his uncle, with whom he lived for a year, knew little about him and was unable to add much to the scant details that Zangara had volunteered about himself.

Childhood

The seeds of his alienation and self-imposed isolation were sown when Zangara's mother died when he was only two years old. His father quickly remarried a widow with six daughters. Giuseppe was soon the outsider in a large peasant family living on the edge of economic survival in southern Italy.

At the age of six, after just beginning school, Giuseppe's father put him to work to help support the family. He described the event bitterly in broken English after his arrest:

> I was two months in school. My father came and take me out like this [makes a rough gesture] and say "You don't need no school. You need to work." He take me out of school. Lawyers ought to punish him—that's the trouble—he send me to school and I don't have this trouble. Government!

Asked if he hated government, Zangara replied "yes" through clenched teeth.[1]

The association between the hostility he felt toward his father and the government expressed so succinctly in this statement provides the clearest indication of Zangara's motives when he opened fire during the political rally at Bayfront Park in Miami. The "trouble" that Zangara referred to was not his arrest but the stomach problem that had plagued him from his childhood on. The malady, Zangara was convinced, was a direct result of being forced to perform hard labor carrying brick and tile as a child. Obsessed with the discomfort his stomach caused him, Zangara placed the blame on authority—to which he attributed an inextricable knot of characteristics shared by his father, wealthy capitalists, and heads of state. So closely entwined were these elements in Zangara's thinking that it was often difficult to determine to whom or to what he was referring. Asked why he hated the rich and powerful, Zangara could not explain without reference to his father:

> ZANGARA: Because rich people make me suffer and do this [stomach pain] to me. My father he sent me to school and then make me work.
>
> QUESTION: Joe, the rich man make you suffer? Since you were how old?

ZANGARA: Six years old.

QUESTION: Six years old?

ZANGARA: Yes, since they sent me to work in a big job.

QUESTION: What makes your belly burn?

ZANGARA: Because when I did tile work it hurt me there. It all spoil my machinery. My stomach—all my insides. Everything inside no good.

QUESTION: All because you worked when you were too young?

ZANGARA: Doctor say so. My father bring me to Doctor. Doctor told my father it spoil me.

QUESTION: The Doctor told your father it would spoil you [or] hurt you?

ZANGARA: Yes.

QUESTION: What did your father say?

ZANGARA: He said nothing because he say he have to send me to work.

QUESTION: Joe, do you like your father or do you hate him? [Do] you love your father?

ZANGARA: I don't know much.

QUESTION: He make you work?

ZANGARA: He didn't have no brains—no-no.[2]

The norms of the patriarchal culture of rural southern Italy and perhaps his small size—he was barely 5 feet tall and weighed only 105 pounds—probably prevented him from expressing his resentment directly toward his father. His only option was to escape the confines of his father's domain. So at the age of sixteen or seventeen (the records are unclear), he left home to join the Italian army. The discipline and drudgery of soldiering did nothing to diminish his growing resentment, but it did expand his perspective. The real causes of exploitation in the world and the incessant burning in his stomach, were, he now believed, political leaders. Thus, near the end of his hitch, he decided he would kill King Victor Emmanuel III of Italy; but he never got the opportunity.[3]

America

The following year, Zangara emigrated to the United States, arriving in Philadelphia on September 2, 1923. He soon found employment as a bricklayer in Paterson, New Jersey, where he and his uncle shared a room. Making as much as fourteen dollars a day, Zangara lived frugally and saved his money.[4] After a year—what proved to be his last year of any sustained social contact—his uncle decided to marry, and Giuseppe moved out because his new aunt, Josephine, didn't care for him.[5] From that time on he lived in almost complete isolation, except for the functional conversations he had with the men he occasionally hired to do subcontract construction work with him.

Working in spite of the stomach pain that gnawed at him constantly, Zangara was an irritable recluse who took no part in the boisterous social life of the Italian neighborhood. He didn't smoke, drink wine, or seek the company of women. His whole life was structured around a hypochondriac's obsession with his health.

In 1926, he had his appendix removed after doctors suggested that it might be causing his discomfort; but it didn't help. By 1927, he had saved enough money to permit some leisure, and he traveled to New Orleans hoping the warmer southern climate would ease his pain. It didn't. He returned and moved in with his uncle again, briefly, on 138 Jersey Street in Paterson but was soon asked to find another place. He began to work irregularly in Hackensack to make a little extra money and to compile a good record for his naturalization hearing. He became a naturalized citizen on September 11, 1929 in the common pleas court in Paterson.

After the stock market crash of 1929, jobs were hard to find and wages were low. But Zangara was not too worried. He was an industrious and competent bricklayer when he had to be, but he hated to work and didn't mind being unemployed. Moreover, he had saved enough to enable a man without demanding vices or a social life to live and travel. In 1930, he took a ship through the Panama Canal to Los Angeles. Not finding things to his liking in California, he returned by rail to Miami in 1931. After a brief stay, he left again for another short visit to Panama.

There is no record of his activities on these trips. It is probable that he lived no differently than he did in New Jersey. Which is to say he spent much time in his room, carefully choosing economical meals, leaving only to take brief strolls and occasionally place a bet—always alone. Then it was back to Paterson briefly before taking two ten-dollar-a-month rooms at 100 Green Street in Hackensack. Zangara lived in one room and kept the other empty to prevent anyone from moving next door.[6]

Anticipating the cold winter weather to come, he returned to Miami by bus in August 1932, where he got a cheap room at the Colonial Hotel. In December, he left the hotel to avoid the higher winter rates and moved into a single room at a house on 126 N.E. 5th Street. He ate frugal fifteen cent meals at Murphy's restaurant.

In New Jersey, Zangara had been getting by on about one hundred dollars a month, which he withdrew at regular intervals from a postal savings account he had in Paterson. After arriving in Miami, he tried to supplement his declining savings with a little judicious betting on the horses and dogs. If his withdrawals are any indication, he seemed to be doing fairly well. On August 23, 1932, he withdrew two hundred dollars and lived on that and his winnings, presumably, until the end of the year. Things apparently started to turn sour at the tracks in December, and on December 30, he withdrew another two hundred dollars. Within two weeks, he was broke again, and on January 20, he was forced to make another two hundred dollar withdrawal. His last deposit had been made on July 1, 1932.[7] Zangara was frustrated and angrier than usual.

By the second week of February, with less than a hundred dollars left and a stomach that permitted no rest, Zangara decided he was going to get even. He would kill that no good capitalist Herbert Hoover in Washington. Everybody was saying Hoover was the cause of the unemployment and the soup lines. Moreover, he was convinced that it was because of men like Hoover that he had to endure the constant misery of his burning stomach.

The Assassination Attempt

On Monday, February 13, Zangara left his room and walked to Davis's Pawn Shop on Miami Avenue and purchased a .32 caliber pistol for eight dollars with the thought that he would take a bus to Washington to meet Mr. Hoover. The next morning on a walk around the docks, he happened to pick up a newspaper and read that President-elect Franklin D. Roosevelt would visit Miami the next day and was scheduled to make an evening speech at the Bayfront Park.[8] Washington is cold in February, he reasoned, so why not remain in warm Miami and take out the President-elect instead. Besides, as he later observed, "Hoover and Roosevelt—everybody the same."[9]

The evening of February 15 was as moonlit and balmy as winter tourists expect February nights in Miami to be. At a little after 9 P.M., the President-elect arrived in a light blue Buick touring car that sparkled in the floodlights as it rolled toward the bandstand. The crippled Roosevelt, speaking from his open car, gave a brief speech and was finished before the diminutive Zangara could position himself among the taller bystanders to get a shot.

Chicago Mayor Anton Cermak and other officials moved toward the car to greet Roosevelt. The frustrated Zangara, unable to see his smiling and waving target, commandeered a rickety wooden folding chair and from this tottering perch opened fire. Five bullets tore into the flesh of as many bystanders—three head wounds, one abdominal wound and Mayor Cermak staggered against the President-elect's car as a bullet smashed into his right lung. Roosevelt miraculously escaped injury. Zangara was mobbed before being rescued by the police and hauled off to jail. He had forty-three dollars left in his pocket.[10]

Trial and Execution

Mayor Cermak lingered in the hospital while Zangara was tried and convicted on four counts of assault with intent to kill. Five days after the attack, he was sentenced to four twenty-year terms. He had pleaded guilty and expressed regret only that he had missed Roosevelt.[11] On the stand, Zangara was at times matter-of-fact and at others defiant. Complaining of his chronic stomach problems, he said: "I decided to kill . . . and make him [Roosevelt] suffer. I want to make it fifty-fifty since my stomach hurt I get even with capitalists by kill the President. My stomach hurt long time."[12]

When Judge E. C. Collins asked if he wanted to live, Zangara, who was still awaiting a possible second trial for murder depending upon the recovery of his victims, replied: "I no care. I sick all time. I just think maybe cops kill me if I kill President. Somebody hit my arm when I try it."[13] The judge asked if he knew what he was doing when he shot at Roosevelt. Scoffing at the idea that he was insane, Zangara answered:

> Sure I know. I gonna kill President. I take picture of President in my pocket. I no want to shoot Cermak or anybody except Roosevelt. I aimed at him. I shoot at him. But somebody move my arm. They fools. They should let me kill him.[14]

Attempting to get at the roots of Zangara's hostility, the judge asked: "Have the *American people* been kind to you?" "No." "Have *they mistreated you?*" "Yes. Everybody." His defense attorney asked him if he was sorry for what he did. "Sure," Zangara replied, "sorry I no kill him" (emphasis added).[15]

On March 6, 1933, Mayor Cermak died. Zangara was immediately indicted for first degree murder, entered a second remorseless guilty plea, and after a brief trial, Circuit Judge Ely O. Thompson sentenced him to die in the electric chair at the Florida State Penitentiary in Raiford. Zangara, his dark eyes flashing, shouted back to the judge:

"You give me electric chair. I'm no afraid that chair. You're one of capitalists. You is crook man too. Put me in electric chair. I no care."[16]

True to form, Zangara walked unaided to the electric chair on March 20, sat down, then spotting observers, shouted, "Lousy capitalists . . . no pictures!" Then after the shroud was placed over his head, his muffled shout was heard seconds before the first charge burned through his central nervous system: "Go ahead. Push the button." With not a single friend, and relatives who disavowed him, Zangara's unclaimed remains were buried in an unmarked prison grave.

Conclusions

In certain respects, Zangara resembled the neurotic Type II assassins. His act could be considered compensatory in a broadly defined sense, if displaced revenge for a bad stomach may be termed compensatory behavior. He also had some qualities of the Type I politically motivated subjects in his conviction that capitalism was the source of all evil. A sanity commission that examined him avoided the sanity issue and referred only to his rejection of social standards—the "distortions" of judgment (for example, capitalists are bad) combined with his at least average intelligence as evidence of a "psychopathic personality."[17]

Zangara's emotions were severely distorted by an obsessive generalized antisocial perspective and rejection of practically everything, including his own very existence. He was, apart from this driving force of negativism, emotionally dead. When asked about his political beliefs, he stated that he thought anarchism, socialism, communism, and fascism were "foolish."[18] He rejected religion, God, Jesus Christ, heaven, hell, and the existence of anything resembling an immortal soul.[19] When asked if he believed anything he read, he replied: "I don't believe in nothing. I don't believe in reading books because I don't think [and] I don't like it. . . . I got everything in my mind."[20]

Thus, unlike the Type I subjects, he had no real cause or ideology, in a positive sense, that he believed in. Unlike the neurotic Type II's, there was no love or anxiety-laden emotional attachment in his lonely, isolated life. He never dated a woman, had no friends, and belonged to a union he disliked only in order to work.[21] Unlike the psychotics, he had no delusions or hallucinations; his grasp of reality was good; his ability to reason was unimpaired, given his premises; and there was no evidence of hereditary mental illness in his family.[22] Intrigued by what this curious angry little man did *not* believe, his interrogators asked what, if anything, he *did* believe. His reply was one that could have been spoken by a Dostoyevskian character: "The land, the sky, the moon—what I see."[23]

His purpose in attacking Roosevelt and killing Cermak was not a political act in the usual sense, it was simply an expression of highly personal outrage against a society he hated: Zangara hated capitalism, and he hated American society because it was capitalistic. He could express that outrage symbolically by killing its leader. To end the miserable life that he had lived in the process was not considered a loss.

Throughout his life his most common emotions were indifference and anger. And he died indifferently, angry only because witnesses were given what he considered to be the privilege of watching. A loveless lifetime of personal torment had destroyed other emotions: happiness, sadness, pleasure, excitement, and fear. Nothing was left except his hatred for a society that had mistreated him, and a perverse satisfaction in his own death.

ARTHUR HERMAN BREMER (1950-)

In the cold, awful Milwaukee January of 1972, a young, marginally employed man began what was to be a deadly odyssey that would end some four months and many miles later in a steamy hot asphalt parking lot in Laurel, Maryland. His victim, Alabama governor and presidential candidate, George Wallace, would recover but would remain paralyzed from the waist down. The bullet that struck his spine and left him a cripple effectively ended George Wallace's controversial and highly successful political career. As a result, the unlikely George McGovern was able to win the Democratic presidential nomination, setting the stage for the 1972 Democratic equivalent of the Republican debacle of 1964. The incumbent, Richard M. Nixon, was swept into a second term in a major political landslide. His impressive victory provided the foundation for a fatal arrogance that would, as it had for his predecessor Lyndon Johnson in 1964, lead to Nixon's political destruction. President Nixon would learn later that he had, as Wallace's attacker's first choice for assassination, narrowly missed mortal destruction on an April presidential visit to Canada.

Frustrated in his attempts to kill the President, the would-be assassin later turned his attention, with some reluctance, to the more accessible presidential candidate, George Wallace. Arthur Herman Bremer was an intelligent, rational, at times even thoughtful, occasionally humorous would-be assassin who knew exactly what he was doing and why—

and it had little to do with politics. On a cognitive level, Bremer was as rational as the doctors who later examined him, but his emotions were stunted and seemed only tangentially consistent with his thoughts. Like Dostoyevsky's narrator in *Notes From Underground*,[24] horrible thoughts and acts triggered pleasurable emotions to define the perversity of his life. Distinctions—pleasure and pain, life and death, love and hate—became blurred in Bremer's mind. The origins of Bremer's perversity can be traced to that awful St. Petersburg night of emotional deprivation that characterized his childhood.

The Wallace Attack

On the warm, humid Monday afternoon of May 15, 1972, George Wallace, governor of Alabama and presidential candidate, walked to his special bullet-proof podium to address an open-air rally at a Laurel, Maryland shopping center. The Governor's talks followed a well-established format: before he would appear, a country western band would warm up the audience as surly, sunglassed, and conspicuous security personnel—the Secret Service as well as Wallace's personal cadre—scrutinized the shuffling, clapping crowds; then Wallace would appear and deliver well-rehearsed remarks about the evils of federal control, permissiveness, and the need for law and order.

The Governor was worried about attempts on his life. Earlier in Wheaton, Maryland, he had been heckled badly and afterward he expressed his concern, as he had on numerous other occasions, about the possibility of an assassination attempt. As a precaution, Wallace usually spoke from behind a specially built, bullet-proof podium and often wore a bullet-proof vest. That afternoon, the heat and humidity were particularly oppressive, especially on the asphalt parking area where he was to speak, and the Governor decided he would forego the vest.

When Wallace appeared shortly before 4 P.M., the crowd cheered and clapped. Unlike the Wheaton Plaza crowd, there was no noticeable heckling. He quickly launched into the familiar law and order theme that had resulted in surprisingly strong victories or showings in primary elections in Florida, Pennsylvania, and Indiana, as well as several deep-South states he had been expected to win easily. The Wallace campaign was rolling, and the fact that he appeared to be the strongest contender on the Democratic ticket was viewed with alarm by liberal Democrats, which, in this case, included most of the party establishment. And with President Nixon's popularity pegged at only 43 percent, even the incumbent was vulnerable to the appeals of the pugnacious little governor from Montgomery. George Wallace was a much more important figure in the 1972 presidential election than many observers, his would-be assassin being one of them, thought possible.

Shortly before the Governor's speech, a blond crew-cut, and pleasant-looking young man parked his 1967 Rambler Rebel in the shopping center lot and joined the gathering crowd. Arthur Bremer was becoming a familiar face at the recent Wallace rallies. Dressed in red, white, and blue combinations of jacket, shirt, and tie, adorned with huge Wallace campaign buttons, and always smiling beneath silvery sunglasses, Bremer appeared to be one of the Governor's most loyal and enthusiastic supporters—a male Wallace groupie of sorts.[25] Applauding, whistling, and shouting enthusiastically, even in indifferent crowds, Bremer was hard to miss.

When the perspiring speaker concluded his speech, he turned to leave. Then drawn by the shouts of the crowd, he turned back, took off his suit jacket, rolled up his sleeves, and walked toward the cheering throng. Bremer, among others, shouted, "Over here. Over here." As Wallace reached for one hand after another, an extended hand suddenly exploded sending a .38 caliber bullet smashing through his midsection. As he fell backward, the explosions continued amid screams of terror as the now grim-faced Bremer continued to fire four more shots hitting his victim in the right arm, shoulder, and chest. Two security men and a woman bystander were also wounded before Bremer was wrestled to the ground.[26]

At the arraignment on May 30, his attorney entered a plea of not guilty, based on insanity, to multiple counts of assault with intent to kill and lesser charges.[27] His victims all survived, but the Governor would never walk again. After jury selection and other legal preliminaries, Bremer's trial began on July 31 in the county courthouse in the village of Upper Marlboro, Maryland. Federal charges were also filed against Bremer in Baltimore.

Under Maryland law, the doctrine of "diminished responsibility" is recognized in such crimes. In other words, the prosecution must prove that the defendant—in this case, Bremer—did *not* lack "substantial capacity" to appreciate the criminality of his act or "conform his conduct" to the law and was, therefore, legally sane and responsible.[28] If a defendant lacks such capacity, he is considered legally insane and cannot, as a consequence, be held criminally responsible.

Coming of Age in Milwaukee

Arthur Herman Bremer was born on August 21, 1950, the fourth of five children. A social worker described Arthur's parents as "an amiable, bland, white unsophisticated couple in their late fifties, of modest height, from a low socioeconomic background, with minimal education, born, raised and now living in Milwaukee, Wisconsin."[29] His mother, Sylvia, had a particularly difficult life, and it showed. Abandoned to a foundling home by her mother, and raised under trying circumstances in a threatening and uncertain world, the very real difficulties she experienced as a youth produced a suspicious, withdrawn woman who was given to erratic hostile outbursts at both her husband and her children. Her husband insulated himself from these attacks with alcohol, which would, in a seemingly never-ending pattern of conflict, result in more hostility from his wife—for example, locking him out of the house, refusing to prepare meals, and so forth.[30] All this had a marked impact on the children. The older two sons and daughter fled to the streets as soon as possible, and their mistakes and misfortunes are recorded in a long history of difficulties with juvenile authorities in Milwaukee.[31] Each of the three older children had minimal contact with the family after adolescence.

Arthur's father, William, was a well-meaning man who worked regularly and tried in his way to be a good father. He took his boys to parades and once on a vacation to a lake, but the overall atmosphere of the family was either one of conflict or passive resignation.

Unlike his older brothers and sister, Arthur did not take to the streets, perhaps because his mother took a special interest in this pretty blond little boy. Seemingly intent on proving she was a good mother with her fourth child, she subjected him to ritualistic forms of attention that were also completely lacking in warmth and communication. For example, he was toilet-trained very early by placing him on the toilet every half hour. Thus he was always "clean" and, to that extent, proof that his mother was a good one.[32] He became a very compliant little boy who "never cried" but also didn't talk until he was four years of age—probably because there was literally nothing to talk about: he was "fed, toileted, clothed on some impersonal, extraneous schedule and never fondled or talked to." His infancy and childhood was characterized by a "gross lack of inter-personal stimulation."[33]

The only real emotional stimulation Arthur and the other children received was the punitive and randomly administered discipline of their mother. When she was questioned about events in Arthur's life, "she knew more about the condition [and] cleanliness of Arthur's underwear than she did about his age, or whether he had ever had a friend, a toy, an interest, or even a nightmare." She was also very proud that he never asked about sex or masturbated—seemingly unaware of the significance of the long hours, during adolescence, Arthur spent alone locked in the bathroom.[34]

Similarly, there was little communication of any sort with his father who appeared to be nothing more in an emotional sense than a benign nonentity who went to work, brought home his pay, skirmished regularly with his wife over financial matters, and got drunk occasionally to relieve his frustrations. He didn't think much beyond the day-to-day realities of earning a living and getting by. One day was pretty much like the next with little prospect of change, so his grasp of things beyond this limited perspective was quite tenuous. He did not understand his children, but, more importantly, he did not seem aware until after Arthur's arrest that there was much to understand. Usually befuddled by outside events when they impinged on his life, he took life a day at a time, passively resigned to the fact that whatever happened, things would go on much as they had before. He speculated during the trial that his son's attack on Wallace might not have occurred if the law providing eighteen-year-olds with the vote had been passed earlier.[35]

The effects of this fragmented, uncommunicative, and conflictive family environment produced a very withdrawn and emotionally warped child who concealed his anxiety under a smiling facade of compliant behavior. By the age of eight or nine, however, Arthur was beginning to have suicide fantasies and contemplated his own death stretched across the railroad tracks near his home. About this time, he seemed to find solace in a neighborhood church and thought for a time that he would become a priest. But the family moved, and he never returned to church. As he told a psychiatrist after his arrest, if the family had not moved, "maybe I would have been a priest by now."[36] Whether he would have or not, the move meant the termination of perhaps the first positive association in his life.

About this time, although it is not clear whether the two events are related, he failed the fifth grade because, he explained simply, "I did failing work."[37] Discouraged, he decided he would end his life before the age of thirteen.

But he didn't. He entered South Division High School, and his years there passed uneventfully. He had few friends, did not date, and, except for a year as a second-string member of the football team, engaged in no school activities.[38] An average student who did not apply his high basic intelligence,[b] Arthur received his diploma in 1968 registering possibly the only success in his life.

[b] Bremer had registered a low average IQ in high school, probably because he did not care about the test. After his arrest, he was variously tested and compiled scores on the Weschsler Adult Intelligence Scale ranging from 114 to 120. These scores place him in the "bright-normal" to "superior" range of intelligence. Only 10 percent of the population score in this range.

During his senior year of high school, his parents noticed a marked change in his behavior: his passivity and compliance disappeared and he became irritable and outspokenly aggressive toward them. He complained about his mother's cooking and made insulting remarks to her about it. A compulsively neat person up until this time, he refused to keep his room clean; moreover, he demanded clean washcloths, towels, and bedding two and three times a week. He also became very extravagant in his dress. He argued with his father over which television programs to watch; he left pornographic material scattered about his room. His entire demeanor shifted from passive compliance to aggressive provocation.[39]

After graduation, he worked at various menial jobs as a busboy at the Milwaukee Athletic Club and the swank Pieces of Eight restaurant and as a janitor at the Story Elementary School in Milwaukee. In all of these jobs, fellow workers testified that they knew little about him except that he did his job and kept to himself. No one could recall more than a brief conversation with him and that Arthur liked to antagonize a supervisor at one of the restaurants by pouring water into glasses from eye level.[40]

In September 1970, Bremer enrolled at the Milwaukee Technical College. He took courses in psychology, art, writing, and photography and turned in indifferent performances.[41] His teachers and fellow students recalled little about him. He made no impression on anyone and dropped out after a year.

Falling in Love

While working and taking courses in his familiar indifferent way, Arthur's behavior at home continued its disruptive course until October 1971, when, in an argument, he struck his father and announced he was moving out.[42] At this time, Arthur was working as a janitor at the Story Elementary School. During this same month, he met his first love, a fifteen-year-old sophomore from West Division High School who worked at Story as a hall monitor. Seizing what seemed to him an opportunity of a lifetime, Arthur got his own apartment and began to chart the course for his first romantic adventure.

After a few weeks of furtive meetings in the halls, the twenty-one-year-old janitor asked the fifteen-year-old hall monitor, Joan Pembrick, for a date—his first—on November 19, 1971. The next day, Saturday, they went to an art museum after missing a movie, then walked around the Lake Michigan beach area before going to a restaurant. He was enthralled with her. But she became angry because of his prying questions about her personal life and his suggestion that her friends really didn't like her. He told her she could confide in him because he knew a good deal about psychology and psychiatry and would help her over her "hang ups."[43]

Bremer's brief relationship with his young girlfriend provides some revealing insights into the continuing development of his Type III antisocial personality. Ms. Pembrick was attracted to Bremer primarily because she was flattered by the attention of this older and presumably more mature man. She very quickly realized that Arthur was not only terribly immature but knew virtually nothing about the ordinary social graces; he also lacked any degree of sexual sophistication.

Bremer's clumsy and inane sexual overtures remind one of a comedy routine. His sexual socialization came primarily from "sex comics" type pornography, which was found in his apartment—and it showed. He thought the way to a girl's heart was through an arousing display of cartoon characters engaged in a variety of sexual acts. His idea of sexual sophistication was an indiscriminate use of vulgar language and terms. For example, on one date at Ms. Pembrick's home, she introduced him to her young cousin. Bremer, who knew neither of the girls very well, began to make what he considered to be amusing and sexually stimulating remarks about the cousin's "big ass and boobs."[44]

A few days before Christmas 1971, Bremer took his young date to a concert featuring the rock group, Blood, Sweat, and Tears. He was elated and could hardly contain his excitement. While they were standing in line outside the concert hall, the normally withdrawn Bremer, who neither smoked, drank, nor experimented with drugs, attempted to demonstrate his man-about-town "cool" by sweeping an unknown girl into his arms and kissing her. He was promptly reported to a policeman, who warned him to control himself. Only momentarily embarrassed, Arthur's attempts to impress his date and her friends continued during the concert where he jumped from his seat, swayed back and forth to the music, and applauded enthusiastically, often at inappropriate times. Ms. Pembrick's young friends, who sat in front of the couple, thought her date was the most absurd person in the hall.[45]

Unaware of such appraisals, Arthur's buoyancy continued after the concert when he slyly complained that he could barely walk because of discomfort in the area of his genitals. He went on to explain to his disbelieving companion that he had to take medication to prevent his hugely distended organ from "rupturing." And then the plaintive clincher: that evening he had forgotten to take his pills. But it didn't work. He had to take his date home without assistance.[46]

These episodes are also reminiscent of the film *Taxi Driver* in which

Robert DeNiro's superbly acted character, a would-be assassin named Travis Bickle, ineptly attempts to develop a relationship with an attractive political campaign worker.[c] The young woman tolerantly agrees to go out with the shy young man only to be appalled when he escorts her with prom-night innocence to a grainy porno film.

Thus, Bremer, like his *Taxi Driver* counterpart, was perplexed when his true love refused to see him again. After some five dates and numerous phone conversations, on January 13, 1972, Joan's mother confirmed to Arthur her daughter's wish that he not bother her again.[47] That same day he went to Casanova Guns and purchased the .38 caliber pistol he would use four months and two days later.[48]

The breakup was devastating for Arthur. The relationship for him had been "the happiest time of my life."[49] And he was desperate. For the girl, the brief friendship and its conclusion meant little. Unable to call as a result of the mother's injunction, he decided on a last desperate scheme to get her attention. On January 15, he shaved his head except for his sideburns. Then confronting the startled teenager, he jerked off a knit cap exposing the incongruous bald head gleaming above the bushy sideburns and wide smile only to have her brush past him without a word. He realized that the first and only person who had meant anything in his empty existence was gone. His life, it seemed, was a complete failure.[50] He brooded in his drab apartment, living on cold cereal, bread and peanut butter, and whatever he could scrounge at the Athletic Club where he worked indifferently until about the middle of February when he quit.[51]

Despair, Perversity, and the Political Targets

During this time, he became preoccupied with suicidal and homicidal fantasies. On one cold evening, he attached a noose around his neck and scrawled "KILLER" across his forehead with a blue felt marker. Then pulling his knit cap down to conceal his forehead and buttoning his heavy coat over the noose he proceeded to a Milwaukee diner for a last meal. His plan was to tie the rope to the railing of a busy midtown bridge, then shoot himself while perched on the rail so that he would drop to hang as a grisly spectacle for passing commuters.

---

[c] This film, which was made after Bremer's diary was published, appears to have drawn heavily on some aspects of Bremer's personality in developing the character of Travis Bickle. The film was subsequently linked in 1981 to the motives of President Reagan's attacker, John Hinckley. Hinckley, claiming love for a teen-age actress in the film, seemingly adopted a role that, in his mind, resembled the would-be assassin. In the film, the DeNiro character expresses his love in an act of violence.

However, a waitress was kind to this strange young man who ate while perspiring heavily in his knit cap and tightly buttoned winter coat. Moved by her attention, he left a generous tip. Shortly after, as he stood in the middle of the bridge about to get on with his plan, the now off-duty waitress walked by and smiled at him. Touched again by her kindness, he decided not to go through with it.[52]

On another occasion during this period, he considered hijacking an armored car, and then with a hostage to hold the police at bay, he planned to park the vehicle in a busy intersection and kill as many people as possible with rifle fire through the vehicle's slit windows. These and similar plans were considered before the decision was made about March 1, 1972 to kill President Nixon.[53] Like another blond crew-cut young man, Charles Whitman, who in 1966 killed thirteen people and wounded thirty-one others from his perch in a clock tower on the University of Texas campus, Arthur Bremer wanted to die in the most outrageous and contemptuous manner possible. He hated society and what it meant to him. There was never much to live for, and now with his only love lost, there was nothing.

But why did he choose Nixon—a political target—when Bremer had never been interested in politics? The reason is understandable within the context of his antisocial Type III perspective and his conclusion that death as well as life was meaningless. Living now without any emotion, save a pervasive contempt for everyone and everything, the distinction between being alive and being dead had become blurred.[54] On an emotional level, Bremer felt nothing—neither joy nor sorrow, pleasure nor pain. He was emotionally dead except for an emerging perverse satisfaction in that condition. Even the pain and depression of his lost love appeared to become submerged in his alienation and contempt for "the basic values of society."[55]

But he remained fully aware of the significance of external actions and events, as well as his own self-interest, given his premises. In his assessment, there was no better way to show his contempt for society than by killing its leader who, incidentally, could have been anyone as far as he was concerned but happened to be the controversial Richard Nixon.

Bremer was not more or less angry with the President than he was with the anonymous pedestrians on the streets of Milwaukee who he had earlier considered killing; nor were Nixon's policies any more offensive to him than the behavior of the war protestors who denounced those policies. He could kill some of them, but who would notice? Or, more importantly, care? They were marginal to society just as he was. He needed an audience for his perversity, and a celebrity like the President would ensure that. Besides who could remember Charles Whitman? On the other hand, who could forget Booth, Oswald and Sirhan?[d] Sometime during this period, he began to keep a diary to log thoughts and events as he began an odyssey that would criss-cross through Michigan, Ontario, and New York and end forty-two days later at the shopping center in Laurel, Maryland.

The Diary

Bremer's diary is interesting because it provides a first-hand glimpse of the frustration, perversity, and reason that motivated him. Some critics have questioned whether he actually wrote the diary, largely because it was widely believed that he was not that intelligent.[56] But, in fact, virtually all the pre-trial psychological testing revealed a very intelligent, if disturbed, young man who had literary aspirations.[57]

The entire diary was read in court by Bremer's attorney with the intent that it would convince the jury that the insanity plea which had been entered in his defense was valid. But the strategy backfired because what the diary reveals is that its author's frustration and anger were reasoned, controlled, and focused: psychopathological, antisocial, but not psychotic.

What also emerges from its pages is a person contemptuous of life, but one who is at the same time able to make sophisticated subjective distinctions where humor and irony, rather than hostility, provide a more effective vehicle for his contempt. And finally, it is clear that Bremer had carefully considered what he was about to do and completely understood the consequences.

The diary begins on April 4, 1972 and describes his thoughts and experiences as he pursued Richard Nixon in Canada where the President was making a state visit. Driving from one location to another, the stalking Bremer never got the chance he needed to carry through with his plans. His random thoughts provide glimpses of a complex, alienated but reasoned person who knew exactly what he was doing and why. His diary reveals a universal contempt for himself and society, a well-developed, if bizarre, sense of humor and irony, and the deep frustration of a misspent life.

Bremer was disdainful of the Nixon protestors in Canada who were constantly milling around waving placards and chanting slogans and, not incidentally, frustrating his efforts to get close to the President:

---

[d] Bremer had read books on each (Trial testimony, pp. 661, 952, 963, 1024, 1027, 1036, 1264).

"They'se nothing. There the new establishmen. To be a rebel today you have to keep a job, wear a suit [as he was] & stay apolitical. Now THAT'S REBELLION!."⁵⁸ᵉ Later these observations about a demonstration leader:

> Mr. Bull Horn bounced his voice off the building with a couple of dozen "Nixon Go Home's." He turned to address the crowd. Some other guys spoke to. A wild shouting idiot shouted some senseless phrases. [He was] The kind of guy Hollywood hires to play the wagon train attacking Indian.⁵⁹

Bremer's contempt was often expressed humorously. Concerned that Canadian customs officials might detect his two concealed pistols and ammunition, he took elaborate precautions before crossing the border. Later he recorded his thoughts as he anxiously drove up to the border station only to be alternately relieved and disappointed by the cursory inspection he received:

> I slowed down to be inspected. Canada had crooked teeth and a moustach. He asked where I was from, where I wanted to go, for how long I wanted to go, for how long and if I had anything to declare. (I was prepared for this last question, I was going to say, "I declair its a nice day." But I just asked, "What should I declair?").⁶⁰

Once in Ottawa, Bremer had difficulty finding a place to stay. He had hoped to stay in the same hotel as the press corps so that it would be easier to determine the President's whereabouts and schedule during his visit. Finding the press corps hotel full, Bremer had to settle for only a drink at the hotel bar. Already frustrated, he was further annoyed by a bartender who failed to serve the Manhattan he ordered on ice. Dubbing the seemingly truculent bartender "Ice-less," Bremer describes an incident that occurred moments later when a reporter asked the same bartender for a drink to take back to the press room:

> Ice-less said it was against the rules. A short argument. The reporter lost.
> "That's Canada for you," I said.
> "It's not Canada, it's just this (points to the bar-keeper) fucking cant!" (Reporter replies) Walks quickly away.

ᵉ In this book, the diary is quoted from the trial transcript, so the page numbers refer to the transcript and not the published version. There are numerous misspellings and these are left uncorrected except in a few instances where to do so would have sacrificed clarity. (See also, Bremer, 1972.)

"A fucking cant is the best kind of cant to be," I say to the amusement of a fat man in glasses.[61]

Such expressions of a fairly well-developed sense of Rabelaisian humor, however, were interspersed with more direct and aggressive statements of frustration and hostility. On April 24, 1972, after failing in his plan to kill the President, he scrawled angrily:

Shit! I am thruerly pissed off. About a million things. Was pissed off befor I couldn't find a pen to write this down. This will be one of the most closely read pages since the Scrolls in those caves. And I couldn't find a pen for 40 seconds & went mad. My fuse about burnt. There's gona be an explosion soon. I had it. I want something to happen. I was sopposed to be Dead a week & a day ago. Or at least in a few hours. FUCKING tens-of-1,000's of people & tens-of-millions of $. I'd just like to take some of them with me &Nixy.

Then scrawled in huge letters:

ALL MY EFFORTS & NOTHING CHANGED.

And on the next page:

Just another god Damn failure.

He continues:

But I want em all to know. I want a big shot and not a little fat noise [the mayor of Milwaukee] I want that god damn [Nixon] tired of writting about it. About what I was gonna do about what I failed to do. About what I failed to do again and again. Traveling around like a hobo or some kind of comical character. I'm as important as the start of WWI [the assassin of Archduke Ferdinand]. I just need the little opening & a second of time. Nothing has happened for so long. 3 months [since his girlfriend broke off their relationship]. the 1st person I held a conversation with in 3 months was a near naked girl rubbing my erect penis & she wouldn't let me put it thru her [refers to an expensive and unrewarding experience in a New York massage parlor].

Then in large letters:

FAILURES.[62]

By his next entry some ten days later on May 4, 1972, he has seen the film "Clockwork Orange" ("Fantasizing myself as the Alek on the screen . . ."), traveled back to Milwaukee, taken long walks to think and get himself settled down, and decided that he would kill presidential candidate George C. Wallace because Wallace was more accessible than Nixon.[63]

After his Milwaukee respite, the Rabelaisian humor returned as he confidently awaited an opportunity to shoot the Alabama governor on a forthcoming Michigan speaking tour. In the following passage, he laments his new target's lack of international visibility, compares Wallace disparagingly to the late FBI director, J. Edgar Hoover, and other possible competing and more newsworthy events:

> It seems I would of done better for myself to kill the old G-man Hoover, In death, he lays with Presidents. Who the hell ever got buried in "Bama" for being great? He certainly won't be buryed with the snobs in Washington. SHIT! I won't even rate a T.V. enterobtion in Russia or Europe when the news breaks—they never heard of Wallace. If something big in Nam flares up I'll end up at the bottom of the 1st page in America. The editors will say—"Wallace dead? Who cares." He won't get more than 3 minutes on network T.V. news. I don't expect anybody to get a big thobbing erection from the news. You know, a storm in some country we never heard of kills 10,000 people—big deal—pass the beer and what's on T.V. tonight.[64]

A few days later, on May 7, he mockingly speculates about the publicity problem and muses about organizing assassins:

> It bothers me that there are about 30 guys in prison now who threatened the Pres & we never heard a thing about 'em. Except that they're in prison.
>
> Maybe what they need is organization. "Make the First Lady a Widow, Inc." "Chicken in Every Pot and Bullet in Every Head, Com., Inc."
>
> They'll hold a national convention every 4 years to pick the exacutioner. A winner will be chosen from the best entry in 40,000 words or less (preferably less) upon the theame "How to Do a Bang-Up Job of Getting People to Notice You" or "Get It Off Your Chest; Make Your Problems Everybody's."[65]

In Dearborn, Michigan, where he had hoped to shoot the Alabama governor, Bremer describes an amusing scene that occurred when he was hurriedly changing into a suit and tie at a gas station on his way to a Wallace rally. In his haste, he can't find his belt and then speculates about the problem this presents because he has nowhere to hide his pistol. He imagines entering the hall beltless, amid security guards, and having one guard return the pistol that has just dropped down his trouser leg clanking on the floor with a polite, "Excuse me sir, is this your gun?"[66]

After his arrest, Bremer's humor appeared to escape two doctors who examined him. When a psychiatrist asked him to explain the meaning of the proverb "people who live in glass houses shouldn't throw stones," Arthur deadpanned: "People who live in glass houses shouldn't." The psychiatrist later cited this as an example of "parahumor" or, as he explained, "verbal behavior with some of the form but without the feeling of ordinary jokes or humorous remarks"; it was symptomatic of Arthur's "schizophrenia."[67]

Later a clinical psychologist viewed Bremer's self-deprecating sense of irony as evidence of "his egocentricity and grandiosity." This conclusion was based on Bremer's habit of mockingly referring to his guards as his "entourage." On other occasions, confined in his cell, facing a hopeless trial on very serious charges, the curious doctors would comment that he seemed depressed and inquire why. His replies to such inquiries: "It's not easy being a star," or "it's lonely at the top." Such remarks were cited as evidence of his delusions of grandeur.[68]

The Motive

But what about his motive? I have suggested throughout that Bremer's motive was the personal and provocative motive of a Type III assassin. Yet in the statements quoted above, he also seems concerned with publicity. Is it possible that Bremer was merely a publicity-seeking weirdo desiring, as the stereotype of assassins suggests, a moment in the limelight? Although Bremer seemingly looked forward to the publicity that his act was calculated to generate, his primary purpose was to insult or outrage society in the most perverse manner possible—and publicity was important only to achieve that end. Bremer wanted to show his contempt for a society he did not fit into and therefore hated. Thus, at one point he wrote: "Ask me why I did it & I'd say 'I don't know,' or 'Nothing else to do,' or 'Why not' or 'I have to kill somebody.' "[69] But Bremer's seeming indifference in these laconic responses are meant to provoke. Here is a man who has committed a calculating, premeditated, and horrible act for no reason other than he felt like it. His act becomes, therefore, that much more outrageous and perverse. This is not the existential estrangement of Camus's murderer, Meursault.[70] Other statements by Bremer contrast sharply with such an image. Not only did Bremer plan to offend and outrage, he wanted the world to witness it and pay for the privilege:

> Hey world! Come here! I wanna talk to ya!
>
> If I don't kill—if I don't kill myself I want you to pay thru the nose, ears, & belly button for the beginning of this manuscript. The 1st pages are hidden & will preserve a long time. If you don't pay me for them, I got no reason to turn 'em over—understand punk!? One of the reasons for this action is money and you the American (is there another culture in the free world?) public will pay me. *The silent majority will be my benifactor in the biggest hijack ever!* [Emphasis added.]

Then predicting, or more accurately, hoping his act would start an epidemic of assassinations, he concluded:

> It was kidnapping in the early part of this century. Then hijack[ing] became popular. . . . I'm gonna start the next crime binge! HA. HA. *And the silent majority will back me all IRONY!! The Way! IRONY!!* [Emphasis added.]

Thus in selecting first Nixon and then Wallace as targets, Bremer was in a very real sense aiming at the values of the so-called silent majority of a hated society. He recognized that the success of his act hinged on the accuracy of his presumption that Nixon and Wallace did symbolize majority sentiment in the country. On one occasion, observing some McGovern gains in the polls, he expressed some misgivings:

> The whole country's going liberal. I can see it in McGovern. You know my biggest failure may be when I kill Wallace. I hope everone screams & hollers and everything!! I hope the rally goes mad!!![71]

The Sanity Question

But was Bremer mad? This was the question before the jury at the courthouse in the sleepy, summer heat of tiny Upper Marlboro, Maryland, in July and August 1972. More specifically, was Arthur Bremer able to distinguish right from wrong, and was he in control of his behavior at the time of the shooting? As might have been predicted, the eight psychiatrists and two clinical psychologists who testified at the trial divided on the issue according to whether their testimony was called by the defense or prosecution. All agreed on the symptoms; the disagreement was on the interpretation of the symptoms and the degree to which Bremer could be held accountable for his act.

The jury decided that Bremer was not only completely aware of what he was doing but that he had coldly considered the various consequences for himself in the most rational manner. His methodical planning, adjustment to change, and ability to exercise appropriate restraint throughout the period he stalked Nixon, and then Wallace, are apparent in his own words. Describing one of his several attempts to shoot Nixon in Ottawa, he writes:

> I didn't want to attrack too much attention standing near the barracade for so long waiting for Nixon. And I was concerned with my appearance [he wore a black business suit and conservative tie] & composure after the bang bangs. I wanted to shock the shit out of the SS [Secret Service] men with my calmness. A little something to be remmened [remembered] by.[72]

Later in Michigan on Wallace's trail, he speculates about his future:

> Really would feel better if Michigan had a death penalty. The trial might be interesting but after visits from the attorneys . . . how will I spend my time in my little cell? You know, suicide is a birth right.[73]

The same day he had written, "1 am one sick assissin. Pun! Pun!."[74]

But was he too "sick" to control his behavior? Hardly. He was calculating, careful, and on one occasion, at least, compassionate. Following the ranting frustration precipitated by his failure to kill President Nixon in Ottawa, Bremer's heart raced with excitement as he stood watching his new target, George Wallace, walk toward him after a May 13 rally in Dearborn, Michigan. As Wallace, waving goodbyes to the cheering crowd, walked to within fifteen feet and a pane of glass from Bremer, the would-be assassin was again frustrated but well under control:

> Two fifteen year old girls had gotten in front of me. Their faces were 1 inch from the glass I would shutter with a blunt-nosed bullet. They [would be] blinded and disfigured. I let Wallace go only to spare these 2 stupid innocent delighted kids. We pounded on the window together at the governor. [There would] be other times.[75]

Throughout the period he stalked Wallace, Bremer frequently speculated rationally about whether he would be killed in the planned attack. On May 8, one week before the shooting, he wrote:

Gotta leave [Milwaukee] soon. I'll stay here long enought to eat all the food up. Still don't know weather its trail [trial] & prison for me or bye bye brains. I'll just have to decide that at the last few seconds. Must seceed. Gota.[76]

Then he speculates about the future value of the diary he is keeping and reaches a typical self-deprecating conclusion. Note that his flights of fancy were always well-grounded in a keen sense of reality and irony. First the fancy:

As late as yesterday I had thought of burying this whole paper [the diary] & reading it after I had gone to Hollywood (I KNOW IT SOUNDS INSANE SO DON'T THINK IT) & making my fortune on the old silver screen.

Then the reality:

Sure! The same way I was gonna fuck 4 million of New York's finest.[77]

Also, it is interesting to observe his awareness of past assassins and their fates—particularly Sirhan's. On May 5, he had checked out two books on Robert Kennedy's assassin: Robert Blair Kaiser's "*R. F. K. Must Die!*" and *Sirhan* by Aziz Shibab.[78] He wrote: "I'm gonna get convicted. It's gonna be very similar to Sirhan. Might as well flaunt the fucker. On second thought, fucing's too good for him [Sirhan]."[79]

While on the Wallace trail, Bremer killed time in a bar, and his thoughts again turned to Sirhan:

Had 2 Manhatins. Drank 2 glasses of water. The drinks didn't bother me much at all. Except financialy. A buck each. Nice little bar. Good bar tender. I thought of Sirhan. He had 4 drinks & was, he claimed drunk when he did his thing.[80]

When doctors examined Bremer after his arrest, they observed his high intellectual capacity, above average vocabulary, excellent perception, good conceptual ability, and absence of any organic brain damage.[81] The most intriguing of the results, however, was Bremer's extraordinary response to the Rorschach test. This procedure requires the subject to interpret what they see in ten ink blots that are presented on cards. The typical response rate is generally between twenty and forty-five interpretations per patient. Bremer recorded over eight hundred responses in his first test and over five hundred in his second.[82] It was the interpretation of this reponse that seemed to provide the most tangible support for a conclusion that Bremer was insane (or lacked the capacity to appreciate the criminality of his act or to conform his conduct to the law). Even on this point, however, the examining psychiatrists and clinical psychologists could not agree on the degree to which such a response rate revealed symptoms of mental illness.[83]

More important, however, was the fact (the significance of which was seemingly overlooked by the doctors) that Bremer had read Robert Blair Kaiser's book on Sirhan.[84] In that book, Kaiser describes the general confusion in interpreting Sirhan's Rorschach test results and comments on the highly subjective scoring procedures. For example, he reports that some of the jurors administered the test to themselves and were surprised to learn that their responses were "startlingly similar to Sirhan's 'paranoid' reactions."[85] Moreover, some ten additional pages were devoted to a discussion of the Rorschach test results and the scoring procedures throughout the book as well as an appendix that reproduced the ten cards with Sirhan's responses noted on them.[86] Given Bremer's interest in Sirhan, it seems reasonable to suspect, as the prosecution did, that this information could have been used by him in a manipulative fashion. Having also had a college level course in psychology, he would probably have learned about the average response rate to this test; and it would not require an advanced degree to conclude that increasing one's responses ten- to twentyfold over the average would be a relatively easy way to raise diagnostic eyebrows if that were the intended result.

With the psychiatrists deadlocked on either side of the sanity issue, the jury made its decision largely on the basis of what Arthur Bremer had written and not on what the doctors had to say about him. They found him guilty on all counts. Before the judge sentenced him to sixty-three years in the Maryland State Penitentiary, he was asked if he had anything he would like to say. Bremer replied in the only statement he ever made that was faintly remorseful:

> Well, Mr. Marshall [the prosecutor] mentioned that he would like society to be protected from someone like me. Looking back on my life I would have liked it if society had protected me from myself. That's all I have to say at this time.[87]

Conclusions: Zangara and Bremer

There is some insight in that laconic statement. Bremer is a young man who grew up in an environment almost devoid of positive emotional experiences. As we have seen, by the age of thirteen he had virtually given up hope of finding any satisfaction and happiness in life. His last chance at happiness was a fifteen-year-old girl he barely knew. But that failed because Arthur simply did not know how—he had never learned—to relate to anyone on an ordinary emotional level. Thus despite the fact of his high intelligence, pleasant appearance, and seemingly good intentions, he was an outcast who had no idea of how to conduct himself in social situations. The girlfriend's rejection and his symbolically shaved head, whether intended or not, confirmed the misfit status he had always known was his. That confirmation was later underscored by his humiliating experience at a New York massage parlor. But unfortunately Bremer never understood why. And his response to the disappointments of his life was simply to shut down emotionally.

Giuseppe Zangara was much the same: the loveless past, the resentment of a father who denied him a normal childhood by forcing him into child labor at the age of six. He, too, never felt part of society. He was, like Bremer, only its victim. Intelligent but emotionless except for the chronic anger and resentment festering beneath an indifferent facade, a description of Bremer appears to fit Zangara equally well.

Because Zangara did not have the extensive psychiatric examination that Bremer received, his case is more speculative, but the similarities are there. Bremer resembles Zangara more than any other assassin. The persona of both was one of detachment, of dealing with life only on a cognitive level. Neither had a real political purpose—any prominent political leader would do, since it was not ideology that motivated them but simply a desire to outrage a society in which they were outcasts. Nor was their act compensatory: it appears that neither one had learned to love because love was something alien—something that had been missing from both their childhoods.

Thus, there were no significant others for whom their ultimate acts were really intended; they were not neurotic in that sense. And the usual symptoms of psychosis were absent: no intellectual impairment, delusions, or hallucinations. Other than their atrophied emotions, they resembled the psychotic Type IV assassins only in their social isolation. But unlike the Type IV subjects, their rage was not focused or personalized: it was diffuse. And they were not divinely inspired. They did not seek to save the Republic as did Guiteau and Schrank, or seek redress for imagined grievances as Lawrence. They scoffed at society, denied its conventions, and, most importantly, rejected its morality. For these reasons, each concluded that the most meaningful comment on a meaningless society was to commit an atrocity; an act vile and reprehensible, planned and publicly executed so there could be no mistake of their perverse intent. But the real outrage, each realized, would come when society understood that the ultimate meaning and significance of their despicable acts was the absence of real meaning or purpose, like their own miserable lives.

So as the self-declared exiles from human society Dostoyevsky wrote about, each was motivated by anger, loneliness, and boredom with lives neither had learned to live. And like those characters, both Bremer and Zangara appeared to derive some satisfaction, perhaps pleasure, in their own debasement. To paraphrase G. K. Chesterton, a Type III subject is not someone who has lost his reason; rather he is someone who has lost everything *but* his reason.

Chapter Seven · The Psychotics

LAWRENCE, GUITEAU, AND SCHRANK

> It is for me, gentlemen, to pass upon you, and not you upon me.
> —Richard Lawrence (to the jury)

> I presume the President was a Christian and that he will be happier in Paradise than here. It will be no worse for Mrs. Garfield, dear soul, to part with her husband this way than by natural death. He is liable to go at any time anyway.
> —Charles Guiteau

> While writing a poem, someone tapped me on the shoulder and said: "Let not a murderer take the presidential chair. Avenge my death." I could clearly see Mr. McKinley's features.
> —John Schrank

OF THE SIXTEEN INDIVIDUALS selected for study, only three possess clear and undeniable symptoms of psychosis. Although each represents a unique case, differing in interesting ways from the others, the symptoms of severe emotional and cognitive distortion, hallucination, delusion, poor reality contact, and, consequently, social isolation are present in each. However, the previously applied label, paranoid schizophrenic, does not fit as neatly as some have suggested.[1] Of the three psychotic assassins—Richard Lawrence, Charles Guiteau, and John Schrank—only Lawrence had symptoms of the extreme and irrational suspicion and hostility that characterize the paranoid schizophrenic. Consider the evidence in each of these three cases.

RICHARD LAWRENCE (c. 1800-1861)

On the cold, gray Friday of January 30, 1835, Richard Lawrence, armed with two pistols, attempted to take the life of President Andrew Jackson. Standing on the east portico of the Capitol, Lawrence calmly waited for Jackson to emerge from the funeral services of Congressman Warren R. Davis. As the elderly and frail Jackson, leaning heavily on the arm of Treasury Secretary Levi Woodbury, walked from the rotunda, Lawrence stepped from the crowd and drawing a pistol from beneath his cloak took aim from a distance of no more than eight feet and pulled the trigger. When the pistol misfired (only the cap exploded noisily but harmlessly), Lawrence pulled a second pistol from his pocket and fired again, this time also with no effect. In both cases, the exploding cap failed to detonate the powder which, from that range, most certainly would have ended the stooped and white-haired President's life. Fortunately for Jackson, the powder and balls in both pistols had apparently fallen out while in Lawrence's pocket.

Lawrence was quickly subdued while the President himself, enraged by the event, struggled to get at him with his cane shouting, "Let me alone! Let me alone! I know where this came from." Jackson had immediately and incorrectly assumed that certain political opponents were behind the attack.[2]

The Attacker

Richard Lawrence was born in England—the date remains uncertain but probably in 1800 or 1801—and came to this country with his parents when he was about twelve years of age. The family settled in the Washington area, and Lawrence seems to have lived an uneventful and normal life as a house painter until November 1832 when he abruptly announced he was returning to England. Until that time, Richard was typically described by the relatives and acquaintances who testified at his trial as "a remarkably fine boy . . . reserved in his manner; but industrious and of good moral habits."[3]

After a month's absence, Lawrence returned to Washington in December explaining that he had decided against the trip to England because the weather was too cold. His brother-in-law, Mr. Redfern, testified that soon after, Lawrence left once again with the intention of going to England to study landscape painting. But soon after his arrival in Philadelphia, he returned a second time, explaining that "people" prevented him from going on to England. He added that the government also opposed his going. He complained that when he arrived in Philadelphia, he found the newspapers so full of attacks on his character and plans that he had no choice but to return to Washington until he could hire his own ship and captain for the trip.[4]

These incidents mark most clearly the first symptoms of Lawrence's advancing mental deterioration. At this point, he gave up his job and first expressed the delusion that was to lead to his attack on President Jackson. He explained to his perplexed sister and her husband, with whom he was living, that he had no need to work because he had large financial claims on the federal government that were now before Congress. The claims were based on his belief that he was in fact King Richard III of England and, as royalty, the owner of two English estates, "Tregear and Kennany that were attached to the crown."[5]

In this deluded state, Lawrence believed President Jackson's opposition to the establishment of a national bank would prevent him from receiving a just settlement for his claims. He reasoned that with Jackson gone, the vice-president would certainly recognize the logic of his case and permit Congress to make the proper remuneration through the national bank so that he could go on to England to settle the claim.

While this seemed to be his primary delusion, there were also other symptoms of his worsening mental state.[6] During the same period, Lawrence, the sober, reliable, and moral young man, suddenly became enamored with fashion. Cultivating a moustache and changing from one extravagant recently purchased costume to another three or four times a day, he would then stand mute in the doorway of his residence for hours, presumably to permit passers-by to gaze upon his sartorial splendor. Neighborhood children picked up on the fancy and addressed him as "King Richard." Lawrence was pleased.

It was also at this time that he first expressed a keen and unbridled, so to speak, interest in the opposite sex. The owner of a livery stable testifed that Lawrence, dressed in decidedly uncharacteristic clothing, would regularly hire two horses, one for himself and another with side-saddle for a young woman of "loose character" with whom he would regally parade the Washington thoroughfares.[7]

In addition to such delusions of grandeur, the paranoia that had gripped Lawrence's senses became manifest during this period. Witnesses testified that this pleasant, mild-mannered young man suddenly became extremely suspicious and hostile. On one occasion, he threatened to kill a black maid because he claimed she was laughing at him; on another, he seized his sister by the shoulders threatening to strike her with a paperweight because he thought she had been talking about him. He was said to have struck his other sisters on numerous occasions during this period. In each instance, his conduct represented a radical departure from previous patterns of behavior. And in each, also, he acted on the basis of imagined grievances.[8]

Doctors and other witnesses testified to marked changes in Lawrence's physical appearance in the two years preceding his attack on the President. The effects of such changes were apparent during his trial. Dressed in a gray shooting coat, black cravat, vest, and brown pantaloons, his eyes reflected a certain strangeness as he made odd gestures or sat motionless with the demeanor of royalty. Others testified to his periodic fits of laughter and cursing, his incoherent conversations with himself, a peculiar gait that would suddenly manifest itself, and his insensitivity to cold while confined in his damp jail cell— all symptoms of severe mental impairment.[9]

At one point during the trial he rose and "addressed himself wildly" to the court. Ranting that the United States had owed him money since 1802 when he claimed his property had been confiscated, Lawrence, suddenly calm, announced with regal contempt, "You are under me, gentlemen." When a deputy marshal tried to seat him, an indignant Lawrence said, "Mr. Woodward, mind your own business or I shall treat you with severity." Then turning slowly back to the court with head held high, he intoned with authoritative solemnity, "It is for me, gentlemen, to pass upon you, and not you upon me." An attempt was made to pacify him with assurances that his rights would be protected. Lawrence replied, "Ay, but when?"; then suddenly with great aplomb he sat down, seemingly lost in thought.[10]

In the weeks preceding his attack on the President, he would sit in his paint shop talking to himself: "Damn him, he does not know his enemy; I will put a pistol. . . . Erect a gallows. . . . Damn General Jackson! Who's General Jackson?" After a boy had delivered a bill, Lawrence, lost in the delusion of his royal status, said "Damn him! He don't know who he's dunning!"[11] Convinced that the nation owed him money, Lawrence refused to pay such bills.

On another occasion, his landlord approached him with a pleasant, "Lawrence, how do you do?" Lawrence replied angrily, "Go to hell! What's that to you?" When the startled landlord explained that his rent was overdue, Lawrence replied, "You mean to warrant me for it, I suppose? [Well] if you do, I will put a ball through your head."[12]

Then on the morning of the day he attacked Jackson, he was seen sitting on a chest in his shop, holding a book and laughing aloud to himself. Suddenly he dropped the book and left the shop chuckling, "I'll be damned if I don't do it."[13]

Conclusions

Underscoring the overwhelming evidence of what would today undoubtedly be diagnosed as paranoid schizophrenia, Lawrence's family history revealed a persistent pattern of mental illness. According to testimony, Lawrence's father had been institutionalized for mental problems and an aunt had died insane.[14] The combined evidence, bolstered by the defendant's bizarre courtroom behavior, was enough to convince the jury and even the prosecutor, national anthem composer Francis Scott Key, that Lawrence could not be held criminally responsible for the crime. He was subsequently acquitted to be confined in mental hospitals for the rest of his life. He died on June 13, 1861 in the Government Hospital for the Insane in Washington.[a]

There can be little doubt that the malady which clouded Richard Lawrence's mind with the delusions, suspicions, and hostility that motivated his attempt to kill the President was genetic in origin and only circumstantially related to events of the time in the most tenuous manner.

CHARLES J. GUITEAU (1841-1882)

With the single exception of Richard Lawrence, there has been no American assassin more obviously deranged than Charles Guiteau. Unlike Lawrence, however, who could be described as a paranoid schizophrenic, Guiteau was not paranoid. Indeed, he possessed a rather benign view of the world until shortly before he was hanged. On the gallows, he did lash out at the injustice of his persecutors, but even then his anger was tempered by a sense of martyrdom, glories anticipated in the next world, and a dying man's belief that in the future a contrite nation would erect monuments in his honor.

That Lawrence was confined in mental hospitals for the remainder of his life and Guiteau hanged can be attributed primarily to two facts: Jackson survived; Garfield did not. For certainly the symptoms of severe mental disturbance in Guiteau's case, although of a different sort, were as striking as in Lawrence's. As we will see, the convenient label and implied motive—"disappointed office-seeker"—that has been

---

[a] Now St. Elizabeth's Hospital.

attached to Guiteau by writers and historians confuses symptoms with causes.[15]

Religion, Law, and Politics

Charles Julius Guiteau was born on September 8, 1841 in Freeport, Illinois. His mother, a quiet, frail woman, died seven years and two deceased infants later of complications stemming from a mind-altering "brain fever" she had initially contracted during her pregnancy with Charles. In addition to Charles, she was survived by her husband, Luther, an intensely religious man and Charles' older brother and sister, John and Frances.[16]

From the beginning, people noticed that little Julius, as he was called (until he dropped the name in his late teens because "there was too much of the Negro about it"), was different.[17] Luther Guiteau soon became exasperated with his inability to discipline his unruly and annoying youngest son and, as a result, Julius was largely raised by his older sister and her husband, George Scoville.[18] Years later, in 1881, Scoville would be called to represent the accused assassin at his trial.

Although plagued by a speech impediment, for which he was whipped by his stern father, Guiteau was, in his fashion, a rather precocious youngster who learned to read quickly and write well. An annoying aversion to physical labor was observed early and remained with him the rest of his life. At the age of eighteen, Charles became interested in furthering his education and, against his father's will, used a small inheritance he had received from his grandfather to enter the University of Michigan.

His father, who was scornful of secular education, had urged his son to seek a scripture-based education at the utopian Oneida Community in New York. The curriculum there focused on study of the Bible. The elder Guiteau had hopes that his errant son might also acquire some self-discipline in a more authoritarian God-fearing environment.[19]

After a couple of semesters at Ann Arbor, Charles, as he was now called, decided to heed his father's advice and transfer to Oneida where, in addition to religious instruction, he had recently learned that they practiced free love. With sex and the Lord on his mind, he enthusiastically entered the New York commune in June 1860. Like his father, Charles now believed that Oneida was the first stage in establishing the Kingdom of God on Earth.

Not long after his arrival, Charles came to believe that he had been divinely ordained to lead the community because, as he announced with a typical lack of humility, he alone possessed the ability. Since no one else had received this revelation, Charles soon found himself at odds with the community leadership. Moreover, the Oneida leaders believed that Charles' vigorously protested need of increasing periods for contemplative pursuits was merely evidence of the slothfulness his father had hoped they would correct.

Other tensions also began to build. Young Charles was becoming increasingly frustrated because the young women of the community were not responding to his amorous overtures. Convinced of his personal charm, this nervous, squirrel-like little man was annoyed because these objects of his intended affection were so unresponsive. Adding insult to injury they soon laughingly referred to him as Charles "Git-out."[20]

As his position within the community continued to deteriorate, Charles became more isolated and alienated until, in April 1865, he left for New York City. He wrote to his father to explain his decision after arriving in Hoboken:

> DEAR FATHER:
>
> I have left the community. The cause of my leaving was because I could not conscientiously and heartily accept their views on the labor question. They wanted to make a hard-working business-man of me, but I could not consent to that, and therefore deemed it expedient to quietly withdraw, which I did last Monday. . . .
>
> I came to New York in obedience to what I believed to be the call of God for the purpose of pursuing an independent course of theological and historical investigation. With the Bible for my textbook and the Holy Ghost for my schoolmaster, I can pursue my studies without interference from human dictation. In the country [Oneida] my *time* was *appropriated*, but now it is at my own *disposal*, a very favorable change. I have procured a small room, well furnished, in Hoboken, opposite the city, and intend to fruitfully pursue my studies during the next three years.[21]

Then he announced a new scheme:

> And here it is proper to state that the energies of my life are now, and have been for months, *pledged to God*, to do all that within me lies to extend the sovereignty of Jesus Christ by placing at his disposal a powerful daily paper. I am persuaded that theocratic presses are destined, in due time, to supersede to a great extent pulpit oratory. There are hundreds of thousands of ministers in

the world but not a single daily theocratic press. It appears to me that there is a splendid chance for some one to do a big thing for God, for humanity and for himself.[22]

With a new suit of clothes, a few books, and a hundred dollars in his pocket, he planned to publish his own religious newspaper that would, he was convinced, spearhead a national spiritual awakening.

In another lengthy letter to his father, Charles continued to detail his plans for the "Theocratic Daily" that would "entirely discard all muddy theology, brain philosophy and religious cant, and seek to turn the heart of men toward the living God." Buoyed with an ill-founded sense of well-being and enthusiasm, Charles went on euphorically: "I claim that I am in the employ of Jesus Christ and Co., the very ablest and strongest firm in the universe, and that what I can do is limited only by their power and purpose." And knowing full well that *he* would edit the paper, he announced confidently:

> Whoever edits such a paper as I intend to establish will doubtless occupy the position of Target General to the Press, Pulpit, and Bench of the civilized world; and if God intends me for that place, I fear not, for I know that He will be "a wall of fire round me," and keep me from all harm.[23]

Confidently expecting to promote the Kingdom of God without the restrictions of the Oneida Community and, not incidentally, also enjoy wealth and fame in the process, Guiteau sought financial backing for the paper in New York City. In a flurry of optimistic salesmanship, he scurried about presenting his proposal to prospective subscribers and advertisers; they, as it turned out, were not impressed with this odd little entrepreneur and his religious views.[24] Soon finding himself short of money, somewhat discouraged, and tiring of a diet of dried beef, crackers, and lemonade that he ate in his dingy Hoboken room, Charles returned to Oneida after only three months in the big city.

But his return only confirmed his original reservations about the place, and he soon left again—this time more embittered by his experiences there than ever before. Again without money, Charles wrote to the Community requesting a $9,000 reimbursement—$1,500 a year for the six years he had spent there. When the Community refused to pay, Charles sued, threatening to make public the alleged sexual, as well as financial, exploitation employed by the Oneida leadership—especially its founder, John Humphrey Noyes.

Undoubtedly bitter about the rejection he had endured in this sexually permissive environment, Charles lashed out in an unintentionally amusing attack on both Noyes and the Oneida women. Charging that Noyes lusted after little girls, Guiteau angrily told a reporter: "All the girls that were born in the Community were forced to cohabit with Noyes at such an early period it dwarfed them. The result was that most of the Oneida women were small and thin and homely."[25]

Obviously stung by such criticism, Noyes threatened to bring extortion charges against Guiteau. In a letter to Charles' father, who was mortified by his son's behavior, he advised that Charles had admitted to, among other sins, stealing money, frequenting brothels, and being treated for a venereal ailment. Noyes added that Charles also had apparently thrown in the towel, so to speak, in an uninspired battle with masturbation. Such appraisals confirmed his father's sad suspicion that Charles' real purpose in going to Oneida was "the free exercise of his unbridled lust." Charles' "most shameful and wicked attack" and subsequent episodes convinced Luther Guiteau that his prodigal son was "absolutely insane." In despair, he wrote to his oldest son John that, unless something stopped him, Charles would become "a fit subject for the lunatic asylum."[26]

Having thus incurred his father's anger and facing the prospects of a countersuit for extortion, Charles abandoned his legal claim and left New York for Chicago. There, given the standards of the day, he began to practice law, after a fashion. In 1869, he married a young woman he had met at the Y.M.C.A., a Miss Annie Bunn. After only one memorably incoherent attempt to argue a case, his practice of law was reduced to collecting delinquent bills for clients. By 1874, the law practice and marriage had both failed, the latter as a result of his adultery with a "high toned" prostitute and the occasional beatings he used to discipline his beleaguered wife.

When his marriage ended, Charles wandered back to New York. Continually borrowing small sums of money that he never repaid voluntarily, Guiteau soon found himself, as usual, in trouble with creditors. Resentful of such unseemly harassment, he wrote an indignant letter to his brother John addressing him as "Dear Sir." This and other letters reveal the unfounded arrogance and unintentional humor of a man with only the most tenuous grasp of the reality of his position:

> Your letter from Eaton . . . dated Nov. 8, '72, received. I got the $75 on my supposed responsibility as a Chicago lawyer. I was introduced to Eaton by a gentleman I met at the Young Men's Christian Association, and it was only incidentally that your name was mentioned.
>
> I wrote to Eaton several times while at Chicago, and he ought

to have been satisfied, but he had the impertinence to write you and charge me with fraud, when he knew he let me have the money entirely upon my own *name and position*. Had he acted like a *"white"* man, I should have tried to pay it long ago. I hope you will drop him.

Yours truly,
CHARLES J. GUITEAU.[27]

A few days after this letter was written, Charles' exasperated brother himself became the target of an angry response when he requested a repayment of a small loan:

J. W. GUITEAU: NEW YORK, March 13th, 1873

Find $7 enclosed. Stick it up your bung-hole and wipe your nose on it, and that will remind you of the estimation in which you are held by

CHARLES J. GUITEAU

Sign and return the enclosed receipt and I will send you $7, but not before, and that, I hope, will end our acquaintance.[28]

Disdainful of the pettiness of such small lenders, Charles confidently launched another major venture in the publishing business: he wanted to purchase the Chicago *Inter-Ocean* newspaper. But businessmen and bankers, from whom he sought financial backing, were unimpressed and not a little skeptical about this seedy little man with a confidential manner. Frustrated but ever the undaunted optimist, Charles turned again to religion.[29]

Impressed with the bountiful collection plates at the Chicago revival meetings of Dwight Moody where he served as an usher in the evening services, Charles decided to prepare himself for the ministry. After a short period of voracious reading in Chicago libraries, he soon had himself convinced that he alone had ascertained the "truth" on a number of pressing theological questions. With familiar enthusiasm, he launched his new career with pamphlets and newspaper advertisements. Adorned with sandwich board posters, Charles walked the streets inviting all who would listen to attend his sermons on the physical existence of hell, the Second-Coming, and so forth. The self-promotion campaign was repeated in one town after another as he roamed between Milwaukee, Chicago, New York, and Boston.

In handbills, Charles proclaimed himself "the Eloquent Chicago Lawyer." His performances, in fact, followed a quite different pattern: a bombastic introduction that soon deteriorated into a series of incoherent nonsequiturs, whereupon he would end inconclusively and abruptly dash from the building amid the jeers and laughter of his audiences—the whole episode lasting perhaps ten to fifteen minutes. With his dubious reputation as an evangelist growing, Charles darted from one town to another leaving in his path a growing accumulation of indignant audiences and unpaid bills. Often arrested, he was periodically jailed for short periods between 1877 and 1880 when he again turned his attention to politics.[30]

The Garfield Connection

Describing himself as a "lawyer, theologian, and politician," Guiteau threw himself into the Stalwart faction's fight for the 1880 Republican presidential nomination in New York. When a third term was denied the Stalwart's choice, Ulysses S. Grant, the nomination went to a darkhorse, James A. Garfield. Guiteau quickly jumped on the Garfield bandwagon. In New York, he began to hang around the party headquarters and, as he was to remind people later, he did work on the "canvass" for the candidate. In his view, his most noteworthy contribution to the campaign and Garfield's subsequent election, however, was an obscure speech he wrote (and may have delivered once in Troy, New York) entitled, "Garfield vs. Hancock." A few weeks before, the same speech had been entitled "Grant vs. Hancock." Undeterred by the change in candidates, the speech, Guiteau later claimed, originated and developed the issue that won the election for Garfield. That issue, in brief, was the claim that if the Democrats gained the presidency it would mean a resumption of the Civil War because the Democrats had only sectional, rather than national, loyalties. In a personal note, dated March 11, 1881, to the newly appointed secretary of state, James G. Blaine, Guiteau explained his claim:

> I think I have a right to claim your help on the strength of this speech. It was sent to our leading editors and orators in August. It was the first shot in the rebel war claim idea, and it was their idea that elected Garfield. . . . I will talk with you about this as soon as I can get a chance. There is nothing against me. I claim to be a gentleman and a Christian.[31]

Indeed, from the moment the election results were in, Guiteau had begun to press his claims in letters to Garfield and Blaine. He also became a familiar figure at the Republican party headquarters in New York, confident that he would be rewarded for his efforts with a consulship appointment; the only question remaining, he believed, was the location. Would it be Paris, Vienna, or some other post of prominence? With this in mind, he moved from New York to Washington on March 5, 1881, where he began to badger not only the President's staff but Blaine and the President himself in the corridors of the White House. Striking a posture of gallingly unwarranted familiarity with those he encountered, he also let loose a barrage of "personal" notes written in the same annoying style. Typical is the following:

[Private.]

GEN'L GARFIELD:

From your looks yesterday I judge you did not quite understand what I meant by saying "I have not called for two or three weeks." I intended to express my sympathy for you on account of the pressure that has been on you since you came into office.

I think Mr. Blaine intends giving me the Paris consulship with your and Gen. Logan's approbation, and I am waiting for the break in the Senate.

I have practiced law in New York and Chicago, and presume I am well qualified for it.

I have been here since March 5, and expect to remain some little time, or until I get my commission.

Very respectfully,
CHARLES GUITEAU.[32]

AP'L 8.

Shortly before he had written to the secretary of state to inquire whether President Hayes' appointments to foreign missions would expire in March 1881, as he expected. Learning that they would, Guiteau became more persistent in pressing his claims for an appointment to the missions of either Vienna, Paris, or possibly Liverpool. Earlier he had written again to Garfield, whom he had never met, to advise him of his plans to wed a wealthy and cultured woman (whose acquaintance, also, he had not at that time, or ever, made). Such unknowingly ludicrous acts were intended, in the bizarre judgment of Charles J. Guiteau, to enhance his already eminent qualifications for a foreign ministry.[33]

In the meantime, the newspapers were filled with the controversy that had developed between the new President and the boss-dominated Stalwart faction of the Republican party over patronage appointments in New York. Finally, on May 13, 1881, the two most powerful of the Stalwart bosses, Roscoe Conkling and Tom "Me Too" Platt of New York, resigned their Senate seats in protest over the President's failure to follow their preferences in his patronage appointments. In so doing, they discounted the fact that Garfield had accepted their man, "Chet" Arthur, as his running mate and vice-president. Angrily condemning the beleaguered Garfield's disloyalty and traitorous tactics, the resignations triggered numerous editorial attacks and denunciations of the President and his mentor Blaine, which were to continue until July 2, 1881.

On the same day the resignations were announced, Guiteau once again approached Blaine with his by now familiar blandishments, only to have the exasperated secretary roar, "Never bother me again about the Paris consulship as long as you live!"[34] But Guiteau persisted. A week later, he wrote again to the President:

[Private]

General GARFIELD:

I have been trying to be your friend; I don't know whether you appreciate it or not, but I am moved to call your attention to the remarkable letter from Mr. Blaine which I have just noticed.

According to Mr. Farwell, of Chicago, Blaine is "a vindictive politician" and "an evil genius," and you will "have no peace till you get rid of him."

This letter shows Mr. Blaine is a wicked man, and you ought to demand his *immediate* resignation; otherwise you and the Republican party will come to grief. I will see you in the morning, if I can, and talk with you.

Very respectfully,
CHARLES GUITEAU.[35]

May 23.

If past behavior is any clue to the future, at this point Guiteau would have begun to consider yet another occupational change, returning again perhaps with his typical enthusiastic optimism to theology or law. Previously, Guiteau had accepted failure with remarkable equanimity, sustained always by the exalted opinion he had of himself. As one scheme after another collapsed—his leadership aspirations at Oneida, his journalistic ventures, the law practice, and the evangelistic crusade— his bitterness and disappointment were short-lived as he moved on to other careers. His confidence in his own ability and the Horatio Alger-like opportunities that abounded in nineteenth-century America remained unshaken. Even his angry exchanges with the Oneida establishment possessed the tone of someone who enjoyed the battle as well as the spoils; certainly these exchanges reflected none of the desperation of the all-time loser that he, in fact, was. In Guiteau's delusional world, these frustrations were merely temporary setbacks in a career that was, he remained convinced, destined for wealth and fame.

Now, for the first time in his oddly chaotic life, Guiteau found himself sharing his outsider status with men he admired: Conkling and Platt and the other Stalwarts. And it was in this realization—not the denial of the various appointments he had sought—that his assassination scheme germinated.[36] Indeed, a month later, on June 16, he wrote in his "Address to the American People":

> I conceived of the idea of removing the President *four weeks ago.* Not a soul knew of my purpose. I conceived the idea myself. I read the newspapers carefully, for and against the administration, and gradually the conviction settled on me that the President's removal was a political necessity, because he proved a traitor to the men who made him, and thereby imperiled the life of the Republic. At the late Presidential election, the Republican party carried every Northern State. Today, owing to the misconduct of the President and his Secretary of State, they could hardly carry ten Northern States. They certainly could not carry New York, and that is the pivotal State.
>
> Ingratitude is the basest of crimes. That the President, under the manipulation of his Secretary of State, has been guilty of the basest ingratitude to the Stalwarts admits of no denial. . . . In the President's madness he has wrecked the once grand old Republican party; and for this he dies. . . .
>
> I had no ill-will to the President.
>
> This is not murder. It is a political necessity. It will make my friend Arthur President, and save the Republic. I have sacrificed only one. I shot the President as I would a rebel, if I saw him pulling down the American flag. I leave my justification to God and the American people.
>
> I expect President Arthur and Senator Conkling will give the nation the finest administration it has ever had. They are honest and have plenty of brains and experience.
>
> [signed] Charles Guiteau[37] [Emphasis added.]

Later, on June 20, he added this even more bizarre postscript:

> The President's nomination was an act of God. The President's election was an act of God. The President's removal is an act of God. I am clear in my purpose to remove the President. Two objects will be accomplished: It will unite the Republican party and save the Republic, and it will create a great demand for my book, "The Truth." This book was written to save souls and not for money, and the Lord wants to save souls by circulating the book.
>
> Charles Guiteau[38]

It is unlikely that Guiteau would have chosen the course of action he did without the sense that he was in good company—"a Stalwart of the Stalwarts," as he liked to describe himself. In his distorted mind, to "remove" the President, as he euphemistically described it, would provide the same status and recognition he had sought in a consulship appointment and, more importantly, in every hare-brained scheme he had botched since the time he first entered the Oneida Community to establish the Kingdom of God on Earth. In this last grandly deluded plan, his aspirations in theology, law, and politics were to culminate in a divinely inspired and just act "to unite the Republican party and save the Republic" and, not incidentally, launch a new career for Charles Guiteau not only as a lawyer, theologian, and politician, but as a national hero with presidential aspirations.[39]

With this in mind, on June 8, Guiteau borrowed fifteen dollars and purchased a silver-mounted English revolver. He planned to have it, along with his papers, displayed after the assassination at the Library of the State Department or the Army Medical Museum. To prepare for the big event, he began target practice on the banks of the Potomac. After stalking the President for several weeks and bypassing at least two opportunities to shoot him, Guiteau rose early on Saturday, July 2, 1881. He had rented a room a few days before at the Riggs House and, on this morning, began preparations to meet the President at the Baltimore and Potomac Railroad Station. The President was scheduled to leave that morning for a vacation trip. Downing a hearty breakfast, which he charged to his room, he pocketed the last of a series of bizarre explanations:

July 2, 1881

To the White House:

The President's tragic death was a sad necessity, but it will unite the Republican party and save the Republic. Life is a fleeting dream, and it matters little when one goes. A human life is of small value. During the war thousands of brave boys went down without a tear. I presume the President was a Christian, and that he will be happier in Paradise than here.

It will be no worse for Mrs. Garfield, dear soul, to part with her husband this way than by natural death. He is liable to go at any time anyway.

I had no ill-will towards the President. His death was a political necessity. I am a lawyer, a theologian, a politician. I am a Stalwart of the Stalwarts. I was with General Grant and the rest of our men in New York during the canvass. I have some papers for the

press, which I shall leave with Byron Andrews and his co-jour-
nalists at 1440 N.Y. Ave., where all the reporters can see them.
I am going to jail.

[signed] Charles Guiteau[40]

Guiteau then walked to the banks of the Potomac where after taking
a few final practice shots he proceeded to the railroad station to await
the President's arrival. Once at the station, he used the men's room,
had his shoes shined, and, after estimating that his assignment would
be completed shortly before the President's train was scheduled to
leave, he reserved a hackman for an anticipated 9:30 arrest and departure to the District Prison. He had already checked the prison's
security, lest in the emotion of the moment he might be attacked by
crowds who had not had time to realize what a great patriotic service
he had just rendered. He was convinced that after his explanation was
published the wisdom and justice of his act would be appreciated.
Until such time, however, he had taken a further precaution of drafting
a letter requesting that General Sherman see to his safekeeping in jail.
The letter, which fell from his pocket during the scuffle that followed
the shooting, read as follows:

TO GENERAL SHERMAN:
I have just shot the President. I shot him several times, as I
wished him to go as easily as possible. His death was a political
necessity. I am a lawyer, theologian and politician. I am a Stalwart
of the Stalwarts. I was with General Grant and the rest of our
men in New York during the canvass. I am going to jail. Please
order out your troops and take possession of the jail at once.

Very respectfully,
[signed] Charles Guiteau[41]

So it was with this completely distorted view of reality that Charles
Guiteau fired two shots into the President's back as he walked arm-
in-arm with Secretary Blaine toward the waiting train. The President,
failing to respond to treatment, lingered two and a half months before
dying on September 19, 1881.

The Trial

Throughout his lengthy seventy-two-day trial, Guiteau's delusional
state was apparent to anyone inclined to acknowledge it. His brother-
in-law, George Scoville, represented him at the trial and entered a plea
of insanity. In Scoville's opening statement for the defense, he described

in some detail the history of mental illness in the Guiteau family: at least two uncles, one aunt, and two cousins, not to mention his mother who died of "brain fever" but was probably insane. He went on to mention the highly eccentric behavior of his father that, at least one physician thought, properly qualified him for this category.[42] It should also be noted that Guiteau's sister, Frances, the wife of George Scoville, behaved so strangely during her brother's trial that her probable insanity was noted by one participating physician who had had occasion to observe her closely.[43] And indeed, her husband later had her declared insane and institutionalized in October 1882, after her brother's execution.

This seemingly overwhelming evidence of an hereditary affliction was ignored or discounted by expert witnesses and finally the jury. Also discounted were the defendant's own delusional symptoms evident in the past schemes, bizarre letters to prominent persons he had never met, and his distorted conception of reality, which was apparent in his remarks throughout the trial and to the day he was executed. Scoville's line of defense was rejected by the defendant himself and greatly resented by John W. Guiteau, Charles' older brother. In a letter to Scoville, dated October 20, 1881, shortly after the trial began, John denied the history of family insanity described by the defense. Rather than heredity, he argued indignantly, most of the cases Scoville cited could be explained by self-induced factors such as insobriety and "mesmerism"; the others, specifically his parents' symptoms, he categorically denied. Falling into line with previous diagnoses of the causes of Charles' problems, most notably that of leaders of the Oneida Community, John Guiteau wrote: "I have no doubt that masturbation and self-abuse is at the bottom of his [Charles'] mental imbecility."[44]

As for Charles himself, thoroughly contemptuous of his brother-in-law's legal abilities, he drafted his own plea, which read as follows:

I plead not guilty to the indictment and my defense is threefold:
    1. Insanity, in that it was God's act and not mine. The Divine pressure on me to remove the President was so enormous that it destroyed my free agency, and therefore I am not legally responsible for my act.[45]

Throughout his trial, Guiteau would acknowledge only this interpretation of insanity; that is, he was insane only in the sense that he did something that was not his will but God's. He did not accept the idea that he was in any way mentally deficient. Typical of his remarks on this issue made throughout the trial is the following:

... the Lord interjected the idea [of the President's removal] into my brain and then let me work it out my own way. That is the way the Lord does. He doesn't employ fools to do his work; I am sure of that; he gets the best brains he can find.[46]

His plea continued describing two rather novel circumstances that, he claimed, were the Lord's will just as the assassination:

2. The President died from malpractice. About three weeks after he was shot his physicians, after careful examination, decided he would recover. Two months after this official announcement he died. Therefore, I say he was not fatally shot. If he had been well treated he would have recovered.[47]

The third circumstance had to do with the court's jurisdiction:

3. The President died in New Jersey and, therefore, beyond the jurisdiction of this Court. This malpractice and the President's death in New Jersey are special providences, and I am bound to avail myself of them in my trial in justice to the Lord and myself.

He went on to elaborate:

I undertake to say that the Lord is managing my case with eminent ability, and that he had a special object in allowing the President to die in New Jersey. His management of this case is worthy of Him as the Deity, and I have entire confidence in His disposition to protect me, and to send me forth to the world a free and innocent man.[48]

The jury's guilty verdict not withstanding, it was clear that Guiteau had no grasp of the reality of his situation. Almost to the last, he believed he would be acquitted, at which point, he planned to begin a lecture tour in Europe and later return to the United States in time to re-enter politics as a presidential contender in 1884. He was confident that the jury, like the great majority of Americans, would recognize that Garfield's "removal" was divinely ordained and that the Almighty himself was responsible. He was convinced they would recognize that he was only an instrument in the Master's hands.

Contrary to some assessments,[49] there was no evidence of paranoia in his behavior. Buoyed by a delusion-based optimism, he mistook the crowds of curious on-lookers at the jail as evidence of respect and admiration: bogus checks for incredible sums of money and ludicrous marriage proposals that were sent to him by cranks were sincerely and gratefully acknowledged; and promotional schemes evolved in his distorted mind to market his ridiculous books and pamphlets—all this while anticipating a run for the presidency in 1884! Meanwhile, in high spirits, the poor wretch ate heartily and slept well in a small cell located both literally and figuratively in the shadow of the gallows.

The Execution

When at the very last he realized that there was no hope for survival, his anger was, considering the circumstances, tempered much as it had been during his dispute with the Oneida Community. There were warnings of divine retribution for the ungrateful new president, Chester Arthur, the unfair prosecuting attorneys, and the jury, but again his anger lacked the intensity and desperation of someone facing death. As the execution date approached, Charles, realizing failure once again, simply set his sights elsewhere as he had on many previous occasions. Eschewing politics, the presidency, the Stalwarts, and the law that had failed him, the lawyer and politician once again became the theologian. Anticipating an other-worldly position at the side of the Almighty, Charles walked serenely to the gallows. Earlier he had given the letter below to the chaplain who stood by him at the last:

Washington, D.C.
June 29, 1882

TO THE REV. WILLIAM W. HICKS:
    I, Charles Guiteau, of the City of Washington, in the District of Columbia, now under sentence of death, which is to be carried into effect between the hours of twelve and two o'clock on the 30th day of June, A.D., 1882, in the United States jail in the said District, do hereby give and grant to you my body after such execution; provided, however, it shall not be used for any mercenary purposes.
    And I hereby, for good and sufficient considerations, give, deliver and transfer to said Hicks my book entitled "The Truth and Removal" and copyright thereof to be used by him in writing a truthful history of my life and execution.
    And I direct that such history be entitled "The Life and Work of Charles Guiteau"; and I hereby solemnly proclaim and announce to all the world that no person or persons shall ever in any manner use my body for any mercenary purpose whatsoever.
    And if at any time hereafter any person or persons shall desire to honor my remains, they can do it by erecting a monument

whereon shall be inscribed these words: "Here lies the body of Charles Guiteau, Patriot and Christian. His soul is in glory."

[signed] Charles Guiteau

Witnesses: Charles H. Reed
            James Woodward[50]

Before the noose was placed around his neck, he was given permission to read his "last dying prayer" to the crowd of faces gazing up at him from the prison yard below. Comparing his situation to that of Christ at Calvary, Guiteau condemned President Arthur's ingratitude "to the man that made him and saved his party and land" and warned of divine retribution.[51]

After completing his prayer, he again looked thoughtfully out over the crowd before announcing in a loud clear voice:

> I am now going to read some verses which are intended to indicate my feelings at the moment of leaving this world. If set to music they may be rendered effective. The idea is that of a child babbling to his mamma and his papa. I wrote it this morning about 10 o'clock.

Then with childlike mournfulness, Guiteau read:

> I am going to the Lordy. I am so glad.
> I am going to the Lordy. I am so glad.
> I am going to the Lordy. Glory, hallelujah;
>   glory hallelujah.
> I am going to the Lordy;
> I love the Lordy with all my soul; glory,
>   hallelujah.
> And that is the reason I am going to the Lord.
> Glory, hallelujah; glory, hallelujah. I am going
>   to the Lord.
> I saved my party and my land; glory, hallelujah.
> But they have murdered me for it, and that is the
>   reason
> I am going to the Lordy.
> Glory, hallelujah; glory, hallelujah. I am going
>   to the Lordy.
> I wonder what I will do when I get to the Lordy;
> I guess that I will weep no more when I get to the
>   Lordy.
> Glory, hallelujah!
> I wonder what I will see when I get to the Lordy,

I expect to see most splendid things, beyond all
  earthly conception.

As he neared completion, he raised his voice to a very high pitch and
concluded with

When I am with the Lordy, glory, hallelujah!
Glory, hallelujah! I am with the Lord.

Whereupon attendants strapped his legs, adjusted the noose, and placed
a black hood over his head as Rev. Hicks prayed, "God the Father
be with thee and give thee peace evermore." Guiteau, according to his
own request, signaled the hangman by dropping a slip of paper from
his fingers. As the trap sprung, Charles Guiteau slipped confidently
into eternity with "Glory, Glory, Glory" on his lips.[52]

Conclusions

Although the debate on the true state of Guiteau's mental condition
was to continue among physicians for some years afterward,[53] a brief
article in the *Medical News* a day after the execution seems to have
been representative of the prevailing view of the medical profession.
While conceding that the neurologists who testified to the assassin's
obvious insanity may have been correct, society would still be better,
the editors reasoned, for having rid itself of such persons.[54] As a further
practical matter, it is unlikely that in 1881 any jury in the country
would have acquitted the President's assassin whatever his mental
condition.

JOHN SCHRANK (1876-1943)

The election of 1912 proved to be a volatile event in the history of
the Republican party. The Progressive wing had formally split from
the party and chose the colorful former president Theodore Roosevelt
as its candidate. The Progressives would oppose the incumbent Republican and Roosevelt's former old friend, William Howard Taft.
Thus divided, the Republicans set the stage for the election of only
the second Democratic president since the Civil War—Woodrow Wilson.

On the evening of October 14, 1912, Colonel Roosevelt, as he liked
to be called, emerged from the Hotel Gilpatrick in Milwaukee and
walked briskly toward a waiting car. He was headed for the municipal

auditorium where he was to speak to an audience of some nine thousand people. A large crowd had gathered in front of the hotel and around the car hoping to catch a glimpse of the charismatic hero of the Spanish American War. As Roosevelt climbed into the open car and was about to seat himself, a shot rang out. In almost the same instant, a short roly-poly and oddly pleasant-looking little man was knocked to the pavement unconscious. A pistol had been kicked from his hand.

Roosevelt staggered briefly when the bullet struck him, pulled out a handkerchief, coughed into it, and observing no blood, called repeatedly to his aides who had grabbed the now dazed assailant, "Do not kill him. Bring him here."[55] The crowd by this time was shouting "Lynch him, kill him," but Roosevelt ordered that the man not be hurt. John Schrank was dragged and carried into the hotel kitchen where he was held until the police arrived.

As one of the Colonel's aides, Henry F. Cochems, provided support, Roosevelt calmly observed, "He *pinked* me, Henry." He then turned to the crowd and shouted over the protestations of his aides, "We are going to the hall; we are going to the hall; start the machine; go ahead; go on."[56] On the way to the speech, it became apparent that the Colonel was bleeding enough to stain his shirt and trousers and to form a puddle in his left shoe, but he insisted on going ahead to the auditorium to give the speech.

As part of his introduction, an aide informed the audience that the former president had been shot. When a heckler boisterously disputed the claim, Roosevelt, grinning defiantly, strode to the podium and with a flourish unbuttoned his vest to expose his bloodstained shirt. As expressions of shock and horror rippled through the auditorium, Roosevelt seized the moment. Drawing himself to full height, he announced:

> It takes more than one bullet to kill a Bull Moose. I'm all right, no occasion for any sympathy whatever, but I want to take this occasion within five minutes after having been shot to say some things to our people which I hope no one will question the profound sincerity of.[57]

Amid cheers from the audience, the Colonel proceeded with a typically bombastic campaign speech. At one point, Roosevelt appeared faint and a doctor rushed to his side pleading with him to stop and get the medical attention he needed. But Roosevelt refused. Then, turning dramatically to the audience he added, "If these doctors don't behave themselves I won't let them look at me at all." The crowd roared; they loved it. So did Roosevelt. "It takes more than one bullet to kill a Bull Moose," he repeated with obvious pride. Shortly after, he again admonished the worried doctors, "Good gracious, if you saw me in the saddle at the head of my troops with a bullet in me you would not mind."[58] The old "rough rider" stayed around long enough to finish his speech and wring the last drop of political advantage from the circumstances.

Later, after treatment at the hospital, doctors announced that the old Bull Moose would have been killed had it not been for the folded fifty-page speech and a spectacle case he had carried in his left breast pocket. These items and his heavy clothing absorbed the shock of the .38 caliber bullet and prevented it from penetrating the rib cage, thus sparing his life. After a brief period of recuperation, he resumed his vigorous campaign schedule.

The Assailant

Roosevelt's thirty-six-year-old assailant was a mild-mannered but troubled man who was offended and obsessed with the threat, he claimed, that the Colonel's bid for a third-term in the White House posed to the nation's democratic institutions. In Schrank's mind, breaking the two-term tradition was the first step toward dictatorship. Although pleading guilty to the shooting, Schrank explained that he did not intend to kill "the citizen Roosevelt" but rather *only* "Theodore Roosevelt, the third termer." "I did not want to kill the candidate of the Progressive Party," he continued, "I shot Roosevelt as a warning to other third termers."[59]

Although Roosevelt's violation of the "third term tradition" was what prompted Schrank's act, there were other grievances in his mind. Prior to the campaign of 1912, Schrank had composed a curious essay on four unwritten laws of government, or as he called them, "The Four Pillars of Our Republic." In it, he discussed the crucial importance of denying a third term to presidents, enforcing the Monroe Doctrine, denying the presidency to Roman Catholics, and avoiding wars of conquest. The "Four Pillars," he reasoned, were fundamental to the nation's well-being.[60] The fact that Roosevelt was a nominal Protestant (whose concept of religion, he once confided, was based almost exclusively on the verse in St. James: "I will show my faith by my works"[61]) and a firm believer in the Monroe Doctrine did not compensate, in Schrank's mind, for his other deficiencies. In addition to the third-term bid, Schrank also resented the Colonel's war of conquest against Cuba: as he called it, "[Roosevelt's] rough-rider masquerade."

On a more personal level, Schrank acknowledged in his confession that while a saloon keeper in New York he had resented the vigorous enforcement of blue laws requiring the closing of bars on Sundays when Roosevelt had been city police commissioner.[62]

Who was this plump and seemingly comfortable little man with the contented, if bovine, appearance and courteous manner who wanted to kill the former president? John Flammang Schrank's short stature, drooping eyelids, and normally pleasant expression were reminiscent of "Dopey," the dull-witted but lovable dwarf who befriended "Snow White." Born in Bavaria in 1876, he came to live with his uncle and aunt in New York City when he was twelve. He was not close to his real parents.

His foster parents operated a respectable and profitable neighborhood saloon in an immigrant section of the city (370 East Tenth Street). They were as good to their kind, well-mannered nephew as he was to them. John helped tend bar and did other chores associated with the family business. He was deeply grieved when his aunt and uncle died within a year of each other in 1910 and 1911, respectively.

After their deaths, he learned, however, that he had inherited the business and real estate valued at some $25,000—a significant sum for the time. He promptly sold the business and lived from that time until his arrest simply and comfortably on his profit.

Having had only five years of schooling in Bavaria, Schrank had quickly enrolled in night classes after arriving in New York. There he learned English and became an avid reader of history, government, and the Bible. His English improved until he was considered quite articulate in his adopted language.

At the age of fifteen or sixteen, John developed an interest in poetry and the writings of the liberal German-American political philosopher and reformer Carl Schurz. Although always courteous and pleasant, Schrank became more withdrawn after the deaths of his aunt and uncle. He spent increasing amounts of his time in solitary strolls in the city parks or just reading and jotting down his thoughts and composing odd poems. A representative sample of the latter is quoted below:

ELECTRIC LIFE

The law that rules electricity
Controls the human life:
The magnitude you possess
Will draw to you a wife.
For positive and negative

Are poles that never meet.
So be sure that she is negative
If you intend to lead.

All matrimonial troubles
Rise from the same defect
Because positive and positive
Are poles that don't connect
Your station and your influence,
The number of friends you control,
Depends upon the power
Of your positive pole.

Your powerhouse is heaven,
The current is your soul,
Your spirit is the wire,
And God your positive Pull;
A sudden death—the failure of heart
Is in other words—a circuit short
But when you die at 90, about
We simply say your fuse burnt out.[63]

It was presumably with such thoughts running through his mind that he retired on the evening of September 15, 1901—the day after President McKinley died from his assassin-inflicted wounds. At 1:30 A.M., John later claimed he was awakened by a vision that he described in a scrawled note:

September 15th, 1901
TO THE PEOPLE OF THE UNITED STATES:
  In a dream I saw President McKinley sit up in his coffin, pointing at a man in a monk's attire in whom I recognized as Theo. Roosevelt. The dead President said, "This is my murderer, avenge my death."[64]

It was during the period following this dream that John had, or imagined that he had, his first and only romance with a neighborhood girl, one Elsie Ziegler, to whom he claimed he had been engaged. But according to Miss Ziegler's brother, Edward, Schrank was never more than a "nodding acquaintance" to her. In any case, John recalled the relationship differently in a conversation with a newspaper reporter after his arrest: "I had a sweetheart once. I haven't any relatives, but I did have a sweetheart once. Her name was Elsie Ziegler. She was a pretty girl. I loved her."[65] He went on to explain that she had died in

1904 when a ferryboat burned and sank in New York harbor. He added that he never wanted a girlfriend after that.

Whether or not John's love affair with Elsie Ziegler was merely a figment of his imagination as her brother and others testified, other delusions were now beginning to dominate his thinking and loosen his grasp on reality. He also began to spend long hours alone at the gravesides of his aunt and uncle. He even moved to an apartment near the Brooklyn cemetery so that he could be closer to them.[66]

According to Schrank, on September 14, 1912, at 1:30 A.M.—almost eleven years to the minute after his first vision—he was once again visited by the spirit of William McKinley on the anniversary of his death. He wrote down a description of the experience:

> September 14, 1912 1:30 a.m.
> While writing a poem, someone tapped me on the shoulder and said: "Let not a murderer take the presidential chair. Avenge my death." I could clearly see Mr. McKinley's features.
> Before the Almighty God, I swear that the above written is nothing but the truth.[67]

Already incensed by what he considered Roosevelt's traitorous bid for a third term, this second visitation and explicit command from the long-dead McKinley convinced Schrank that it was time to act. He bought a .38 caliber pistol for fourteen dollars and a steamship ticket to Charleston, South Carolina where Roosevelt was scheduled to campaign. On September 21, 1912, he embarked on his pursuit of the campaigning candidate following a trail that would lead him eventually from Charleston to Augusta, Atlanta, Birmingham, Chattanooga, Nashville, Louisville, Evansville, Chicago, and Milwaukee before he finally got his chance.[68]

After his arrest, Schrank, citing the divinely inspired visions of Moses and Joan of Arc as comparable to his own, denied his insanity. He explained that such experiences were common to the select few chosen to do God's bidding. Convinced that he now enjoyed such status, he sought to legitimize his claim by requesting that his pistol and the bullet that struck Roosevelt be given to the New York Historical Society for public display. When a sheriff's deputy explained that doctors had decided against removing the bullet from Roosevelt's rib cage, Schrank was furious:

> That is my bullet. In after years when I am regarded as a hero, the bullet will be valuable and I want it to go to the New York Historical Society. I want the gun to go with it also and I am putting that in my will.[69]

The Verdict and Aftermath

Statements such as this considered along with the McKinley visitations left little doubt that Schrank was psychotic. Further investigation also revealed an hereditary strain of insanity in his family: an aunt and possibly his father and grandfather had been afflicted. Thus, there was little controversy when a panel of alienists concluded that John Schrank was insane and was therefore exempt from criminal proceedings.

Although labeled a paranoid by the panel,[70] apart from his view of Roosevelt's possible third term, Schrank appeared to possess a remarkably benign view of the world. There was no evidence of either physical or verbal aggression in his past. Witnesses recalled him as a quiet but pleasant man who didn't bother anyone. Indeed, until a few minutes before the shooting, he sat in Herman Rollfink's saloon talking pleasantly with the bartender Paul Thume. According to Thume:

> He . . . asked the bar musicians to play some song, something with *stripes* in it, and then he bought each one a drink. [Schrank later chuckled openly as the bartender related the incident at a pre-trial hearing recalling that the song with "stripes" was the popular patriotic march, "Stars and Stripes Forever."]

Enjoying the company, Schrank danced merrily around as they played, perhaps feeling the effects of the beer he had been drinking. He then bought another jovial round of drinks and left. A few minutes later, he shot Roosevelt.[71]

During his confinement in the Milwaukee jail, his friendly thoughtfulness soon made him a favorite with the other prisoners. A pleasant conversationalist on most topics except the shooting, which he would not discuss with anyone but authorities, he laughed and joked while he taught fellow inmates and guards the finer points of checkers.

Apparently the only thing offensive about John Schrank was his odor—even by the lenient standards of that era. He did not like to bathe. After a week or so in confinement, the sheriff directed that he be required to wash. Schrank's smelly clothes were destroyed and new ones issued with the strict injunction that he bathe regularly.[72]

Later when the panel of doctors announced their insanity verdict, the agreeable Schrank, shaking hands and thanking each, informed them that while he disagreed with their diagnosis, he felt that they had done their best. Similarly, as he was being transferred from the jail for his trip to the state mental hospital, he thanked the sheriff and a jailer for their kindness adding, "I hope I haven't caused you much

trouble." "Not a bit," the sheriff replied. "You've been the best prisoner we have had here since I have been in office."[73]

As the train rolled across the wooded Wisconsin countryside en
route to the state mental hospital, he was asked whether he liked to
hunt. "Only Bull Moose," he replied wryly.[74]

Schrank lived the remainder of his years as an inmate in the prison
hospital at Waupon, Wisconsin, where he became known as "Uncle
John." He was described as a model patient when he died at the age
of sixty-seven on September 15, 1943—the anniversary of the two
visions that had so influenced his life, if not the nation's history as he
had intended.

John Schrank never received a card or visitor in over thirty years
of confinement. When he died, unlike his heroes, Moses and St. Joan,
in death John Schrank became just another cadaver at the Marquette
University Medical School.

Conclusions

There can be little doubt that Richard Lawrence, Charles Guiteau,
and John Schrank were insane. But even among these rather obvious
cases there are differences. Lawrence was the most severely afflicted,
experiencing constant and total emotional and cognitive distortions;
hallucinations and delusions of major proportions virtually destroyed
his contact with reality. He actually did not know who he was, and
was not fully aware of what he was doing. His behavior had assumed
a random quality. He even seemed insensitive to the realities of his
physical environment: for example, he seemed impervious to the cold
temperatures of his jail cell. For Lawrence, the world was a hostile
place—everyone was out to get him. He was completely isolated in a
mental vacuum of overwhelming fear and suspicion. In retrospect, he
alone seems to have possessed the all-consuming qualities diagnosed
as paranoid schizophrenia.

Charles Guiteau and John Schrank were less severely afflicted than
Lawrence. Although both suffered from delusions and a markedly
distorted perception of the world and their place in it, neither possessed
the severe loss of contact with reality experienced by Lawrence. While
both were motivated by grandiose delusions of their own importance,
the darker side of that phenomenon—persecutory delusions—never
occurred. Both acted in concert with remarkably benign views of society. They saw good not only in themselves but in most others. Indeed
one of the symptoms of cognitive distortion in each was their expectation that, in time, society would view their actions sympathetically

and favorably. Almost to the end, Guiteau felt the nation would come around to his point of view and consequently spare his life. His sense of injustice before his execution was simply a reflection of the disappointment of an optimist whose expectations no sane person would have entertained. And even then, he died believing he would be honored eventually by a repentant nation. And Schrank, living the rest of his life in confinement, without bitterness, became the kindly old "Uncle John" he probably had always been, making almost believable his belief that his aggression on that cool October evening in 1912 came not from within but from above.

There is simply no evidence to support the contention commonly put forth that Guiteau and Schrank were motivated by persecutory delusions as was Lawrence. Insane and deluded, yes, but only in the grandiose sense that each was convinced he had been selected by God to implement His will.

Chapter Eight · Family and Money

WEISS AND RAY

. . . how could he have left the wife and baby that he loved above everything?
— A relative of Carl Austin Weiss, 1935

. . . If he done it there had to be a lot of money involved because he wouldn't do it for hatred or just because he didn't like somebody, because that is not his line of work.
— Jerry Ray, 1968

IN MY ANALYSIS of sixteen assassins, only two defy classification, and these two atypical subjects are as different from each other as they are from the classifiable fourteen. Carl Austin Weiss was the most unlikely of all American assassins. Happily married, a doting parent, and a prosperous, respected physician, no one could have predicted that he would kill the flamboyant United States senator and presidential aspirant, Huey P. Long in 1935. At the opposite end of the sociological spectrum, we find the other atypical case, James Earl Ray, the convicted slayer of civil rights leader Martin Luther King, Jr. Unlike Weiss, Ray was notably unsuccessful, even compared to other assassins. Born into poverty and crime, Ray had spent most of his life in prison for clumsily executed robberies. His whole life can be understood, in one sense, as a futile attempt to reach the height of material comfort and respectability that Carl Weiss acquired at birth.

Just as their lives differed, so did their motives: Weiss killed in order to remove what he considered to be an eminent threat to the family he loved; Ray killed for the basest of reasons—money. It is interesting to note in the following how far each of these cases depart from the assassin stereotype.

CARL AUSTIN WEISS (1905-1935)

Senator Huey P. Long was shot on the evening of September 8, 1935 in a corridor of the capitol building in Baton Rouge. His assassin was killed immediately by his bodyguards; Long died shortly after, on September 10. So unlikely was his assassin, that to this day there are those who question whether he actually shot Long, in spite of the scores of persons who witnessed the shooting in the crowded corridor. And even among those who accept that he did, no one is completely sure why. Carl Austin Weiss remains, without question, the most improbable of American political assassins.

Although the life of his colorful victim has been the subject of numerous books, among them Robert Penn Warren's novel *All The King's Men*[1] (which later became an Oscar-winning movie) and T. Harry Williams' biography *Huey Long*[2]—both of which won Pulitzer Prizes— comparatively little is known or remembered about his assassin.[3] Few official records were kept; only the most perfunctory of inquests were held in both deaths.

The first detailed accounts of the actual assassination were published coincidentally in 1963 in two books: David Zinman's *The Day Huey Long Was Shot*,[4] and Hermann B. Deutsch's *The Huey Long Murder Case*.[5] Both books attempt to reconstruct the assassination and possess the authenticity of primary sources. Deutsch's book is based on his notes and recollections of the event and its aftermath as a New Orleans newspaperman who knew Long and many of his associates personally. Zinman's book is the first and only account based on extensive interviews in the early sixties with the families of the slain assassin and his wife.

It is indicative of the improbable qualities of the event that both of these carefully researched books arrive at different conclusions: Deutsch ends convinced that Weiss undoubtedly shot Long on that warm Sunday evening in 1935 for personal reasons, whereas Zinman believes, along with Weiss's family, that Long was shot accidentally by his own trigger-happy bodyguards after he was accosted by Weiss. T. Harry Williams, in his respected biography *Huey Long*, relies heavily on the work of both Deutsch and Zinman, agreeing with Deutsch that Weiss did kill Long but differing in that Williams believed it was for political rather than personal reasons. The variations in the conclusions of these factually consistent books can be traced directly to the mysterious motives of Dr. Carl Austin Weiss. The purpose of my essay is to draw together, for the first time, important facts presented separately by

Deutsch, Zinman, and Williams that provide a more plausible and complete explanation for Long's death.

A Good Life

On December 18, 1905, Viola Maine Weiss gave birth to her first child, a son, in Baton Rouge, Louisiana. Her husband, Carl Adam Weiss, was a young physician who had just started to practice in Baton Rouge. Two years and another child (Olga Marie) later, the family moved to New Orleans where Dr. Weiss had decided to return to medical school to specialize in eye, ear, nose, and throat medicine. About 1916, he and his family returned to Baton Rouge where he began what was to become a respectable and profitable medical practice. In 1917, their third and last child was born, another son, Thomas Edward.

The Weiss family settled into a comfortable but unpretentious life in warm, sleepy Baton Rouge. Strict German Catholics, the family attended church regularly and took their religion seriously. The elder Weiss was a self-satisfied, stern, no-nonsense but loving father who attended Mass daily at 5:15 A.M. and imposed a strong belief in punctuality on all the activities of his family.

His oldest son, Carl Austin, appeared to be his favorite. A quiet, obedient, and highly intelligent youngster, he developed an early interest in mechanics, electricity, and music. He would spend long hours alone playing with erector sets and radios, and eventually learned to play the piano, clarinet, and saxophone. At the age of eight, he disassembled and repaired a family heirloom clock without assistance. Later he was to impress his chums by surreptitiously running electricity from a streetcar stop into their clubhouse. At the age of twelve or thirteen, he wired his grandaunt's house. His competence was later verified by a qualified electrician he agreed to have check his work.

Carl was a curious youngster, interested in many things. An early and avid reader, he injured his eyes as a result of his refusal to stop reading while he had the measles. He made sketches, dabbled in photography and woodcarving, played tennis, and fished. He also liked guns, although he never hunted, preferring instead to test his skill on targets rather than living creatures.[6]

Carl's very obvious talents enabled him to graduate from St. Vincent's Academy as valedictorian at the age of fifteen in 1921. He entered Louisiana State University at the end of that summer to major in engineering. In two years, he accumulated a B-plus average in his classes but decided he would switch from engineering to pre-med. The change also meant that he would have to transfer down the river to Tulane because Louisiana State had no medical program.

As a child and adolescent, Carl had been somewhat introverted. Always polite and courteous, he seemed to be more comfortable with things rather than people. During college, however, he became much more sociable. A wry sense of humor, his musical ability, and above-average intelligence made him a popular person with his fraternity brothers. Never possessing the personal dynamics to carry him into a demanding social life, he was, nonetheless, elected secretary-treasurer of the Sigma medical fraternity. He was also public-spirited in his quiet way and regularly gave up his evenings to play the organ for songfests that were held in a nearby old folks home.[7]

Graduating with a bachelor of science degree in 1925, Carl continued on with his medical training at Tulane winning an internship in pathology at the Touro Infirmary in New Orleans. In 1927, at the early age of twenty-one, he received his M.D. He was invited to remain on another year at the infirmary. In 1928, the impressive young doctor was awarded a prestigious internship to study at the American Hospital in Paris. On September 19, 1928, Carl sailed from Hoboken, bound for France on the *George Washington*. While in Europe, he also studied briefly in Vienna and found time to tour Italy, Hungary, and Yugoslavia, where he witnessed the first ripples of the fascist tide that was to sweep over Europe. But in Europe, he was much more interested in art, music, architecture, and professional matters than he was in politics. His brother was to recall later:

> He felt that politics, as he saw it, was an awful lot of wheels spinning and it really didn't get you very far. He always seemed to have more interesting things to talk about. . . . In fact, I never recall he ever had any strong political philosophy. Just right and wrong. And that was it.[8]

Returning to the states in May 1930, Weiss accepted an internship at Bellevue Hospital in New York where, like his father, he specialized in eye, ear, nose, and throat medicine. At Bellevue, he impressed virtually everyone, even the cynics, who had heard about the impressive young surgeon from Baton Rouge. Describing Weiss as "really a brilliant man," one of his colleagues there added:

> He did some of the most constructive work ever performed in Bellevue clinic. Strong-willed, or even hot-headed, as some might call it, he had a certain charm of manner with troublesome patients. I remember that several times patients were turned over to him when nobody else could handle them. He did.[9]

His colleagues at Bellevue also recalled that he had political opinions, but they agreed that politics was not a central concern with him. When asked about Senator Long, Weiss made it clear that he didn't care for Long, but the feelings were not intense, merely those of any number of other professional people in Louisiana who found the Senator's politics and coarse style more offensive to their taste rather than any direct threat to their interests.[10]

In 1932, Carl decided he would return to Baton Rouge and practice with his father. Baton Rouge at that time was a small, southern town with a population of about thirty thousand—a far cry from New York, but the quieter small-town life appealed to Carl and, besides, he was very close to his parents. When he arrived, the town gave one of its favorite sons a typically folksy welcome. An article in the Baton Rouge *Morning Advocate* reported:

Dr. Weiss has always wanted to practice in Baton Rouge, his birthplace, and on his return two weeks ago went into the office with his father, Dr. C. A. Weiss. He jokingly declared that a few gray hairs would aid him immeasurably. However, his large, capable hands, his serious eyes, and friendly smile inspire confidence.

When asked whether the girls in Baton Rouge and America compared favorably with foreign girls, he answered: "Well, I could hardly be called an expert on that subject. But you see I didn't bring any back with me."[11]

The young, twenty-seven-year-old doctor went through the usual jitters experienced by professional persons who decide to practice in their home towns. The need to establish a professional identity that would gently replace the more familiar boy-next-door image was expressed in growing a moustache, shaving it, aging his satchel through deliberate abuse, joining the Kiwanis Club, and, in general, attempting to appear older and more mature. Such activities, combined with regular church attendance, his father's well-established practice and reputation—he was elected president of the Louisiana Medical Society in 1933—and his own professional skill soon made young, handsome Dr. Weiss one of the most respected members of the community, and perhaps the most eligible bachelor in Baton Rouge.

Louise Yvonne Pavy was born and raised across the Mississippi and down U.S. 190 west through the pine-cypress swamps in the little town of Opelousas. Yvonne—she used her middle name—was one of seven children of Judge Benjamin Pavy and his wife. The Pavys lived in the quiet elegance of prosperous French Louisianans. The Judge presided over the Thirteenth Judicial District composed of St. Landry and Evangeline parishes. He campaigned in French, won the judgeship in 1910 and every election after that until 1936 when he was gerry-mandered out of office by the Long organization. One of the Judge's brothers was a member of the state legislature. The Pavys were a well-seasoned political family in Louisiana and at odds with Huey Long's organization.

Yvonne was an attractive dark-haired young woman who graduated from Tulane's Newcomb College for Women in 1929 with a degree in French. After graduation, she taught school briefly before applying for and being awarded a scholarship to study at the Sorbonne in 1931, after Carl, unknown to her at the time, had returned to the United States.[12] Following a marvelous social year in Paris, Yvonne returned home in 1932 without the advanced degree she had sought. Feeling guilty, she promptly applied for graduate work at Louisiana State in Baton Rouge, determined to make up for the misspent year abroad.

Yvonne's commitment to her studies was real. In November 1932, she walked into the Weiss and Weiss office suite on the seventh floor of the Reymond Building for treatment of eyestrain. The elder Weiss, impressed with his attractive patient, inquired about her studies and brightened when she told him she had spent a year at the Sorbonne. Seizing upon the common experience, he promptly introduced the well-bred and educated young woman to his bachelor son.[13]

About four months later, the cautious Carl sent her an Easter egg and asked her for a date. After a very traditional courtship of evening strolls, porch-swing conversations, and Sunday dinners, they were engaged in the summer of 1933. Their families were delighted. A more attractive couple was difficult to imagine. Two days after Christmas they were married in the St. Landry Parish Catholic Church in Opelousas.[14]

It was to be a close and loving relationship that began with a Florida honeymoon and grew with first year happiness in a cozy apartment near the capitol. When Yvonne became pregnant the following September, they moved to an attractive three-bedroom house at 527 Lakeland Drive to await happily the birth of their child. The house was conveniently located only a few blocks from Our Lady of the Lake Hospital where Carl did most of his surgery and only a short walk from St. Joseph's Church where the young couple attended Mass every Sunday. It was also less than two blocks from the capitol.

According to Yvonne, Carl was more than a doting father to the son born in June 1935. He adored the child and happily participated in every aspect of the little boy's care. Not content with the traditional father's role he could have easily adopted, Carl prepared and gave bottles at all hours, changed diapers, pushed the carriage on contented strolls through the tree-shaded neighborhood, and recorded his happiness with numerous photographs.[15] Even the hot, humid Louisiana summer that had enveloped Baton Rouge could not dampen the happiness of the little family that summer of 1935 as they enjoyed their lives together and planned optimistically for the future.

But apparently Huey Pierce Long could. The Senator and unquestioned political boss of Louisiana had long been at odds with Yvonne's father. Old Ben Pavy, secure in the loyalty of the Cajun voters of Louisiana's Thirteenth Judicial District, was a man the Long organization could not control. Long associates in St. Landry and Evangeline Parishes had convinced the Senator that Pavy had to go, one way or another. It seemed clear that he could not be beaten in an honest election. During the summer, Long ordered a bill drafted that would effectively dilute the Judge's electoral strength by redrawing the boundaries of the Thirteenth District. Irritated by Judge Pavy's quiet contempt and self-confidence, it was widely rumored that Long, not content with just a gerrymander, would also "tar brush" the Judge with a racial smear dredged up from the Judge's distant political past.[16] The slur, simply stated, was that there was black ancestry in the Pavy family. Although this old lie had not worked against the Judge—he hadn't lost an election in nearly thirty years—and had been seemingly forgotten, the fact remains that the charge had never been invoked by anyone approaching the political skill and influence of Huey Long. Although Long associates have denied their leader's plan to smear Pavy in this underhanded way, there can be no doubt that there was precedent for such tactics in Long's political repertoire.[17]

Since virtually all Louisiana newspapers opposed Long, he created his own weekly, the *Louisiana Progress*, to set forth his views and attack his opponents. It was widely read, and the use of racial innuendo was common. For example, he always referred to a New Orleans political opponent as "Kinky," a nickname Huey had coined to convey his view of the man's lineage. The term "shinola" was also regularly used for the same purpose.[18] And he publicly criticized another opponent, Dudley LeBlanc, because the latter employed blacks as fellow officers in his burial insurance company.[19]

The Pavy family, accustomed to the rough and tumble of southern politics, reported that they were not disturbed by the rumor.[20] The Judge had survived many a campaign. The Judge's brother, a member of the Long-dominated legislature, acknowledged that the issue had been discussed in the family but that it had been taken "lightly rather than otherwise."[21]

Carl Weiss, however, was not a political person himself and he was not especially interested in the politics of others. But he had a devout Catholic's concern about right and wrong and good and evil, and certain of Long's actions during that summer of 1935 left little doubt about the powerful Senator's contempt for the Pavys: the gerrymander bill had been introduced on September 7 in a special session of the legislature; this followed in the wake of the Long organization's recent and abrupt termination of the contracts of Paul Pavy, Yvonne's uncle, who was principal of the high school in Opelousas, and Yvonne's sister, Marie, an elementary school teacher, allegedly because neither had been properly certified by the Long-controlled state board of education.[22]

The Victim

On Sunday, September 8, 1935, Huey P. Long was one of the most powerful, loved and feared men in the United States. His rise from obscure beginnings in Winn Parish, Louisiana, through the State Railroad Commission in 1918, the governor's mansion in 1928, and on to the United States Senate in 1932 remains one of the more colorful tales of political success in America. According to his biographer, T. Harry Williams, he was probably the most powerful political boss in American history.[23] A southern populist with a way with words, he was a William Jennings Bryan with brains. Long launched his political career by attacking the big corporate special interests that controlled the state and struck a responsive cord with the people when he followed through with positive action on his campaign promises: the "Kingfish," as he referred to himself, delivered. He demanded and got legislation and appropriations to pave roads, build bridges, improve hospital services, supply free textbooks and other educational services, expand educational opportunities for adults, and abolish the poll tax. More significant, perhaps, he made the depression-weary plain folks of Louisiana feel that they were important. And they have not forgotten him. His death removed one of the most powerful and effective spokesmen for the poor in American history. It also assured Franklin Roosevelt an extended tenure in the White House. With Long dead, the only effective challenge from the political left ended.

President Roosevelt was worried about Long. It was clear that the outspoken and irreverent senator was staking out a position from which to challenge him in the 1936 presidential election.[24] A secret poll commissioned by the President revealed that Long could attract as many as six million votes; moreover, his appeal was not restricted to the South. And the politically astute Long had not yet begun to campaign.[25]

But the Kingfish did have his eye on a national constituency. As early as 1933, the year Roosevelt took office, he began to develop his claim as the only candidate of the people. The populist appeal that had been so successful in Louisiana would be projected on the national scene. Quoting the Bible and damning privilege, Long had the name of his weekly newspaper changed from the *Louisiana Progress* to the *American Progress*. In 1933, he published his autobiography, *Every Man a King*, which, in a self-congratulatory manner, detailed his campaign against special interests and his accomplishments in behalf of common people. In a public letter, he demanded that his name be removed from the Washington *Social Register*. In February 1934, he announced the establishment of local chapters for a "Share the Wealth" campaign around the country and commissioned rabble-rousing evangelist Gerald L. K. Smith as his chief organizer. Long was now clearly directing his appeals beyond the rural South to the depression-ravaged centers of discontent in the urban Northeast and Midwest. Advocating a four-million-dollar limit on personal fortunes and stiff corporate taxes, Long promised to convert the excess into a home, an automobile, a radio, and two thousand dollars a year for every poor family.[26] Hollow-eyed victims of the depression found the promise appealing.

In the spring of 1935, Long dictated his second book entitled *My First Days in the White House*.[27] In it, he outlined with greater specificity how he intended to implement his share-of-the-wealth philosophy once in the White House. In addition to the programs already mentioned, he promised a ten-billion-dollar public works program to build roads and eliminate slums, to promote national health care, and to establish tuition-free college education for all children with requisite ability. Moreover, he announced that he would nationalize corporations that did not operate in the public interest. He also promised to appoint a highly qualified cabinet that would include Franklin D. Roosevelt—as secretary of the Navy.[28]

Long was aware that his outspoken and heavy-handed politics had created many bitter enemies; he was concerned about his safety and always had himself accompanied by a loyal cadre of heavily armed bodyguards. On August 9, 1935, only a month before his death, he rose in the U.S. Senate to announce that a conspiracy to kill him had been uncovered in Louisiana: he referred to what has become known as the "Desoto plot." The plot supposedly unfolded in a meeting of anti-Long forces that had met in mid-July at the Desoto Hotel in New Orleans. Although the actual murderous intent of this meeting has been questioned, there can be no doubt that Long's removal through violence or other means was a frequent and continuing topic at meetings of Long opponents.[29]

Huey Long represented a direct threat to the nation's political and economic establishment: compared to him, the patrician-reformer in the White House—by way of Groton, Harvard, and Hyde Park—was clearly preferable. There is also every reason to think that when Long died on September 10, 1935 there was a collective sigh of relief in the White House as well as on Wall Street. But at no time was evidence ever substantiated that the Senator died as a result of a conspiracy of his opponents.[30]

Possible Explanations

Why then did Dr. Carl Weiss, an apolitical man with seemingly nothing to gain and everything to lose, kill Huey Long? What were his motives? The answers to these questions have brought forth various explanations that can be listed briefly as follows:

1. Long died as a result of a conspiracy in which Weiss had been selected through a drawing of straws as his assassin.
2. Weiss killed Long to end the career of a politically dangerous demogogue. His act was idealistically inspired. He was in this sense a zealot and a willing martyr for a political ideal.
3. Weiss did not kill Long. He had no sufficient motive. Rather, Long was killed by his own bodyguards in the melee that followed after Weiss struck the Senator in the mouth.
4. Long's death was an impulsive, unpremeditated case of homicide. Weiss was angry about Long's treatment of his wife's family but did not intend to kill the Senator.
5. Weiss killed Long in a willful, premeditated manner in retaliation for his actions, real and anticipated, against his wife's family.

Briefly consider each of these explanations.

The conspiracy explanation simply has not been substantiated. There has been no evidence to show that Dr. Weiss attended the Desoto Hotel meeting in spite of rumors to the contrary. Weiss's office records and patients, as well as family testimony, confirm that on the days of the New Orleans conference he was in Baton Rouge and Opelousas.[31]

Foremost among the proponents of the second explanation that Weiss killed Long for patriotic reasons is the historian T. Harry Williams. Suggesting that the young doctor and his family were unaware of the rumored racial slur, Williams concluded that Long died because

"Carl Weiss was a sincere and idealistic young man who agonized over the evils that he believed Huey Long was inflicting on his class and his state."[32] Similarly, *Playboy* author James McKinley also concludes that "it could only have been the impulse of idealism, a hatred and fear of oppression, of Long's fascism [that motivated Weiss]."[33] Both of these views are consistent with the explanation offered by the perplexed family spokesman, Dr. Octave Pavy, who told the press immediately after the tragedy:

> Our only explanation for his action is that this [Long's] suppressive type of rule preyed on his mind until it unhinged, and he suddenly felt himself a martyr, giving his life to the people of Louisiana. He must have felt that way, else how could he have left the wife and baby that he loved above everything?[34]

The family later changed its view and concluded that their loved one simply had no motive for killing Long. Rather, they contended he was killed along with the Senator during a confrontation that resulted in a wild shooting spree by Long's bodyguards who inadvertently fatally wounded their boss while killing the young man who had punched him in the mouth. This is the explanation presented by Zinman in a most convincing manner.[35] But it doesn't quite bear the weight of conflicting evidence.

According to the family's explanation, they were not that upset about Long's actions against them. While acknowledging that the gerrymander was discussed during a pleasant Sunday dinner the day of the killings, it was almost in a joking manner,[36] although Carl did say to his wife, "You know Long is out to get your father. Your father is going to be gerrymandered out of office." The morning paper, which they all read, described the bill that had been introduced the evening before. The family claimed, however, that they were not aware of the racial slur rumor until after the assassination—a statement echoed by Long's associates.[37] In any case, according to this explanation, the slur was something that Carl had not discussed with anyone and was therefore probably unaware of it.

The family also points to a number of inconsistencies beyond their most central argument that the young doctor lacked a sufficient motive. First, the bullet that killed Long was never recovered, raising doubts about its origin and the probability that it came from the gun of one of his over-zealous bodyguards. Second, an autopsy that could have provided more information on this point was not performed; rather, the Senator's body was viewed from across the room by a quickly appointed coroner's jury who, from the distance of approximately twelve feet, were given a very brief view of the tiny exit wound in his back.[38] Indeed, except for a very cursory inquest, an official investigation into the assassination was never conducted. Third, no convincing explanation was ever given for the cut on Long's mouth, which he reportedly explained to a nurse as "That's where he hit me." The failure to address this issue suggests that Weiss did strike the Senator rather than shooting him as Long's associates claimed.[39] These and other bits of circumstantial inconsistencies in the official version of the events, however, only underscore the family's central claim that Carl Weiss had no motive for doing what the state concluded he did. According to his own words and actions prior to the slayings, there was every reason to conclude that Carl Weiss did not anticipate his own death. He appeared on September 8, 1935 to be a happy, content young man looking forward to the future.

Consider the following. On the day of his death, he attended Mass as usual with his wife. After a pleasant Sunday dinner with his parents, the two couples drove to the elder Weisses' river cottage where they spent the remainder of the warm afternoon swimming, playing with the baby, and in easy conversation on the screened porch viewing the river. Driving back to Baton Rouge that evening, Carl and Yvonne said goodbye to Carl's parents and went home, where Carl ate heartily— a couple of sandwiches and two glasses of milk—while his wife bathed their son and got him ready for bed. He then fed the dog, called an anesthetist who was to assist him in a tonsillectomy the next morning to confirm the arrangements, and, as his wife read the Sunday comics, he showered. Later he emerged in the white linen suit and accessories he had worn that morning to Mass. After some light banter about whether they would rock the baby to sleep as usual or let him cry, Carl told Yvonne he had a call to make but would return shortly. He kissed his wife and son and left at about 9 P.M. Although his activities beyond this point remain obscure, it appears that he drove across town to Baton Rouge General Hospital where he was to operate the next morning. A nurse reported having a brief conversation with him there that evening, but there was some confusion concerning the time.[40]

Earlier that week, Weiss had gone with his wife to Kornmeyer's furniture store and purchased a new dining room suite. He also planned to purchase a new gas furnace for the house. He told his mother, who had questioned the wisdom of investing money in a small house he would probably want to leave as his family grew, that he and Yvonne planned to remain there "for ten years at least."[41] There was not a single clue in the words or behavior of the young doctor that he was planning to confront Huey P. Long.

A number of commentators on the killings have concluded that Weiss must have killed for personal rather than political reasons and differ only on whether or not the act was premeditated.[42] Of this group, most are somewhat skeptical of the premeditation theory because both the Weiss and Pavy families had denied a major concern over Long's vendetta against the Pavys. When asked about whether the vendetta might have motivated Weiss, Dr. Octave Pavy, speaking for the family, replied: "In the first place, none of us would kill anyone over such a matter as the loss of a public office."[43] Years later when Yvonne was asked how her family responded to news of the gerrymander, she replied:

> Mother was delighted because Papa didn't make much money as a judge. He had wonderful connections and my brother was practicing law. My mother was elated. The ambition of her life was to get him out of that judgeship. Get him off the bench. So there was no great grief. Nobody was complaining. Judge Pavy himself, never felt an injustice was being done to him personally. It was just the fact that it wasn't legally right. He didn't feel that he was personally suffering from it.[44]

Thus, to a politically seasoned family such as the Pavys, political actions were not taken personally: if one wanted to pursue a political career, it was just part of the game. But unlike the Pavys—and the Longs—Carl Weiss was not capable of such detachment. Carl's world was defined by moral principles and personal concerns. Even so, the loss of a political office alone was not a cause for his martyrdom.

The Motive

Running through the substance of these various theories is a thread of facts and circumstances that provides the most reasonable explanation for the young doctor's behavior. Although most commentators on the killings have focused on a single explanation for Weiss's motives or lack of them, it is probable that he was driven by a combination of factors.

First, it is true that Weiss and people of his class did not like the coarseness and demagogy of Huey Long. But, as we have seen, Weiss was no political zealot; therefore political ideology alone could not have triggered the events of that day.

Second, given Weiss's quiet, intense personality and his strict Catholic sense of right and wrong, it is reasonable to suggest that Long's well-publicized intent to gerrymander his wife's father out of office, following on the heels of the Long-inspired dismissal of her uncle and sister, angered him more than he let on: his seemingly impatient and somewhat condescending remark on the matter at the dinner table is suggestive of this anger. But even this threat was too far removed from the young doctor's primary concerns to have singularly motivated him. In addition, there was an undeniably impulsive quality about the doctor's behavior: the relaxed day with his family, his plans for surgery the next morning, his assurance to his wife that he would return shortly after a quick hospital visit to help with the baby. Also the fact that the special session of the legislature had been called only the day before (Saturday) and that Long's arrival at the session on the fateful next day (Sunday) was unplanned provided little opportunity for a carefully premeditated assassination. Something must have occurred after the doctor left home that warm Sunday evening to cause him to seek out Long.

Third, most observers who discount the racial slur motive are unaware that on Sunday afternoon Long had telephoned his New Orlean's printer, Joe David, that he would be sending down an important story on Judge Pavy for the *American Progress*.[45] One can only conclude that this story would have been a vintage Long racial smear against the Judge to justify and provide a capstone for the forthcoming gerrymander. And "tar brushing," as such racial slurs were called, was a familiar tactic with the Kingfish. In all probability, Weiss heard of Long's intentions after leaving home that evening. Since he normally carried a pistol in his car for night calls, the fact that he was armed was not unusual. What the self-satisfied Long didn't realize as he joked with his protégés in the capitol was that his systematic attacks on the Pavy family—which were politics as usual for Long and even the Pavys—had now extended into an area of vital concern to an intense and now deadly serious young husband and father. Long, always concerned about his personal safety, had no idea that he would be killed by a man with whom, as far as he knew, he had no quarrel.

Irate after hearing Long's plan (from an unidentified source who afterward would be unlikely to come forth with the story), and aware that it fit into a well-known pattern of his vindictive behavior, Weiss quickly considered his options. Given Long's recent attacks on the Pavys, he had no reason to doubt the story. Weiss realized he had little time: he had to act at once to prevent Long from publicizing a charge throughout the state that would jeopardize the future of a wife and son he loved literally, as he would momentarily demonstrate, more than life.

To appreciate the immediacy and salience of this threat, one must consider the virulent form of racism that existed throughout the South in the 1930s. Lynchings, for example, were occurring in unprecedented numbers as the economic hardship of the depression aggravated racial tensions. To be black in the South of the 1930s meant relegation to a sub-human existence.[a] Weiss, who probably shared in the racial prejudices of his fellow white southerners, recognized that even the suspicion of black ancestry was enough to ruin the lives of his wife and son. Long had to be stopped.

The Event

Driving to the capitol from the hospital,[b] Weiss entered the building armed with the .32 caliber pistol he had brought back from Europe along with his fencing equipment and two old battle swords. Like the European standards those swords represented and he admired, what he was about to do was a matter of honor.[46]

In the capitol corridor, Weiss spoke pleasantly to a young woman who happened by, patted the former patient on the head, and walked quickly toward the corridor outside the governor's office.[47] Reaching the office, he stood quietly in a tiny alcove opposite the double doors that led into the governor's anteroom.[48] Moments later, Long and his entourage entered the corridor after a quick walk from the legislative chamber. Long planned to use Governor O. K. Allen's office to issue a press release blaming President Roosevelt for the deaths of Civilian Conservation Corps youths in a Florida hurricane.[49] Coat unbuttoned, elbows swinging, and belly bouncing, Long was bellowing over his shoulder to aides as his bodyguards scrambled to keep up with him, when a slight figure in a white linen suit appeared. Long's eyes bulged in fear, and as he began to recoil, Carl Weiss, without a word, fired from a distance of a few feet. Long screamed, clutching his abdomen, and ran from the corridor moments before bedlam broke loose. As aides grappled with Weiss knocking him to the floor, he fired again

---

[a] Recall that the legal basis for the "separate but equal" doctrine of racial segregation was established by the Supreme Court in its ruling on a Louisiana case, *Plessy* v. *Ferguson* (1896). The *Plessy* decision upheld the Louisiana law which specified that a person with even one thirty-second of black blood was considered black and was therefore forbidden to use "white only" facilities. *Plessy* remained the law of the land until it was overturned in 1954 in the famous *Brown* decision.

[b] Some have questioned why he took his car when he lived less than two blocks from the capitol and the parking lot was invariably jammed when the legislature was in session.

at his assailants.[c] Then the corridor exploded in gunfire and smoke as Weiss, who had regained his feet, crouched facing the onslaught before being slammed to the floor under the impact of the .44 and .45 caliber hollow-point bullets that tore through his face, neck, and torso.[50] Seemingly crazed with frustration and anger, Long's bodyguards continued to fire into the lifeless body causing it to lurch crazily across the marble floor as it was torn apart by some thirty-two to sixty bullets fired at point-blank range.[51]

Long raced down a stairway to the ground floor where, on the verge of collapse, he met an aide who flagged down an unknown car in the parking lot and escorted the wounded Senator to Our Lady of the Lake Hospital. Dr. Arthur Vidrine, a political appointee and friend of Long's who had been at the special session, arrived soon after and decided to operate. Vidrine, who had little training in surgery, failed to perform the standard pre-operative diagnosis of the wound and, as a result, the surgery failed to reveal a hemorrhaging kidney. And Long was too weak to survive a second operation. Doctors arriving after the surgery had been completed quickly observed the fatal error that resulted in the Senator's death some thirty odd hours later on Tuesday, September 10, 1925.[52] Senator Huey Long was buried in front of the skyscraper capitol he had built after the largest funeral in Louisiana history.

Carl Weiss was given a church burial the day after he died. His funeral, the largest of any assassin in American history, was attended by several hundred friends, former patients, civic leaders, a former governor, a congressman, the district attorney, and virtually the entire Baton Rouge medical profession. Thousands stood in a pouring rain at Roselawn Cemetery. Most of the mourners could not believe he had killed Long; many of those who did considered him a martyr.[53]

Conclusions

The most improbable of American assassins, Carl Weiss bore no resemblance to the stereotyped, mentally ill assassin so often characterized in the literature of such events. Those who would label him a zealot who killed for political purposes have ignored the apolitical qualities of his life. He was a highly individualistic person. He was not drawn to, nor was he motivated by, political causes. Carl Weiss killed Huey Long somewhat impulsively when he learned that Long threatened direct harm to those he loved.

---

[c] It is probable that Long was struck in the mouth by one of his own men during the confusion of this brief scuffle. Weiss never got close enough to strike him.

The only case that resembles this one, and then only in some respects, is the 1978 murders of Mayor George Moscone and Supervisor Harvey Milk of San Francisco. Like Long, Moscone and Milk did not realize that their decision to deny Dan White's seat on the board of supervisors meant much more to White than merely losing a political office. For White, it was not merely "the breaks" in a rough and tumble world of politics, it meant everything—his future, his family, and his self-respect. Like Carl Weiss, he was not temperamentally suited for politics: he was much too intense. He didn't have the emotional slack to handle defeat, especially when he considered it unfair. There was also no real separation of political and personal for White either. In other words, he too did not have the emotional resiliency and moral flexibility to handle politics as usual. Just as the politically tough and sophisticated Pavy family could not imagine killing Long for what he did, or was threatening to do, most Bay Area politicians could not understand why Dan White would do what he did. But the Carl Weisses and Dan Whites of the world are wired too tightly for the stresses of political life. And in each case that wire of constraint snapped at the personal level with tragic and totally unanticipated consequences.

A wheeling and dealing style in political life always involves risks, and overcoming those risks makes winning even more satisfying; it is a political aphrodisiac for many practitioners. But unfortunately, tough successful politicians like Long, Moscone, and Milk fail to realize that the stakes of the game can reach intolerably high limits with unanticipated rapidity for those who are not emotionally prepared to play such a high-stakes game. It is the unpredictable risks represented by improbable killers such as Carl Weiss and Dan White that define a thin, white-hot thread of emotion that marks the sometimes too subtle and fatal boundary between political and personal life.

JAMES EARL RAY (1928-)

Unlike the relatively unknown Carl Weiss, a good bit has been written about James Earl Ray, the convicted killer of Dr. Martin Luther King, Jr. Ray was arrested at Heathrow Airport in London on June 8, 1968, some sixty-five days and an international manhunt after Dr. King was fatally shot in Memphis, Tennessee. Except for John Wilkes Booth, Ray is the only other subject who had planned and implemented an elaborate escape.

After a succession of lawyers and controversy surrounding deals to market the James Earl Ray story, an anti-climactic guilty plea was entered, and Ray was sentenced to ninety-nine years imprisonment. The plea was unexpected because Ray had the nationally known criminal lawyer Percy Foreman representing him, and the expectation was that there would be a well-publicized trial rather than a brief ceremony in which Ray admitted his guilt and was sentenced.

The case against Ray was overwhelming: evidence that he had been stalking King; that he had purchased the murder weapon; that he had rented a room adjacent to the bathroom from which the fatal shot was fired; that witnesses saw a person matching Ray's description fleeing the scene; and that Ray's fingerprints were the only ones found on the rifle and personal belongings dropped in a doorway near the scene of the crime. The only thing that could have strengthened the case against him, it seemed, was a witness who actually saw him pull the trigger. Everything else was there.[54] But the fact that there was no trial to speak of and that Ray subsequently claimed he was not the killer, as he had admitted, has contributed to the strong suspicion that Ray did not act alone.

Two of Ray's better known biographies are William Bradford Huie's *He Slew the Dreamer*[55] and George McMillan's more recent *The Making of an Assassin*.[56] Huie's book is based largely on written statements that Ray gave to him as well as his own investigation of Ray's story. McMillan's book relies heavily on Huie's research, supplemented with information obtained through interviews with members of Ray's family, especially his brothers John and Jerry. Both writers conclude that Ray acted alone and disagree only in their interpretation of his motive. Huie believes Dr. King was killed to enable Ray to achieve fame—a familiar explanation for many assassins.[57] Imposing a rather strained psychoanalytic interpretation, McMillan concludes that Ray killed the civil rights leader to satisfy an obsessive racist hatred of blacks which had somehow become tangled up with the unresolved oedipal conflicts Ray had with his father. Thus, oddly enough according to McMillan, Dr. King had become a father figure to Ray and had died as a result.[58] Both books have drawn criticism and lawsuits from Ray and outright denials of accuracy by Ray's brothers. Jerry Ray also acknowledged that he had deliberately lied to McMillan and referred to the book as "a joke."[59]

Although there are obvious risks in writing books based on paid interviews with known criminals, taken together, the two books provide an intriguing view of the man James Earl Ray up to the time of his escape from Missouri State Penitentiary on April 23, 1967. Other sources provide a more complete and convincing account of activities from that time to his arrest and conviction for the King assassination. What follows is an attempt to present a collage of James Earl Ray's background selectively drawn from these primary, if controversial, accounts.

A Hard Life

James Earl Ray was born on March 10, 1928 to poor parents in Alton, Illinois. He was the first of the nine children of George and Lucille Ray. Drab river towns and hard-clay farms with deteriorating, unpainted buildings marked the boundaries of their existence on the Missouri-Illinois border. The Rays were the poorest of the poor. In fact, the depression did not substantially change their life for the worse as it did for many people of that era. The failures of George Ray, or "Speedy," as he was called, were complete before the depression. Speedy was the kind of person who wanted to run a farm but actually spent most of his time just trying to keep his truck running. He always had the appearance of someone who had spent a good part of his life under dilapidated vehicles. His wife had the drawn, hollow-eyed appearance of a woman who was having too many children too fast and had too little to support them with. Even more than her husband, she was being overwhelmed by the harsh realities of what she saw happening but was unprepared to handle. Before long she would turn to drink.

Many who grew up during those times can remember a James Earl Ray in grade school. In a roomful of shabbily-hand-me-down dressed school children, his clothes were the most colorless. His shoes were "clodhoppers"—cheap, sturdy, rural-looking shoes that kids who could not afford rubber galoshes for snow and slush in the winter wore year round. Kids like this seemed to have constantly running noses that, because they rarely had handkerchiefs, were wiped on sleeves or the backs of their hands. And they always had the damp, musky smell of urine, regardless of personal habits, because in many cases they slept in the same beds with little brothers and sisters. It didn't matter, however: teachers invariably blamed them and expressed their contempt in low grades in "health" or "citizenship," not to mention unsubtle remarks to the class about cleanliness.

Confronted with such obstacles, it is little wonder that many of these children became withdrawn, just as the six-year-old Jimmy Ray did. Missing a lot of school and possessing none of the endearing social graces middle-class teachers prefer, he flunked the first grade in spite of his normal I.Q. of 105 to 108.

The old farm in Ewing where the Ray's lived represented the rural equivalent of the wrong side of the tracks. It was the place anyone in Ewing could contemplate and feel a little bit better about his or her lot in life. Living under such a stigma makes children bitter. Little boys become tough—not bullies usually—but kids who do not back away from a fight, and, once engaged, battle with a ferocity and abandon that, regardless of skill, is likely to cause alarm among better-dressed, sweeter-smelling rivals. Jimmy Ray was no exception.

Often children in these circumstances don't have a lot of close friends the way middle-class children do. Friendships are less intimate because there is so little in the home environment to share with friends: few outsiders want to share adversity. Paradoxically, however, the same adversity often seems to meld a common bond between siblings—particularly those closest in age and experience. Jimmy Ray was always closer to his family than to anyone else. In spite of his loner ways, he would remain in regular contact with his brothers, John and Jerry, and also his sister, Carol, throughout his life.[60]

Jimmy also got along well with his parents in spite of the hardships that would eventually destroy the family. He liked to sit by his dad as they clattered along in a succession of old trucks. He also watched with pride as Speedy defeated opponents at the local pool hall and listened carefully as his hero taught him to play the game.[61]

His mother, too, loved and cared for the little boy as best she could with all the other younger children. But in family situations such as the Ray's, attention was received only when absolutely required, not because there was no love, but simply because there was no time or energy: attention spans were constrained by necessity. There was a quiet, nonconflictive resignation to the bad hand they had been dealt as a family, interrupted occasionally only by some additional crisis—a little daughter dying from household burns, or Jimmy breaking his leg in the schoolyard. It was only on these occasions that love and compassion were released from beneath the insulating layers of emotional dormancy that had been created by the unrelieved pressures of poverty.

But the pressures were eventually too great to endure, and the family collapsed when Jimmy was in eighth grade. He quit school and went to live with his grandmother, eventually winding up where he was born in Alton. The three youngest children were placed in the Catholic Children's Home in Alton, and his mother took the older ones with her to Quincy, Illinois. Speedy took up with another woman.

The Rays provide a classic example of the sociological conception of a family that accepted culturally defined goals of success but was denied the socially structured means of achieving it. They would run a convulsively destructive course of desertion, neglect, despair, alcoholism, and crime, with only a daughter, Carol, managing to cling tenaciously to a remnant of stability and respectability. The rest would be destined for mental hospitals, prisons, and premature graves.

There was a point when Jimmy tried to make it in a conventional sense. At the age of sixteen, in 1944, he got a job at a tannery in Hartford, Illinois. He was a good, reliable worker who saved his money for almost two years before he was laid off in January 1946. Six weeks later, he joined the Army and, after basic training, was sent to serve with the occupation forces in Germany. But Army life did not agree with him. Soon after his arrival in Bremerhaven, his main pursuits became drinking, fighting, whoring around, and financing most of it through the black market sale of cigarettes—hardly the activities of "a young political idealist," as George McMillan describes him, looking for ideological answers in bombed-out Germany.[62]

The fact is there is little evidence of Ray's ideological concerns during this period beyond a friendship with an alleged crypto-Nazi he worked with at the Hartford tannery and questionable hearsay evidence of rather ordinary racist remarks attributed to him.[63] Such remarks could have been made by any number of white Americans in 1946, not to mention whites on the lower rungs of society such as Ray.

Although Ray could be considered a tough kid, he was not a bully, and his subsequent criminal record reveals no tendency toward personal violence.[64] Rather, that record, which begins after his discharge from the Army and continues consistently to his arrest for the King slaying, is a record of bungled and ludicrously inept robberies and burglaries during which no one was ever hurt or seriously threatened with bodily harm.

He served time for stealing a typewriter in Los Angeles in 1949, robbing a Chicago cab driver in 1952, stealing money orders in Hannibal, Missouri and cashing them on a carefree trip to Florida in 1955, and robbing a St. Louis supermarket in 1959. The $120 he lifted from the Kroger's cash register got him twenty years in the Missouri State Penitentiary in Jefferson City. After two unsuccessful escape attempts in 1960 and 1966, he finally made it through the gates concealed in a bread truck on April 23, 1967.

There is not much in the record to suggest that after the age of twenty-one James Earl Ray ever thought of going straight. Prison authorities considered him an habitual criminal with only a marginal chance of changing.[65] He wanted success—to experience the American Dream. But he was also smart enough to see that the reality of success in America was defined in dollars, the magnitude of which was far beyond the potential offered through honest hard work.

The Alleged Racist Motive

The five years and few months Ray spent in the Missouri State Penitentiary figure importantly in some attempts to explain his subsequent behavior. George McMillan, for example, claims Ray's motive for killing Dr. King was an obsessive racist hatred and describes events in Ray's prison experience to support his claim. Ray, for example, supposedly declined a desirable opportunity for transfer to a prison farm because it was racially integrated. However, Ray claims he declined the transfer to avoid the possibility of trouble, which could jeopardize his chances for parole, due to the extensive drug dealing among the farm inmates.[66] Other accounts refer to the verbal rages Ray allegedly went into when Dr. King appeared on the prison television screens.[67] Such behavior is attributed to the Nazi sympathies Ray supposedly acquired in his youth. Both Ray and his family have denied these allegations, and their denials have been essentially substantiated. In fact, the prison warden reported that Ray and other inmates did not have access to television.[68]

Other examples of the depths of Ray's acknowledged racism have also been questioned. After his escape from prison, Ray left on an odyssey of sorts that carried him from Chicago to Puerto Vallarta, with stops in Montreal and Birmingham, Alabama before arriving in Los Angeles on November 19, 1967. Authors Huie and McMillan have cited a number of events during his travels to underscore their contention that Ray was aggressively hostile toward blacks.[69]

In Montreal, Ray had a brief affair with a young and very attractive Canadian woman. In the course of their relationship, Ray was described as having made racist remarks to her about "niggers." But the woman later denied that she had ever reported that Ray had made any such statements: "He never mentioned the name Martin Luther King and never indicated any hatred toward Negroes."[70]

Two racially motivated altercations at bars also have been attributed to Ray. The first of these occurred in Puerto Vallarta sometime in October or November 1967, where Ray allegedly tried to provoke a fight with some black sailors who were celebrating at a nearby table. According to Ray's companion, a prostitute, Ray did not try to provoke a fight. What actually happened was that a drunken black sailor, who had gotten up to leave the boisterous table, stumbled and fell into Ray's table and, in the process, grabbed the prostitute by the shoulders in a vain attempt to prevent his fall. Ray became angry, swore at the sailor—"son-of-a-bitch"—and later showed the prostitute a pistol he intended to use if they were bothered again. In explaining the incident later, however, his companion claimed that Ray's anger was over the intrusion and not because the drunk was black.[71]

The second incident occurred later, after Ray had traveled to Los Angeles from Mexico. During his stay there—November 19, 1967 to March 18, 1968—he frequented a couple of bars. The incident occurred at one of these during a discussion in which Ray argued that a white person would not be safe in the Watts section of Los Angeles. According to an FBI report,[72] Ray became angry and attempted to drag a female participant in the discussion out of the bar, supposedly to drop her off in Watts. The story has been questioned, and although the FBI agent still claims its accuracy, a bartender who witnessed the discussion claims, in a signed statement, that the FBI report is a distortion. According to him, a discussion did occur involving a number of people at the bar—including blacks—but it was not a heated discussion, nor did Ray accost, or attempt to drag, anyone from the bar; nor was he subsequently attacked by a black in the parking lot. Rather the evening ended without incident.[73]

Also interesting in this context is the fact that the two bars Ray favored in Los Angeles—the Rabbit's Foot and the Sultan Room—were racially integrated. It was estimated that approximately half the regular clientele of the Rabbit's Foot and a third of the Sultan Room's customers were black. If this bothered Ray, it was not to a degree sufficient to cause him to select another from the hundreds of bars in the Los Angeles area. Moreover, a woman who knew Ray during his stay in Los Angeles revealed that, for a period, he dated a black woman he met in the Sultan Room and gave no overt indication of any racism in his conduct toward her.[74]

Although these accounts do not deny Ray's basic racism, they do raise doubts about its alleged intensity. And in so doing, one must question whether an obsessive racist rage provides a convincing explanation of his assassination of Dr. King.[75] As a lower-class white from the rural-southern culture of Missouri, it is not surprising that Ray held racist views. But it is doubtful that Ray's racism alone could have motivated him to leave Los Angeles on March 18, 1968 to begin a single-minded and deadly journey that would eventually lead to a cracked and dirt-stained bathroom window in a seedy rooming house in Memphis, Tennessee.[76]

As we will see, his racism did, however, alter his view of the seriousness of his crime and, to that degree, his assessment of his ability to get away with it. In other words, it was not James Earl Ray's white, lower-class resentment of what Martin Luther King, Jr. represented—a prominent national leader, a recipient of a Nobel Peace Prize, and a person who was invited to counsel with presidents—that drove him obsessively to the assassination. Rather, Dr. King was killed, in part, because he was *merely* a "nigger." And killing a nigger in the South was an act a man could get away with, even if caught: it was, therefore, worth doing if the *price* was right.

The Family Connection

With a single significant qualification—his family—Ray's relationships with other people were invariably brief; he was a loner. Over the years, however, he faithfully maintained contact with his brothers John and Jerry as well as his sister Carol. It was a curious bond, probably formed by the adversity they shared as children, nurtured in adulthood by a common knowledge that life was unfair and the belief that there were precious few people they could count on except each other. John's description of his brother shortly after his arrest in 1968 characterizes the relationship: "James would do anything for us and we for him. But he wasn't particularly sociable with strangers."[77]

Other than the mysterious "Raoul," who, according to Ray's story, suddenly appeared after Ray's escape from Missouri State Penitentiary in April 1967 and simply vanished—literally without a trace—after the King slaying, Ray had no sustained relationships with anyone but his two brothers and sister. For example, Jerry and John were the only persons who visited James Earl in prison. He corresponded only with his sister Carol.[78]

There is an overwhelming amount of evidence of the interaction between the Ray brothers. Moreover, the coincidental nature between these interactions and those attributed by Ray to the puzzling Raoul is revealing. Consider the following chronology of Ray's activities from the time of his prison escape until a few days before King's death.[79]

April 22, 1967. John visited James Earl on the day before his escape on April 23, 1967, and this suggests a strong probability that he assisted his brother in the escape.[80]

April 30 to July 13, 1967. The *brothers* remained in contact after the escape and possibly discussed some joint enterprises during Ray's stay in the Chicago area.[81]

July 13, 1967. Ray probably participated with *one or both brothers* in the $27,000 robbery of the Bank of Alton, Illinois. From this point on, Ray appeared to have plenty of money.[82]

July 14 to August 21, 1967. After the robbery, Ray went to Montreal, where he remained. It is probable that he maintained contact with his *brothers* while in Canada. Ray told a girlfriend there that he was working for his *brother*.[83]

August 21 to August 30, 1967. Returning to the states, Ray met with his *brother* Jerry in Chicago enroute to Birmingham, Alabama. During this period, Ray received three payments totalling $4,500 from someone—*he claims Raoul*.

October 7 to November 18, 1967. Ray traveled to Mexico in the white Mustang he had purchased in Birmingham. It is not clear what the purpose of this trip was. It has been suggested that he hoped to get started in the pornography business with his newly purchased photography equipment and the availability of less expensive Mexican prostitutes.[84] He may have also been exploring the possibilities of a burgeoning marijuana market, although this has been denied.[85]

November 19, 1967. Ray arrived in Los Angeles and soon established contact with one or both of his *brothers* by mail and telephone.

December 14 or 15, 1967. Ray cancelled an appointment with a psychologist explaining that he had to *meet his brother* in New Orleans about a job. *Ray called Jerry* twice on his way to New Orleans. He then received a payment of five hundred dollars from someone in New Orleans—*he claims Raoul*.

December 1967. After returning to Los Angeles on December 21, Ray made a $364 payment for dancing lessons and casually mentioned to the instructor that he had just returned from visiting his *brother* in Louisiana. An anonymous witness later testified that Jerry had told him that he had been in New Orleans with his *brother* the third week of December 1967.[86]

February 1968. Sometime this month someone wrote or called Ray in Los Angeles—*allegedly Raoul*—and instructed him to return to New Orleans in March. Ray then called New Orleans for more complete information.

March 2 to March 19, 1968. He again casually mentioned to someone in the bartending school he was attending that he was going to Birmingham to see his *brother*. He repeated this story when he declined a bartending job on March 9. Then on March 17, Ray left Los Angeles, indicating his ultimate destination on a postal change of address order as Atlanta—Dr. King's home and headquarters, rather than New Orleans, as he later claimed.[87]

March 20-28, 1968. Arriving in New Orleans on March 20, Ray received a message to meet someone—*he claims Raoul*—in Birmingham. Ray left for Birmingham the next day but took a suspiciously round-about route through Selma, Alabama, where he spent the night on March 22. Dr. King had just left the area the day before. That morning Ray drove to Birmingham where he met someone—*allegedly Raoul*—before driving on together to Atlanta on March 23. During this time, Ray was armed only with a .38 caliber pistol. After a day together, Ray's accomplice—*allegedly Raoul*—left and did not return until March 28 or 29. During his stay in Atlanta, Ray circled the area of Dr. King's home, office, and church on an Atlanta map.[88]

March 29-30, 1968. Sometime during this period, Ray and *his accomplice* decided it would be easier and safer to kill Dr. King with a long-range rifle rather than a pistol. On March 29, Ray received $750 from his accomplice—*allegedly Raoul.* That same day, according to attorney Percy Foreman, *Ray and his brother Jerry* drove to Birmingham together where Ray purchased a .243 Remington rifle at Aeromarine Supply Company. Later that day, Ray called the Aeromarine salesman to say that his *brother* had convinced him that he needed a larger caliber rifle. The next day, the exchange was made, and Ray left with a Remington 30.06—the murder weapon.[89] From this point until the assassination Ray was alone.

Following the rifle purchase, Ray returned to Atlanta still on Dr. King's trail. On March 31, he paid his room rent, and on April 1, he dropped off some clothing at the Piedmont Laundry. Ray later denied making this trip back to Atlanta since it would provide strong circumstantial evidence that he was, in fact, stalking Dr. King. He stated flatly before the House Select Committee on Assassinations: "If I did return to Atlanta on those dates, I will just take responsibility for the King case here on TV." The committee then presented the laundry receipt as undeniable evidence.[90]

After learning in the Atlanta papers of Dr. King's plan to be in Memphis on April 3 and 4, Ray left Atlanta on April 2 and drove to Memphis, arriving on April 3 when he checked into the New Rebel Motel. Then reading in the Memphis *Commercial Appeal* that Dr. King was staying at the Lorraine Motel, Ray rented another room in Bessie Brewer's rooming house only a short distance and an unobstructed view across a back alley from King's room.[91]

Again, it is clear that throughout the period extending from his prison escape until he shot Dr. King James Earl Ray's *only* consistent contacts were with his *brothers*—and especially Jerry—unless one accepts the Raoul story. His own testimony and written statements, the testimony of others he happened to talk with (for example, the woman in Canada), acquaintances in Los Angeles, the policeman who guarded him after his arrest in England, his attorneys, author William Bradford Huie, *Playboy* Magazine, and Dan Rather of CBS News substantiate the pattern and exclusivity of this association.[92]

Moreover, not one shred of evidence has ever been produced to verify the existence of a "Raoul"—not a fingerprint, witness, telephone call, or even a reasonable circumstantial clue. Beyond this, there is some evidence that contact was maintained between the brothers *after* the assassination. For example, it is probable that John Ray knew his brother was in London *before* Ray's arrest and planned to join him there.[93] James Earl Ray was, and continues to be, close to and protective of his family.

Thus it would appear that there is a considerable amount of evidence indicating that James Earl Ray killed Martin Luther Kng, Jr. with the probable knowledge and assistance of his two brothers. But the question why remains. Having found little support for the notion that Ray's undeniable racism was a primary motive, one must consider the probability that what motivated James Earl Ray was what had always motivated him throughout his criminal life—money.

The Contract

Two days before Ray was arrested in London, a companion asked Jerry Ray if he thought his brother had actually killed Dr. King. Jerry acknowledged later that he replied, in effect: "If I was in his position and had 18 years to serve and someone offered me a lot of money to kill someone I didn't like anyhow, and get me out of the country, I'd do it." When asked if there was money involved, he replied: ". . . if he done it there had to be a lot of money involved because he wouldn't do it for hatred or just because he didn't like somebody, because that is not his line of work."[94] Brother John expressed the same view in a June 9, 1968 interview with the *St. Louis Post-Dispatch*.[95]

Given this acknowledged history of James Earl Ray's past motives and behavior, consider the outline of a probable conspiracy that was not revealed for some ten years and a curiously conducted FBI investigation after Dr. King's death.

Sometime early in 1967, a St. Louis underworld figure, Russell G. Byers, was approached by an acquaintance, John Kauffmann, and asked if he was interested in making fifty thousand dollars.[96] John Kauffmann, a jowly-faced, bald, paunchy man in his early sixties was fairly well-known among people operating outside of the law in the St. Louis area. Kauffmann, a sometime stockbroker, actually ran a fencing operation for stolen cars and other goods out of a motel he owned in Barnard, Missouri, near St. Louis.[97] His main activity, however, was drug dealing through a licensed drug company he owned. Kauffmann would purchase drugs wholesale and then market them illegally, making a considerable profit on the mark-up. As a result of these activities, he came into contact with many known criminals and ex-convicts in St. Louis.[98]

One of Kauffmann's more interesting friends was Dr. Hugh Maxey, a physician at Missouri State Prison where James Earl Ray and Russell Byers' brother-in-law, John Paul Spica,[d] knew each other as fellow inmates.[99] Spica also worked in the prison hospital with Dr. Maxey as an orderly. It is probable that the functional basis of the friendship between John Kauffmann and Dr. Maxey was prison-related drug dealing.[100] In any case, this was one segment of a pattern of associations that existed when John Kauffmann approached Russell Byers about a fifty-thousand-dollar job.

During this same period, Carol Ray Pepper, the Ray brothers' sister, owned the Grapevine Tavern in St. Louis. The tavern was managed by her brother John. A fairly rough bar in the rundown southside of the city, it was, as its name suggests, a place where one could go for information and contacts with the St. Louis underworld. John Kauffmann used to drop by the tavern occasionally for that reason.[101] It was also a distribution point for George Wallace's 1968 American Independent party campaign literature, located as it was, just across the street from the Wallace campaign headquarters in that section of the city.[102]

Outside of St. Louis in a rural area near Imperial, Missouri lived white-haired, distinguished-looking John Sutherland. Born in Virginia in 1905, and a 1926 engineering graduate of Virginia Military Institute, the ambitious and hard-working Sutherland went on to earn both a bachelor's and a master's degree in law before establishing a successful practice as a patent attorney in St. Louis. Active in social, fraternal, and professional activities in the area, Sutherland was proud of a southern family heritage he traced back to the early colonists. He was also the organizer of a segregationist white citizens' council and an avid supporter of Governor Wallace's presidential campaign in 1968. Sutherland alone paid the six-hundred-dollar-a-month salary for the AIP's state chairman.[103]

Sutherland's right-wing affiliations extended to the ultraconservative Southern States Industrial Council and its president, Thurman Sensing, with whom he shared concerns, friendship, and correspondence in 1968.[104] Less than two weeks after Dr. King's death, Thurman Sensing would address the Daughters of the American Revolution in a tasteless

---

[d] Spica was killed after his release from prison in a car bombing on November 7, 1979.

speech that did, however, draw a very favorable response from the FBI and its director, J. Edgar Hoover.[105] In the speech, Sensing stated, in part: "It is not too much to say, in fact, that Martin Luther King, Jr., brought this crime [his assassination] on himself." He went on to speculate sympathetically that Dr. King's assassin may have reasoned: "I think Martin Luther King should be killed. I realize there is a law against murder, but in this case, I think the law is unjust."[106]

Mr. Sutherland's politics were also reflected in the decor of his home and at times even in his dress. When John Kauffmann led Russell Byers into Sutherland's richly furnished den on that evening in early 1967, they took an almost farcical step back in time. As they walked across a rug replica of the Confederate flag amid other trappings and memorabilia of an era a hundred years past, the wealthy attorney greeted them in the uniform of a Confederate officer complete with a colonel's hat.[107] One can only wonder what crossed the minds of Kauffmann and Byers who were more accustomed to the revolving illuminated Clydesdales, pickled eggs, and calendar nudes of places like the Grapevine.

In any case, after some somewhat awkward pleasantries, Sutherland addressed the purpose of the gathering: would Byers arrange the murder of Martin Luther King for fifty thousand dollars? The surprised Byers asked where the money was going to come from. Sutherland's reply: "A secret Southern organization."[108] After declining the offer, Byers testified that he was never approached again about the matter and did not think much about it until Dr. King's death.[109] Concerned at that time that he might be implicated, he related the incident to two of his attorneys who advised him just to remain quiet. Then sometime during late 1973, some five and a half years after the assassination, Byers happened to mention the incident unknowingly to an FBI informant. The latter reported the story to the St. Louis FBI office a few months later in March 1974. For strange and mysterious reasons, this important information was not investigated by the Bureau. Byers was never questioned despite the fact that he was a known criminal figure. And it was not until March 13, 1978—four years later—that the information was finally reported to the House Select Committee on Assassinations. The FBI explained this breakdown in an important investigation as nothing more than an administrative error.[110]

The probable communication between Sutherland and Kauffmann and members of the Ray family is fairly direct: word that a contract was out on Dr. King need not have depended on chance and rumor. The link between Kauffmann and Dr. Maxey extended to Russell Byers' brother-in-law John Spica, an inmate acquaintance of James

Earl Ray; Spica was also an associate of one Robert Regazzi whose ex-wife, Naomi, was employed as a barmaid at Carol and John Ray's Grapevine Tavern. Recall that the tavern was a watering hole for the Wallace organization people headquartered across the street. And Wallace's American Independent party in St. Louis was bankrolled in part, as we have seen, by John Sutherland. Consequently, the Wallace party also had close contact with, and financial support from, the segregationist Citizens' Council of St. Louis, which counted Mr. Sutherland as one of its founders and most committed members.[111]

Although it is unlikely that the respectable, middle-class John Sutherland ever bellied-up to the bar at the Grapevine to discuss anything directly with its sleazy clientele, it is probable that John Kauffmann did from time to time. His underworld activities required that he make the kind of contacts available in a place like the Grapevine where criminal transactions were a well-known pattern of activity.[112] Another of Mr. Sutherland's friends, Glen Shrum, a Wallace organizer, enjoyed the ambience of the Grapevine and regularly crossed the street for a drink or two and some congenial conversation. A Bircher as well as a Minuteman, there was no question about where Glen Shrum stood on the race issue, and John Sutherland liked men like that— men ready to use whatever means available to save the "Republic" from the evils of civil rights and race mixing. Drinking their beer amid the Wallace bumper stickers, campaign pamphlets, and stale bar odors of John Ray's tavern, there was no doubt in the minds of these angry supporters about the threat posed by the black minister from Atlanta.[113]

At this time—the middle of March 1968—James Earl Ray, who had become mildly interested in the possibility of a Wallace presidency while living in Los Angeles, was driving to New Orleans after receiving word from someone (allegedly Raoul, but as we have seen, most likely his brother Jerry) about a big deal: the contract had been picked up. From this time on, James Earl Ray began his systematic stalk of Dr. King, following his movements and plans in newspaper accounts that recorded his activities in and out of his Atlanta headquarters. The hunt would end on the balcony of the Lorraine Motel in Memphis on April 4.[114]

Escape and Arrest

Ray's seemingly well-planned and executed escape after the assassination was marred by the same sort of blunders that had characterized his previous criminal activity. As he ran from Bessie Brewer's rooming house after firing the fatal shot, he spotted a police car and instinctively discarded the murder weapon and a number of personal belongings he had wrapped in a bedspread in the doorway of Canipes Amusement Company.[115] He had not planned to do this. The fingerprints on these articles eventually led to his arrest on the morning of June 8, 1968 as he was preparing to board a Brussels-bound jet in London. Except for this immediate evidence, it is unlikely that authorities could have pieced together other clues in time to prevent him from making good his ingenious escape through Canada and England to some anticipated sanctuary in Angola, Rhodesia, or South Africa.[116]

A second major blunder of Ray and those who conspired with him was the way they bungled the payoff. Operating under the assumption that once King was dead and he was safely out of the country the bounty could be claimed, Ray and his accomplices, in typical Ray fashion, failed to work out the details. It is interesting to note that after his arrest, neither John nor Jerry Ray attempted to deny their brother's guilt. Instead they stated simply that if he had killed Dr. King, he had done it for money[117]—a hint, perhaps, to those now silent partners of the contract.

However, the bumbling Ray brothers were victims of a double-cross situation they themselves created. Having acted precipitously on the assumption that the fifty-thousand-dollar payoff would be made after Dr. King's death, they failed to realize that they were not dealing with honorable men. Once King was dead and Ray arrested, there was no reason to make the payoff and risk exposure. Since John and Jerry had less at stake in the murder, the two brothers, whom Percy Foreman referred to as "a couple of morons," had only to be kept quiet.[118] And that was fairly easy to do, since both had everything to lose and nothing to gain from talking. Almost immediately after Ray's arrest, Jerry was quickly befriended and employed by Ku Klux Klan attorney J. B. Stoner,[e] who also offered to represent James Earl Ray free of charge.[119]

The problem, however, was James Earl, who with an overwhelming and indisputable amount of evidence indicating that he was the assassin, might be inclined to talk. Subsequently, two curious events occurred. First, Ray dismissed segregationist attorney Arthur Hanes when the internationally-known criminal lawyer, Percy Foreman, volunteered his services for what promised to be the kind of well-publicized trial the colorful Houston attorney preferred. Oddly enough, however, Foreman, whose reputation is based on his shrewd, exciting, and successful courtroom performances on very difficult cases, immediately advised Ray to enter a guilty plea in return for a ninety-

---

[e] In 1980, seventeen years later, J. B. Stoner was convicted for his part in the 1963 bombing of a black church in Birmingham, Alabama, that killed four children. He was given a ten-year sentence.

nine year sentence or risk the electric chair. Foreman acted quickly after a reportedly very casual examination of the evidence.[120] Second, Foreman convinced author William Bradford Huie, to whom Ray had sold his story, that Ray acted alone killing King for the all-too-familiar reasons attributed to assassins—fame and notoriety.[121] Ray, who had assumed he would receive a light sentence because of southern sympathy for what he had done and the past record of acquittals and light sentences in civil-rights-related killings, was shaken by the authoritative and persuasive Foreman prognosis. According to Foreman, Ray had "mistakenly" believed that if he was part of a conspiracy, he could not be convicted of murder. Ray also believed that the combined seventy-percent Nixon-Wallace vote in Shelby County, Tennessee and the numerous letters of support he received nationwide would translate into a very favorable jury verdict.[122]

Ray's assessment was not as foolish as Foreman suggested, given the record at the time. The trial of Mississippi civil rights leader Medgar Evers' accused killer ended in a hung jury in 1964. The accused killers of civil rights worker Viola Liuzzo were convicted only on conspiracy charges and received ten-year sentences. Of the eighteen accused participants in the 1964 abduction and slaying of civil rights workers James Chaney, Andrew Goodman, and Michael Schwerner, only seven were convicted and, again, only on conspiracy charges—not murder—on October 20, 1967.[123]

In any case, Ray was plea-bargained a ninety-nine-year sentence only to protest feebly and in vain after he was sentenced that there was *more* to it. Three days later he wrote the judge, angrily denouncing "that famous Houston attorney Percy Fourflusher" for having deceived and pressured him into the guilty plea.[124] Only an attorney with Foreman's reputation could have closed this explosively controversial case so quickly and skillfully without a trial. Ray had been had, and he knew it. He had to be careful about his protests, however, because a slip could mean the arrest of his brothers who had been involved, the facts suggest, in everything but the actual shooting.

But, paradoxically, he soon realized that he had no tangible evidence of conspiracy without them. Why? Because one or both had put him on to the St. Louis contract offer as a relatively easy way for them to crack into some big money—nearly twice the money as the Alton, Illinois bank job and, they miscalculated, it would probably involve fewer risks. After all, virtually everyone they knew or heard about wished King was dead. And this impression was not merely a reflection of the subterranean haunts of the sleazy bars and whorehouses where the Ray brothers circulated: King was widely hated by whites regardless of social background.[125] Ray resolved the dilemma concerning his brothers by doing the only thing he could, inventing a surrogate—the mysterious, enigmatic, and nonexistent Raoul, whose alleged movements, as we have seen, so closely paralleled those of his brother Jerry.[126]

A Curious Investigation

A considerable amount of circumstantial evidence suggested that other persons were involved with James Earl Ray when he shot and killed Martin Luther King, Jr. Yet the intense and thorough FBI investigation that led to Ray's arrest curiously failed to pursue the most obvious clues leading back from the bathroom in the Memphis rooming house on April 4, 1968 to a mysterious February message to the convicted killer in Los Angeles and the killer's return to New Orleans to discuss a big money deal. Ray, who had been casting about looking for such an opportunity since his prison escape, had embarked on a number of self-improvement schemes—self-confidence counselling, a correspondence course, bartenders' school, dancing lessons, even a nose job. But he dropped everything and left for New Orleans on March 17. The deal, as indicated earlier, was the fifty-thousand-dollar contract on the life of Martin Luther King, Jr.

Although the identity of the "Secret Southern Organization" that put out the contract remains obscure, it seems reasonably certain that the word-of-mouth transactions can be traced logically up the Mississippi to south St. Louis and the dingy confines of the Grapevine Tavern and on out to the comfortable, flag-adorned sanctuary of attorney John Sutherland in Imperial. The obvious target for such an investigation was the Ray family. But once the arrest was made, the FBI chose to ignore all conspiracy leads associated with Ray's family—despite a clear and persistent pattern of interaction between the Ray brothers that the Bureau was aware of.[127]

Even the March 19, 1974 FBI memorandum detailing the Russell Byers' story remained buried for four years in the Bureau's St. Louis files. By the time it was revealed, both the main suspects, Sutherland and Kauffmann, were dead.[f] Also dead were the number one and two men at the FBI who directed the investigation of King's assassination—Director J. Edgar Hoover and his associate director and companion, Clyde A. Tolson. Others of the Bureau's top leadership were also either dead or retired by 1978.[128]

[f] John Sutherland died in 1970 and John Kauffmann in 1974. Both died from natural causes.

It is perhaps only coincidental that the Bureau's failure to pursue this obvious line of investigation occurred in the wake of its illegal counterintelligence program designed to harass and discredit Dr. King and the civil rights movement.[129] But even J. Edgar Hoover's well-documented and virtually pathological hatred and harassment of Dr. King—which is outlined in the Justice Department's 1977 investigation of the Bureau's activities (and also presented in some detail during the 1978 assassination hearings)—are not enough to explain the breakdown in the investigation.[130]

Although it is unlikely that there was direct collusion between the FBI and those persons who instigated the King assassination, it is probable that there was a common perception of the threat posed by the civil rights movement and its leader. Few people hated Dr. King more than J. Edgar Hoover. Also, Hoover's admiration for the values espoused by groups such as the Southern States Industrial Council has been established—an admiration shared by John Sutherland.[131]

It must be assumed that J. Edgar Hoover had mixed feelings when he heard the news of King's death. On the one hand, he no longer had to worry about what he believed was the Communist threat posed by his black adversary—a man he had labeled a "sexual degenerate" and "the most notorious liar in the country"[132]—a concern, incidentally, that the Justice Department concluded was unsupported by the facts.[133] On the other hand, however, given his well-publicized disputes with Dr. King, it was imperative that the FBI get the killer before existing suspicions about the FBI's vendetta could build.[g] But as soon as Ray was apprehended, the Bureau showed little interest in pursuing the investigation into a possible conspiracy. Relieved and content with a lone-assassin explanation, as he was in President Kennedy's death, Hoover did not want to follow a path of investigation when he was gravely concerned about where that rather well-defined path might lead. He did not want to know, nor, in his fashion, did he think it would be in the national interest for the country to know. King was dead, his killer in prison; the case was, to his relief, closed.

Conclusions

There is no question that racism was behind Dr. King's death; but it was not what motivated James Earl Ray: he expected to make the kind of big money on this job that had eluded him throughout his

---

[g] And the concerns about the FBI's purposes in the South during this period were not unfounded. In 1978, Gary Thomas Rowe, a paid FBI informant, was finally indicted and subsequently convicted of the 1965 murder of civil rights worker Viola Liuzzo.

penny ante life of crime. Racism was a factor in Ray's behavior only to the following extent. First, he and his brothers assumed that they could get away with killing a "nigger" even respectable people hated: after all, respectable people were putting up the money. Racism was the primary motive in *their* behavior—it was not in his. Second, he believed there was not a southern white jury in the target areas—Mississippi, Alabama, Georgia, and Shelby County, Tennessee—that would convict him of anything more serious than conspiring to violate King's civil rights. If arrested, he was confident that, at worst, he would be out of prison in no more than ten years with money to spend and the folk-hero status accorded previous slayers of civil rights workers during that ugly era of southern history.

James Earl Ray possessed none of the characteristics of other assassins. He fits none of the four types. His decision to kill Dr. King and his conduct to the present has been that of a coldly rational and shrewd, if not highly competent, hit man. His miscalculations concerning the payoff were probably, in large part, a result of his unwarranted confidence in the competence of his inept brothers. His stress-induced decision to discard the fingerprinted murder weapon and personal belongings is consistent with a long history of such incidents that had led to his imprisonment for lesser crimes.

Except for the pre-eminence of his victim, Ray might have still gotten away with the crime, just as had the accused killers of Medgar Evers, James Chaney, Andrew Goodman, Michael Schwerner, Viola Liuzzo, and scores of nameless black persons over the years. Given that record in the southern courts and the fifty-thousand-dollar bounty, it seemed like a reasonable venture to Ray. The risks were well within the range of acceptability for a man who, in the past, would gamble twenty years of his life for a hundred dollars or so in a supermarket cash register. What he did not know that could have changed his mind was that, paradoxically, Dr. King's well-placed enemies would insist that his assassin, who had so well served their purposes, be given a quick and unequivocal conviction to avoid the threatening implications of a trial.

Meanwhile, the contract money was never paid and James Earl Ray languishes in a Tennessee prison betrayed by the ineptitude he shares with his slow-witted brothers. They remain free thanks to their older brother's loyalty, J. Edgar Hoover's concerns, and the statute of limitations. So it ends for James Earl Ray in a cramped cell, convicted for a crime he had good reason to think was not punishable in the South, ensnared by a web of circumstances he could not have foreseen, or perhaps understood.

Chapter Nine · Conclusions

IN THE PRECEDING CHAPTERS I have raised a number of questions about our understanding of assassinations in America; I have also tried to suggest some answers. Let me summarize the major points addressed at the beginning of the book. Most past studies of American assassins are biased. First, there is an unmistakable *political* bias toward a highly individualistic psychopathological explanation of the motives of assassins. Thus, at the official level there is a strong inclination to "explain" assassinations in terms of the personalities of allegedly mentally ill individuals. To do otherwise would be to risk acknowledging the rationality of some political grievances.

The political bias can be traced back historically to the act of John Wilkes Booth; more recently it was reflected in President Johnson's pressure on the Warren Commission to conclude its investigation of the Kennedy assassination quickly with a "lone assassin" explanation even though Johnson himself believed otherwise. It was also apparent in attempts to discount the possible rationality of Sirhan Sirhan's motives five years later.

Second, this political bias has been supported by a *psychiatric* bias that tends to view any deviation from social norms as ipso facto evidence of pathology. In instances of extreme and offensive acts, such as assassination, the bias is pronounced. The effects of this bias are also compounded by the common failure of psychiatrists and examining clinicians to consider the motives and behavior of their subjects in the *total context* of his or her life experiences.

The combination of such political and psychiatric biases results in highly *reductionist* explanations of American assassinations. Upon closer examination of individual cases, I have suggested the *tautological* or circular quality of these reductive interpretations: the act of assassination is presumed to be evidence of the pathology that is subsequently verified by the highly selective and questionable presentation of other so-called symptoms of mental illness. And we have seen how such work has contributed to a cumulative body of misinformation based upon the *pyramiding* effect of inaccurate secondary literature.

The Alternative Approach

In this study, I have questioned both the political bias and its psychiatric support. I have done this by attempting to reconstruct both the *subjective* realities of the subjects and the *objective* realities of the times they experienced. Then by examining, rather than presuming, the difference or congruence between these two definitions of reality, I was able to make some judgments about the motives of the subjects. Were the motives *rational* or *irrational* and to what degree? And in that sense, were they *political* or *personal*? Beyond this, I looked for specific symptoms, as they are ordinarily defined, of mental illness. Through this process, I searched for *themes* in each subject's life; if present, I tried to trace these themes, in an etiological sense, to their *sources* in the *total* context of their lives—not merely to their immediate family or social situations. In other words, I was equally concerned with the press of historical and cultural forces on their behavior.

Obviously, in a comparative work of this scope, it is impossible to present an exhaustive biography of each subject. But not all events in a person's life are of equal importance. I have attempted, on the basis of the best information available, to select only those events and circumstances in each life that seemed to be important—that is, those events which contributed in a developmental manner to an understanding of their motives. Thus, I have tried to be definitive, not exhaustive, in the presentation of material.

Motives

In Chapter One, I have expounded a number of significant exceptions to conventional wisdom concerning the motives of assassins. First, I contend that there are important distinctions that can be observed among assassins and would-be assassins. Moreover, these distinctions are patterned enough to define, with some qualifications, the four basic types defined in Figure 2. Only two of the sixteen subjects depart in unique ways from this typology. To this extent, the actual meaning and understanding conveyed by common clinical labels such as paranoid schizophrenia becomes suspect. Even if all these subjects satisfy some definition of "paranoia" or "schizophrenia" (which, I claim, most do not) what is the operational utility, not to mention validity, of diagnostic concepts that include so many diverse individuals?

Similarly, the variety of legal definitions of criminal responsibility—e.g., the M'Naghten and Durham rules—also contribute little to an understanding of these subjects because they fail to recognize nuance. To the degree that the Moral Penal Code attempts to include nuance— e.g., notions of "diminished capacity"—it verges into the ambiguity of psychiatric labeling. Such issues define the conflict between legalistic definitions that are narrowly conceived, stubbornly structured, and coldly insensitive to nuance, and psychiatric appraisals that, in contrast, tend to be excessively subjective and devoid of operational structure. This latter problem is further complicated by the tendency of many courtroom psychiatrists and psychoanalysts to explain their diagnoses in the all-too-familiar, nonempirical language of unresolved oedipal conflict that has tantalized them for so long with so little success.

FIGURE 2
Types of Assassins: A Comparison

CHARACTERISTICS	TYPE I	TYPE II	TYPE III	TYPE IV
Emotional Distortion	Mild	Moderate	Severe	Severe
Cognitive Distortion	Absent	Absent	Absent	Severe
Hallucination	Absent	Absent	Absent	Present
Delusion	Absent	Absent	Absent	Present
Reality Contact	Clear	Clear	Clear	Distorted
Social Relations	Varied	Disturbed	Isolated	Isolated
Primary Motive	Political	Personal/ Compensatory	Personal/ Provocation	Irrational

Moving on to a consideration of the specific types of persons involved in these acts, other departures from conventional wisdom were also revealed. First, only the three Type IV subjects—Lawrence, Guiteau, and Schrank—possessed the symptoms of delusion and reality distortion associated with the schizophrenia so frequently attributed to all of these subjects. It is important to note that they are also the only subjects with convincing evidence of hereditary insanity in their families. Although the term psychotic, which can be applied to the Type IV subjects, conjures up images of axe murderers as well as assassins, except for their final acts, Lawrence, Guiteau, and Schrank were more amusing or piteous than frightening. The poetry of Guiteau and Schrank, for example, typifies the hopelessly muddled condition of their minds.

The Type III assassin represents an important departure from such cognitive confusion. Such assassins resemble the remorseless sociopathic killer. They sought to assassinate only for the perverse satisfaction they hoped to experience from venting the only emotion left in empty, meaningless lives—rage. There is no evidence of delusion or reality distortion in the lives of Giuseppe Zangara and Arthur Bremer any more than there was in the lives of other seemingly sociopathic killers such as Gary Gilmore and Steven Judy. Such persons, devoid of empathy or remorse, seek only to outrage a society they hate and to which they cannot adjust. Their targets are simply representatives of that larger society. Personalized animosity is absent; virtually any symbol of the society is a potential victim. Zangara and Bremer selected prominent political figures who represented respectively "capitalists" or "the silent majority" they hated. Recall that earlier Bremer had considered killing lunch-time shoppers in downtown Milwaukee. In 1977, Gary Gilmore killed, in execution style, two ordinary young men who only happened to symbolize the moral, clean-living, self-righteousness of a Mormon society he hated. As he said to one of the perplexed victims, "Your money, son, *and* your life."[1] A remorseless Judy was executed in 1981 for the senseless and merciless murder of a young woman and her three children. In each case, an aggressive universal contempt seemed to be the only emotion these tormented individuals were capable of experiencing. But they *understood* what they were doing.

If Type III subjects are devoid of ordinary emotions of love, empathy, remorse, and guilt, their Type II counterparts are overwhelmed by such feelings. Beset with seemingly unmanageable problems in their personal lives, these subjects project and displace their personal frustrations onto paradoxically *less* threatening *public* targets. Thus Lee Oswald and Samuel Byck both translated their very real—not imagined—domestic difficulties into political extremism. Each displaced occupational frustration and projected spousal rejection onto political surrogates and acted on the basis of such grievances. Their primary purposes were not to kill Presidents Kennedy and Nixon but to place guilt and a sense of responsibility for what they did on the women who turned them away. In Oswald's case, however, he also wanted to prove himself, for the same reasons, to a Cuban government that had viewed him no more seriously than his wife had.

The two women who have been classified as Type II subjects represent different dimensions of anxiety-based behavior. Sara Jane Moore attacked President Ford because she was alone and afraid for her own life. Rejected by her Bay Area radical friends after admitting her role as an FBI informant, and fearing retaliation, she sought again the protective sanctuary of the FBI. Worthless now that she was a known informant, the FBI had no further interest in her. Desperate, Moore had two primary objectives when she raised her pistol that September afternoon, and neither was to kill the President. President Ford's death was simply an unavoidable potential consequence at that point. First, she wanted to demonstrate her sincerity and commitment to the radicals she had deceived; in essence, she was saying I'm sorry and I'll prove it; please forgive me. Second, her act would mean that she would be safely removed to the protective custody she had previously, and unsuccessfully, sought. It was the interplay of such emotions that accounts for her motive, although it was typically rationalized in terms of larger political ideals.

Lynette Fromme illustrates a different, noncompensatory aspect of this neurotic dimension. Fromme could reasonably be defined as a Type I because of her fanatical commitment to a cause or an ideal. But because her commitment seemed to be primarily to a person—Charles Manson—rather than an ideology, and also because of the obsessive/compulsive nature of that commitment, I believe she can be more accurately described as a Type II. Highly personalized commitments to charismatic individuals such as Manson are difficult to decipher. Would the commitment to the cause remain without the man, as it has with the great religions of the world? In Fromme's case, the key appears to be not the cause but the man. Her attack on the President can only be understood in terms of her consuming personal affection for Manson—her savior—and her obsessive desire to obtain his release from prison through any means.

It is unlikely, in this sense, that Lynette Fromme intended to shoot the President because to do so would have been self-defeating. Her objective was only a trial that could provide a forum and, hopefully, a new trial for Manson and, at worst, a short prison term for herself. After which, if all went well, they would be reunited again. It was a long and desperate chance that did not work. Like the other Type II subjects, emotion rather than reason dictated her actions. But she had no illusions about either the game she was playing or the stakes. It was a desperate gamble. Misguided, perhaps, but not insane.

The least understood of all are the Type I subjects because they represent the primary notion official explanations have sought to deny: that is, some assassins are rational extremists who have acted for political rather than personal reasons. It is difficult for many Americans to acknowledge this fact. In the case of each of the persons described as Type I's, there is a strong unmistakable motive linked to rational political concerns: nationalism (Collazo, Torresola, and Sirhan), class conflict (Czolgosz), and sectionalism (Booth). Moreover, the strong ethnic, class, and sectional grievances associated with the motives of these subjects were shared by millions of others, either in this country or elsewhere. It is from such reservoirs of resentment that these assassins spring—not the broken homes, unresolved oedipal crises, delusions, paranoia, desire for recognition, and so forth that form the basis for most previous explanations of their acts. The only qualification of this conclusion is that the primary political motives of Booth and Sirhan were accompanied by an intense personal hatred of their victims.

Nor do such gross pathological explanations account for the motives of the two atypical assassins, Carl Weiss and James Earl Ray. Weiss, as we have seen, killed impulsively for highly personal reasons that were only tangentially related to politics: politics was involved only to the extent that Huey Long's politics had become too personal. Weiss had a reasonable personal motive that can be explained in the context of the history and culture of Louisiana in the third decade of the twentieth century. Ray also killed for personal reasons that were, like Weiss's, only indirectly related to politics. It was not racist politics that accounts for James Earl Ray's motive—which was only a criminal's rational desire for more money; but it was racist politics behind the financial inducement that made King's assassination attractive. Only in that larger political context can James Earl Ray's act be explained as being the result of racism. Ray's own racism was incidental.

FAMILY INFLUENCES

In past studies of American assassins, much has been made of the critical etiological significance of family relations. Psychiatrists and psychoanalysts especially have placed a great deal of emphasis on this aspect of the socialization of assassins and would-be assassins. As I suggested in Chapter One, considerable attention has been given to the centrality of weak fathers and unresolved oedipal conflicts in the motives of *male* assassins. And, as I indicated in earlier chapters, family conflict during childhood seemed to be a critical element in the socialization of both Type II and Type III assassins. While there may be disagreements on theoretical perspectives and implications, there can be little doubt that most of the subjects of this study experienced troubled family relations of one form or another. Some, however—Booth, Schrank, Weiss, Collazo, and Torresola—seemed to enjoy normally affectionate relations with their respective families.

On the negative side, the subjects are distributed along a continuum ranging from the total rejection of family expressed by Zangara, Fromme, and Moore to the milder forms of selective withdrawal from specific family members of Czolgosz (only his stepmother), Ray (only his parents), and Sirhan (only his father). In between these two extremes are the actively conflictive and disturbed relations of Oswald, Bremer, and Byck. Although Lawrence and Guiteau could be included in this last group, it is obvious that their family difficulties were directly a result of their own severe mental disturbances.

But how important were these family influences in a direct causal sense? What evidence is there, for example, to support the commonly held assumption that these domestic conflicts and anger were generalized or displaced onto political figures? The answers to these questions reveal that direct causal associations of this kind are present in only four of the sixteen subjects. Only the acts of the Type III subjects—Zangara and Bremer—and the Type II males—Oswald and Byck—seemed to be directly associated with family hostilities in the manner described here. Weiss's murder of Huey Long was obviously family-related, but not, as we have seen, in the negative sense. No such direct influences were observed in any of the remaining subjects.

Consistent with the typology described in Chapter One, and summarized in Figure 2, the attacks of subjects classified as Type I's and Type IV's, as well as the two atypical cases, were not directly associated with domestic difficulties. Rather, politics (Type I), insanity (Type IV), and uniquely personal reasons (the atypicals) account for their actions. This is not to deny the unquestionable importance of family influence in a more general sense. The family is usually the most important agent in the socialization process, and assassins are no exception. But for most of these individuals, it cannot be considered a *direct* causal influence in their violent crimes—at least no more so than the failed fathers in the lives of so many American writers, such as Hemingway, Faulkner, and Steinbeck, to name only a few, can be credited with their sons' literary success.

GENESIS OF THE ASSASSINS' PERSONALITIES

Another difficult related question has to do with the factors of nature and nurture that produce the types of assassins identified in this research. Where in the backgrounds of these various types did the distinguishing aggressive features and values of their personalities begin to emerge?

There can be little question about the Type IV subjects. The delusions of Lawrence, Guiteau, and Schrank appeared to emerge from a documented history of hereditary mental illness. Unable for physiological reasons to distinguish between reality and their delusions, they were prompted to their extreme acts by totally illusory (Lawrence) or the most innocuous (Guiteau and Schrank) political circumstances.

The aggressive and perverse emotional unidimensionality of the Type III subjects appears to have had its origins in the loveless, emotional deprivation of their childhoods. Unprepared by early socialization to deal with life on a mature emotional level, both Zangara and Bremer withdrew into a shell of self-centered moral indifference and smoldering resentment toward, what was to them, an alien society. Then when in the crucible of their tortured psyches this resentment became rage, it was expressed in self-destructive and criminally indifferent acts that were designed to offend and outrage a society that both men blamed for the misery of their lives.

Similarly, a common theme runs through the lives of the Type II assassins and would-be assassins. Although the emotionally searing deprivation of the Type III's was not present in early childhood (Oswald's childhood, however, comes close), love and affection in their early socialization was *conditional*. When behavior did not conform to parental expectations—whether those expectations were erratic (Oswald) or rigid (Fromme and Moore)—love was withheld. The resulting anxieties about approval and affection followed them into adulthood and, as I have suggested, culminated in their extreme compensatory acts of violence. Although less is known about Byck's childhood, his tapes revealed a deep-seated resentment toward a mother who was not reluctant to acknowledge her disappointment in him, just as she apparently had with his father.

As we have seen, the aggression of the Type I subjects has little to do with the mental, family, and social problems associated with their Type II, III, and IV counterparts. Booth, Czolgosz, Collazo, Torresola, and Sirhan were motivated by larger historical and political forces. The only characteristic they share is an intense ideological commitment that was directly linked to personal political experiences and partisan loyalties that were contrary to those represented by the political figures they attacked.

The two atypical subjects—Weiss and Ray—were poles apart in socialization and background. Similarly, neither of their lives resembled the lives of any of the other subjects. Weiss, the successful physician and contented family man, and Ray, the only assassin from the dregs of society who had spent a good part of his life in prison, hold down the extremes in any sociological ranking of American assassins.

And each killed for reasons associated with the values of these extremes: Weiss killed impulsively out of a profound feeling of responsibility and protectiveness for his wife and son; Ray killed for money in the calculating manner of a hardened criminal.

What Can Be Done?

An obvious question that arises in this kind of research is why there are so relatively few assassinations when there must be scores of people that possess all or most of the characteristics associated with assassins? The answer to this has to do with circumstances and chance: many potential assassins have not killed simply because they have not had an opportunity. Thus the typology that is presented in this book is essentially nonpredictive unless circumstantial factors can be identified, and even then, chance remains a major determinant that can only be assessed after that fact. But the dramatic increase in assassinations and assassination attempts since 1963 does reveal certain associated factors that, if considered, provide some further insights into the problem—insights that bear directly on questions of security and criminal responsibility.

At the beginning of this book, I identified four types of variables that must be considered in order to understand the complex political behavior of an assassin or would-be assassin: thus, in addition to the personality of the subject, the situational, social, and cultural contexts of his behavior must be analyzed. With this perspective in mind, let me summarize the potentially manageable factors that affect the personal safety of national leaders.

A major argument in this book has been that the model that defines our present understanding of the assassination phenomenon in America is deficient to the extent that it focuses on similarities among assassins and would-be assassins while ignoring important differences. These differences are central to their motives and thus are key factors in identifying them, assessing the potential threat they pose, and, at least to a degree, minimizing that threat as well as assessing their culpability should preventative measures fail.

As we have seen, subjects identified as Types II, III, and IV were motivated by situations, some imagined, some real, that had little to do with politics. And it is important to note that five of the seven incidents since 1963 involved Type II and III subjects—specifically, Oswald, Bremer, Byck, Fromme, and Moore. And it also appears (at this writing) that the motives of President Reagan's would-be assassin,

John Hinckley, were at their core highly personal. Only Sirhan and Ray—who struck in that year of great political turbulence, 1968—killed for reasons that were not primarily related to personal problems.

Media Exposure

The one characteristic that the post-1963 Type II and III subjects shared was a need to do something spectacular that would guarantee the public exposure each desired. It has only been since the advent of television that such immediate and saturating exposure has become possible. The dramatic possibilities of television only became apparent with President Kennedy's assassination. Prior to 1963, newspapers and even radios in some cases simply did not provide the spectacular coverage of assassinations and attempted assassinations that television has made possible.

Thus it appears that the cultural context of a television-dominated era has greatly increased the probability of assassination attempts by Type II and III subjects who seek exposure and public attention, although for different kinds of personal reasons.[a] For example, the personal frustrations of Oswald, Fromme, and Moore, combined with the threats each made before their attacks, should not have been ignored or discounted as they were. It follows that a prime consideration in determining the threat posed by suspects should be a careful analysis of any configuration of personal characteristics and situational circumstances that would predispose a person toward such actions. Obviously, security investigations that rely primarily on data regarding political affiliations and beliefs would be more likely to miss or min-

---

[a] Another interesting pattern of cultural and psychological influence appears to link Arthur Bremer and John Hinckley in spite of the vast sociological differences between the two. Recall that Bremer had been fascinated with the Stanley Kubrick film "Clockwork Orange" prior to his attempted assassination of George Wallace. Bremer wrote that in his fantasies he identified with the main character in the film "Alek," a perverse young man who expresses his frustrated sexuality and alienation in sadistic violence. Some nine years later, John Hinckley developed a fantasized love relationship with a young actress, Jodie Foster, who plays a teen-age prostitute in the Martin Scorcese film, "Taxi Driver." The script draws heavily from Bremer's diary in developing the alienated main character. Hinckley appears to have identified with the Bremer-like taxi driver, who attempts to assassinate a presidential candidate and subsequently rescues the young prostitute he loves by killing her pimps in a disturbingly graphic shooting spree. Apparently Hinckley saw the film more than once and the last time within a few weeks of his attempt on President Reagan's life. A love letter written to Ms. Foster shortly before the shooting was found in Hinckley's hotel room: "Dear Jodie, There is a definite possibility that I will be killed in my attempt to get Reagan. . . . I love you forever." (*Washington Post*, April 5, 1981, A19.)

imize the importance of this kind of complex, highly personal information.

This raises a question concerning whether media coverage of assassinations and assassination attempts should be restricted in order to minimize its attractiveness to Types II and III potential assassins. The question again bears directly on the form and substance of American political culture. How much of the openness and access we value in a democratic society must be sacrificed to protect leaders from such troubled individuals? Tighter security would reduce the probability of assassinations as it has in more authoritarian societies, but it is unlikely that political leaders, or the public, would be willing to make that kind of sacrifice. To accept such restrictions on access and movement would violate a national conception of what politics and politicians should be in a free society.

Similarly, one can ask whether the schedules of Presidents and candidates should be kept from the press and public in order to reduce the likelihood of assassinations. We have seen that most of the subjects of this research were very attentive to such schedules in planning their attacks. Again, the question focuses attention on the fundamental nature of our political culture and would involve—as the previous question, if answered in the affirmative—a disheartening admission of what American society has become.

Domestic Surveillance?

An even more troubling question involves whether domestic surveillance should be expanded, as advocated by some politicians after the attack on President Reagan, to enhance the security information of law enforcement agencies. It is unlikely that the benefits of such increased surveillance would outweigh the social and political costs. As indicated earlier, the FBI and/or the Secret Service were aware of the activities of Oswald, Byck, Fromme, Moore, and Hinckley before their attacks and apparently did not consider them to be sufficiently dangerous to warrant special attention. Thus, the problem seems to be one of faulty or incomplete analysis of extant information rather than a need for additional data obtained through increased electronic surveillance. Moreover, in most incidents, the subjects acted alone in a manner unlikely to have been detected through such surveillance. Of the more recent cases (when such technology was available) only the King assassination conspiracy conceivably might have been detected through these means. Ironically, however, the FBI had focused its surveillance efforts on the victim—the nonviolent King—and the danger he, in the mind of FBI director J. Edgar Hoover, represented.

Further, there is no convincing evidence that these methods were employed by the FBI to conduct a thorough investigation of James Earl Ray's links to other persons after his arrest.

It seems highly improbable that increased domestic surveillance would have any effect on the destructive capabilities of persons who in most cases acted alone and in other cases should have been recognized as potential security risks on the basis of information already in the files of law enforcement agencies at the time of the attack. The fact that in two cases—Oswald and Ray—such information was destroyed or suppressed after the assassinations should also give pause to the thoughtful observer.

Handguns

Much has been written about the so-called "culture of violence" in America. And it is difficult to discount a history that includes a relentless and brutal subjugation of American Indians, a revolution, a civil war that was fought, in part, over the issue of human slavery, a turbulent and bloody period of labor conflict, and a civil rights struggle that over the years saw many lynched, bombed, shot, and beaten. Part of this tradition of domestic violence can be explained in terms of the conquest and internal political struggles among competing groups in a new nation. Few emerging nations have avoided similar experiences. Such experiences are unfortunate, seemingly inevitable, but hardly uniquely American. Another part of this gloomy history can be understood as one of the costs associated with a free and open society where good intentions and innocence are assumed until proven otherwise and the potential criminal as well as the law-abiding citizen enjoy the same liberties. But a significant abuse of these cherished liberties is the strongly defended and fictitious constitutional "right" to own handguns. The realities of handgun-related violence are so immediate and intimidating that only the most courageous or foolish walk city streets at night. Of the sixteen assassins and would-be assassins discussed in this study, fourteen used the easily concealed handgun. And on March 30, 1981, John Hinckley shot and inflicted nearly fatal wounds on President Reagan and three others with a handgun. Of all the measures that could be taken to decrease the probability of future assassinations, the most significant would be the confiscation of privately owned handguns.

Would such legislation be unconstitutional as the gun lobby claims? The Second Amendment to the Constitution reads: "A well regulated Militia, being necessary to the security of a free state, the right of the people to keep and bear Arms shall not be infringed." Note that the gun lobby—ignoring that the purpose of the amendment was to prevent Congress from disarming state militias, not individual gun owners—restricts its own and the public's attention to only the second phrase of the amendment. It should be obvious that unregulated handgun possession has little to do with "a well regulated Militia." As Justice William O. Douglas observed in his dissent in *Adams* v. *Williams*:

> A powerful lobby dins into the ears of our citizenry that . . . gun purchases are constitutional rights protected by the Second Amendment. . . . There is under our decisions no reason why stiff state laws governing the purchase and possession of pistols may not be enacted. There is no reason why pistols may not be barred from anyone with a police record. There is no reason why a State may not require a purchaser of a pistol to pass a psychiatric test. There is no reason why all pistols should not be barred to everyone except the police.[2]

Handguns are dangerous because they can be concealed in the belt or pocket of a Sirhan Sirhan, a Samuel Byck, an Arthur Bremer, or a John Hinckley, in the purse of a Sara Jane Moore or under the skirts of a Lynette Fromme—all of them innocuous-looking would-be assassins. Handguns could be confiscated without infringing on the sportsman's desire to own a shotgun or rifle, or the homeowner's perceived need to own a weapon for security purposes. In short, shotguns and rifles should satisfy the desires of persons who feel they have need for firearms. But, more importantly, such weapons cannot be as readily concealed by potential assassins and murderers: and the law-abiding citizen, presumably, has no need for concealment.

Although handgun control would not eliminate the threat of a determined assassin, such as Lee Harvey Oswald or James Earl Ray, it would have the significant virtue of reducing the probability of such attacks by *all* types of assassins—even the politically motivated Type I. In so doing it would ease the tremendous pressure on security personnel and the risks to which they are exposed not only by reducing the number of persons possessing these weapons but by making weapons detection much easier than it is now.

FINAL OBSERVATIONS

In this book I have tried to look at the nature of assassination in America in a somewhat different and more systematic manner than many previous studies. The act of taking a life in the calculating, premeditated, and public manner of a political assassin is a chilling and disturbing prospect. But it is an important and complex subject that deserves more serious scholarly attention than it has received. Assassins cannot be easily stereotyped. The differences among them are significant not only in a theoretical sense but also because of the very practical problem of ensuring, as much as possible, the personal safety of political figures. Such differences are also crucial, as I have tried to demonstrate, in determining the criminal responsibility of persons who commit these crimes.

The incidence of these attacks has increased significantly since 1963. This fact, combined with the unsettling realization that five of the last seven attackers were known to authorities—Oswald, Byck, Moore, Fromme, and President Reagan's would-be assassin, John Hinckley—and were not considered serious enough threats to warrant surveillance or protective custody, underscores the nature of the problem. The tasks of security are enormous, and the brave persons shouldering that difficult burden should have the best information available. At present, they do not.

Notes

CHAPTER ONE

1. See, for example, Robert J. Donovan, *The Assassins* (New York: Harper & Brothers, 1952); Lawrence Z. Freedman, "Assassination: Psychopathology and Social Pathology," *Postgraduate Medicine* 37 (June 1965): 650-658; Donald W. Hastings, "The Psychiatry of Presidential Assassination, Part I: Jackson and Lincoln," *The Journal-Lancet* 85 (March 1965): 93-100; "The Psychiatry of Presidential Assassination, Part II: Garfield and McKinley," *The Journal-Lancet* 85 (April 1965): 157-162; "The Psychiatry of Presidential Assassination, Part III: The Roosevelts," *The Journal-Lancet* 85 (May 1965): 189-192; "The Psychiatry of Presidential Assassination, Part IV: Truman and Kennedy," *The Journal-Lancet* 85 (July 1965): 294-301; G. Wilse Robinson, "A Study of Political Assassinations," *American Journal of Psychiatry* 121 (May 1965): 1060-1064; John Kaplan, "The Assassins," *Stanford Law Review* 59 (May 1967): 1110-1151; Sidney J. Slomich and Robert E. Kantor, "Social Psychopathology of Political Assassination," *Bulletin of the Atomic Scientists* 25 (March 1969): 9-12; Alfred E. Weisz and Robert L. Taylor, "American Presidential Assassinations," *Diseases of the Nervous System* 30 (October 1969) 658-668; James F. Kirkham, Sheldon G. Levy, and William J. Crotty, *Assassination and Political Violence: A Report to the National Commission on the Causes and Prevention of Violence* (New York: Praeger and the *New York Times*, 1970); Lawrence Z. Freedman, "Psychopathology of Assassinations," in *Assassinations and the Political Order*, ed. William J. Crotty (New York: Harper & Row, 1971), pp. 143-160; Thomas C. Greening, "The Psychological Study of Assassins," in *Assassinations and the Political Order*, ed. William J. Crotty (New York: Harper & Row, 1971), pp. 222-268; William J. Crotty, "Presidential Assassinations," *Society* 9 (May 1972): 18-29; David Abrahamsen, *The Murdering Mind* (New York: Harper & Row, 1973); Conrad V. Hassel, "The Political Assassin," *Journal of Police Science and Administration* 4 (December 1974): 399-403; and James McKinley, *Assassination in America* (New York: Harper & Row, 1977).

2. William R. Smith, *Assassination and Insanity: Guiteau's Case Examined and Compared with Analogous Cases from the Earlier to the Present Times* (Washington, D.C., 1881), p. 4.

3. Stanley Kimmel, *The Mad Booths of Maryland* (1940; reprint ed., New York: Dover Publications, 1969).

4. L. Vernon Briggs, *The Manner of Man that Kills* (Boston: The Gorham Press, 1921).

5. Abrahamsen, *The Murdering Mind.*

6. Donovan, *The Assassins*, p. 9.

7. Kirkham et al., *Report to the National Commission.*

8. Thomas S. Szasz, *The Myth of Mental Illness* (New York: Harper & Row, 1961); *Law, Liberty and Psychiatry* (New York: Macmillan & Co., 1963); *Ideology and Insanity* (Garden City, N.Y.: Doubleday & Co., 1970); *Schizophrenia: The Sacred Symbol of Psychiatry* (New York: Basic Books, 1976).

9. For an extended discussion of these problems as they impinge upon the criminal justice system see, for example, Jay Ziskin, *Coping with Psychiatric and Psychological Testimony* (Beverly Hills, Ca.: Law and Psychology Press, 1975; supplement, 1977); Robert Spitzer, Jean Endicott, and Eli Robins, "Clinical Criteria for Psychiatric Diagnosis and DSM-III," *American Journal of Psychiatry* 132 (November 1975): 1187-1192; and Daniel J. Robinson, *Psychology and Law: Can Justice Survive the Social Sciences?* (New York: Oxford University Press, 1980).

10. D. L. Rosenhan, "On Being Sane in Insane Places," *Science* 179 (January 1973): 250-258.

11. See, for example, Anthony Davids, "Projective Testing: Some Issues Facing Academicians and Practitioners," *Professional Psychology* 4 (November 1973): 445-453; Denis G. Lewandowski and Dennis P. Saccuzzo, "The Decline of Psychological Testing," *Professional Psychology* 7, no. 2 (May 1976): 177-184; Sidney E. Cleveland, "Reflections on The Rise and Fall of Psychodiagnosis," *Professional Psychology* 7, no. 3 (August 1976): 309-318; and Robert W. Wildman and Robert W. Wildman II, "An Investigation into the Comparative Validity of Several Diagnostic Tests and Test Batteries," *Journal of Clinical Psychology* 31 (July 1975): 455-458.

12. Daniel M'Naghten's Case, 10 Clark and Fin. 200, 8 Eng. Rep. 718 (1843). See also W. C. Townsend, *Modern State Trials* (London: Longman, Brown, 1850).

13. Durham v. United States, 214 F.2d, 862 (U.S. Court of Appeals, D.C., 1954).

14. MacDonald v. United States, 312 F.2d 847, 851 (D.C. Cir., 1962).

15. See, for example, Fritz A. Henn, Marian Herjanic, and Robert H. Vanderpearl, "Forensic Psychiatry: Diagnosis and Criminal Responsibility," *The Journal of Nervous and Mental Disease* 162 (June 1976): 423-429; Seymour Pollack, "Principles of Forensic Psychiatry for Psychiatric-Legal Opinion Making," in *Legal Medicine Annual*, ed. C. H. Wecht (New York: Appleton-Century-Crofts, 1971), ch. 14; Ziskin, *Coping with Psychiatric*, ch. 1; and Robinson, *Psychology and Law*, ch. 2.

16. Model Penal Code 4.01 (P.O.D. 1962). See S.1, 93d Cong., 1st Sess., 1-302, 1973.

17. Quoted in John M. MacDonald, *Psychiatry and the Criminal*, 2d ed. (Springfield, Illinois: Charles C. Thomas, 1969), p. 43.

18. Szasz, *Schizophrenia*, pp. 3, 190 (emphasis added). See also Seymour

Halleck, "American Psychiatry and the Criminal," in *The Psychological Foundations of Criminal Justice*, ed. Robert W. Rieber and Harold J. Vetter (New York: The John Jay Press, 1978), 1:8-42.

19. See, for example, P. B. Medawar, *The Hope of Progress* (London: Methuen, 1972); Ziskin, *Coping with Psychiatric*; and Robinson, *Psychology and Law*.

20. M. Brewster Smith, "A Map for the Analysis of Personality and Politics," *The Journal of Social Issues* 24 (July 1968): 15-28.

21. The classic exposition of the frustration-aggression hypothesis is J. Dollard et al., *Frustration and Aggression* (New Haven: Yale University Press, 1939).

22. Harold D. Lasswell, *Power and Personality* (New York: The Viking Press, 1948), ch. 3.

CHAPTER TWO

John Wilkes Booth

1. Stanley Kimmel, *The Mad Booths of Maryland* (1940; reprint ed., New York: Dover, 1969).

2. Edward Hyams, *Killing No Murder* (Camden, N.J.: Thomas Nelson & Sons, 1969), pp. 69-70.

3. See, for example, George W. Wilson, "John Wilkes Booth: Father Murderer," *The American IMAGO* 1 (June 1940): 49-60; Phillip Weissman, "Why Booth Shot Lincoln," in *Psychoanalysis and the Social Sciences* (New York: International Universities Press, 1958), 5:99-115.

4. James G. Randall, *The Civil War and Reconstruction* (Boston and New York: D. C. Heath, 1937), p. 65.

5. Ella V. Mahoney, *Sketches of Tudor Hall and the Booth Family* (Belair, Md.: Ella V. Mahoney, 1925), p. 33.

6. Kimmel, *The Mad Booths*, pp. 66-78.

7. Asia Booth Clarke, *The Unlocked Book* (New York: G. P. Putnam's Sons, 1938), pp. 74, 91; Kimmel, *The Mad Booths*, p. 70.

8. Kimmel, *The Mad Booths*, pp. 341-342.

9. Clarke, *The Unlocked Book*, pp. 73-74.

10. Ibid., pp. 72-73.

11. Kimmel, *The Mad Booths*, pp. 150-153, 158.

12. Ibid., p. 153.

13. Ibid., p. 168.

14. Ibid., p. 170.

15. Ibid., p. 172.

16. Ibid.

17. Ibid., p. 173.

18. Ibid., p. 177.

19. Clara Morris, *Life on the Stage* (New York: McClure, Phillips & Co., 1901), p. 103.

20. Kimmel, *The Mad Booths*, p. 180.

21. Louis J. Weichmann, *A True History of the Assassination of Abraham Lincoln and the Conspiracy of 1865*, ed. Floyd E. Risvold (New York: Vintage Books, 1975; written in the 1890s), p. 42.

22. Asia Booth Clarke, *The Elder and the Younger Booth* (Boston: James R. Osgood & Co., 1882), pp. 66-67.

23. Morris, *Life on Stage*, p. 103.

24. Francis Wilson, *John Wilkes Booth* (New York: Benjamin Bloom, Inc., 1929, 1972), pp. 7, 10.

25. Ibid., pp. 15-16.

26. Ibid., pp. 11-12, 16.

27. Quoted in Kimmel, *The Mad Booths*, p. 169.

28. Quoted in the Washington *Evening Star*, April 20, 1865; complete letter quoted in Wilson, *Booth*, pp. 50-54, and Weichmann, *A True History*, pp. 49-52.

29. Kimmel, *The Mad Booths*, pp. 179-181, 184-185, 187, 204.

30. New Orleans *Times*, March 17, 1864; cited in Kimmel, *The Mad Booths*, p. 180.

31. Kimmel, *The Mad Booths*, p. 187.

32. David Donald, *Lincoln Reconsidered* (New York: Vintage Books, 1961), pp. 188-196; Charles A. and Mary R. Beard, *The Rise of American Civilization* (New York: Macmillan & Co., 1927), pp. 94-97.

33. Randall, *The Civil War*, pp. 222-223, 597, 602.

34. Joel Tyler Headley, *The Great Riots of New York, 1712 to 1873* (1873; reprint ed., New York: Dover, 1971).

35. Randall, *The Civil War*, pp. 412-414.

36. William Dusinbeere, *Civil War Issues in Pennsylvania* (Philadelphia: University of Pennsylvania Press, 1965), p. 157; Randall, *The Civil War*, pp. 643-645.

37. Wilson, *Booth*, pp. 117-118.

38. Randall, *The Civil War*, p. 620.

39. T. Harry Williams, *Lincoln and the Radicals* (Madison: University of Wisconsin Press, 1941), pp. 316-333.

40. Williams, *Lincoln*, pp. 328-329; William R. Brock, *Conflict and Transformation: The United States, 1844-1877* (New York: Penguin Books, 1973), pp. 280, 294.

41. For example, the *Chicago Times* panned the President's second inaugural speech as so bad it did not "conceive it possible that even Mr. Lincoln could produce a paper so slipshod, . . . so puerile, not alone in literary construction, but in its ideas, its sentiments, its grasp. . . . By the side of it, mediocrity is superb" (editorial, *Chicago Times*, March 6, 1865; quoted in Randall, *The Civil War*, p. 644). For a detailed discussion of Lincoln's unpopularity, see also Randall's *Lincoln the Liberal Statesman* (New York: Dodd, Mead & Co., 1947), esp. ch. 3.

42. Randall, *The Civil War*, pp. 642-645; Brock, *Conflict and Transformation*, pp. 292-293.

43. Quoted in John Cottrell, *Anatomy of an Assassination* (London: Frederick Muller, 1966), p. 35.

44. Clarke, *The Elder*, pp. 123-124.

45. Ibid., pp. 115-117, 119; Kimmel, *The Mad Booths*, p. 179.

46. Benn Pitman, *The Assassination of President Lincoln and the Trial of the Conspirators: The Courtroom Testimony* (1865; reprint ed., New York: Funk & Wagnalls, 1954); hereafter cited as *Trial Testimony*.

47. Ibid., pp. 47-57.

48. Letters of John Wilkes Booth, Attorney General's Papers, Lincoln Assassination, RG No. 60, National Archives.

49. For example, see Otto Eisenschiml, *Why Was Lincoln Murdered?* (Boston: Little, Brown, 1937).

50. Weichmann, *A True History*, p. 137; Wilson, *Booth*, pp. 70-71.

51. Randall, *The Civil War*, p. 683.

52. Kimmel, *The Mad Booths*, p. 218.

53. Pitman, *Trial Testimony*, pp. 154-168, 144-153.

54. Diary of John Wilkes Booth, Attorney General's Papers, Lincoln Assassination, RG No. 60, National Archives.

55. Ibid.

56. Kimmel, *The Mad Booths*, p. 249.

57. Pitman, *Trial Testimony*, p. 92.

58. Ibid.

59. Ibid., p. 93.

60. Jefferson Davis, *The Rise and Fall of the Confederate Government* 1881; reprint ed. (South Brunswick, N.J.: Thomas Yoseloff, 1958).

Leon Czolgosz

61. *People v. Leon F. Czolgosz* (1901), Courthouse Archives, Erie County, Buffalo, New York. Reprinted in *American State Trials*, ed. John D. Lawson (St. Louis: Thomas Law Book Co., 1923), 14: 169-170. Hereafter cited as *Trial*.

62. Carlos F. MacDonald, "The Trial, Execution, Autopsy, and Mental Status of Leon F. Czolgosz, Alias Fred Nieman, the Assassin of President McKinley," *The American Journal of Insanity* 58 (January 1902): 375; Walter Channing, "The Mental State of Czolgosz, the Assassin of President McKinley," *The American Journal of Insanity* 59 (October 1902): 274.

63. Joseph Fowler, Floyd S. Crego, and James W. Putnam, "Official Report of the Experts for the People in the Case of the People v. Leon F. Czolgosz" (1901). Reprinted in *American State Trials*, ed. John D. Lawson (St. Louis: Thomas Law Book Co., 1923), 14: 195-199. Hereafter cited as "Fowler Report." "Report of Dr. Carlos F. McDonald and Dr. Arthur Hurd, Experts for the Prisoner" (1901), in Lawson, ed., *American State Trials*, 14: 196-203. Hereafter cited as "McDonald and Hurd Report."

64. Channing, "The Mental State."

65. Ibid., pp. 261-266.

66. L. Vernon Briggs, *The Manner of Man that Kills* (Boston: The Gorham Press, 1921).

67. Robert J. Donovan, *The Assassins* (New York: Harper & Brothers, 1952).

68. Donald W. Hastings, "The Psychiatry of Presidential Assassination, Part II: Garfield and McKinley," *The Journal-Lancet* 85 (April 1965): 157-162.

69. See, for example, James McKinley, *Assassination in America* (New York: Harper & Row, 1977).

70. Allan McLane Hamilton, *Recollections of an Alienist* (New York: George H. Dolan, 1916), pp. 363, 365-366; Briggs, *The Manner of Man that Kills*, pp. 252-253.

71. Briggs, *The Manner of Man that Kills*, p. 338.

72. Ibid.

73. Ibid., pp. 321-331.

74. Ibid., p. 290.

75. Emma Goldman, *Living My Life* (Garden City, N.Y.: Garden City Publishing Co., 1931), p. 355.

76. Robert V. Bruce, *1877: Year of Violence* (Chicago: Quadrangle Books, 1959); Philip S. Foner, *The Great Labor Uprising of 1877* (New York: Monad Press, 1977), pp. 231-240.

77. Goldman, *Living*, pp. 355-356; Briggs, *The Manner of Man that Kills*, p. 290.

78. Henry David, *The History of the Haymarket Affair*, 2d ed. (New York: Russell & Russell, 1958), p. 463.

79. Goldman, *Living*, p. 304.

80. Briggs, *The Manner of Man that Kills*, p. 303.

81. Thomas Bell, *Out of the Furnace* (1941; reprint ed., Pittsburgh: University of Pittsburgh Press, 1976), p. 418.

82. Joseph G. Rayback, *A History of American Labor* (New York: The Free Press, 1959, 1966), pp. 194-197.

83. Briggs, *The Manner of Man that Kills*, p. 302.

84. Ibid., pp. 279, 304-305.

85. Ibid., pp. 260, 305.

86. Almont Lindsey, *The Pullman Strike* (Chicago: The University of Chicago Press, 1942), p. 359.

87. Ibid., pp. 90-95.

88. Lawrence Goodwyn, *Democratic Promise: The Populist Movement in America* (New York: Oxford University Press, 1976).

89. Ibid., p. 555.

90. V. O. Key, "A Theory of Critical Elections," *The Journal of Politics* 17 (February 1955): 3-18.

91. Briggs, *The Manner of Man that Kills*, p. 306.

92. Michael Novak, *The Guns of Lattimer* (New York: Basic Books, 1978), p. xvi.

93. Ibid., pp. 18-19, 111-112.

94. Ibid., pp. 125-134.

95. Victor R. Greene, *The Slavic Community on Strike* (Notre Dame, Ind.: University of Notre Dame Press, 1968), pp. 141-142.

96. Novak, *The Guns*, pp. 201, 235-236.

97. Channing, "The Mental State," p. 239.

98. Briggs, *The Manner of Man that Kills*, p. 307.

99. Channing, "The Mental State," p. 241; Briggs, *The Manner of Man that Kills*, p. 308.

100. Channing, "The Mental State," pp. 241-242; Briggs, *The Manner of Man that Kills*, pp. 293-294, 306, 313.

101. Briggs, *The Manner of Man that Kills*, p. 311.

102. Ibid., p. 300.

103. Ibid., p. 306.

104. Ibid., pp. 313-314.

105. Novak, *The Guns*, pp. xv-xvi.

106. Briggs, *The Manner of Man that Kills*, p. 313.

107. *Trial*, p. 194.

108. Channing, "The Mental State," p. 263.

109. Briggs, *The Manner of Man that Kills*, p. 308.

110. Ibid., p. 321; *Cleveland Plain Dealer*, May 6, 1901, p. 8.

111. Briggs, *The Manner of Man that Kills*, p. 317.

112. Ibid.

113. Richard Drinnon, *Rebel in Paradise: A Biography of Emma Goldman* (Chicago: The University of Chicago Press, 1961), p. 68.

114. Briggs, *The Manner of Man that Kills*, pp. 274, 309.

115. Ibid., pp. 321-322.

116. Ibid., p. 278.

117. "Fowler Report," p. 196.

118. Briggs, *The Manner of Man that Kills*, p. 277.

119. Ibid.

120. Drinnon, *Rebel in Paradise*, p. 69.

121. A. Wesley Johns, *The Man Who Shot McKinley* (South Brunswick and New York: A. S. Barnes, 1970), p. 60.

122. *Trial*, pp. 184-185.

123. Johns, *The Man Who Shot McKinley*, p. 91.

124. *Trial*, p. 179.

125. Ibid., p. 191.

126. Ibid., pp. 175-176.

127. Ibid., pp. 175, 178. See also Selig Adler, "The Operation on President McKinley," *Scientific American* 208 (March 1963): 118-130.

128. *Trial*, pp. 184, 186.

129. MacDonald, "The Trial, Execution, Autopsy," p. 384.

130. "Fowler Report," p. 196.

131. Ibid., p. 198.

132. MacDonald, "The Trial, Execution, Autopsy," p. 375.

133. Ibid., p. 386.

134. Edward A. Spitzka, "The Post-Mortem Examination of Leon F. Czolgosz, the Assassin of President McKinley," *American Journal of Insanity* 58 (January 1902): 386-387.

135. *Trial*, pp. 163-164.

136. Briggs, *The Manner of Man that Kills*, p. 327.

137. Ibid., pp. 322-323.

138. Goldman, *Living*, pp. 306, 324-325. See also, Emma Goldman, "The Tragedy at Buffalo," *Mother Earth* 1 (October 1906): 11-16.

139. Goldman, *Living*, pp. 316-317.

140. Channing, "The Mental State," p. 271; Briggs, *The Manner of Man that Kills*, pp. 336-343.

141. Briggs, *The Manner of Man that Kills*, pp. 331, 337.

142. Channing, "The Mental State," p. 272. In his *Recollections*, Hamilton argues the same totally unsubstantiated position.

143. Margaret Leech, *In the Days of McKinley* (New York: Harper & Row, 1959), p. 594.

144. Briggs, *The Manner of Man that Kills*, p. 259.

145. Quoted by Briggs in ibid., p. 343.

146. See, for example, Hastings, "The Psychiatry of Presidential Assassinations," and McKinley, *Assassination in America*.

147. Quoted by Briggs, *The Manner of Man that Kills*, p. 74.

CHAPTER THREE

Oscar Collazo and Griselio Torresola

1. "Incidents Preceding November 1, 1950, Attempted Assassination of President Truman," Federal Bureau of Investigation, File No. 62-7721-1695, p. 17. Hereafter cited as FBI Document 62-7721-1695.

2. Ibid., p. 32.

3. "Origin of Nationalist Party of Puerto Rico (NPPR), Including the Rise of Pedro Albizu Campos," Federal Bureau of Investigation, Document 94-50590-2, p. 10. Hereafter cited as FBI Document 94-50590-2.

4. Trial testimony (United States v. Oscar Callazo [February-March 1951], United States District Court for the District of Columbia), Collazo, vol. 8, p. 745.

5. FBI Document 94-50590-2, pp. 1-7.

6. "Nationalist Party of Puerto Rico," Federal Bureau of Investigation, File No. 100-7689, pp. 35-36. Hereafter cited as FBI Document 100-7689.

7. FBI Document 94-50590-2, p. 9.

8. Puerto Rican Nationalists, Oscar Collazo, Federal Bureau of Investigation, File No. 3-36-A, November-December 1950. Hereafter cited as FBI Document 3-36-A.

9. FBI Documents 3-36-A, 94-50590-2, and 100-7689, p. 21.

10. FBI Document 100-7689.
11. Ibid., pp. 7-8.
12. Ibid., p. 8.
13. Ibid., p. 7.
14. Ibid., pp. 9-10.
15. Ibid., p. 10.
16. Trial testimony, Collazo, vol. 7, pp. 702-704.
17. FBI Document 100-7689, p. 11.
18. Ibid., pp. 10-11.
19. Trial testimony, Collazo, vol. 7, p. 711.
20. Ibid., pp. 711-712.
21. Ibid., p. 712.
22. FBI Document 100-7689, pp. 14, 21.
23. Ibid., p. 15; Trial testimony, Collazo, vol. 7, pp. 714-716.
24. FBI Document 100-7689, pp. 12-13.
25. Trial testimony, Collazo, vol. 8, p. 752.
26. FBI Document 100-7689, p. 17; Trial testimony, Collazo, vol. 7, p. 717.
27. Trial testimony, Collazo, vol. 7, p. 718.
28. Ibid., vol. 8, p. 763.
29. Ibid., vol. 7, p. 719.
30. Ibid., vol. 7, pp. 717, 722; vol. 8, p. 740.
31. Ibid., vol. 7, p. 720.
32. Ibid., pp. 722-723.
33. Ibid., p. 724.
34. FBI Document 94-50590-2, p. 8.
35. Trial testimony, Rover, vol. 7, pp. 725-726.
36. Trial testimony, Collazo, vol. 7, p. 726.
37. Ibid., p. 727.
38. *New York Times*, September 11, 1979, A16.
39. Ibid.
40. *New York Times*, September 12, 1979, A1, A14.
41. Ibid.
42. *New York Times*, September 13, 1979, B23.
43. *New York Times*, December 4, 1979, A1.
44. Trial testimony, Collazo, vol. 8, p. 766.
45. *Chicago Daily News*, November 1, 1950, 1.

Sirhan Sirhan

46. Robert Blair Kaiser, "*RFK Must Die!*" A History of the Robert Kennedy Assassination and its Aftermath (New York: Dutton, 1970), pp. 419-422; 425.
47. Ibid.
48. Trial testimony (The People of the State of California v. Sirhan Bisbara

Sirhan [1969], Superior Court, Crim. Case No. 14026), Lubic, vol. 19, p. 5525.

49. People's Exhibit 78, Autopsy Report.

50. Trial testimony: Unruh, vol. 12, pp. 3283, 3291; Sirhan, vol. 18, p. 5217.

51. Godfrey Jansen, *Why Robert Kennedy Was Killed* (New York: The Third Press, 1970), ch. 11.

52. Trial testimony, Mary Sirhan, vol. 16, pp. 4671-4729; Hashimeh, vol. 16, pp. 4591-4622; Sirhan, vol. 17, pp. 4810-4833.

53. Trial testimony, Nahas, vol. 16, pp. 4575-4588.

54. Trial testimony, Mary Sirhan, vol. 16, pp. 4704-4707; Sirhan, vol. 17, pp. 4815, 4832-4833.

55. Trial testimony, Hashimeh, vol. 16, pp. 4599-4607.

56. Ibid., p. 4621.

57. Ibid., p. 4616.

58. Ibid. Trial testimony, Sirhan, vol. 17, p. 4869.

59. Trial testimony, Hashimeh, vol. 16, pp. 4591-4622.

60. Trial testimony, Mary Sirhan, vol. 16, pp. 4712-4713.

61. Trial testimony, Sirhan, vol. 17, pp. 4970-4971.

62. For a discussion of this period, see Richard H. Rovere, *Senator Joe McCarthy* (New York: World Publishing, 1960).

63. Trial testimony, Sirhan, vol. 17, pp. 4856, 4937.

64. Defendant's Exhibit D.

65. Ibid.

66. Trial testimony, Harris, vol. 16, pp. 4625-4644.

67. Trial testimony, Lewis, vol. 17, pp. 4787-4802; Defendant's Exhibit G.

68. Trial testimony: Weidner, vol. 19, pp. 5427-5445; Sirhan, vol. 17, p. 4878.

69. Trial testimony, Weidner, vol. 19, pp. 5427-5445.

70. Trial testimony, Strathman, vol. 19, pp. 5381-5406.

71. Trial testimony, Sirhan, vol. 17, p. 4898.

72. Ibid., p. 4937; Trial testimony, Strathman, vol. 19, pp. 5381-5406.

73. Defendant's Exhibits II and JJ.

74. Trial testimony, Sirhan, vol. 17, pp. 4924-4937.

75. Ibid., p. 5026.

76. Trial testimony: Weidner, vol. 19, pp. 5431-5434; Sirhan, vol. 18, pp. 5236-5254.

77. Trial testimony, Sirhan, vol. 17, pp. 4905-4924.

78. Ibid., pp. 4919-4920; Defendant's Exhibits H and I.

79. Defendant's Exhibit J.

80. Trial testimony, Sirhan, vol. 17, pp. 4931, 4971, 4977.

81. Defendant's Exhibit RR.

82. Trial testimony, Sirhan, vol. 17, pp. 4969, 4971.

83. Ibid., p. 4905.

84. Trial transcripts, Sirhan tapes, vol. 21, pp. 5948-6170.
85. Defendant's Exhibit RR.
86. People's Exhibit 71.
87. Ibid.
88. Ibid.
89. Defendant's Exhibit HH.
90. Kaiser, "*RFK Must Die,*" pp. 111-112.
91. Trial testimony: Sirhan, vol. 18, p. 5125; Erhard, vol. 13, pp. 3747-3755.
92. Trial testimony, Clark, vol. 14, pp. 4010-4017.
93. Kaiser, "*RFK Must Die,*" pp. 164-165.
94. Ibid., pp. 163-164, 228-229.
95. People's Exhibit 71.
96. Kaiser, "*RFK Must Die,*" p. 219.
97. Trial testimony, Sirhan, vol. 17, pp. 4970-4971.
98. Kaiser, "*RFK Must Die,*" p. 533.
99. Ibid., p. 534.
100. Trial testimony: Placentia, vol. 12, pp. 3482-3511; White, vol. 13, pp. 3810-3832.
101. Trial testimony, Sirhan, vol. 17, pp. 4977-4978.
102. Trial testimony, Bryan, vol. 19, pp. 5459-5464.
103. Trial testimony: Sirhan, vol. 18, pp. 5125-5126; Erhard, vol. 13, pp. 3747-3755; People's Exhibits 22-23.
104. Trial testimony, Sirhan, yol. 18, pp. 5131-5143.
105. Kaiser, "*RFK Must Die,*" p. 534.
106. Trial testimony, Sirhan, vol. 18, pp. 5152-5171.
107. Ibid., pp. 5182-5187, 5200-5202, 5214-5215.
108. Trial testimony, Bidstrup, vol. 19, pp. 5465-5484.
109. Trial testimony: Rabago, vol. 19, pp. 5490-5491; Cordero, vol. 19, pp. 5499-5505.
110. Trial testimony: Perez, vol. 12, pp. 3374-3375; Patrusky, vol. 19, p. 3881.
111. Trial testimony, Jordon, vol. 16, p. 4448; Trial transcripts, Sirhan tapes, vol. 21, pp. 5971-6011.
112. Trial transcripts, Sirhan tapes, vol. 21, pp. 5971-6170.
113. Ibid., pp. 5971-6170; Kaiser, "*RFK Must Die,*" p. 56.
114. Trial transcripts, Sirhan tapes, vol. 21, pp. 5971-6170.
115. Trial testimony, Jordan, vol. 16, pp. 4430-4434.
116. Trial transcripts, Sirhan tapes, vol. 21, pp. 5985-5986.
117. Kaiser, "*RFK Must Die,*" p. 94.
118. Trial testimony, Evans, vol. 15, pp. 4317-4326.
119. Defendant's Exhibits H, S, T, U, R.
120. People's Exhibit 99.
121. Defendant's Exhibit U.
122. People's Exhibit 102.

123. Ibid., pp. 2-3.

124. Kaiser, "*RFK Must Die*," pp. 242-243, 293; see also Trial testimony, Schorr, vol. 19, p. 5547.

125. Defendant's Exhibit T.

126. People's Exhibit 102.

127. Trial testimony, Diamond, vol. 25, p. 7197.

128. Kaiser, "*RFK Must Die*," p. 388.

129. Ibid., pp. 243, 343-345.

130. Trial testimony, Sirhan, vol. 16, pp. 4646-4650; Cooper statement, vol. 16, p. 4645; Berman statement, vol. 15, pp. 4381-4384.

131. Trial testimony: Nahas, vol. 16, pp. 4575-4588; Hashimeh, vol. 16, pp. 4591-4622; Mary Sirhan, vol. 16, pp. 4671-4719.

132. Trial testimony, Sirhan, vol. 17, pp. 4931-4937.

133. Defendant's Exhibit H; People's Exhibit 102.

134. Kaiser, "*RFK Must Die*," pp. 218-219.

135. Ibid., p. 440.

136. Ibid., pp. 290, 345.

137. Trial testimony, Diamond, vol. 24, p. 6998; emphasis added.

138. Ibid., p. 6994.

139. Trial testimony, Diamond, vol. 24, pp. 7099-7100.

140. People's Exhibit 111.

141. Trial testimony, Diamond, vol. 24, p. 6998.

142. Trial statement, Howard, vol. 31, pp. 8887-8888.

143. Kaiser, "*RFK Must Die*," Appendix H.

144. Ibid., p. 466.

145. James McKinley, "Inside Sirhan," *Playboy*, April 1978, p. 96.

146. *Arizona Daily Star*, September 27, 1980, A2.

147. *Tucson Daily Citizen*, February 4, 1981, A1.

148. Kaiser, "*RFK Must Die*," p. 422.

149. Ibid., pp. 26, 230, 265, 294, 466, 514, 524.

150. Cynthia Gorney, "Sirhan," *Washington Post*, Aug. 21, 1979, B3.

151. Ibid.

CHAPTER FOUR

Lee Harvey Oswald

1. Elton B. McNeil, *Neuroses and Personality Disorders* (Englewood Cliffs, N.J.: Prentice-Hall, Inc., 1970), pp. 3-22.

2. Harold D. Lasswell, *Power and Personality* (1948; reprint ed. New York: The Viking Press, 1962).

3. Ibid., pp. 39-58.

4. President's Commission on the Assassination of President Kennedy, *Hearings on the Investigation of the Assassination of President John F. Kennedy* (Washington, D.C.: U.S. Government Printing Office, 1964), vols. 1-26:

testimonies of John Pic, vols. 11, 12; and Marguerite Oswald, vol. 1, p. 254. Hereafter cited as Hearings 1964.

5. Hearings 1964: testimonies of Marguerite Oswald, vol. 1, pp. 250-252; and John Pic, vol. 11, pp. 27-29.

6. Hearings 1964: R. Hartogs, Deposition (Dep.) 1.

7. Hearings 1964: J. Carro, Dep. 1, pp. 3, 6; E. Siegel, Dep. 1, p. 3.

8. Hearings 1964: J. Carro, Dep. 1, p. 2.

9. Hearings 1964: testimony of John Pic, vol. 11, p. 809.

10. Hearings 1964: E. Siegel, Dep. 1, pp. 2, 3.

11. Hearings 1964: testimonies of K. Thornley, vol. 11, pp. 89, 101; A. D. Graef, vol. 8, p. 318; J. R. Heindell, vol. 8, p. 318; M. Osborne, vol. 8, p. 321; and J. E. Donovan, vol. 8, pp. 292-293.

12. Hearings 1964: testimony of D. Powers, vol. 8, pp. 270, 287.

13. Hearings 1964: testimonies of D. Powers, vol. 8, p. 277; and K. Thornley, vol. 11, pp. 93-94.

14. Hearings 1964: testimonies of D. Murray, vol. 8, p. 319; J. Botelho, vol. 8, p. 315; and M. Osborne, vol. 8, p. 321.

15. Hearings 1964: A. Folsom, Dep. 1, pp. 31-34, and vol. 8, p. 308.

16. President's Commission on the Assassination of President Kennedy, *Report of the President's Commission on the Assassination of President John F. Kennedy* (Washington, D.C.: U.S. Government Printing Office, 1964, 1967), Commission Exhibit 295, pp. 4, 7, 8; Commission Exhibit 294, p. 1. Hereafter cited as CE, 1964.

17. CE 24, 1964, pp. 1-2; CE 985, 1964.

18. CE 985, 1964; Hearings 1964: testimony of Marina Oswald, vol. 5, p. 589; CE 24, 1964; CE 25, 1964.

19. CE 24, 1964, p. 9.

20. CE 92, 1964.

21. CE 94, 1964, p. 1.

22. Hearings 1964: testimonies of Marina Oswald, vol. 1, pp. 5-7; and A. D. Graef, vol. 10, pp. 186-189.

23. Priscilla Johnson McMillan, *Marina and Lee* (1977; reprint ed., New York: Bantam, 1978), pp. 341-342, 350-355, 426, 452-453.

24. CE 97, 1964.

25. McMillan, *Marina*, p. 646, n. 17.

26. CE 97, 1964.

27. CE 133, 134, 1964.

28. McMillan, *Marina*, p. 367.

29. Hearings 1964: testimony of Marina Oswald, vol. 1, pp. 15-16.

30. U.S. Congress, House, Select Committee on Assassinations, *Hearings on the Investigation of the Assassination of President John F. Kennedy*, 95th Cong., 2d Sess., 1978, vol. 2, pp. 242-249. Hereafter cited as Hearings 1978.

31. McMillan, *Marina*, pp. 373-375.

32. Ibid., pp. 368-369, 376.

33. Ibid., p. 384.

34. Ibid., p. 378.

35. CE 1, 1964.

36. McMillan, *Marina*, p. 380.

37. Ibid., p. 383.

38. Ibid., p. 384.

39. Ibid., p. 394.

40. Ibid., pp. 395-396.

41. Hearings 1964: testimony of N. Delgado, vol. 8, pp. 233, 240.

42. Hearings 1978: vol. 4, p. 480; Appendix, vol. 10, pp. 123-136.

43. Hearings 1964: testimony of A. Alba, vol. 19, p. 220.

44. Hearings 1964: testimony of W. Stuckey, vol. 11, pp. 165-166.

45. CE 1349, 1964; Hearings 1978: statement of G. R. Blakey, vol. 3, p. 3.

46. Hearings 1978: statement of G. R. Blakey, vol. 4, pp. 484-485; and vol. 10, pp. 131-132.

47. Hearings 1978: vol. 19, pp. 5-35.

48. Ibid., vol. 3, pp. 33-60, 130-147.

49. McMillan, *Marina*, p. 504.

50. Hearings 1964: vol. 25, pp. 768-769.

51. McMillan, *Marina*, pp. 505-506.

52. Hearings 1964: testimony of R. Truly, vol. 3, pp. 216-218.

53. McMillan, *Marina*, p. 509.

54. Hearings 1964: testimonies of George and Jeanne de Mohrenschildt, vol. 9, pp. 233, 309-314; and Ruth Paine, vol. 11, p. 396.

55. McMillan, *Marina*, p. 511.

56. Ibid., p. 517.

57. Ibid.

58. Ibid., pp. 514-515.

59. Ibid., p. 529.

60. Ibid., pp. 535-537. See also U.S. Congress, House, Subcommittee on Civil and Constitutional Rights of the Committee of the Judiciary, *Hearings on Federal Bureau of Investigation*, 94th Cong., 2d Sess., 1975-1976, serial no. 2, pt. 3: testimony of James P. Hosty, pt. 3, pp. 124-129. Hereafter cited as Hearings 1975-1976.

61. CE 103, 1964.

62. Hearings 1975-1976: testimony of Nancy L. Fenner, pt. 3, p. 37.

63. Ibid.

64. Hearings 1964: testimony of Marina Oswald, vol. 1, pp. 54, 63.

65. Hearings 1964: testimony of A. C. Johnson, vol. 10, pp. 297-298.

66. Hearings 1964: testimony of Marina Oswald, vol. 1, pp. 46, 63, 65.

67. CE 1361-1380, 1964.

68. Hearings 1964: testimony of B. W. Frazier, vol. 2, p. 222.

69. McMillan, *Marina*, pp. 559-560.

70. Ibid., pp. 562-563.

71. Ibid., p. 564.

72. U.S. Congress, House, Select Committee on Assassinations, *Report on Findings and Recommendations, 1979,* 95th Cong., 2d Sess., 1979, HR 95-1828, pt. 2, pp. 65-93.

Samuel Byck

73. Documents, Samuel Byck, Department of Transportation Federal Aviation Administration, Security Summary (SE-1600-20) ASE-74-4.

74. Documents, Samuel Byck, Small Business Administration, 1973. Hereafter cited as Documents, SBA.

75. Letter dated October 22, 1972, Documents, Samuel Byck, United States Secret Service, 1972-1974. Hereafter cited as Documents, Secret Service.

76. Samuel Byck, Recorded Tapes, Federal Bureau of Investigation, February 21, 1974. Hereafter cited as Tape.

77. Documents, Secret Service, report dated November 21, 1972.

78. Documents, Samuel Byck, Federal Bureau of Investigation, File No. BA 164-170. Hereafter cited as Documents, FBI.

79. Documents, Secret Service, January 26, 1973.

80. Documents, SBA, February 8, 1979.

81. Documents, Samuel Byck, Federal Communications Commission, File No. 8310-100, C6-1833, August 8, 1973.

82. Documents, Secret Service, October 12, 1973.

83. Documents, Samuel Byck, Office of Pardon Attorney, U.S. Department of Justice, January 9, 1974.

84. Documents, FBI.

85. Documents, Secret Service.

86. Documents, FBI and Secret Service.

87. Tape, February 5, 1974.

88. Ibid., February 21, 1974.

89. Ibid., February 5, 1974.

90. Ibid., January 30, 1974.

91. Ibid., February 5, 1974.

92. Ibid., February 8, 1974.

93. Ibid., February 22, 1974.

94. Ibid.

CHAPTER FIVE

Lynette Alice Fromme

1. Sara Jane Moore, "Playboy Interview," *Playboy,* June 1976, p. 70.

2. Lynette Fromme, untitled manuscript, *Time,* September 15, 1975, p. 12. Hereafter referred to as Untitled Manuscript.

3. Ibid.

4. Vincent Bugliosi, with Curt Gentry, *Helter Skelter* (New York: W. W. Norton & Co., 1974).

5. *Sacramento Bee,* September 17, 1975, B1.

6. *Sacramento Bee*, September 12, 1975, A3.

7. Trial (United States v. Lynette Alice Fromme [November-December 1975], United States District Court for the Eastern District of California, CR. No. 5-75-451, vols. 1-10), Exhibit No. 24.

8. Trial transcripts, pp. 1899-1900.

9. Ibid.

10. *Sacramento Bee*, September 10, 1975, A14.

11. Untitled Manuscript, p. 17.

12. *Sacramento Bee*, September 7, 1975, A20.

13. Trial transcript, p. 1631.

14. Ibid. See also Untitled Manuscript, p. 17.

15. Trial transcript, p. 1622.

16. Ibid., pp. 1622-1623.

17. Ibid., pp. 1623-1624.

18. Ibid., p. 1624.

19. Ibid., p. 1625.

20. Ibid., pp. 1626-1628.

21. Ibid., pp. 2250-2258.

22. *Sacramento Bee*, September 7, 1975, A20.

23. Ibid., September 9, 1975, A3.

24. Trial transcript, p. 2365.

25. *Sacramento Bee*, September 10, 1975, A1.

Sara Jane Moore

26. *Charleston Gazette*, September 24, 1975, A1, B1.

27. Ibid., p. A16.

28. Ibid., September 25, 1975, A1.

29. Ibid., p. A2.

30. Ibid., September 24, 1975, A3.

31. Ibid., September 24-25, 1975, A1, A3.

32. *Los Angeles Times*, September 23, 1975, I-3.

33. Ibid., p. I-1.

34. Ibid.

35. Ibid.

36. Moore, "Interview," p. 78.

37. *Los Angeles Times*, September 23, 1975, I-19.

38. Moore, "Interview," p. 80.

39. Ibid., pp. 80-81.

40. Ibid., p. 82.

41. *Newsweek*, October 6, 1975, 24.

42. Moore, "Interview," p. 82.

43. Ibid., p. 82.

44. Ibid., p. 84.

45. Ibid., pp. 84-86.

46. Ibid., p. 72.

47. *Los Angeles Times*, September 25, 1975, I-3, I-29; Moore, "Interview," p. 77.

48. *Los Angeles Times*, September 24, 1975, I-1.

49. Ibid., p. I-18; ibid., September 25, 1975, I-29.

50. Ibid., September 23-24, 1975, I-1, I-3.

51. Moore, "Interview," pp. 70-71.

52. *Los Angeles Times*, September 25, 1975, I-1.

Chapter Six

Giuseppe Zangara

1. Giuseppe Zangara, "Sworn Statement of Joseph Zangara," Miami, Dade County, Florida, February 16, 1933, p. 22. Hereafter cited as "Sworn Statement."

2. Ibid., pp. 13-14.

3. Documents, Giuseppe Zangara, Federal Bureau of Investigation, File No. 62-28219-1-61, February 16, 1933. Hereafter cited as FBI Documents.

4. Ibid., February 18, 1933.

5. *Newark Evening News*, February 16, 1933, 1.

6. Ibid., p. 2.

7. FBI Documents, March 18, 1933.

8. "Sworn Statement," pp. 10-11.

9. Ibid., p. 9.

10. FBI Documents, February 16, 1933.

11. *Newark Evening News*, February 20, 1933, 1.

12. Ibid., February 21, 1933, 3.

13. Ibid.

14. Ibid.

15. Ibid.

16. Ibid., March 10, 1933, 1.

17. *Miami Herald*, February 21, 1933, 1.

18. "Sworn Statement," pp. 6, 14.

19. Ibid., pp. 7, 11.

20. Ibid., p. 12.

21. Ibid., pp. 8, 14, 23.

22. Ibid., p. 12.

23. Ibid., p. 7.

Arthur Herman Bremer

24. Fyodor Dostoyevsky, *Notes From Underground*, ed. Robert G. Durgy, trans. Serge Shishkoff (New York: Thomas Y. Crowell, 1969).

25. Trial (State of Maryland v. Arthur Herman Bremer [July-August 1972], Circuit Court for Prince George's County, Maryland, Crim. Tr. Nos. 12376-12379) testimony, Laurence Pierce, p. 205.

26. Trial testimony, Joseph Schanno, pp. 380-381.

27. Trial transcripts, p. 4.

28. Annotated Code of Maryland, Article 59, section 25.

29. Report by Eloise M. Agger, Trial transcripts, p. 831. Hereafter cited as Agger Report.

30. Ibid., pp. 566-567, 831-835.

31. *Milwaukee Journal*, May 21, 1972, 1.

32. Agger Report, p. 837.

33. Ibid.

34. Ibid., pp. 838-839.

35. Ibid., p. 844.

36. Trial testimony, Eugene B. Brody, p. 637.

37. Ibid., p. 654.

38. Ibid., p. 708.

39. Ibid., pp. 639-642.

40. Trial statements: Kay Johannes, Peter Holmes, and FBI reports, pp. 894-932.

41. Trial testimony, Eugene B. Brody, p. 641; Trial statement, James Johannes, pp. 934-937.

42. Trial testimony, Eugene B. Brody, p. 642.

43. FBI interview of Joan Marie Pembrick, Trial transcripts, pp. 865-868.

44. Trial statement, Joan Pembrick, pp. 870-871.

45. Trial statement, Darlene Lemberger, p. 887.

46. Trial statement, Joan Pembrick, pp. 868-869.

47. Trial statement, Margaret Pembrick, p. 877.

48. FBI report, Trial transcripts, p. 875.

49. Trial testimony, Eugene B. Brody, p. 644.

50. Ibid.

51. Trial testimony, William Heely, pp. 897-899.

52. Trial testimony: James E. Olsson, pp. 509-510; Eugene B. Brody, p. 645.

53. Trial testimony, Eugene B. Brody, pp. 645-646.

54. Trial testimony: James E. Olsson, p. 488; William N. Fitzpatrick, p. 542; Eugene B. Brody, pp. 636, 650, 654-655, 659-660.

55. Trial Testimony: James E. Olsson, p. 489; Jonas Rappeport, p. 581; Eugene B. Brody, p. 636.

56. Gore Vidal, "Now For the Shooting of George Wallace," *New York Review of Books* 20 (December 13, 1973): 17-19; and James McKinley, *Assassination in America* (New York: Harper & Row, 1977).

57. Trial Testimony: James E. Olsson, pp. 483-532; Eugene B. Brody, pp. 669-740; Eugene C. Stammeyer, pp. 741-754.

58. Diary, Trial transcripts, pp. 1006-1007. Hereafter cited as Diary.

59. Ibid., pp. 1009-1010.

60. Ibid., p. 994.

61. Ibid., p. 1012.

62. Ibid., pp. 1019-1021.

63. Ibid., pp. 1023-1024.
64. Ibid., pp. 1024-1025.
65. Ibid., p. 1035.
66. Ibid., p. 1040.
67. Trial testimony, Eugene B. Brody, pp. 633, 656.
68. Trial testimony, James E. Olsson, p. 482.
69. Diary, p. 1034.
70. Albert Camus, *The Stranger* (New York: Alfred A. Knopf, 1946).
71. Diary, p. 1026.
72. Ibid., p. 1008.
73. Ibid., p. 1036.
74. Ibid.
75. Ibid., p. 1042.
76. Ibid., p. 1027.
77. Ibid., pp. 1027-1028.
78. Ibid., pp. 952, 1027.
79. Ibid., p. 1037.
80. Ibid., p. 1045.
81. Trial testimony: James E. Olsson, pp. 483-485; Eugene B. Brody, pp. 669-670; Eugene C. Stammeyer, p. 754.
82. Trial testimony: James E. Olsson, p. 514; Eugene C. Stammeyer, p. 755.
83. Trial testimony: James E. Olsson, p. 515; Eugene B. Brody, p. 668.
84. Trial testimony, Eugene B. Brody, pp. 696-697.
85. Robert Blair Kaiser, *"RFK Must Die!" A History of the Robert Kennedy Assassination and its Aftermath* (New York: Dutton, 1970), p. 512.
86. Ibid., pp. 412, 440, 447-478, 464, 467, 475-476, 481, 492, 597-609.
87. Statement, Arthur H. Bremer, p. 1277.

CHAPTER SEVEN

Richard Lawrence

1. Donald W. Hastings, "The Psychiatry of Presidential Assassination, Part I: Jackson and Lincoln," *The Journal-Lancet* 85 (March 1965): 93-100; "The Psychiatry of Presidential Assassination, Part II: Garfield and McKinley," *The Journal-Lancet* 85 (April 1965), 157-162; and "The Psychiatry of Presidential Assassination, Part III: The Roosevelts," *The Journal-Lancet* 85 (May 1965): 189-192.

2. "Trial of Richard Lawrence," in *Assassination and Insanity: Guiteau's Case Examined and Compared with Analogous Cases from the Earlier to the Present Times*, ed. William R. Smith (Washington, D.C., 1881), pp. 26-80. See also United States v. Richard Lawrence (March 1835), Circuit Court, District of Columbia, Case No. 15, 577; *Niles Register*, vol. 48, 1836; and *Criminal Appearances* 119 (March 1835), United States District Court of the District of Columbia, Record Group 21, National Archives.

3. Smith, ed., "Trial," p. 33.

4. Ibid., pp. 30-31.

5. Ibid., p. 31.

6. Ibid., p. 30.

7. Ibid., p. 35.

8. Ibid., p. 31.

9. Ibid., pp. 32, 34, 38.

10. Ibid., p. 30.

11. Ibid., p. 32.

12. Ibid., p. 34.

13. Ibid., p. 32.

14. Carlton Jackson, "Another Time, Another Place—The Attempted Assassination of President Andrew Jackson," *Tennessee Historical Quarterly* 26 (Summer 1967): 188.

Charles J. Guiteau

15. See, for example, James McKinley, *Assassination in America* (New York: Harper & Row, 1977), p. 42; and Samuel Eliot Morison and Henry Steele Commager, *The Growth of the American Republic* (New York: Oxford University Press, 1950), 2:221.

16. Trial (United States v. Charles J. Guiteau [June 1882], Supreme Court of the District of Columbia, Criminal Case No. 14056, National Archives) statement of George Scoville, p. 294.

17. Trial testimony, Charles Guiteau, p. 311.

18. Trial statement, George Scoville, pp. 294-295.

19. Ibid.

20. Ibid., pp. 297-298.

21. John W. Guiteau, "Letters and Facts Not Heretofore Published, Touching the Mental Condition of Charles J. Guiteau Since 1865," Document submitted to the President of the United States by John W. Guiteau in the Matter of Application for a Commission De Lunatico Inquirendo, June 23, 1882, File No. 14056, National Archives, p. 11.

22. Ibid.: See also Charles J. Guiteau, "The New York Theocrat," prospectus, File No. 14056, National Archives.

23. J. Guiteau, "Letters and Facts," p. 11.

24. C. Guiteau, "The New York Theocrat."

25. Charles E. Rosenberg, *The Trial of the Assassin Guiteau* (Chicago: The University of Chicago Press, 1968), p. 26.

26. J. Guiteau, "Letters and Facts," p. 23.

27. Ibid., p. 22.

28. Ibid.

29. Trial statement, George Scoville, pp. 2115-2116.

30. Ibid., pp. 305-307, 2118-2119.

31. Letters of Charles J. Guiteau, File No. 14056, National Archives.

32. Ibid.

33. Ibid.
34. Trial transcript, p. 211.
35. Letters.
36. Trial testimony, Charles Guiteau, pp. 56-57.
37. Trial exhibit, p. 216.
38. Letters.
39. Trial testimony, Charles Guiteau, p. 2206.
40. Letters.
41. Ibid.
42. Charles F. Folsom, *Studies of Criminal Responsibility and Limited Responsibility* (Boston: Privately printed, 1909), p. 20; and Trial testimony, George Scoville, pp. 291-293.
43. Edward C. Spitzka, "A Contribution to the Question of the Mental Status of Guiteau and the History of His Trial," *Alienist and Neurologist* 4 (April 1883): 204.
44. J. Guiteau, "Letters and Facts," p. 2.
45. W. W. Godding, *Two Hard Cases: Sketches from a Physician's Portfolio* (Boston: Houghton Mifflin, 1882), p. 46.
46. "The Trial of Charles J. Guiteau for the Murder of President Garfield, in *American State Trials*, ed. John D. Lawson (St. Louis: Thomas Law Book Co., 1923), 14:68.
47. Godding, *Two Hard Cases*, pp. 46-47.
48. Ibid., p. 47.
49. Hastings, "The Psychiatry of . . . Part II."
50. Letters.
51. "The Trial of Guiteau," pp. 156-157.
52. Ibid., p. 157.
53. John Purdue Gray, "The United States vs. Charles J. Guiteau," *American Journal of Insanity* 38 (January 1882): 303-448; Spitzka, "A Contribution"; Allan McLane Hamilton, "The Case of Guiteau," *Boston Medical and Surgical Journal* 106 (March 9, 1882): 235-238; Stewart Mitchell, "The Man Who Murdered Garfield," *Proceedings of the Massachusetts Historical Society* 68 (1941-1944): 452-489; and Rosenberg, *The Trial of the Assassin Guiteau.*
54. "Guiteau-Finis," *Medical News* 41 (July 1882): 12.

John Schrank

55. Oliver E. Remy et al., *The Attempted Assassination of Ex-President Theodore Roosevelt* (Milwaukee: The Progressive Publishing Co., 1912), p. 147.
56. Ibid., p. 148.
57. Ibid., p. 20.
58. Ibid., pp. 42, 45.
59. Ibid., pp. 101-102.
60. Ibid., pp. 224-234.

61. George E. Mowry, *The Era of Theodore Roosevelt and the Birth of Modern America* (New York: Harper & Row, 1958), p. 48, citing Elting E. Morison, ed., *The Letters of Theodore Roosevelt*, 8 vols. (Cambridge, Mass.: Harvard University Press, 1951), 3:xvi.

62. *Milwaukee Journal*, October 15, 1912, 1-2.

63. Ibid., November 13, 1912, 1-2.

64. Arthur MacDonald, "The Would-Be Assassin of Theodore Roosevelt," *Medical Times* 62 (April 1914): 100.

65. *Milwaukee Journal*, October 15, 1912, 1.

66. Ibid., October 16, 1912, 1, 4.

67. MacDonald, "The Would-Be Assassin," p. 100.

68. Remy et al., *The Attempted Assassination*, p. 202.

69. *Milwaukee Journal*, October 18, 1912, 1.

70. MacDonald, "The Would-Be Assassin," p. 101.

71. Remy et al., *The Attempted Assassination*, pp. 108-109.

72. *Milwaukee Journal*, October 18, 1912, 1.

73. Ibid., October 17, 1912, 1-2; November 25, 1912, 1; Remy et al., *The Attempted Assassination*, p. 111.

74. *Chicago Tribune*, November 26, 1912, 1.

CHAPTER EIGHT

Carl Austin Weiss

1. Robert Penn Warren, *All the King's Men* (New York: Harcourt, Brace & Co., 1946).

2. T. Harry Williams, *Huey Long* (New York: Bantam Books, 1969).

3. Other interesting accounts of the Long era would include Carleton Beals, *The Story of Huey Long* (New York: Lippincott, 1935); Harnett Kane, *Louisiana Hayride* (New York: Morrow, 1941); Allan P. Sindler, *Huey Long's Louisiana* (Baltimore: Johns Hopkins, 1956); Stan Opotowsky, *The Long's of Louisiana* (New York: Dutton, 1960); Arthur M. Schlesinger, Jr., *The Politics of Upheaval*, vol. 3 (Boston: Houghton Mifflin, 1960); and V. O. Key, *Southern Politics in State and Nation* (New York: Alfred A. Knopf, 1949).

4. David H. Zinman, *The Day Huey Long Was Shot* (New York: Ivan Oblensky, Inc., 1963).

5. Hermann B. Deutsch, *The Huey Long Murder Case* (Garden City, N.Y.: Doubleday & Co., 1963).

6. Zinman, *The Day*, pp. 55-57.

7. Ibid., p. 60.

8. Ibid., pp. 64-65.

9. Ibid., pp. 66-67.

10. Ibid., p. 66.

11. Quoted in ibid., p. 71.

12. Ibid., p. 77.

13. Ibid., p. 76.
14. Ibid., pp. 78, 81.
15. Ibid., p. 83.
16. Deutsch, *The Long Murder Case*, p. 129.
17. Williams, *Huey Long*, p. 913.
18. Zinman, *The Day*, p. 280.
19. Deutsch, *The Long Murder Case*, p. 164.
20. Ibid., p. 128.
21. Ibid., pp. 128, 162.
22. Ibid., p. 71.
23. Williams, *Huey Long*, p. 896.
24. Ibid., p. 886.
25. Ibid., p. 887.
26. Reinhard H. Luthin, *American Demagogues* (Boston: The Beacon Press, 1954), pp. 263-267.
27. Huey P. Long, *My First Days in the White House* (Harrisburg, Pa., 1935); published posthumously.
28. Williams, *Huey Long*, p. 888.
29. Deutsch, *The Long Murder Case*, pp. 161-162; Williams, *Huey Long*, pp. 880-883, 900-901.
30. For a detailed discussion of the rumors circulating at the time, see Deutsch, *The Long Murder Case*, and Williams, *Huey Long*.
31. Zinman, *The Day*, pp. 234-235; Williams, *Huey Long*, p. 915.
32. Williams, *Huey Long*, p. 915.
33. James McKinley, *Assassination in America* (New York: Harper & Row, 1977), p. 97.
34. Deutsch, *The Long Murder Case*, p. 128.
35. Zinman, *The Day*.
36. Deutsch, *The Long Murder Case*, p. 162.
37. Zinman, *The Day*, pp. 85-86, 279-280.
38. Deutsch, *The Long Murder Case*, pp. 132-133.
39. Zinman, *The Day*, p. 284.
40. Ibid., pp. 85-92; Deutsch, *The Long Murder Case*, pp. 82-83.
41. Zinman, *The Day*, pp. 83-84.
42. Harvey G. Fields, *The Life of Huey Pierce Long* (Farmerville, La.: Fields Publishing Agency, 1944); Luthin, *American Demagogues*; Deutsch, *The Long Murder Case*; Jack Pearl, *The Dangerous Assassins* (Derby, Conn.: Monarch Books, 1964); Murray C. Havens et al., *The Politics of Assassination* (Englewood Cliffs, N.J.: Prentice-Hall, Inc., 1970); Lauran Paine, *The Assassins' World* (New York: Taplinger Publishing Co., 1975); and Sandy Lesberg, *Assassinations in Our Time* (London: Peebles Press International and Bobbs-Merrill, 1976).
43. Deutsch, *The Long Murder Case*, p. 128.
44. Zinman, *The Day*, p. 155.
45. Williams, *Huey Long*, p. 905.

46. For various immediate newspaper descriptions and interpretations of the event, see the following papers for September and October 1935: Baton Rouge *Morning Advocate* and *State-Times*, and the New Orleans *States Item* and *Times-Picayune*.

47. Zinman, *The Day*, p. 112.

48. Deutsch, *The Long Murder Case*, p. 89.

49. Williams, *Huey Long*, p. 906.

50. Deutsch, *The Long Murder Case*, p. 151.

51. Williams, *Huey Long*, p. 908.

52. Zinman, *The Day*, pp. 148-154; Deutsch, *The Long Murder Case*, pp. 108-110, 120-121.

53. Zinman, *The Day*, p. 158.

James Earl Ray

54. U.S. Congress, House, Select Committee on Assassinations, *Hearings on the Investigation of the Assassination of Martin Luther King, Jr.*, 95th Cong., 2d Sess., 1978, vols. 1-12, pp. 346-351. Hereafter cited as Hearings.

55. William Bradford Huie, *He Slew the Dreamer* (New York: Delacorte Press, 1970).

56. George McMillan, *The Making of an Assassin* (Boston: Little, Brown, 1976).

57. Huie, *The Dreamer*, p. 173.

58. McMillan, *Assassin*, pp. 70, 246-247.

59. Hearings: testimony of Jerry Ray, vol. 7, pp. 395, 400, 436-437, 499-500, 520-521.

60. Hearings: narration of James Wolf, vol. 8, pp. 1-13, 33.

61. McMillan, *Assassin*, pp. 69-71.

62. Ibid., p. 106.

63. Hearings: testimony of Jerry Ray, vol. 7, p. 500.

64. Ibid., vol. 4, p. 195.

65. Huie, *The Dreamer*, p. 11.

66. Hearings: narration of G. Robert Blakey, vol. 4, pp. 112, 132, 147-149.

67. McMillan, *Assassin*, pp. 206-207.

68. Hearings: testimony of James Earl Ray, vol. 1, pp. 230, 329-330, 334; narration of G. Robert Blakey, vol. 4, p. 112; testimony of Jerry Ray, vol. 7, pp. 500, 520-521.

69. Hearings: testimony of James Earl Ray, vol. 4, pp. 112-113.

70. Hearings: narration of G. Robert Blakey, vol. 4, pp. 117-121.

71. Hearings: Exhibit F-172, vol. 4, pp. 155, 158; Exhibit F-166, vol. 4, pp. 171-175.

72. Hearings: Exhibit F-171, vol. 4, pp. 144-145.

73. Hearings: narration of G. Robert Blakey, p. 124; Exhibit F-170, vol. 4, pp. 130-134.

74. Hearings: Exhibit F-166, vol. 4, pp. 148-154.

75. McMillan, *Assassin*, pp. 221-227.
76. Hearings: narration of G. Robert Blakey, vol. 4, pp. 112-113, 194.
77. *St. Louis Post-Dispatch*, June 9, 1968, A31; see also Hearings: testimony of John Larry Ray, vol. 8, pp. 589, 600.
78. Hearings: testimony of Jerry Ray, vol. 7, pp. 338-340; narration of James Wolf, vol. 8, p. 3; testimony of John Larry Ray, p. 57. See also *Report of the Department of Justice Task Force to Review the FBI Martin Luther King, Jr. Security and Assassination Investigations* (Washington, D.C.: U.S. Department of Justice, January 11, 1977); hereafter cited as *Justice Report.*
79. Contradictions in Ray's various accounts of his activities are detailed in U.S. Congress, House, Select Committee on Assassinations, *Compilation of the Statements of James Earl Ray*, 95th Cong., 2d Sess., August 18, 1978.
80. Hearings: testimony of John Larry Ray, vol. 8, pp. 57-66.
81. Hearings: testimony of James Earl Ray, vol. 3, pp. 169-174; *Justice Report*, pp. 101-103.
82. Hearings: testimonies of James Earl Ray, vol. 2, pp. 486-487; Jerry Ray, vol. 7, p. 520; narration of James Wolf, vol. 8, pp. 9-12.
83. Hearings: narration of G. Robert Blakey, vol. 4, pp. 118-120, and vol. 7, p. 313.
84. Ibid., vol. 4, pp. 156-157, 182.
85. Ibid., p. 176.
86. Hearings: testimony of James Earl Ray, vol. 3, p. 203; narration of G. Robert Blakey, vol. 7, pp. 315, 317.
87. Hearings: narration of G. Robert Blakey, vol. 7, pp. 315, 317; testimony of James Earl Ray, vol. 1, p. 303, and vol. 2, pp. 48-53.
88. Hearings: testimony of James Earl Ray, vol. 3, pp. 213-214; narration of G. Robert Blakey, vol. 7, pp. 316-318.
89. Hearings: testimony of James Earl Ray, vol. 1, pp. 100-101, and vol. 3, pp. 215-222; narration of G. Robert Blakey, vol. 4, p. 8; vol. 5, pp. 219-220, 331; and vol. 7, pp. 316, 318; testimony of Jerry Ray, vol. 7, p. 440.
90. Hearings: testimony of James Earl Ray, vol. 2, p. 61 (see also pp. 62-67, 70-95); statement of Annie Estelle Peters, vol. 3, pp. 302-512.
91. Hearings: testimony of James Earl Ray, vol. 2, pp. 96-101, and vol. 1, pp. 76-82.
92. Ibid., vol. 1, pp. 87-112, 258, 333; vol. 2, pp. 26-27, 44; vol. 3, p. 271; vol. 4, introduction, p. 6; narration of G. Robert Blakey, pp. 21, 118-120; testimony of Percy Foreman, vol. 5, pp. 101-103, 116, 206, 219, 326, 330-332; narration of G. Robert Blakey, vol. 7, pp. 313-317; testimony of Jerry Ray, vol. 7, pp. 338-340, 396-401, 439-444; narration of James Wolf, vol. 8, pp. 3, 31; testimony of John Larry Ray, vol. 8, pp. 57-66, 600-604; and vols. 9, 10, 11, and 12, which contain eight intensive interviews with Ray in 1977 and his "20,000 word" handwritten statement.
93. Hearings: testimony of John Larry Ray, vol. 8, p. 601.
94. Hearings: testimony of Jerry Ray, vol. 7, p. 462.
95. Hearings: testimony of John Larry Ray, vol. 8, pp. 589, 599.

96. Hearings: testimony of Russell George Byers, vol. 7, p. 181.

97. Ibid., p. 187.

98. Ibid.

99. Ibid., pp. 194, 294.

100. Ibid., pp. 194, 198; narration of Edward Evans, vol. 7, pp. 250, 294-295.

101. Hearings: narration of Edward Evans, vol. 7, p. 310.

102. Ibid., p. 297.

103. Ibid.

104. Ibid., pp. 250-251.

105. Ibid., pp. 252-253.

106. Ibid., p. 263.

107. Ibid., p. 249.

108. Hearings: testimony of Russell George Byers, vol. 7, pp. 181-183, 188-189, 245-246.

109. Ibid., p. 191.

110. Ibid., p. 199; testimony of Edward Evans, vol. 7, pp. 247-248, 305.

111. Hearings: testimony of Edward Evans, vol. 7, p. 293.

112. Ibid., p. 310.

113. Ibid., pp. 293-302; Hearings: testimony of John Larry Ray, vol. 8, pp. 586-593.

114. Hearings: testimony of James Earl Ray, vol. 2, pp. 45-102.

115. Hearings: narration of Gene Johnson, vol. 1, p. 84; testimonies of James Earl Ray, vol. 3, p. 274; and Alexander Eist, vol. 4, p. 22.

116. Hearings: testimony of James Earl Ray, vol. 3, pp. 239-253; narration of G. Robert Blakey, vol. 4, pp. 113-116.

117. Hearings: narration by G. Robert Blakey, vol. 4, p. 195; testimony of Jerry Ray, vol. 7, p. 462; Exhibit F-642, vol. 8, p. 589.

118. Hearings: testimony of Percy Foreman, vol. 5, p. 208.

119. Hearings: testimony of Jerry Ray, vol. 7, pp. 328-329.

120. Hearings: Dan Rather interview of James Earl Ray, vol. 1, p. 343; testimony of Percy Foreman, vol. 5, pp. 300-302, Exhibit 47, p. 303.

121. Hearings: deposition of Percy Foreman, vol. 5, pp. 200-203; testimony of Percy Foreman, vol. 5, pp. 323, 329; Huie, *The Dreamer*, p. 170.

122. Hearings: interview with Alexander Eist, vol. 3, pp. 274-275; testimony of Alexander Eist, vol. 4, pp. 22-23; deposition of Percy Foreman, vol. 5, pp. 94-95; Huie, *The Dreamer*, pp. 207-212.

123. *Congressional Quarterly*, "Revolution in Civil Rights, 1945-1968," June 1968, pp. 11-12.

124. Hearings: Dan Rather interview, vol. 1, pp. 283-291; Huie, *The Dreamer*, pp. 198-199.

125. James W. Clarke and John W. Soule, "Southern Children's Reaction to King's Death," *Trans-Action 5* (October 1968): 35-40.

126. Hearings: Exhibit F-607, vol. 7, pp. 313-316.

127. *Justice Report*, pp. 101-110.

128. Hearings: testimony of Arthur L. Murtagh, vol. 6, p. 112.

129. *Justice Report*, p. 115.

130. Ibid., pp. 115-120, 125-142; Hearings: prepared statement of G. Robert Blakey, vol. 6, pp. 59-80; testimony of Arthur L. Murtagh, vol. 6, pp. 91-105.

131. Hearings: testimony of Edward Evans, vol. 7, p. 251; Exhibit F-578, pp. 252-268; Exhibit F-578A, vol. 7, pp. 269-292; testimony of Edward Evans, vol. 7, p. 293.

132. *Justice Report*, p. 126.

133. Ibid., pp. 123-125.

CHAPTER NINE

1. Norman Mailer, *The Executioner's Song* (Boston: Little, Brown, 1979), p. 357.

2. Adams v. Williams, 407 U.S. 143 (1972).

Bibliography

GENERAL

Books and Articles

Abrahamsen, David. *The Murdering Mind*. New York: Harper & Row, 1973.

Briggs, L. Vernon. *The Manner of Man that Kills*. Boston: The Gorham Press, 1921.

Cleveland, Sidney E. "Reflections on the Rise and Fall of Psychodiagnosis." *Professional Psychology* 7, no. 3 (August 1976): 309-318.

Crotty, William J. "Presidential Assassinations." *Society* 9 (May 1972): 18-29.

Davids, Anthony. "Projective Testing: Some Issues Facing Academicians and Practitioners." *Professional Psychology* 4 (November 1973): 445-453.

Dollard, J.; Doob, L.; Miller, N.; Mowrer, O.; and Sears, R. *Frustration and Aggression*. New Haven: Yale University Press, 1939.

Donovan, Robert J. *The Assassins*. New York: Harper & Brothers, 1952.

Freedman, Lawrence Z. "Assassination: Psychopathology and Social Pathology." *Postgraduate Medicine* 37 (June 1965): 650-658.

―――. "Psychopathology of Assassinations." In *Assassinations and the Political Order*, edited by William J. Crotty, pp. 143-160. New York: Harper & Row, 1971.

Goodwyn, Lawrence. *Democratic Promise: The Populist Movement in America*. New York: Oxford University Press, 1976.

Greening, Thomas C. "The Psychological Study of Assassins." In *Assassinations and the Political Order*, edited by William J. Crotty, pp. 222-268. New York: Harper & Row, 1971.

Halleck, Seymour. "American Psychiatry and the Criminal." In *The Psychological Foundations of Criminal Justice*, edited by Robert W. Rieber and Harold J. Vetter, vol. 1, pp. 8-42. New York: The John Jay Press, 1978.

Hassel, Conrad V. "The Political Assassin." *Journal of Police Science and Administration* 4 (December 1974): 399-403.

Hastings, Donald W. "The Psychiatry of Presidential Assassination, Part I: Jackson and Lincoln." *The Journal-Lancet* 85 (March 1965): 93-100.

―――. "The Psychiatry of Presidential Assassination, Part II: Garfield and McKinley." *The Journal-Lancet* 85 (April 1965): 157-162.

―――. "The Psychiatry of Presidential Assassination, Part III: The Roosevelts." *The Journal-Lancet* 85 (May 1965): 189-192.

―――. "The Psychiatry of Presidential Assassination, Part IV: Truman and Kennedy." *The Journal-Lancet* 85 (July 1965): 294-301.

Henn, Fritz A.; Herjanic, Marian; and Vanderpearl, Robert. "Forensic Psychiatry: Diagnosis and Criminal Responsibility." *The Journal of Nervous and Mental Disease* 162 (June 1976): 423-429.

Kaplan, John. "The Assassins." *Stanford Law Review* 59 (May 1967): 1110-1151.

Kimmel, Stanley. *The Mad Booths of Maryland.* 1940. Reprint. New York: Dover, 1969.

Kirkham, James F.; Levy, Sheldon G.; and Crotty, William J. *Assassination and Political Violence: A Report to the National Commission on the Causes and Prevention of Violence.* New York: Praeger and the *New York Times,* 1970.

Lasswell, Harold D. *Power and Personality.* 1948. Reprint. New York: The Viking Press, 1962.

Lesberg, Sandy. *Assassinations in Our Time.* London: Peebles Press International and Bobbs-Merrill, 1976.

Lewandowski, Denis G., and Saccuzzo, Dennis P. "The Decline of Psychological Testing." *Professional Psychology* 7, no. 2 (May 1976): 177-184.

MacDonald, John M. *Psychiatry and the Criminal.* 2d ed. Springfield, Ill.: Charles C. Thomas, 1969.

McKinley, James. *Assassination in America.* New York: Harper & Row, 1977.

McNeil, Elton B. *Neuroses and Personality Disorders.* Englewood Cliffs, N.J., Prentice-Hall, Inc., 1970.

———. *The Psychoses.* Englewood Cliffs, N.J.: Prentice-Hall, Inc., 1970.

Mailer, Norman. *The Executioner's Song.* Boston: Little, Brown, 1979.

Medawar, P. B. *The Hope of Progress.* London: Methuen, 1972.

Miller, Milton H. "Classification in Psychiatry: Neurosis, Psychosis, and the Borderline States." In *Comprehensive Textbook of Psychiatry,* edited by Alfred M. Freedman and Harold I. Kaplan, pp. 589-592. Baltimore: The William and Wilkins Co., 1967.

Morison, Samuel Eliot, and Commager, Henry Steele. *The Growth of the American Republic.* Vol. 2. New York: Oxford University Press, 1950.

Paine, Lauran. *The Assassins' World.* New York: Taplinger Publishing Co., 1975.

Pollack, Seymour. "Principles of Forensic Psychiatry for Psychiatric-Legal Opinion Making." In *Legal Medicine Annual,* edited by C. H. Wecht, ch. 14. New York: Appleton-Century-Crofts, 1971.

Robinson, Daniel J. *Psychology and Law: Can Justice Survive the Social Sciences?* New York: Oxford University Press, 1980.

Robinson, G. Wilse. "A Study of Political Assassinations." *American Journal of Psychiatry* 121 (May 1965): 1060-1064.

Rosenhan, D. L. "On Being Sane in Insane Places." *Science* 179 (January 1973): 250-258.

Slomich, Sidney J., and Kantor, Robert E. "Social Psychopathology of Political Assassination." *Bulletin of the Atomic Scientists* 25 (March 1969): 9-12.

Smith, M. Brewster. "A Map for the Analysis of Personality and Politics." *The Journal of Social Issues* 24 (July 1968): 15-28.

Smith, William R. *Assassination and Insanity: Guiteau's Case Examined and Compared with Analogous Cases from the Earlier to the Present Times.* Washington, D.C., 1881.

Spitzer, Robert; Endicott, Jean; and Robins, Eli. "Clinical Criteria for Psychiatric Diagnosis and DSM III." *American Journal of Psychiatry* 132 (November 1975): 1187-1192.

Szasz, Thomas S. *The Myth of Mental Illness.* New York: Harper & Row, 1961.

————. *Law, Liberty and Psychiatry.* New York: Macmillan & Co., 1963.

————. *Ideology and Insanity.* Garden City, N.Y.: Doubleday & Co., 1970.

————. *Schizophrenia: The Sacred Symbol of Psychiatry.* New York: Basic Books, 1976.

Townsend, W. C. *Modern State Trials.* London: Longman, Brown, 1850.

Weisz, Alfred E., and Taylor, Robert L. "American Presidential Assassinations." *Diseases of the Nervous System* 30 (October 1969): 658-668.

White, Theodore H. *The Making of the President 1964.* New York: Atheneum Publishers, 1965.

Wildman, Robert W., and Wildman, Robert W. II. "An Investigation into the Comparative Validity of Several Diagnostic Tests and Test Batteries." *Journal of Clinical Psychology* 31 (July 1975): 455-458.

Ziskin, Jay. *Coping with Psychiatric and Psychological Testimony.* Beverly Hills, Ca.: Law and Psychology Press, 1975; supplement, 1977.

Court Cases

Adams v. Williams, 407 U.S. 143 (1972).

Durham v. United States, 214 F.2d 862 (U.S. Court of Appeals, D.C., 1954).

MacDonald v. United States, 312 F.2d 847, 851 (D.C. Cir., 1962).

Daniel M'Naghten's Case, 10 Clark and Fin. 200, 8 Eng. Rep. 718 (1843).

Smith v. Schlesinger, 13 F.2d 462 (D.C. Cir., 1975).

Document

Model Penal Code 4.01 (P.O.D. 1962). See S.1, 93d Cong., 1st Sess., 1-302, 1973.

JOHN WILKES BOOTH

Books and Articles

Beard, Charles A., and Beard, Mary R. *The Rise of American Civilization.* New York: Macmillan & Co., 1927.

Brock, William R. *Conflict and Transformation: The United States, 1844-1877.* New York: Penguin Books, 1973.

Clarke, Asia Booth. *The Elder and the Younger Booth.* Boston: James R. Osgood & Co., 1882.

Clarke, Asia Booth. *The Unlocked Book*. New York: G. P. Putnam's Sons, 1938. Originally written in 1888.

Cottrell, John. *Anatomy of an Assassination*. London: Frederick Muller, 1966.

Davis, Jefferson. *The Rise and Fall of the Confederate Government*. 1881. Reprint. 2 vols. South Brunswick, N.J.: Thomas Yoseloff, 1958.

Donald, David. *Lincoln Reconsidered*. New York: Vintage Books, 1961.

Dusinbeere, William. *Civil War Issues in Pennsylvania*. Philadelphia: University of Pennsylvania Press, 1965.

Eisenschiml, Otto. *Why Was Lincoln Murdered?* Boston: Little, Brown, 1937.

Headley, Joel Tyler. *The Great Riots of New York, 1712 to 1873*. 1873. Reprint. New York: Dover, 1971.

Hyams, Edward. *Killing No Murder*. Camden, N.J.: Thomas Nelson & Sons, 1969.

Kimmel, Stanley. *The Mad Booths of Maryland*. 1940. Reprint. New York: Dover, 1969.

Mahoney, Ella V. *Sketches of Tudor Hall and the Booth Family*. Belair, Md.: Ella V. Mahoney, 1925.

Morris, Clara. *Life on the Stage*. New York: McClure, Phillips & Co., 1901.

Pitman, Benn. *The Assassination of President Lincoln and the Trial of the Conspirators: The Courtroom Testimony*. 1865. Reprint. New York: Funk & Wagnalls, 1954.

Randall, James G. *The Civil War and Reconstruction*. Boston and New York: D. C. Heath, 1937.

———. *Lincoln the Liberal Statesman*. New York: Dodd, Mead & Co., 1947.

Weichmann, Louis J. *A True History of the Assassination of Abraham Lincoln and the Conspiracy of 1865*. Edited by Floyd E. Risvold. New York: Vintage Books, 1975; originally written in the 1890s.

Weissman, Phillip. "Why Booth Shot Lincoln." In *Psychoanalysis and the Social Sciences*, vol. 5, pp. 99-115. New York: International Universities Press, 1958.

Williams, T. Harry. *Lincoln and the Radicals*. Madison: University of Wisconsin Press, 1941.

Wilson, Francis. *John Wilkes Booth*. New York: Benjamin Bloom, Inc., 1929, 1972.

Wilson, George W. "John Wilkes Booth: Father Murderer." *The American IMAGO* 1 (June 1940): 49-60.

Documents

Diary of John Wilkes Booth, Attorney General's Papers, Lincoln Assassination. RG No. 60, National Archives.

"Investigation and Trial Papers Relating to the Assassination of President Lincoln." Microfilm No. 599, National Archives.

Letters of John Wilkes Booth, Attorney General's Papers, Lincoln Assassination. RG No. 60, National Archives.

Newspapers

Chicago Times. March 6, 1865.
New Orleans Times. March 17, 1865.
Washington Evening Star. April 20, 1865.

LEON CZOLGOSZ

Trial Transcript

People v. Leon F. Czolgosz (1901). Courthouse Archives, Erie County, Buffalo, New York. Reprinted in *American State Trials*, edited by John D. Lawson, vol. 14, pp. 159-231. St. Louis: Thomas Law Book Co., 1923.

Books and Articles

Adler, Selig. "The Operation on President McKinley." *Scientific American* 208 (March 1963): 118-130.

Bell, Thomas. *Out of the Furnace.* 1941. Reprint. Pittsburgh: University of Pittsburgh Press, 1976.

Briggs, L. Vernon. *The Manner of Man that Kills.* Boston: The Gorham Press, 1921.

Bruce, Robert V. *1877: Year of Violence.* Chicago: Quadrangle Books, 1959.

Channing, Walter. "The Mental State of Czolgosz, the Assassin of President McKinley." *The American Journal of Insanity* 59 (October 1902): 233-278.

David, Henry. *The History of the Haymarket Affair.* 2d ed. New York: Russell & Russell, 1958.

Donovan, Robert J. *The Assassins.* New York: Harper & Brothers, 1952.

Drinnon, Richard. *Rebel in Paradise: A Biography of Emma Goldman.* Chicago: The University of Chicago Press, 1961.

Fine, Sidney. "Anarchism and the Assassination of McKinley." *American Historical Review* 60 (July 1955): 777-799.

Foner, Philip S. *The Great Labor Uprising of 1877.* New York: Monad Press, 1977.

Goldman, Emma. "The Tragedy at Buffalo." *Mother Earth* 1 (October 1906): 11-16.

————. *Living My Life.* Garden City, N.Y.: Garden City Publishing Co., 1931.

Greene, Victor R. *The Slavic Community on Strike.* Notre Dame, Ind.: University of Notre Dame Press, 1968.

Hamilton, Allan McLane. *Recollections of an Alienist.* New York: George H. Dolan, 1916.

Hastings, Donald W. "The Psychiatry of Presidential Assassination, Part II: Garfield and McKinley." *The Journal-Lancet* 85 (April 1965): 157-162.

Hughes, Charles H. "Medical Aspects of the Czolgosz Case." *Alienist and Neurologist* 23 (January 1902): 40-52.

Johns, A. Wesley. *The Man Who Shot McKinley*. South Brunswick and New York: A. S. Barnes, 1970.

Key, V. O. "A Theory of Critical Elections." *The Journal of Politics* 17 (February 1955): 3-18.

Lawson, John D., ed. *American State Trials*. Vol. 14. St. Louis: Thomas Law Book Co., 1923.

Leech, Margaret. *In the Days of McKinley*. New York: Harper & Row, 1959.

Lindsey, Almont. *The Pullman Strike*. Chicago: The University of Chicago Press, 1942.

MacDonald, Carlos F. "The Trial, Execution, Autopsy and Mental Status of Leon F. Czolgosz, Alias Fred Nieman, the Assassin of President McKinley." *The American Journal of Insanity* 58 (January 1902): 369-386.

McKinley, James. *Assassination in America*. New York: Harper & Row, 1977.

Novak, Michael. *The Guns of Lattimer*. New York: Basic Books, 1978.

Rayback, Joseph G. *A History of American Labor*. New York: The Free Press, 1959, 1966.

Spitzka, Edward A. "The Post-Mortem Examination of Leon F. Czolgosz, the Assassin of President McKinley." *American Journal of Insanity* 58 (January 1902): 386-388.

Documents

Fowler, Joseph; Crego, Floyd S.; and Putnam, James W. "Official Report of the Experts for the People in the Case of the People v. Leon F. Czolgosz" (1901). Reprinted in *American State Trials*, edited by John D. Lawson, vol. 14, pp. 195-199. St. Louis: Thomas Law Book Co., 1923.

"Report of Dr. Carlos F. MacDonald and Dr. Arthur Hurd, Experts for the Prisoner" (1901). Reprinted in *American State Trials*, edited by John D. Lawson, vol. 14, pp. 196-203. St. Louis: Thomas Law Book Co., 1923.

Newspaper

Cleveland Plain Dealer. May 6, 1901, 8.

OSCAR COLLAZO AND GRISELIO TORRESOLA

Trial Transcript

United States v. Oscar Collazo (February-March 1951). United States District Court for the District of Columbia.

Documents

"Incidents Preceding November 1, 1950, Attempted Assassination of President Truman." Federal Bureau of Investigation, File No. 62-7721-1695.

"Nationalist Party of Puerto Rico." Federal Bureau of Investigation, File No. 100-7689.

"Origin of Nationalist Party of Puerto Rico (NPPR), Including the Rise of Pedro Albizu Campos." Federal Bureau of Investigation, Document 94-50590-2.

Puerto Rican Nationalists, Oscar Collazo. Federal Bureau of Investigation, File No. 3-36-A, November-December 1950.

Newspapers

Chicago Daily News. November 1, 1950, 1.

New York Times. September 11, 1979, A16; September 12, 1979, A1, A14; September 13, 1979, B23; December 4, 1979, A1.

SIRHAN SIRHAN

Trial Transcript

The People of the State of California v. Sirhan Bisbara Sirhan (1969). Superior Court, Crim. Case No. 14026.

Books and Articles

Jansen, Godfrey. *Why Robert Kennedy Was Killed.* New York: The Third Press, 1970.

Kaiser, Robert Blair. *"RFK Must Die!" A History of the Robert Kennedy Assassination and its Aftermath.* New York: Dutton, 1970.

McKinley, James. "Inside Sirhan." *Playboy,* April 1978.

Rovere, Richard H. *Senator Joe McCarthy.* New York: World Publishing, 1960.

Newspapers

Arizona Daily Star. September 27, 1980, A2.

New York Times, September 8, 1970, A1.

Tucson Daily Citizen. February 4, 1981, A1.

Gorney, Cynthia. "Sirhan." *Washington Post.* August 20-21, 1979, B1, B3.

LEE HARVEY OSWALD

Books

Lasswell, Harold D. *Power and Personality.* 1948. Reprint. New York: The Viking Press, 1962.

McMillan, Priscilla Johnson. *Marina and Lee.* 1977. Reprint. New York: Bantam, 1978.

McNeil, Elton B. *Neuroses and Personality Disorders.* Englewood Cliffs, N.J.: Prentice-Hall, Inc., 1970.

———. *The Psychoses.* Englewood Cliffs, N.J.: Prentice-Hall, Inc., 1970.

Schorr, Daniel. *Clearing the Air.* Boston: Houghton Mifflin, 1977.

Documents

President's Commission on the Assassination of President Kennedy. *Hearings on the Investigation of the Assassination of President John F. Kennedy*, vols. 1-26. Washington, D.C.: U.S. Government Printing Office, 1964.

———. *Report of the President's Commission on the Assassination of President John F. Kennedy*. Washington, D.C.: U.S. Government Printing Office, 1964.

U.S. Congress, House, Select Committee on Assassinations. *Hearings on the Investigation of the Assassination of President John F. Kennedy*, vols. 1-12. 95th Cong., 2d Sess., 1978.

U.S. Congress, House, Select Committee on Assassinations. *Report on Findings and Recommendations, 1979*, HR 95-1828, part 2. 95th Cong., 2d Sess., 1979.

U.S. Congress, House, Subcommittee on Civil and Constitutional Rights of the Committee on the Judiciary. *Hearings on Federal Bureau of Investigation Oversight*, Serial No. 2, pt. 3. 94th Cong., 1st and 2d Sess., 1975-1976.

Newspaper

New Orleans Times-Picayune. August-September 1963.

SAMUEL BYCK

Documents

Byck, Samuel. Recorded Tapes. Federal Bureau of Investigation, 1974.

Documents, Samuel Byck. Department of Transportation Federal Aviation Administration, Security Summary (SE-1600-20) ASE-74-4.

Documents, Samuel Byck. Federal Bureau of Investigation, File No. BA 164-170.

Documents, Samuel Byck. Federal Communications Commission, File Nos. 8310-100, C6-1833.

Documents, Samuel Byck. National Park Service, National Capital Parks, 1973.

Documents, Samuel Byck. Office of Pardon Attorney, U.S. Department of Justice, January 9, 1974.

Documents, Samuel Byck. Small Business Administration, 1973.

Documents, Samuel Byck. United States Secret Service, 1972-1974.

Newspapers

New York Times. February-March 1974.
Philadelphia Inquirer. February 1974.
Washington Post. February-March 1974.
Washington Star. February-March 1974.

LYNETTE ALICE FROMME

Trial Transcript

United States v. Lynette Alice Fromme (November-December 1975). United States District Court for the Eastern District of California, CR. No. 5-75-451, vols. 1-10.

Book

Bugliosi, Vincent, with Curt Gentry. *Helter Skelter*. New York: W. W. Norton & Co., 1974.

Document

Fromme, Lynette. Untitled Manuscript. Quoted in *Time*, September 15, 1975, p. 12.

Newspaper

Sacramento Bee. September 1975.

SARA JANE MOORE

Article

Moore, Sara Jane. "Playboy Interview." *Playboy*, June 1976.

Newspapers

Charleston (West Virginia) *Gazette*. September 1975.
Los Angeles Times. September 1975.

GIUSEPPE ZANGARA

Documents

Documents, Giuseppe Zangara. Federal Bureau of Investigation, File No. 62-28219-1-61, February-March 1933.
Zangara, Giuseppe. "Sworn Statement of Joseph Zangara." Miami, Dade County, Florida, February 16th, A.D. 1933. Federal Bureau of Investigation.

Newspapers

Miami Herald. February-March 1933.
Newark Evening News. February-March 1933.

ARTHUR HERMAN BREMER

Trial Transcript

State of Maryland v. Arthur Herman Bremer (July-August 1972). Circuit Court for Prince George's County, Maryland, Crim. Tr. Nos. 12376-12379.

Books and Articles

Bremer, Arthur H. *An Assassin's Diary*. Harper's Magazine Press, in association with Harper & Row, New York, 1972.

Camus, Albert. *The Stranger*. New York: Alfred A. Knopf, 1946.

Dostoyevsky, Fyodor. *Notes From Underground*. Edited by Robert G. Durgy. Translated by Serge Shishkoff. New York: Thomas Y. Crowell, 1969.

Kaiser, Robert Blair. *"RFK Must Die!": A History of the Robert Kennedy Assassination and its Aftermath*. New York: Dutton, 1970.

Vidal, Gore. "Now for the Shooting of George Wallace." *New York Review of Books* 20 (December 13, 1973): 17-19.

Document

Annotated Code of Maryland.

Newspaper

Milwaukee Journal. May 1972.

RICHARD LAWRENCE

Trial Transcript and Record

United States v. Richard Lawrence (March 1835). Circuit Court, District of Columbia, Case No. 15,577; also, *Niles Register*, vol. 48, 1836.

Lawrence, Richard. *Criminal Appearances* 119 (March 1835). United States District Court of the District of Columbia. Record Group 21, National Archives.

Books and Articles

Hastings, Donald W. "The Psychiatry of Presidential Assassination, Part I: Jackson and Lincoln." *The Journal-Lancet* 85 (March 1965): 93-100.

Jackson, Carlton. "Another Time, Another Place—The Attempted Assassination of President Andrew Jackson." *Tennessee Historical Quarterly* 26 (Summer 1967): 184-190.

Smith, William R., ed. "Trial of Richard Lawrence." In *Assassination and Insanity: Guiteau's Case Examined and Compared with Analogous Cases from the Earlier to the Present Times*, pp. 26-80. Washington, D.C., 1881.

Newspaper

Daily National Intelligencer. January 31, 1835; April 13, 1835, 1.

CHARLES J. GUITEAU

Trial Transcript

United States v. Charles J. Guiteau (June 1882). Supreme Court of the District of Columbia, Criminal Case No. 14056. National Archives.

Books and Articles

Folsom, Charles F. *Studies of Criminal Responsibility and Limited Responsibility.* Boston: Privately printed, 1909.

Godding, W. W. *Two Hard Cases: Sketches from a Physician's Portfolio.* Boston: Houghton Mifflin, 1882.

Gray, John Purdue. "The United States vs. Charles J. Guiteau." *American Journal of Insanity* 38 (January 1882): 303-448.

"Guiteau-Finis." *Medical News* 41 (July 1882): 12.

Hamilton, Allan McLane. "The Case of Guiteau." *Boston Medical and Surgical Journal* 106 (March 9, 1882): 235-238.

————. *Recollections of an Alienist.* New York: George H. Doran, 1916.

Hastings, Donald W. "The Psychiatry of Presidential Assassination, Part II: Garfield and McKinley." *The Journal-Lancet* 85 (April 1965): 157-162.

Lawson, John D., ed. "The Trial of Charles J. Guiteau for the Murder of President Garfield." In *American State Trials.* Vol. 14. St. Louis: Thomas Law Book Co., 1923.

Mitchell, Stewart. "The Man Who Murdered Garfield." *Proceedings of the Massachusetts Historical Society* 68 (1941-1944): 452-489.

Rosenberg, Charles E. *The Trial of the Assassin Guiteau.* Chicago: The University of Chicago Press, 1968.

Smith, William R. *Assassination and Insanity: Guiteau's Case Examined and Compared with Analogous Cases from the Earlier to the Present Times.* Washington, D.C., 1881.

Spitzka, Edward C. "A Contribution to the Question of the Mental Status of Guiteau and the History of His Trial." *Alienist and Neurologist* 4 (April 1883): 201-220.

Documents

Guiteau, Charles J. "The New York Theocrat" (prospectus). File No. 14056, National Archives.

Guiteau, John W. "Letters and Facts Not Heretofore Published, Touching the Mental Condition of Charles J. Guiteau Since 1865." Document submitted to the President of the United States by John W. Guiteau in the Matter of Application for a Commission De Lunatico Inquirendo, June 23, 1882. File No. 14056, National Archives.

Letters of Charles J. Guiteau. File No. 14056, National Archives.

JOHN SCHRANK

Books and Articles

Hastings, Donald W. "The Psychiatry of Presidential Assassination, Part III: The Roosevelts." *The Journal-Lancet* 85 (May 1965): 189-192.

MacDonald, Arthur. "The Would-Be Assassin of Theodore Roosevelt." *Medical Times* 62 (April 1914): 97-101.

Morison, Elting E., ed. *The Letters of Theodore Roosevelt.* Vol. 3. Cambridge, Mass.: Harvard University Press, 1951.

Mowry, George E. *The Era of Theodore Roosevelt and the Birth of Modern America.* New York: Harper & Row, 1958.

Remy, Oliver E.; Cochems, Henry F.; and Bloodgood, Wheeler P. *The Attempted Assassination of Ex-President Theodore Roosevelt.* Milwaukee: The Progressive Publishing Co., 1912.

Newspapers

Chicago Tribune. November 26, 1912.

Milwaukee Journal. October 10, 1912; October 15, 1912, 1-2; October 16, 1912, 1-4; October 17, 1912, 1-2; October 18, 1912, 1; November 13, 1912, 1-2; November 25, 1912, 1.

CARL AUSTIN WEISS

Books

Beals, Carleton. *The Story of Huey Long.* New York: Lippincott, 1935.

Deutsch, Hermann B. *The Huey Long Murder Case.* Garden City, N.Y.: Doubleday & Co., 1963.

Fields, Harvey G. *The Life of Huey Pierce Long.* Farmerville, La.: Fields Publishing Agency, 1944.

Havens, Murray C.; Leiden, Carl; and Schmitt, Karl M. *The Politics of Assassination.* Englewood Cliffs, N.J.: Prentice-Hall, Inc., 1970.

Kane, Harnett. *Louisiana Hayride.* New York: Morrow, 1941.

Key, V. O. *Southern Politics in State and Nation.* New York: Alfred A. Knopf, 1949.

Lesberg, Sandy. *Assassinations in Our Time.* London: Peebles Press International and Bobbs-Merrill, 1976.

Luthin, Reinhard H. *American Demagogues.* Boston: The Beacon Press, 1954.

Optowsky, Stan. *The Longs of Louisiana.* New York: Dutton, 1960.

Paine, Lauran. *The Assassins' World.* New York: Taplinger Publishing Co., 1975.

Pearl, Jack. *The Dangerous Assassins.* Derby, Conn.: Monarch Books, 1964.

Schlesinger, Arthur M., Jr. *The Politics of Upheaval.* Vol. 3. Boston: Houghton Mifflin, 1960.

Sindler, Allan P. *Huey Long's Louisiana.* (Baltimore: Johns Hopkins, 1956).

Warren, Robert Penn. *All The King's Men*. New York: Harcourt, Brace & Co., 1946.

Williams, T. Harry. *Huey Long*. New York: Bantam Books, 1969.

Zinman, David H. *The Day Huey Long Was Shot*. New York: Ivan Obolensky, Inc., 1963.

Newspapers

Baton Rouge Morning Advocate. September-October 1935.

Baton Rouge State-Times. September-October 1935.

New Orleans States Item. September-October 1935.

New Orleans Times-Picayune. September-October 1935.

James Earl Ray

Books and Articles

Clarke, James W., and Soule, John W. "Southern Children's Reactions to King's Death." *Trans-Action 5* (October 1968): 35-40.

Huie, William Bradford. *He Slew the Dreamer*. New York: Delacorte Press, 1970.

McMillan, George. *The Making of an Assassin*. Boston: Little, Brown, 1976.

Documents

Congressional Quarterly. 4th ed. "Revolution in Civil Rights, 1945-1968." June 1968.

Report of the Department of Justice Task Force to Review the FBI Martin Luther King, Jr. Security and Assassination Investigations. Washington, D.C.: U.S. Department of Justice, January 11, 1977.

U.S. Congress, House, Select Committee on Assassinations. *Compilation of the Statements of James Earl Ray*. 95th Cong., 2d Sess., August 18, 1978.

————. *Final Report of the Select Committee on Assassinations*. 95th Cong., 2d Sess., January 2, 1979.

————. *Hearings on the Investigation of the Assassination of Martin Luther King, Jr.*, vols. 1-12. 95th Cong., 2d Sess., 1978.

Newspaper

St. Louis Post-Dispatch. June 9, 1968, A31.

Index

Abel, Rudolph, 99
Adams v. *Williams*, 270
"Address to the American People" (Guiteau), 207
Aeromarine Supply Co., 248
Aldrich, Nelson W., 42
Alexandra of Russia, 155
Al Fatah, 91-92
Allen, O. K., 237
All the King's Men (Warren), 224
American Civil Liberties Union (ACLU), 96, 122
American Independent party, 250, 252
American Law Institute, 11
American Progress (formerly *Louisiana Progress*), 231, 236
American Railway Union, 47
anarchist movement, 42, 53-56, 59-62
Ancient Mystical Order of the Rosae Crucis (Rosicrucian Society), 86-88, 94
Anderson, Jack, 134
Arab-American Relations Committee, 101
Arab-Israeli conflict, 79-82, 86-87, 92, 132
Arab nationalism, 79-82, 86-88, 91-92, 101-104, 262-263
Arnold, Samuel, 33, 35n
Arthur, Chester A., 206, 212-213
assassin, origin of word, 88n, 101
Associated Press (AP), 78, 93, 102
atypical assassins, 16-17, 223, 263-268. *See also* types of assassins; Weiss; Ray
Atzerodt, George, 33-35
Azcue, Eusebio, 120

Bandowski, Frank, 47-49, 52-53, 61n
Baton Rouge, La., 225-229
Bay of Pigs invasion (1961), 117, 126
behavior patterns, 13-17, 105-107. *See*

also psychopathic behavior; *specific assassins*, psychological appraisal
Bell, John, 25
Bell, Thomas, 45
Bellamy, Edward, 47
Bellevue Hospital, 226-227
Bender-Gestalt Test of Intelligence, 96
Berkman, Alexander, 46
Berman, Emile Zola, 77, 102
Bernstein, Leonard, 134
Bidstrup, Hans, 95
Birdzell, Donald T., 72, 75
Black Liberation Army, 130
Black September terrorists, 104
Blaine, James G., 42, 204-206
Blood, Sweat, and Tears (rock group), 180
B'nai B'rith Messenger, 87n
"Bonny" (Byck's friend), 132-135, 138-139, 142
Booth, Asia, 20, 24, 29
Booth, Edwin, 19, 21-23
Booth, John Wilkes: abduction letter, 30-32; acting career, 20-25; Confederate sympathies, 19, 22, 28-34; diary, 35-37; family relations, 21-22, 263; hatred of Lincoln, 28-34, 76, 263; political motives, 25-28, 183, 262-263, 265; psychological appraisal, 6n, 7n, 8n, 19-20, 24-25, 38-39, 258; as Type I assassin, 19, 262-263; and women, 24
Booth, Junius Brutus, 20-21
Booth, Junius Brutus, Jr., 19-21, 23
Boro, Harold, 146
Boston Globe, 82
Boston Strangler, 95-96
Breckenridge, J. C., 25
Bremer, Arthur: background and family, 176-181, 264; diary, 183-191, 267n; homicidal fantasies, 181-183, 188-

Bremer, Arthur (*cont.*)
189, 270; humor, 185-187; love af-
fair, 179-181; motivation, 187-188,
266; psychological appraisal, 9, 12-
13, 77, 166-167, 174-176, 182-183,
186-193; Rorschach tests, 190-191;
suicidal fantasies, 178, 181-183, 188-
189; as Type III assassin, 260-261,
264-265, 267, 270; Wallace assassina-
tion attempt, 174-176
Bremer, Sylvia, 176-181
Bremer, William, 176-181
Bresci, Gaetano, 53
Brewer, Bessie, 248, 252
Briggs, L. Vernon, 39-41, 60, 62
Brown, Jerry, 152
Brown, John, 31
Brussel, James A., 98
Bryan, William Jennings, 48
Bryant, William Cullen, 27
Bugliosi, Vincent, 152
Bundy, Theodore, 166
Bunn, Annie, 202
Burger, Warren E., 12
Butler, Benjamin, 27
Byck, Samuel: hijacking attempt, 128-
129; marriage and family, 130-133,
264, 270-271; Operation Pandora's
Box, 133-135; political motives, 130-
141, 261; psychological appraisal, 8n,
9, 106, 129-133, 135, 266; tapes,
133-141, 265; as Type II assassin,
106, 142, 261, 264, 266, 268, 270
Byers, Russell G., 249-251, 255

Cafaro, Vincent, 167-170
Campos, Pedro Albizu, 64-67, 73, 76
Camus, Albert, 187
Cancel-Miranda, Rafael, 74
Canipes Amusement Co., 253
Carnegie, Andrew, 42
Carnegie Steel Co., 45-46
Carter, Jimmy, 74
Casanova Guns, 181
Case Book of a Crime Psychiatrist, A
(Brussel), 98
Castro, Fidel, 7n, 113, 117-120, 126
Central Intelligence Agency (CIA), 118,
126
Cermak, Anton, 167, 171-172, 174

Chaney, James, 254, 257
Channing, Walter, 39-40, 60
Chase, Salman P., 27, 33
Chesterton, G. K., 193
Choate, Raymon, 149-150
Christieson, Sanderson, 41
Citizens' Council of St. Louis, 252
Clark, Alvin, 91, 99
Clarke, John Sleeper, 29
classification of assassins, 14-17, 105-
107, 259-269. *See also* types of assas-
sins
classification of mental illness, 10-13
Clemente, Roberto, 133
Cleveland, Grover, 47
"Clockwork Orange," 185, 267n
Cochems, Henry F., 215
Coffelt, Leslie, 73
Cohn, Roy, 82
Collazo, Oscar: alias Anthony de Silva,
71; background, 64-66, 263; national-
ism as motive, 63, 71-73, 262-263,
265; October Insurrection, 66-71;
psychological appraisal, 7n, 73-76;
trial and sentence, 73-76, 98; Truman
assassination attempt, 67-73; as Type
I assassin, 76, 262-263, 265
Collective, The (Oswald), 111-112
Collins, E. C., 172
Communist Labor party, 160
Communist party, 91-92, 119, 122
compensatory behavior, 163-165, 173-
174, 191-193, 261-262
Confederacy and Booth, 19, 28-34
Conkling, Roscoe, 205, 207
conspiracy theory: and Kennedy assassi-
nation, 126-128; and King assassina-
tion, 240-241, 249, 253-256, 269
Constitutional Union party, 28
Cordero, Humphrey, 95
Cortelyou, George, 57
criminal responsibility, 10-13, 259-260.
See also diminished capacity
Crowe, Walter, 91-92
Cuba, 113, 116-120, 126-127
Cuban Revolutionary Junta, 118
cultural context of assassination, 4, 12-
17, 266-268
Czolgosz, Leon: alias Fred C. Nieman,
46, 55, 61; background and family,

42-49, 53, 62, 264; class conflict, 61-
62, 262-263; hereditary insanity, 61;
McKinley assassination, 56-58; nervous breakdown, 51-53; political motives, 39-49, 52-56, 60-62, 265; psychological appraisal, 6n, 7n, 8n, 39-
42, 58-63; and stepmother, 49, 53,
61, 264; trial and sentence, 58-59; as
Type I assassin, 61, 262, 264-265
Czolgosz, Waldek, 46-49, 51-53, 59,
61n

Dallas Morning News, 116
Daughters of the American Revolution
(DAR), 250
David, Joe, 236
Davis, Jefferson, 33, 36
Davis, Warren, 195
Davis's Pawn Shop, 171
Day Huey Long Was Shot, The (Zin-
man), 224
Debs, Eugene, 47-48
Deir Yassin, 80, 104
Democratic party, 27, 78-79
de Mohrenschildt, George, 114
DeNiro, Robert, 181
"Desoto plot," 231-232
Deutsch, Hermann B., 224
Diamond, Bernard, 77, 99-100
"diminished capacity," 11-13, 77, 97,
99, 176, 188-191, 259-261. *See also*
criminal responsibility
Dolores, Carmen, 66, 70
Donovan, Robert, 7-8, 40
Dostoyevsky, Feodor, 175, 193
Douglas, Stephen A., 25
Douglas, William O., 270
Downs, Joseph H., 73
draft resistance, 26-27
Duran, Sylvia, 119-120
Durham Rule, 11, 259

El Diario de Nueva York, 68
Electric Tower (Pan-American Exposi-
tion), 58n
Ellsler, John, 23
Emancipation Proclamation, 26-28
Engel, George, 44
Eshkol, Levi, 87n
Essex, Mark "Jimmy," 131, 134, 167

Evers, Medgar, 254, 257
Every Man a King (Long), 231

Fair Play for Cuba Committee, 117-120
family influence on assassins, 263-266.
See also specific assassins
Faulkner, William, 264
Federal Bureau of Investigation (FBI), 8-
9, 13, 268-269; and King, 255-256,
268-269; and Moore, 160-163, 261-
262; and Oswald, 122-124, 126-127,
268-269; and Ray, 245, 249, 251,
255-256, 268-271
Federal Communications Commission
(FCC), 132, 134
Fenner, Nancy Lee, 123
Fernwood, Mark, 164
Ferrie, David, 118, 126
Fifteenth Amendment, 43
Figuero-Cordero, Andres, 74
Fischer, Adolph, 44
Fitts, David, 99-100
Flores-Rodriguez, Irving, 74
Ford, Gerald R., 133, 144-145, 152-
154, 156, 163-164, 261
Ford's Theatre, 35
Foreman, Percy, 239-240, 248, 253-254
Forrest, Edwin, 23
Foster, Jodie, 180-181, 267n
Foster, Marcus, 161
Fourteenth Amendment, 43
Free Society, 55-56, 61-62
Fremont, John C., 27
Frick, Henry Clay, 42-46
Friends Psychiatric Hospital, 130
Fromme, Lynette Alice: background and
family, 144-146, 263-265, 267; Ford
assassination attempt, 144-145, 152-
154, 163-164; and Manson, 144-155,
262; political beliefs, 147-153, 155-
156; psychological appraisal, 8n, 9,
106, 143-145; tapes, 148-149; terrorist activities, 148-152; trial, 153-154;
as Type II assassin, 143, 261-263,
265-266
frustration and assassination, 13-14,
149-155, 261-262, 267

Gacy, John Wayne, 166-167
Garfield, James, 204-212

Garry, Charles, 162
Gettysburg, Battle of, 28
Gilmore, Gary, 166-167, 261
Goldberg, Arthur, 90
Goldman, Emma, 42, 45, 53-56, 59-60
Good, Sandra, 147-148, 150, 152
Goodman, Andrew, 254, 257
Gould, Jay, 42
Grant, Ulysses S., 34-35, 204
Grapevine Tavern, 250-252, 255
Greeley, Horace, 27
Guiteau, Charles: background and family, 198-204, 264; feelings for Garfield, 204-212; Garfield assassination, 208-209; hereditary insanity, 210, 260; newspaper venture, 201-202, 206; notes and speeches, 205-214; political beliefs, 204-214; psychological appraisal, 6n, 7n, 8n, 11-12, 41, 60, 77, 192, 206-212, 222, 260; religious beliefs, 199-204, 206, 208, 210-214; speech impediment, 199; trial and execution, 209-214; as Type IV assassin, 194, 260, 265
Guiteau, Frances, 210
Guiteau, John, 202-204, 210
Guiteau, Luther, 199-204, 210
gun control, 269-270

Hamilton, McLane, 40-41
Hanes, Arthur, 253
Hanna, Marcus, 42, 48
Harris, William and Emily, 162
hashish and assassins, 88n, 101
Hastings, Donald, 40
Hayes, Rutherford B., 205
Haymarket Square riot, 44-45, 59-60
Hearst, Patty, 149, 159, 161-163
Hearst, Randolph, 159
Helter Skelter (Bugliosi), 149, 152
Hemingway, Ernest, 264
Herold, David, 33-35
He Slew the Dreamer (Huie), 240
Hicks, William, 212-214
Hinckley, John, 181n, 267, 269-271
Hoffa, James, 83
Holmes, Mary Ann, 20
Holt, Henry, 62
Homestead strike (1892), 45-46
Hoover, Herbert, 171

Hoover, J. Edgar, 251, 255-257, 268-269
Hosty, James, 122-124
House of Representatives, 74
Howard, John E., 100
Huey Long (Williams), 224
Huey Long Murder Case, The (Deutsch), 224
Huie, William Bradford, 240, 248, 254
Humbert I (king of Italy), 53-54
Humphrey, Hubert, 88

Independent Star-News, 93
Indians (American), 42-44, 269
industrial revolution (U.S.), 42-49
"International People's Court of Retribution," 148
Inter-Ocean (newspaper), 203
Irgun terrorists, 80
Isaak, Abe, 55, 62
Israeli-Arab conflict, 79-82, 86-87, 92, 132

Jackson, Andrew, 3, 5, 195-196
Jackson, Popeye, 159-160, 163
Jansen, Godfrey, 78
Jews, 83, 86, 93-94
Joan of Arc, 219, 221
Johnson, Andrew, 34-35
Johnson, Lyndon B., 83, 87n, 88, 174, 258
Johnston, Joe, 34
Judy, Steven, 261

Kahn, Olaf, 156-159
Kahn, Sara Jane, 156-157. *See also* Moore, Sara Jane
Kaiser, Robert Blair, 77, 92, 97, 101, 103, 190-191
Kauffmann, John, 249-252, 255-256
Keating, Kenneth, 83
Kennedy, Edward, 101-102
Kennedy, John F., 82, 107, 117-118, 124-126, 256, 261, 267
Kennedy, Joseph P., 82
Kennedy, Robert F., 78-79, 82-83, 87-88, 92-93, 102
Key, Francis Scott, 198
KFWB-Radio, 93
Kimmel, Stanley, 19-20, 22, 25

King, Martin Luther, 16-17, 91, 223, 239-240, 251-254, 263; FBI harassment, 245-249, 255-256, 268-269
Kirschke, Jack, 95-96
Kubrick, Stanley, 267
Kulthum, Umm, 84

labor movement, 43-51
Lasswell, Harold, 105-107, 143-144
Lattimer Mines Massacre, 49-51, 58
Lawrence, David, 93
Lawrence, Richard: background and family, 195-198, 264; psychological appraisal, 3, 5, 10, 12, 60, 222; as Type IV assassin, 17, 192, 260, 264-265
"Leaves of Grass" (Whitman), 109
LeBlanc, Dudley, 229
Lebron, Lolita, 74
Lee, Robert E., 28-29, 34
Leech, Margaret, 61
Library of Congress, 13
Lincoln, Abraham: abduction plot, 28-34; assassination plot, 34-39; executive actions, 26-28; unpopularity of, 18, 20, 25-28, 38-39
Lingg, Louis, 44
Liuzzo, Viola, 254, 256-257
Lock, Stock, and Barrel Gun Shop, 94
Long, Huey: assassination, 16-17, 237-238; Pavy vendetta, 229-236, 263; political machine, 223-224; racism, 229, 232-237
Lopez, Manuel, 68
Lorraine Motel, 248, 252
Louisiana Medical Society, 227
Louisiana Progress (later *American Progress*), 229, 231
Lutheran Church, 80-82

McBride, Thomas J., 153-154
McBroom, Marcus, 78
McCarthy, Eugene, 83, 88
McCarthy, Joseph, 82, 106
McClellan, George, 27
McGovern, George, 131, 133, 174
McKinley, James, 233
McKinley, William, 18, 48, 56-58, 60, 62, 218-220
McMillan, George, 240, 243-244

McMillan, Priscilla Johnson, 109n, 112
Mafia and JFK, 118, 126-127
Making of an Assassin, The (McMillan), 240
Manson, Charles: background and family, 157; as Christ figure, 147-153, 155-156; and Fromme, 143-145, 153-154; press release, 150
Marxism, 108, 112-113
Matthews, John, 34-37
Maxey, Hugh, 250-252
May First Movement, 160
media exposure and assassinations, 267-268
Medical News, 214
Melcher, William, 154
Mercado, Rosa, 66, 70
methodology of research, 5-17, 259, 266-267
Milburn, John G., 58
Militant, The, 114, 117
Milk, Harvey, 12n, 103, 239
mind control, 86-90, 101
Minnesota Multiphasic Personality Inventory, 96
M'Naghten Rule, 10-11, 259
Model Penal Code, 11
Moody, Dwight, 203
Moore, Sara Jane: guilt and penance as motive, 161-165, 261-262, 266-267; as informant, 160-164, 261-262; marriage and family, 156-158, 264-265; political beliefs, 158-160, 165; psychological appraisal, 8n, 9, 17, 106, 143-144, 161-165; as Type II assassin, 143-144, 261-262, 265, 267-268
Morgan, J. P., 48
Morning Advocate, 227
Morris, Clara, 24
Moscone, George, 12n, 103, 239
Moses, 219, 221
motives for assassination, 13-17, 259-263. *See also specific assassins*
Moyne, Lord, 104
Mroz, Vincent P., 73
Mudd, Samuel, 35n
Murphy, Susan, 147
Murret, Dutz, 118n
My First Days in the White House (Long), 231

Nasser, Gamal Abdal, 86
National Archives, 13
National Intelligencer, 34, 36
nationalism as motive. *See* Collazo; Torresola; Sirhan; Arab and Puerto Rican nationalism
Newberg Wire Mills, 46
New Rebel Motel, 248
newspapers: and assassins, 267-268; and Lincoln, 26-27
New York Central Railroad, 48
New York Life, 48
New York Times, 87
Nicholas II (Czar of Russia), 155
1984 (Orwell), 109
Nixon, Richard Milhous: and Bremer, 174-175, 182-183; and Byck, 131-134, 261; and Manson, 147, 150-153; and Oswald, 116
Notes from Underground (Dostoyevsky), 175
Nowak, John, 55
Nowak, Walter, 53
Noyes, John Humphrey, 201-202

objective reality, 13, 259. *See also* reality and psychopathic behavior
October League, 160
October 30 Insurrection (Puerto Rico), 64-71
Odio, Silvia, 118-119
O'Laughlin, Michael, 35n
Olney, Richard, 47
Olympic Games (1972), 104
Oneida Community, 199-202, 206, 212
Organization of Arab Students, 86, 91
Orwell, George, 109-110
Oswald, John, 107
Oswald, Lee Harvey: alias O. H. Lee, 122, 124; court-martial, 109-110; Cuban sympathies, 111, 113, 116-120, 126-127, 261; dyslexia, 110n; emigration attempt, 119-120; family and marital difficulties, 107-109, 112, 114-117, 120-128, 264-267; FBI and, 122-124, 126-127, 268-269; Kennedy assassination, 120, 124-125, 183; Marine stint, 109-110, 117; political beliefs, 107-108, 110-113, 117-122, 261; psychological appraisal, 6n, 7n,

61, 106-107, 126-128; Soviet Union visit, 110-113, 126; suicide attempt, 110, 119; as Type II assassin, 105-107, 261, 264-268; Walker assassination attempt, 113-117, 119, 126-127; writings, 110-113
Oswald, Marguerite, 107-109
Oswald, Marina, 111-112, 114-118, 120-128
Oswald, Robert, 107, 109, 112

Paine, Michael, 120, 122-123
Paine, Ruth, 118, 120, 123
Palestine Liberation Organization (PLO), 101n
Pan-American Exposition (1901), 56-58
paranoia, 39-41, 194, 196, 198, 211-212, 221-222, 259-261
Parsons, Albert, 44
Parsons, Russell E., 96-97
pathological theory of assassination, 3-10. *See also* political bias and psychoanalysis; psychiatric bias
Patrusky, Martin, 95
Pavy, Benjamin, 227, 232-233
Pavy, Louise Yvonne, 227-229, 234
Pavy, Marie, 230
Pavy, Octave, 233, 235
Pavy, Paul, 230
Payne, Lewis, 33-35
Pembrick, Joan, 179-181
Pennsylvania Railroad, 48
People in Need, 159-160
Perez, Jesus, 95
Philadelphia, Pennsylvania, 133
Philadelphia General Hospital, 132
Pic, John, 107
Piedmont Laundry, 248
Placentia, Art, 78
Platt, Tom, 205, 207
Playboy Magazine, 248
Plessy v. *Ferguson*, 237
political bias and psychoanalysis, 76-79, 258
political context of assassination, 9-17, 262-263, 267-268. *See also specific assassins*
political personality, 15, 105-107, 153, 165, 262-263. *See also* Type II assassins

Pollack, Seymour, 100
Populist party, 48
Powers, Francis Gary, 99
Prairie Fire Organizing Committee, 160
Progressives, 214-216
psychiatric bias, 6n, 7n, 8-17, 258-259
psychopathic behavior, 6-10, 15-17,
    105-107, 166-167, 173, 188-191,
    194, 208-214, 217-219, 221-222,
    258-262, 264-266. *See also* political
    bias and psychoanalysis; psychiatric
    bias; *specific assassins*
Puerto Rican nationalism, 7n, 63-76,
    262
Pullman, George, 47
Pullman strike (1894), 47-48

Rabago, Enrique, 95
Rabbit's Foot (bar), 245
radio and assassination, 93, 267
Rafferty, Kathleen, 89n
railroads, 48
railroad strike (1877), 44
"Raoul" (alleged Ray accomplice), 246-
    249, 252, 255
Rasputin, Grigori Y., 155
Rather, Dan, 248
Ray, Carol, 242-243, 246, 250, 252
Ray, George, 241
Ray, James Earl: as atypical assassin,
    223, 257, 265-266; background, 239-
    248; brothers as accomplices, 246-
    249, 253, 264; criminal activities,
    243-244, 254, 265; conspiracy, 240-
    241, 249, 253-256, 269; contract,
    249-252, 254, 257, 270; escape and
    arrest, 252-255; political beliefs, 243;
    psychological appraisal, 6n, 7n, 13-14,
    16-17, 223, 240; racism, 240, 243-
    246, 248-249, 254, 256-258, 263,
    267; trial, 239-240, 254-255
Ray, Jerry, 240, 242, 246-250, 252-253
Ray, John, 240, 242, 246-250, 252-253
Ray, Lucille, 241
Reagan, Ronald: assassination attempt
    on, 3n, 181n, 266, 267n, 268-269
reality and psychopathic behavior, 106-
    107, 167, 194, 208-214, 217-219,
    259-262, 264-266. *See also* social iso-
    lation of assassins

reductive conclusions, 9-10, 258
Regazzi, Naomi and Robert, 252
*Report to the National Commission on
    the Causes and Prevention of Vio-
    lence*, 8, 134
Republican party, 48, 204-209, 214-216
Ribicoff, Abraham, 134
Riggs House, 208
Rio Piedras riots, 65
Rizzo, Frank, 133
Rockefeller, John D., 42, 48
Roesch, William, 148-149
Rollfink, Herman, 220
Roosevelt, Franklin Delano, 71, 171-
    172, 174, 230-232, 237
Roosevelt, Theodore, 214-219
Rorschach tests, 9-10, 96, 190-191
Rosenberg, Julius and Ethel, 106
Rossie, Charles, 151-152
Rowe, Gary Thomas, 256n
Ruby, Jack, 8n, 127

St. Louis Post-Dispatch, 249
Salk, Jonas, 134
San Gabriel Valley Gun Club, 94
San Quentin Six, 162
Schilling, Emil, 54
schizophrenia, 10-13, 39-42, 58-63,
    106-107, 194, 198, 221-222, 259-261
Schorr, Daniel, 120n
Schorr, Martin M., 96-98
Schrank, John Flammang: background
    and family, 216-221, 260; delusions
    and visions, 216-220, 260; hereditary
    insanity, 220-260; incarceration, 220-
    221; political beliefs, 216-221; psy-
    chological appraisal, 11-12, 192, 216-
    221, 260; Roosevelt assassination at-
    tempt, 214-216; as Type IV assassin,
    260, 263, 265; writings, 217-220
Schurz, Carl, 217
Schweiker, Richard, 132-133
Schwerner, Michael, 254, 257
Scorsese, Martin, 267
Scoville, George, 199, 209-210
Secret Service, 8-9, 13, 131-133, 164,
    268-271
Sensing, Thurman, 250
Seward, William H., 34-35
Seymour, Horatio, 27

Sherman, William Tecumseh, 28-29, 34, 209
Shibab, Aziz, 190
Shrum, Glen, 252
Sirhan, Adel, 84
Sirhan, Bisbara, 81-82, 264
Sirhan, Mary, 80-82, 101
Sirhan, Munir, 94
Sirhan, Saidallah, 81
Sirhan, Sharif, 81
Sirhan, Sirhan: admiration for JFK, 87; arrest and trial, 95-101; death of sister, 84-85; family and identity, 79-85, 264; hatred of RFK, 76-77, 263; Kennedy assassination (Robert), 78-79, 88-95, 183, 190-191, 270; nationalism as motive, 63, 79-82, 84-88, 91-92, 98-104, 262-263, 265, 267; 1979 interview, 102-103; notebook, 88-96, 102; psychological appraisal, 6n, 7n, 8-9, 11-13, 76-82, 88-101; Rorschach tests, 191; as Type I assassin, 17, 101-104, 262-263; and women, 89, 103
Six Day War, 86-87, 91-92
slavery, 26-34, 43
Slavic culture, 49-53, 55, 61
Small Business Administration (SBA), 132, 134, 142
Smith, Gerald L. K., 231
social context of assassination, 13-17, 266-268
social isolation of assassins, 6n, 7n, 8n, 71, 129-135, 166-167, 192-194, 217-221, 260-262, 264-266. *See also specific assassins*, psychological appraisal
Social Register, 231
Soliah, Kathy, 159
Soliah, Steve, 163
Southern Reconstruction, 43
Southern States Industrial Council, 250, 256
Spangler, Edward, 35n
Spanish American War, 215
Speck, Richard, 166
Spica, John Paul, 250-252
Spies, Henry, 44
Stalwarts, 204-209
Standard Oil, 48
steel industry, 45-46
Steinbeck, John, 264

Stern Gang, 80
Stoner, J. B., 253
Students for a Democratic Society (SDS), 91
subjective reality, 13, 259. *See also* reality and psychopathic behavior
Sultan Room (bar), 245
Surratt, John, 33, 35
Surratt, Mary, 35n
surveillance, 268-269
Sutherland, John, 250-252, 255-256
Symbionese Liberation Army (SLA), 149, 159-163
Szasz, Thomas, 12

Taft, William Howard, 214
Tate-LaBianca murders, 145-147, 149, 151-152, 155
"Taxi Driver," 180-181, 267n
television and assassination, 267
Texas School Book Depository, 120, 124-125
Thematic Apperception Tests, 9-10, 96
Thirteenth Amendment, 43
Thompson, Ely O., 172
Thume, Paul, 220
Tilton, Theodore, 27
Tolson, Clyde A., 255-256
Torresola, Elio, 64
Torresola, Griselio: alias Charles Gonzalez, 71; background and family, 63-66, 70, 263; nationalism as motive, 71-73, 262, 265; October Insurrection, 66-71; psychological appraisal, 7n; Truman assassination attempt, 71-73; as Type I assassin, 17, 76, 262-263, 265
Touro Infirmary, 226
Truman, Harry S, 63, 71-74
types of assassins: Type I, 14, 17, 61, 76, 155, 173, 259-267; Type II, 14-15, 17, 61, 76, 105-107, 142-144, 155-156, 167, 173, 187, 259-268; Type III, 15-17, 76, 166-167, 173-174, 180-183, 191-193, 259-268; Type IV, 16-17, 76, 104, 167, 192, 259-267

United Nations, 75
United Press International (UPI), 78

United Prisoners Union, 159
United States Cavalry, 42-44
Unruh, Jesse, 78

Vallandigham, Clement L., 27
Vanderbilt, Cornelius, 42
Vandervort, Edward, 148-149
Victor Emmanuel III (king of Italy), 169
Vidrine, Arthur, 238
Vietnam War, 83

Walker, Edwin A., 113-117, 119, 121, 126-127
Wallace, George C., 174-176, 186, 250-252, 267n
Warren, Robert Penn, 224
Warren Commission, 258
Watson, Tom, 58
Watson, Van, 157
W.E.B. DuBois Club, 91
Weidner, John, 86
Weiss, Carl Adam, 225-227
Weiss, Carl Austin: as atypical assassin, 223, 238-239, 263-266; background, 223-230; conspiracy theory, 231-232; feelings for Long, 227-239, 263-264; Long assassination, 224-225, 237-238; marriage and family, 227-229, 233-235, 263; political beliefs, 226-228, 232-235, 238-239; possible innocence, 232-235; premeditation theory, 233-236; psychological appraisal, 8n, 16-17, 76

Weiss, Olga Marie, 225
Weiss, Thomas Edward, 225-226
Weiss, Viola Marie, 225
Weschler Adult Intelligence Scale, 178n
White, Dan, 239
White, Theodore, 7n
White, Travis, 78
Whitman, Charles, 167, 182-183
Whitman, Walt, 109
Wilderness Campaign (Civil War), 28
Williams, Tennessee, 151
Williams, T. Harry, 224, 230, 232
Wilson, Woodrow, 214
Woodbury, Levi, 195
Worker, The, 114, 117
working class, 19, 39-49
Wyndham, Charles, 24

Yoshimura, Wendy, 163

Zangara, Giuseppe: background and family, 167-174; medical problems, 168-172; psychological appraisal, 6n, 7n, 8n, 71, 166-167, 192, 262-264; Roosevelt assassination attempt, 171-172; trial and execution, 172-173; as Type III assassin, 17, 173, 260-261, 263-265
Ziegler, Edward, 218
Ziegler, Elsie, 218-219
Zinman, David, 224, 233
Zionist movement, 79-82, 86-88, 104

Library of Congress Cataloging in Publication Data

Clarke, James W., 1937-
American assassins.

Bibliography: p.   Includes index.
1. Assassins—United States—Biography.
I. Title.
HV6278.C57   1982   364.1'524'0922 [B]   81-47912
ISBN 0-691-07637-5   AACR2